MODERNIZATION

MODERNIZATION

The Humanist Response to Its Promise and Problems

Selected Readings from the
Proceedings of the International Conferences
on the Unity of the Sciences

Edited by Richard L. Rubenstein

PARAGON HOUSE

Washington

093895

Printed in the United States of America

International Standard Book Number: 0-89226-015-7

Library of Congress Catalogue Card Number: 82-083241

The International Cultural Foundation, Inc. (ICF, Inc.)

International Headquarters:
G.P.O. Box 1311, New York, NY 10116

Tokyo Office:
Rm. 1006, TBR Bldg., 2-10-1 Nagata-cho
Chiyoda-ku, Tokyo, Japan

London Office:
44 Lancaster Gate,
London W23NA, England

— CONTENTS —

Preface

With a single exception, the essays included in this book have been selected from papers originally presented at the Committee on Religion and Philosophy of the Sixth and Seventh meetings of the International Conference on the Unity of the Sciences that took place November 25-27, 1977 in San Francisco and November 24-26, 1978 in Boston.[1] These two conferences were convened in the shadow of dramatic events which colored the experience of each participant. The 1977 meetings took place immediately after the late Anwar Sadat's first historical visit to Jerusalem. The initial hopefulness inspired by that event was very much a part of the atmosphere of the meeting in San Francisco. The ICUS is one of a small number of continuing international conferences where Israeli and Arab scholars can present their views in an atmosphere of absolutely strict neutrality with regard to the political issues that divide them. There was, unfortunately, a very different atmosphere at the Boston meeting, which took place almost immediately after the mass suicide of the followers of the Rev. Jim Jones in Jonestown, Guyana. At the time, there was considerable negative reaction against all of the newer religious movements which were linked together by the media as "the cults." Since the sponsor of ICUS, the International Cultural Foundation, Inc., receives contributions from the Unification Church, one of the most highly publicized of the newer religious movements, the Jonestown tragedy was very much on everyone's mind. During the Boston meeting, over one hundred scholars took part in an informal discussion of the Jonestown tragedy. Since the group included sociologists, psychologists, historians of religion, and officials of both the government of Guyana and the United States Department of State, it was both memorable and enlightening. Unfortunately, no record of the discussion remains because of the spontaneous way in which the group came together.

---

[1] *The exception was a paper by this author entitled "The Elect and the Preterite" which was originally read at the Fifth meeting of the ICUS which met November 26-28, 1976 in Washington, D.C.*

Over the past few years, the International Conference on the Unity of the Sciences has been the object of much debate both in the media and within the academy. Unfortunately, much of that debate has been carried on with little regard for what has actually transpired at the meetings of the Conference. The papers presented in this book offer an excellent overview of the range of issues considered, as well as the level and quality of the sessions of the Committee on Religion and Philosophy of the ICUS during the period in which it was this author's privilege to serve as chairman. This volume is not likely to end the debate, but it does make the record publicly accessible.

In conclusion, I would like to express my gratitude to all those who made these conferences a reality. They are too numerous to name, but they include the leadership of the sponsoring organization, those who wrote papers, their commentators, and the invited participants and observers.

Richard L. Rubenstein
Tallahassee

Richard L. Rubenstein

Introduction

This collection of essays examines aspects of the modernization process and its religious, social, environmental and political consequences. By modernization I mean the growth and diffusion of a distinctive set of institutions and values rooted in the technological transformation of the economy and the organization of the state. Alternatively, the phenomenon to which I refer can be understood as an expression of the triumph of functional rationality, a rationality of means rather than ends, as the predominant mode of problem solving in human affairs. All of the authors are humanists in the sense that they are fundamentally concerned with the quest for values by which men and women can sustain themselves. None of our authors are merely technicians whose fundamental concern is the solution of practical problems apart from any consideration of value or social cost. They come from a very wide variety of national, religious, cultural, and professional backgrounds. Moreover, most of the authors had no previous contact with each other before attending the ICUS. Yet, the majority of the papers reflect an underlying concern with the impact of the worldwide trend toward the modernization of the economy and society on contemporary religion, ethics and politics. Because of the diversity of perspectives from which the authors write, a wide variety of topics are explored. Nevertheless, one is struck by the unanimity that is manifest in their concern with the problems brought about by modernization.

Part I. Contemporary Images and the Quest for Values

A. Technological Civilization and the Environment

The first group of papers are concerned with the impact of modernization on our relation to the environment. Paul Shephard, John Rodman and Joseph Meeker are in agreement that the relationship between contemporary technological civilization and the environment is self-destructive. Our current mode of relating to the environment involves large-scale exploitation and spoliation of ecosystems. If unrestrained, such behavior is bound ultimately to destroy the very basis of human life itself. Shephard argues that we are engaged in a world-wide devastation of ecosystems that can only be reversed by a radical transformation of consciousness. Such a transformation would do away with the current value-neutral, relativistic attitudes which predominate in technological civilization and would result in a re-visioning of mankind as intrinsically related to "the whole community of species." For Shephard, the choice is either a restoration of fellowship between humanity and all that partakes of and sustains life or a diminished, impoverished, desert-like existence for those who survive the ecological disasters which contemporary civilization inevitably entails.

Commenting on Shephard, Sigmund Kvaloy of Oslo, Norway sees this restoration as taking place "only after the abundant industrial energy flows of the present Euro-American society have dried up." Kvaloy's position is thus very close to Shephard's. He argues that the displacement of the current capital-intensive economy by a restored labor-intensive economy is indispensable if humanity is ever again to live in harmony with itself and nature.

John Rodman argues that those who share a common concern to preserve the environment are often motivated by very different conceptions of the human/nature relationship. These conceptions include the following: (a) *resource conservation*, in which natural resources are preserved for homocentrically-defined, utilitarian purposes; (b) *wilderness preservation*, in which non-utilitarian religious and aesthetic motivations predominate; (c) *nature moralism*, a position that argues that nature as well as man has rights; (d) *ecological resistance*, which is Professor Rodman's own position. Rodman counsels resistance to the exploitation of the natural environment because such exploitation is a threat to the self, or, put differently, to "the principle of diversity and spontaneity that is the endangered side of the basic balance that defines and sustains the very nature of things."

Joseph Meeker appeals for an end to specialization and professionalism. He calls upon us to give up what he describes as "fields of danger" and to return to the "wilderness of wisdom." He contends that the roots of the ecological crisis are very old, that they go back to the earliest agrarian and urban revolutions of the ancient world. Although today the term field usually denotes a specialized domain in intellectual endeavor, fields were originally "devices invented for taming reality and reducing natural complexity." Meeker argues that the first fields made possible the single crop agriculture of the neolithic period. These farmers' fields laid the basis for civilization as we know it, by making possible the domestication of plants and animals, permanent human settlements, and stratified societies. According to Meeker, field specialization displaced the older, nonspecialized occupations of hunting and gathering. This increased the goods available for consumption but had the effect of radically diminishing the capacity of most men and women to be "fully in touch with a whole natural setting" and to develop their own powers to the fullest. Fields, whether agrarian or intellectual, lead to specialization and the abandonment of human wholeness. Put differently, according to Meeker, alienated, fragmented, specialized labor had its origins in the invention of the neolithic agricultural field.

Meeker argues that field specialization has become one of the most dangerous threats to the healthy continuation of both man and nature because such specialization leads to fragmentation and the inability to perceive context. As a result, we are unable to foresee the natural and social consequences of our exploitation of the environment. According to Meeker, if we are to survive, we must develop a wisdom that is conscious of wholeness and an integrity that transcends both narrow fields and specialized disciplines. Meeker calls upon us to return to the "wilderness of wholeness." Meeker's analysis of contemporary society recalls Emile Durkheim's contrast between the non-specialized "mechanical solidarity" of pre-modern society and the specialized "organic solidarity" of modern society. Perhaps because he writes several generations later, Meeker's prognosis is far more pessimistic than Durkheim's.

All three scholars offer a negative judgment on technological civilization. In their view, humanity may come to realize its integral relationship with the environment only when it is too late, that is, when it has so thoroughly destroyed our common habitat that human existence can no longer be sustained or sustained only in a mutant form that most men and women living today would regard as hardly worth survival. As we have noted, an important element in these papers is their criticism of specialization, professionalism, and ultimately, the division of labor. Whereas most sociological critics of modern society have stressed the alienating character of the processes by which men and women were uprooted from their traditional religious, social, and cultural moorings, Shephard, Rodman, and Meeker see the damage largely in terms of a loss of the *sense of context* in which all human endeavor must take place.

Nevertheless, one is struck by the fact that, while Shephard, Rodman, and Meeker have much insight into the costs of technological civilization, they have little to say concerning the social costs that would be involved in dismantling it. Although they express the conviction that, if we continue on our current path, we will be faced with large-scale ecological catastrophe, nowhere in their papers do they deal with the very real possibility that large-scale demographic catastrophe is likely to ensue if technological civilization is abandoned. Is it, for example, possible to abandon contemporary techniques of food production without bringing about world-wide famine? What would happen to the populations of the world's urban centers were the specialization of labor universally abandoned? Where would they go? How would they live?

It may be that those who regard the abandonment of industrial society as mankind's only hope of averting catastrophe understand the costs and do not realistically expect a shift away from technological civilization until after it has run its destructive course. If that is the case, as indeed I suspect it is, it would follow that there is a strongly apocalyptic element in what has been called the Deep Ecological Movement. According to this perspective, one way or another modern civilization is fated to end catastrophically. Sooner or later nature will correct the distortions mankind has introduced into the ecological balance.

I am not persuaded of the inevitability of such a dire outcome. While I share many of the scholars' forebodings concerning the long-range costs of technological civilization, I am, for better or for worse, persuaded that technological civilization is our destiny, if only because the costs of dismantling it appear far higher than those involved in maintaining it while attempting to ameliorate its worst effects. I would agree that large-scale demographic catastrophe is one possible outcome of contemporary civilization. Nevertheless, it remains a *possible* outcome, whereas the deliberate dismantling of contemporary industry and technology renders demographic catastrophe not merely possible but *certain*. It is for that reason that, while I regard the ecological thinkers as important in making us aware of one dimension of the hazards of contemporary civilization, I am unwilling to entertain seriously the more radical proposals suggested by some of their number for an end to science, technology, and the division of labor.

B. The 'Legitimation Crisis' and the Quest for a New Consensus

The response to modernization is also a fundamental issue in the three papers dealing with Religion and Society at ICUS-VI in San Francisco. Anthropologist Mary Catherine Bateson addresses the problem of modernization from the perspective of metaphors of kinship. According to Professor Bateson, in almost every instance, premodern societies have been bound together by a sense of common origin and destiny. In these societies, relationships within the family offered an analogical basis for both political and social ethics. The larger community was normally regarded as an extended kinship group whose members were bound together by a myth of descent from a common ancestor. Such communities were usually led by a figure whose authority was ultimately derived from a paternal model. With the breakdown of traditional society, the world-wide shift to the nuclear family, greater equality of women, and the rise of mass urbanization, older metaphors of kinship have lost their credibility. The situation described by Professor Bateson has been characterized succinctly by the late Benjamin Nelson as a shift "from tribal brotherhood to universal otherhood." Professor Bateson sees the world of universal otherhood as offering no viable basis for ethics such as that once provided by the family model. She argues that we need new metaphors that do not possess the built-in biases and exclusions of the older metaphors of kinship, yet which are not rootless and hence meaningless. Bateson finds none of the currently available metaphors of either kinship or affinity satisfactory. She expresses the hope that newer experiments in parenting, which are taking place all over the world, may eventually offer familial models which can be carried over to the larger community. In these experiments, the partners, though different in gender, are nevertheless regarded as equal within the relationship. This, however, is only a very tentative expression of hope.

Bateson concludes that our civilization lacks a key image that asserts "both equality and difference," "complementarity without exploitation," and which refers to a "common future and a common responsibility" rather than a common past. She thus leaves us with insight into yet another dimension of the predicament of modern civilization. We see our dilemmas through the eyes of a noted anthropologist who is especially sensitive to the breakdown of a binding sense of affiliation, relatedness, and responsibility, which in the past enabled at least those men and women who shared a common origin to live and work together.

The issue of metaphors of kinship raised by Professor Bateson has a direct bearing on the political history of the twentieth century. The search for a viable basis for community has had some devastating results in our era. The fact that we lack adequate metaphors of fellowship and community does not eliminate the urgent need for such symbols. Nazism was one such attempt to offer new symbols of kinship. Its racist ideology can be understood as an attempt to create a basis of community through the myth of shared origins. It was also a thoroughly modern response to the fragmented affiliations of modern society. More than any other socio-political ideology, it was based upon the built-in biases and exclusions common to metaphors of kinship and shared origins that Professor Bateson rightly finds wholly inadequate to our current needs. Nevertheless, the fact that such an ideology had the enormous potency it did is evidence of the urgency of the need for credible metaphors of affiliation and fellowship, if not kinship, in contemporary society. Both racism and nationalism are attempts to answer the question, "Who is my brother?" in a world of well-nigh universal otherhood. Because contemporary society is unable to overcome otherhood, it does not follow that the thirst for brotherhood has disappeared. On the contrary, in times of extreme stress, it is likely to take extremely violent and xenophobic forms. Even a movement as vicious as Nazism can be seen as a distorted attempt to offer Germans and others of related origin the hope for a common life, albeit one that involved the extermination of those excluded from the magic circle of kinship.

Nevertheless, in modern times even when members of a society share a common origin, there is no assurance that they will inhabit a common world. It is to this aspect of contemporary civilization that Lonnie D. Kliever addresses himself in his paper. Professor Kliever asks, "What happens when the monopoly on world-definition is broken within a society? Can the common life survive without a common world-view and moral system?" Is it ever possible, Kliever asks, for an individual to form a stable identity when he no longer inhabits a world that guarantees him meaning and structure? In the past, meaning and structure were guaranteed by religious institutions that usually had a monopoly of reality definition. As we know, this is no longer the contemporary situation. Most men and women today live in societies in which a multiplicity of world-views compete for public acceptance. Following Jurgen Habermas and Ernest Gellner, Kliever sees modern man as faced with a "legitimation crisis" that arises from the very plurality of reality-definitions confronting him.

This crisis does not appear to Kliever to be entirely without an element of promise. Kliever sees contemporary pluralism as offering the possibility of "a world and a society freed for diversity..." Such pluralism can lead to "an enriched and enlarged sense of the possibilities of life here and now." Nevertheless, Kliever holds contemporary pluralism to be imperilled. He tells us that "a new rage for order and meaning" has been let loose as a result of traditional religion's loss of authority. Thus, religion persists precisely because religion has ceased to be credible. With the demise of its authority and its monopoly on reality definition, the needs that religion once met have become ever more urgent. Were such a situation left unchecked, it is altogether possible that contemporary pluralism might yield to a new intolerant absolutism and self-destruct. Kliever therefore suggests several ways in which the continued viability of pluralism might be assured. These include rational monotheism, non-dualistic mysticism, and the epistemological relativism of the sociology of knowledge. He recognizes that each of these positions is problematic and calls upon us to join in searching for ways to sustain the continuing viability of our pluralistic situation.

One of the most significant aspects of Kliever's paper is his wholehearted willingness to accept contemporary civilization. He is undeceived about its problems. He would undoubtedly find merit in much of the criticism offered by Shephard, Rodman, Meeker and Bateson. Yet, Kliever accepts modern pluralism in all of its complexity. What makes his position important is that his choice is lucid, informed and serious. Nor is it likely that Kliever would ever regret his choice, no matter how many unpleasant surprises the modern world might have in store for him.

While Canada's distinguished philosopher, George Grant, finds the pluralism embraced by Kliever to be the destiny of western man, he regards it as profoundly at odds with those values which are of greatest importance to him as a faithful Christian. Grant portrays the conflict as one between the values intrinsic to Christian faith and the values to which the modern multiversity is fundamentally committed. Note that Grant does not use the term university. He uses the term multiversity in order to stress the pluralism of values and viewpoints co-existing in the contemporary academy. For Grant, faith is "the experience that intelligence is illuminated by love." By contrast, the multiversity is committed to science which is "the project of reason to gain objective knowledge." In modern academic and scientific research, Grant observes, knowledge qua knowledge is detached from love qua love. The objectivity demanded by research in the multiversity, even in the study of religion, is in conflict with "the experience that intelligence is illuminated by love." Grant further observes that today's multiversity has become an institution whose primary function is to certify professional competence rather than one in which knowledge is likely to lead to faith.

Like Kliever, Grant recognizes that the pluralism, secularity, and objectivity of modern institutions cannot satisfy the religious hunger of large sectors of the population. Like Kliever, he is not surprised at the growth of pietism, fundamentalism, and the new religions as responses to the contemporary situation. Nevertheless, the secular, pluralistic culture Kliever would embrace is seen by Grant as at best a harsh destiny he cannot avoid. Finally, Grant expresses the hope that the culture of scientific objectivity may yet yield a new experience of faith. However, if such a renewal is to take place, it will involve crossing through the "web of necessity" that science has bequeathed to the modern world. As a Christian, Grant apparently sees in the message of the cross the hope that the death of the spirit in contemporary civilization will be followed by its resurrection, not by avoiding the "iron cage" of modernity, but by experiencing it to its fullest. It is that insight which apparently allows Professor Grant to be both a professor at a multiversity and a faithful Christian.

C. The Individual and the Political Order

The group of papers by Andrew Reck, Gerald McCool and Klaus Rohmann respectively were presented at a session on "Freedom and Sources of Authority" at ICUS-VII in Boston. The authors of all three papers examine the problematics of contemporary culture from the perspective of political philosophy. Reck argues for the reciprocal relationship between liberty and authority in a healthy society. According to Reck, following Solzhenitsyn, contemporary Russia exhibits a want of liberty; contemporary America a lack of moral and political authority to balance personal freedom. Reck argues that when men fail to maintain the reciprocity, the fabric of common life is endangered. McCool divides the evolution of western ethical and social thought into three stages. In the first stage, the interpretive model for the relation of society to its individual members is taken to be the relation of a living organism to its parts; in the second, the model is that of the relation of a machine to its parts. Since the parts are adventitiously rather than intrinsically related, the claims of the unrestricted individual could, and often did, take priority over the well-being of the commonwealth. At the same time, the individual had no protection against the all-powerful state when its leaders were moved by purposes that took precedence over the requirements of human dignity, freedom, and even life itself. In the third stage, McCool sees a reaction against the mechanism and individualism of the Enlightenment, as well as an attempt to find an organic model for the relation of the individual and society that could be appropriate to our age. If that venture proves unsuccessful, McCool fears that the temptation of Marxist totalitarianism may prove irresistible.

According to Klaus Rohmann, in the Middle Ages man considered himself to be "relatively absolute," that is, absolute by virtue of his relation to the Absolute. In the modern period, man himself has become absolute without qualification. Since such godlike autonomy is impossible for the single individual to sustain, it has been taken over by science, economics, politics and the arts. These in turn have been made subordinate to the ends of the wholly autonomous state. Though science and technology pretend to bestow prosperity, they actually achieve dominion, first over nature and then, as an instrument of the state, over man. In the century of genocide, slave labor camps, nuclear warfare, and value-free bureaucratic domination, the absolute power of the autonomous state stands fully revealed. This has led to a phenomenon that Rohmann calls *"Staatsverdrossenheit"* or weariness of the state, which is in reality a weariness of all kinds of state administration. As a result, the state has lost its authority but not its power. Moreover, the absolute dominion possessed by the state is both anonymous and irresponsible, since it is not linked to identifiable persons. Rohmann concludes that our fundamental task is that of "getting dominion over dominion." Rohmann suggests that the means of achieving this may be a new asceticism. According to Rohmann, such an asceticism involves neither hostility to life nor a retreat into privatism. It is rather "self-education to gain freedom from possession 'as though' we possessed not; freedom to a reduction of one's claims; freedom to fight against the automatism of advertisement, against the inundation of sensations; freedom to independence of judgement, to resistance against what one says, one does . . . Asceticism means self-education for distance."

It is interesting to note that Rohmann, a Catholic thinker living in Essen, Germany, sees a way out of the problematics of the modern period that greatly resembles the Buddhist way as interpreted by Hawaiian scholar David Kalupahana. As we noted, Kalupahana holds that Buddhism regards excessive desire as the cause of human suffering and counsels that unnecessary desire, not genuine human need, be abandoned. The convergence of important Buddhist and Christian themes is also noted by a number of our scholars but never as strikingly as in the papers of Rohmann and Kalupahana.

The final paper of this section is one that this author prepared for ICUS-V, which met in Washington, D.C. in 1976. It deals with another aspect of the modernization process: in a time of growing population and diminishing resources, who is likely to survive and even prosper?

D. Contemporary Images of Death

One of the topics originally scheduled for the Boston meeting was "Death and Suicide in Contemporary Thought." Professor Walter Kaufmann was chairman of the session which was planned months before the Jonestown tragedy. Nevertheless, in the aftermath of the tragedy, the special relevance of this session was apparent to everybody. At the beginning of this essay, I observed that most of the papers presented in the Religion and Philosophy section of ICUS-VI and VII can be seen as responses to problematic aspects of the modernization process and technological civilization. That observation was especially true of the conference papers dealing with death and suicide. With the decline of the power of traditional religious sources of consolation and confidence in the face of death, the stark opacity and inevitability of death confront modern man as never before. There is much irony in the fact that the culture of science and technology, which has enhanced the physical comfort of large sectors of mankind, has done so at the price of rendering infirm the beliefs, values and institutions that have in the past alleviated humanity's anxiety before its terminal necessity.

In his essay on "The Anatomy of Death," Ninian Smart points to yet another dimension of the problematic character of technological civilization. Smart argues that death mocks us because it not only threatens our individual substance, but also the substance of the community and the values with which we identify and which offer us a sense of meaning and purpose that transcends the narrow limits of our own individual lives. For those who no longer find any meaning in the hope for personal immortality, such transcendent identifications can give their lives some sense of meaning and value. Unfortunately, in our era the possibility of collective death through nuclear war or other demographic catastrophes threatens even these latter values. As Smart comments, collective death "renders our teleological values empty and our attributive values without social basis." Commenting on Smart, Alfred Alvarez argues that "death itself has become not only another aspect of omnipotent technology, but it has become absurd." The random character of modern collective death renders it totally without personal meaning. Collective death destroys all possibility of martyrdom. It also puts an end to personal heroism. There is nothing heroic about nuclear incineration. Thus, collective death threatens to put an end even to those existential and social values which in the past gave the individual meaning after he or she had lost his or her traditional faith.

Nor can meaning be affirmed by a romantic choice of "artistic suicide" argues novelist Joyce Carol Oates. Whoever choses death choses neither liberation nor transcendence, but "brute deadness." While Professor Oates admits that there are situations in which the deliberate choice of self-destruction is the only move whereby one can preserve one's dignity, she asserts that the act of suicide is "a consequence of the atrophying of the creative imagination: the failure of imagination: not to be confused with gestures of freedom, rebellion, or originality, or transcendence." In the aftermath of the Jonestown tragedy, Professor Oates' paper seemed especially appropriate to the mood and preoccupations of the conferees.

E. Contemporary Images of Salvation

The failure of traditional institutions of consolation and hope before the dead-end character of the human condition has not lessened the thirst for redemption in technological civilization. On the contrary, that hope may have been intensified precisely because of contemporary civilization's spiritual failure. Moreover, the consolations that have been offered in our time, have tended to be this-worldly and, hence, socio-political. In his essay, Etienne Trocme explores the question of whether contemporary ideas of redemption have New Testament roots. Surprisingly, Trocme rejects the idea that Christianity was originally a religion of redemption, although he concedes that it later became one. Catholic theologian Maurice Boutin argues that the theme of "man's salvation is central for Karl Marx." Boutin counsels us to see Marxism "as a peculiar, yet crucial version of a secularized Christianity." Boutin further argues that salvation demands a severance from the present order of things. Relying heavily on Marx's critique of industrial capitalism, Boutin argues that man's salvation in this world must be located in overcoming the human and social dilemmas arising from the shift in the modern period from use-value to exchange-value as the basis for the disposition and consumption of human resources. Put differently, for Boutin, following Marx, redemption would mean the overcoming of industrial capitalism. Nevertheless, although Boutin joins the ecologists in their negative assessment of contemporary civilization, he advocates its transformation, not its dismantling. To that end, Boutin sees nothing in the Biblical tradition which is capable of dealing with the problem of salvation as it arises in the contemporary world. Even Marxism falls short. According to Boutin, Marxist analysis can help us to understand industrial capitalism and its problems, but by itself it is no longer adequate to deal with a far more complex civilization than that which Marx attempted to analyze a century ago. Nevertheless, by pointing to the conflict between man's activity and man's being under industrial capitalism, Marx identified the arena in which man's quest for salvation must be situated. According to Marx, under industrial capitalism, man's activity is for the sake of exchange values, even when those values threaten man's very being individually and collectively. Following Marx, Boutin argues that salvation in industrial capitalism involves overcoming the fundamental contradiction between exchange values and use values.

Part II.   Religious Responses To Modernization

F.   The Persistence of Religious Aspects of Consciousness

Religious consciousness continues to manifest itself in a non-religious age, according to Edward Robinson. Robinson's contention that the religious consciousness is a universal aspect of human experience is challenged by commentator R. Zwi Werblowsky who expressed doubt that we can speak of anything more than "the religious aspects of consciousness." Perhaps someday that issue may be resolved, if Nobel Laureate Eugene Wigner's hope is fulfilled that physics may eventually become a universal science encompassing all of reality. In any event, whether we speak of a religious consciousness or "the religious aspects of consciousness," we note once again the persistence of powerful religious elements in our secular culture.

G.   Comparative Religious Responses to Modernization

The next group of papers were originally read in a section dealing with the general theme of Comparative Religious Responses to Modernization. In contrast to Rodman, Shephard, and Meeker, each of the scholars in this section appears to assume that, whatever its problems, modernization is here to stay. This shared opinion is especially significant because all of the religious traditions under discussion are non-western. Moreover, there is general agreement among the scholars that technological civilization, indeed the modernization process itself, is endogenic to the Judaeo-Christian west and exogenic to the cultures of Hinduism, Islam, and Buddhism. In the paper dealing with Hinduism and modernization, Ravi Ravindra holds that in India modernization has meant primarily westernization, especially in the areas of science and technology. In spite of its foreign origin, Ravindra maintains that western values have come to predominate over the entire globe because of their success and because of military and economic pressures. An important example of the way in which military pressures foster the development of technological civilization, even at the risk of ecological hazard, is the progressive proliferation of nuclear-powered generating plants throughout much of the so-called Third World.

Since these plants are capable of producing material for nuclear weapons, one can never be certain whether they have been built for military or civilian purposes. In any event, once in place they alter the military balance between the nation with a nuclear capability. None of the scholars concerned with the ecological effects of contemporary civilization discusses the way in which military pressures are likely to compel contemporary societies to become more rather than less reliant on technology in the future. Just as unilateral disarmament by a single power is infeasible and utopian, so too unilateral abandonment of technology appears to be totally unrealistic. On the contrary, military considerations are far more likely to compel the great powers to accelerate their technological development. Ravindra's observations on the relation of military pressure to technological civilization offers a convincing reason for believing that technological civilization is likely to be our destiny for good or ill.

Ravindra's observations come from a non-westerner whose native cultural heritage is diametrically opposed to the dominant values in technological civilization. Although Ravindra questions whether there is any such "religion" as "Hinduism," he does maintain that the Sanskrit words *dharma* and *yoga* approximate what we in the west understand to be religion. According to Ravindra, the word *dharma* has a larger community component in it whereas *yoga* refers to a more individual quest. He offers a tentative definition of Hinduism as *dharma* and *yoga* leading to *moksa* or liberation. Thus, the goal of Hinduism transcends the this-worldly concerns and aspirations that characterize western technological civilization. Not only is technological civilization alien in origin to Hinduism, but its values, especially its conceptions of both individual and group achievement, are antithetical to those of Hinduism. In spite of this, Ravindra sees no possibility that science and technology will be rejected in India. Because of the prevalence of mass poverty in contemporary India, few intellectuals are disposed to forego western technology. I would add that military pressures from India's neighbors preclude the abandonment of science and technology.

Nevertheless, Ravindra does not believe that it is possible for India altogether to abandon its own heritage, if only because of the impoverishment of the spirit that is everywhere visible in the western world. At a time when thousands of young westerners, dissatisifed with their own religious culture, flock to India in search of spiritual nourishment, it is hardly likely that India's embrace of western values could be wholehearted. Thus, the picture Ravindra draws is one of a culture divided against itself more thoroughly than ever before. That a somewhat comparable internal division is also to be found in the west is evident both in the pervasive dissatisfaction with the fruits of science and technology, of which most of the papers in this volume are representative, as well as what theologian Harvey Cox has called the "turn east" taken by so many westerners in recent times.

Mohamed Al-Nowaihi's paper is concerned with a distinctive aspect of the encounter of Islam with modernization, namely, the intellectual modernization of his tradition or *modernism in religion.* Like Ravindra, Al-Nowaihi is as convinced of the irreversibility of modernization. His primary concern is to spell out a strategy of interpretation by which religious modernism in Islam can be reconciled with Islam's sacred scripture, the Koran. For the Jewish and Christian reader, Al-Nowaihi's interpretive strategies will seem reminiscent of similar strategies employed by Jewish and Christian scholars who sought to reconcile modern culture with the authority of Scripture. Professor Al-Nowaihi's paper was written before the Islamic revolution in Iran. Moreover, it reflects attitudes to be found in the most cosmopolitan center of Islam, Egypt. Reconciling strategies such as Al-Nowaihi's were bound to prove unacceptable to large numbers of his co-religionists, just as was the case with similar Jewish and Christian reconciling strategies. Where Ravindra and Al-Nowaihi see their traditions as capable of harmonization with the modern spirit, fundamentalists in Judaism, Christianity and Islam reject at the very least the intellectual modernization of their traditions. All three traditions have witnessed the rise of powerful counter-modernization movements, the most spectacular being that of the Ahatollah Khomeini. Incidentally, insofar as the participants of the ecological movement advocate an end to technology and specialization, they too can be regarded as counter-modernizing, although they are seldom fundamentalist in religion. Both the fundamentalists and the ecologists find an irreconcilable conflict between their most important values and the predominant values of modernity.

The tensions between the forces making for modernization and Buddhism especially Theravada Buddism, are discussed by Israeli scholar R. Zwi Werblowsky and his respondent David J. Kalupahana of Hawaii. Werblowsky sees contemporary Buddhism caught between Buddhism's classical attitude of "indifference" to the world and the inner-worldly concerns of western science and technology. Werblowsky limits the "indifference" of Buddhism to an elite of religious virtuosi and asserts that the average householder was "rarely obsessed with Nirvana." By contrast, Kalupahana rejects Werblowsky's claim that there is a tension between Buddhism and the values intrinsic to modernization. He also rejects Werblowsky's notion of a two-tier religiosity in Buddhism. Like Al-Nowaihi, Kalupahana sees no inherent conflict between modernization and, if not all forms of Buddhism, at least its very earliest form. For Kalupahana, modernization is a "regression" to Buddhism's earliest sources. Arguing that the theory of causation or "dependent arising" is central to Buddhism and leads to a thorough-going empiricism and naturalism, Kalupahana maintains that on the basis of experiential knowledge, Buddhism came to the conclusion that human suffering is caused by excessive desire or attachment. This conclusion does not result in a rejection of the material world and a quest for a transcendent domain. The goal of Buddhism, according to Kalupahana is thoroughly naturalistic. It seeks happiness here and now rather than through some transcendent state of bliss. Such happiness is to be attained not by an otherworldly denial of human needs but a rejection of unrealistic desires. Kalupahana concludes that Buddhism has no difficulty in adapting to modernization. Whether Werblowsky is correct or Kalupahana, many of the Asian countries in which Buddhism has flourished have in fact proven capable of a sustained capacity to master the techniques of modernization. They have also proven capable of successfully competing with the west in the area of science and technology.

H. Religion and Science:
Convergent or Divergent Definitions of Reality

The collision between the objective posture demanded by scientific research and the commitment of faith is discussed by Donald R. Ferrell in his paper. Professor Ferrell speaks for a group of influential religious thinkers who identify themselves as revisionist theologians. The position of the revisionists differs from that of the neo-Orthodox and the Orthodox on the one hand and the radicals and liberals on the other. It rejects the position of those who assert that there is an exclusively religious form of knowledge or revelation, as well as those who deny all possibility of a viable conception of God. Where both the fundamentalists and the radicals tend to see an inherent conflict between science and religion, the revisionists see the scientific enterprise as possessing "a genuinely religious dimension which points to a universal religious dimension within the whole of science." It is religion's task to make that dimension "as explicit as possible through its own symbolic language." The revisionists thus see their role as essentially one of reconciliation.

It is interesting to note a certain agreement between the revisionists' position, as described by Ferrell, and Ben Ami Scharfstein, who is interested in the question of why the great philosophers chose their vocations. Instead of focussing on the *teachings* of philosophers, religious thinkers, and scientists, Scharfstein focuses on the biographies of twenty of the greatest of their number. Although Scharfstein's work is susceptible of misunderstanding by those who accuse him of psychological reductionism, he raises an entirely legitimate question—why did these thinkers pursue their distinctive vocations? Tentatively, he has concluded that "their need to create philosophy has been a response to anxiety, isolation, perhaps the result of the early death of a parent." Scharfstein sees similar motives at work in both the religious thinkers and the scientists. He concludes that, whatever their differences, the philosophers, scientists, and religious thinkers were impelled by common personal needs. Scharfstein would thus concur with Ferrell's contention that a common element binds those engaged in scientific inquiry and religious thought. Where Scharfstein utilizes the insights of psychology to arrive at his conclusion, Ferrell and the revisionist theologians appear to rely heavily on the sociology of knowledge for theirs. Nevertheless, Scharfstein's paper must be seen as adding weight to Ferrell's conclusions.

In conclusion, when one compares the way in which the ICUS has been conducted over the years with so many other international conferences, especially those sponsored by inter-governmental agencies concerned with political, economic, and social issues, with their politically-motivated, doctrinaire, ideologically-intolerant overt and covert agendas, it becomes readily apparent that ICUS can easily serve as a model of how international conferences ought to be conducted. Thanks are due to the officers and staff of the International Cultural Foundation for making the conferences possible. The ICF staff is largely drawn from a religious community with a very clear and definite theological and intellectual orientation, but even a cursory perusal of the papers in this volume will show that the ICF staff has been scrupulous in its commitment to open, forthright dialogue and honest intellectual interchange. All responsible points of view have been welcomed and their exponents have been treated with courtesy. Unlike so many international conferences, there have been no walk-outs and no one has been compelled to leave the podium before completing his or her presentation. Both in tone and substance, the conferences have been characterized by the kind of openness that alone can make possible a genuine trans-cultural exchange of ideas.

Truro, Massachusetts

About the Authors

Paul Shepard is Avery Professor of Natural Philosophy and Human Ecology, Pitzer College, Claremont, California.

Sigmund Kvaloy is Research Associate in Human Ecology and Ecophilosophy, Oslo School of Architecture, Oslo, Norway.

John Rodman is Professor of Political Studies, Pitzer College and the Claremont Graduate School, Claremont, California.

Joseph W. Meeker is Interdisciplinary Professor, Athabasca University, Edmonton, Alberta.

Ravi Ravindra is Associate Professor of Physics and Religion, Dalhousie University, Halifax, Nova Scotia.

Mohammed Al-Nowaihi is Professor of Arabic Language and Literature, The American University, Cairo, Egypt.

David J. Kalupahana is Professor of Philosophy and Chairman of the Department, University of Hawaii, Honolulu, Hawaii.

R.J. Zwi Werblowsky is Professor of Comparative Religion, The Hebrew University, Jerusalem, Israel.

Mary Catherine Bateson is Dean of Faculty and Professor of Anthropology at Amherst College.

Lonnie D. Kliever is Professor of Religion and Chairman of the Department, Southern Methodist University, Dallas, Texas.

Joseph D. Bettis is Dean and Professor of Philosophy, Fairhaven College, Western Washington University, Bellingham, Washington.

Gabriel Vahannian is Jeanette K. Watson Professor of Religion, Syracuse University, Syracuse, New York, and Strasbourg, France.

George P. Grant is Professor of Religious Studies, McMaster University, Ontario, Canada.

Herbert Richardson is Professor of Religion, St. Michael's College, University of Toronto, Toronto, Ontario.

Donald R. Ferrell is Associate Professor of Religion and Philosophy, Doane College, Crete, Nebraska.

Morris I. Berkowitz is Professor of Sociology, Brock University, St. Catherine's, Ontario.

Ben-Ami Scharfstein is Professor of Philosophy, Tel Aviv University, Tel Aviv, Israel.

Etienne Trocme is President and Professor of New Testament Exegesis, Universite des Sciences Humaine, Strasbourg, France.

Maurice Boutin is Associate Professor of Fundamental Theology, University of Montreal, Montreal, Quebec.

Edward A. Robinson is Director, Religious Experience Research Unit, Manchester College, Oxford, England.

Eileen V. Barker is Professor of Sociology, the London School of Economics and Politics, London, England.

Eugene P. Wigner, Nobel Laureate, is Professor of Physics Emeritus, Princeton University, Princeton, New Jersey.

Ninian Smart is Professor of Religious Studies, University of California at Santa Barbara, Santa Barbara, California, and Professor of Religious Studies, Furness College, University of Lancaster, Lancaster, England.

Alfred Alvarez is Advisory Editor of *The Observer*, London, England.

Joyce Carol Oates, novelist, is Professor of English, Creative Writing Program, Princeton University, Princeton, New Jersey.

Jean-Guy LeMarier is Dean, Faculty of Theology, St. Paul University, Ontario, Canada

Andrew J. Reck is Professor of Philosophy, Tulane University, New Orleans, Louisiana.

Gerald McCool is Professor of Philosophy, Fordham University, Bronx, New York.

Klaus Rohman is Supervisor of Graduate Teacher-Training Programs, University of Essen, Essen, West Germany.

Richard L. Rubenstein is Robert O. Lawton Distinguished Professor of Religion, Florida State University, Tallahassee, Florida.

PART I:

Contemporary Images And The Quest For Values

A Technological Civilization and the Environment

B The 'Legitimation Crisis' and the Quest for a New Consensus

C The Individual and the Political Order

D Contemporary Images of Death

E Contemporary Images of Salvation

Section A:
Technological Civilization and the Environment

— A1 —
The Conflict of Ideology and Ecology
Paul Shepard/Sigmund Kvaloy

— A2 —
Theory and Practice in the Environmental Movement: Notes Towards an Ecology of Experience
John R. Rodman

— A3 —
Fields of Danger and the Wilderness of Wisdom
Joseph W. Meeker

Paul Shepard

— A1 —
The Conflict of Ideology and Ecology

In recent years there has been a concentrated effort in many disciplines to locate those ideas and sentiments in history which underlay the exploitation and destruction of ecosystems. This widespread riffling of the documents and institutions upon which modern presuppositions about the relationship of man and nature are founded was preceded by a less introspective explanation based on the "gospel of efficiency," a creed espoused by the early conservationists which postulated the origin of the difficulty in poor laws, bad management, inadequate planning and wasteful habits. It was a view that all the major institutions of government and business were comfortable with, predicated on the controlled expansion of an economy geared to evermore efficient conversion of ecosystems and habitats into jobs and products. Indeed, in America, conservation was conservative, a rich-man's hobby and big foundation playground.

When doubts arose about these premises and it began to appear that deep weaknesses in the system and not simply the system's priorities were at fault, there was an academic scramble to open up the history of ideas, doctrines of theology, origins of esthetics, and the confines of "linear thought" so as to lay bare the root causes of our environmental dilemmas. Out of this rich lode came monographs on the theory and practice of the domination of nature, Greek and Roman hubris, the arrogance of patriarchal, pastoral civilizations under whose feet the world was washing way, Judaic historicism and Christian other-worldliness, the mechanizations of science and illusions of homocentrism. It was a big rock that scholarship turned over and many of its cryptic denizens hunched there have yet to be collected. It is apparent that, like ecosystems, the web of our perception of nature ramifies without end, pervading thought and value in all the arts and sciences. In all fields it has become possible, even somewhat fashionable, to attend to those components heretofore ignored.

One of the consequences of this new exploration is that C.P. Snow's widely heralded "two-cultures" version of the modern world breaks down. Science does not always compel a vision of nature different than that of the humanities. Both are strongholds of the hierarchic view of the world, mankind as the privileged species, and the subordination of the non-human for the benefit and exaltation of people. Conversely, both contain minorities in which a more organic model and more humble philosophy prevail.

Another consequence is in the ways in which science influences the non-sciences, and it is one of these to which I wish to draw attention. It occurs as an aspect of the style of modern thought which, in effect, is detached and ostensibly non-judgmental, not so much noncommital as an extension of the view that all ideas have their merits and should be heard. Nothing objectionable about it on the surface, but it is the strategy of the calculating intellect which enables the individual to deliberate on the assumption that he is restraining his personal preferences from matters of public discussion and is open to divergent views.

This cherished posture, in its modern form, is interconnected with the discovery of culture. That discovery occurred in the twentieth century as the social sciences realized that the world's ethnic groups do not constitute evolutionary stages which culminate in Western Europe, but are in fact equally valid ways of life. It is not this premise itself which is at issue but a corollary flowing from it, that appraisals must be withheld about the practices of other people because such valuing is biased and culture-bound. Carried one step further, this view is that, even within a single society, no absolute values are possible. As academics we live in a world dominated by the fallout from this relativism which flourishes in a multinational political environment but which castrates the educational process by depriving it of any commitment except to its own unflinching pliancy.

Oddly enough, it is a style inextricably connected to the myth of ideology. Nothing might seem farther from the militant assertion of one's own beliefs than the determined flaccidity of commitment which I have described. But the myth of ideology is that the human animal is engaged in a lifelong process of choosing sides, mobilizing conviction in dialectics, collating opinions, dipping in and out of beliefs and disbeliefs and in short creating a concept of the self in terms of selective preference. To that end the academics and intellectuals see themselves as the agents of internal and external dialogues, committed only to the ideal of identity by belief and will.

Although one is identified with a "position" in such a culture, its actual basis is incipient abandonment of positions. The individual articulates a thesis of identity the way a lawyer takes a case, as though it were detachable: one may take the opposite side tomorrow from a hotly-defended position today. The myth holds all those elements constituting the self or group as equally detachable: politics, social role, "life-style," gender, and relationships in a wider ecological context. But the ease of detachment is merely a supposition, and it is quite possible that we are not that kind of animal at all. If so, attempts to change ecological relationships may be very different in consequences than detachment from a legal position. The kinds of damage that are possible in exercising this philosophy of casual disengagement have not been much studied.

Today every field of the study of mankind is deeply committed to environmental relativism. Even the concept of "environmentalism" has become a psychological doctrine denying inherent constraints on the human organism. Geography, with its blase endorsement of economic determinism; history, our study of the "rise" of civilization on a Promethean theme; the arts, which have separated abstract qualities from content; anthropology and sociology, with their social process and ethnological cataloguing on the theme of "everything's possible," and the natural sciences, with their posture of value-free fact-finding; all seem to confirm that "man makes himself" no matter how the world is made.

I am fully aware of the crippling effect on thought of the unwillingness to consider alternatives or the indulgence of whim and emotion. Turning the mind over to the arbitrary acts of irrational behavior and rationalizing mindlessness would be to surrender qualities which are precious, rare and hard-won. Tyranny lies in that direction. And yet, we are engaged in a world-wide devastation of ecosystems and other species on the grounds that people are related to the natural world only by "paradigms," "models," "schemata," or other constructs which are at best variations on archetypes and

at worst fickle opinions shared by a group. Thus the biological concept of evolution is seen not as a scientific formulation of the inte-
grative processes of nature but as one more construct in a
marketplace of ideas. Myths are viewed in a framework of comparative mythology, prose as comparative literature. Any and all
aspects of human life assume this mantle of footless disposition—the human population, the existence of other species, the use
of soils, forests and waters, the manipulation of watersheds, the
regulation of energy and nutrient systems, the fate of public lands
and public air.

Each of these becomes in this mode of thought a bundle of
"issues" in which coalitions of political power rise and fall, working
out their compromises on the shared assumption that the world has
no inherent structure, no given, but only an order projected upon it
which makes it seem coherent. One chooses ecological relationships
the way one chooses a political party or chooses brands of groceries.

As unrealistic as this attitude may seem it is the position of
modern scholarship. It is the intellectual manifestation of the Faus-
tian premise of human destiny by the assertion of will and the
domination of nature—stoutly defended on the grounds that 1) man
is a special case and therefore free to make a world according to his
desires, and 2) that the notion of "determinism" (taken to mean any
constraint by the non-human) is a cold hand on imagination,
creativity, or the human spirit, and is inevitably abused to justify
injustice.

On the grounds that one culture is intrinsically no better than
another we are therefore expected to accept, for instance, that goat-
pastoralism is no worse than any other land use, and that it cannot,
in fact, be judged by members of outside cultures. Consequently we
have created a free-association fantasy-land for every area of
thought touching on either the "cradle" lands of civilization in the
Middle East, or on the present "Third World." Back-to-the-land
movements, bearing ecological banners and celebrating simplified
"life styles" are widely adopting the goat on the misapprehension
that all the attributes of pre-industrial agriculture are ideological.

Because it has given the world a 5000 year lesson in environmental catastrophe, one might expect that goat-keeping and its effects
would represent a generally understood and accepted principle. But

the goat remains immune. It is sanctioned on government lands, given as foreign aid, praised by peace corps and missionaries, idealized by literary enthusiasts for classical allusions, defended by geographers, and cuddled by sub-culture groups who refuse to accept that any animal so cute and sociable is not a friend to man.

This is but one example in the whole realm of man-nature relationships. Lacking a true cultus to undergird our thought and discussion, we have instead a cult of relativity with its glaze of humane affirmation of brotherhood, the unwillingness to commit beyond dialectics on the grounds that personal choice and cultural context are the only absolutes. Fearful of appearing provincial or prejudiced, the intellectual style holds only to the right of equivocation.

The observation that a society based on cultural relativism inexorably extends its withdrawal of judgment and appraisal to all of its areas of interest, including the relationship of man to nature, precipitates us into a serious double-bind. How can we divest ourselves of that autotelic posture which says in effect that there is no evolutionary context of human life, no inherent constraints on our freedom to do as we please in the natural world, throw off that hubris in which the world is viewed as inert stuff for our manipulation and still retain our tolerance for the views of other peoples? If peace in the world is to be based on mutual respect, a willingness to live in a world of many races and many customs, how can we avoid the accommodative attitude which I have just been criticising? How can we be at once committed and yet affirm the diversity of peoples?

In short, the advocacy of an absolute sense of human ecology and a relativistic one of human cultures seems contradictory. But I think it need not be. The conservationists have held that the attribution of things as resources was primarily a cultural designation, and that may be so, but the reality of ecosystems and biomes, the interdependent community of species, the roles of soil and sea as the matrix of life are not cultural concepts. They are previous to cultures. It may indeed be chauvinistic for one people to ridicule an alien notion that, for instance, the mistletoe, a shrubby parasite, is spiritually potent, but the extermination of whales or pollution of the stratosphere is another matter.

What is the difference? How can we forebear on the grounds of universal brotherhood and local customs on the one hand and be adamant about natural systems on the other? Within the context of modern existential relativism, there is no resolution of this dilemma. To those who accept all things on the grounds of the privilege of personal or cultural conviction, for whom reality is created wholly anew with each perceiving agent, and alike for those committed to the homocentric destiny in which mankind transcends the usual order of nature, the contradiction can only be resolved by the assertion that all such actions carry the rights of tribal hegemony. Carried to its logical end in a democracy of individualism, everyone's private vision is as valid as every other; this is precisely where academic, intellectualist thought has brought us.

If ecological thought—that is, natural philosophy or ecosophy—is seen as part of that neutral matrix to be shaped according to the circumstances and impulses of each tradition then there can be no prior understanding. It means, in effect, that there is no such thing as the human species, except as a kind of transmitter or container for fluid thought. It follows that there are no other species either, since, like us, they cannot be studied *as a species*, but only as specific and particular instances. The parable of the blind men and the elephant becomes appropriate in a strange way: reality depends on your perspective and the occasion, therefore there is no elephant, only a word by which different individuals, groups, cultures refer to a kind of experience.

Geographer David Lowenthal asserted that the American concern for wilderness had nothing to do with insight into the foundations of our existence but was only a matter of taste—and rather poor taste at that. "The bison," he wrote, "is not a great shaggy beast. It is only a congeries of feelings."

The poor bison! It does not exist except in the multifold ways that different cultures choose to see it. In the same spirit, the typical trick for impressing freshmen in introductory psychology is to suggest that the tree falling on an island where there are no people makes no sound.

Thus things cannot have an enduring relationship with their environment if their reality depends on the contingent mind. Art, in this view, has no communicative function except by ideosyncratic chance. This capriciousness, or "the cult of eccentric originality" as

Sibyl Moholy-Nagy calls it, is shared by the artists themselves, as when la Corbusier or Soleri build cities or buildings unrelated to the surroundings. History itself is often seen as a collage of such extraneous acts, a transcendent creativity answering only to seemingly illogical whim.

Because the central question concerning the relationship of man to nature is the nature of nature, that is, of the Other, its reciprocal aspect is the nature of the self. All concepts of the natural thus turn on the definition of man. If man is indeed a member of ecosystems and not their god then his evolution should illuminate his membership, and we would expect paleo-anthropology to interpret the fossil human record accordingly. A small group of anthropologists have indeed fostered our understanding of the genus *Homo* as an evolving, biological species. The mainstream of anthropology, however, clings tenaciously to the dazzle of comparative ethnology, the striving for cultural analysis pioneered by Boas and given brilliant recent articulation by Clifford Geertz, who says that since human behavior is only manifest in a particular culture then the underlying species-specific behaviors are not only unavailable but virtually nonexistent. Thus has anthropology, like the other social sciences, surrendered its opportunities to define what it means to be human except by intra-species comparisons; that is, by human difference. Man may indeed have food habits, they seem to say, but all we can study are his knives, forks and spoons.

In this way a field with the brightest possibilities for defining human ecology yielded to the dialectics of ideology and the ideology of dialectics. Ideology, the master myth of our time, is the cloak of reasoned partisanship in a world where there are allowed only internally logical options. Within the frame of competing world religions (or what Gary Snyder has called "the cosmopolitan religions"), isms, ologies, parties, sects, and a dime-store counter of psychological trinket-theories of the self we seem to have settled for the deep premise that the only environment is a kind of ambience or closet from which we choose today's reality-costume.

The modern imagination, as Louis Halle has said, is ideological. Thought is so grossly confused with consciousness that a prominent psychologist can write on the "origin of consciousness" as an existential dilemma occuring in historical times, a view woefully deficient in what Robert Ardrey terms the sense of "four-dimensional man."

It has been widely observed that, since about the time of Francis Bacon, the West abandoned its preoccupation with paradise past and fixed its attention on future utopias, to be created by the reign of politician-scientists. Having turned our back on the past as the primal element in our identity, we entered a wonderland of possibilities. Liberated from 1,500 years of desultory regret and lament for the lost Eden, the energies of hope and optimism sprang up in the name of Progress. It is not surprising that Darwin's theory of evolution has had so little impact on the modern consciousness. The Church may have fought it, but to the secular mind the image of aeons of proto-human bestiality was no more attractive than a world degenerating since Adam. Only in one respect was Darwin preferable: he seemed to support the theory of Progress, though of course evolution has nothing whatever to do with that concept.

That abuse of Darwinian thought may prove in the long run to be more destructive than social Darwinism. From the confusion of progress and evolution we derive the corollaries of the normalcy of perpetual change and the idea of adaptability. Shorn of their time perspectives these aspects of evolution appear to justify change for its own sake, unlimited human flexibility, and therefore the commercial exploitation of our adolescent side in its relentless restructuring, the permutation of things and brands as novelty, and the curiously intolerant pursuit of fashion.

Further, there is a reintrojection of the idea of transient forms and values into evolutionary settings, so that it can be argued with solemn authority that for man biological evolution has ended and its place taken by "cultural evolution." The ideological, stratigraphic mind leaped to this marvelous discovery that social change, transmitted by learned information, has supplanted an objectionable biological process dependent on (the much too slow) genetic transmission.

It was just what society needed to disengage itself from the unsavory determinism of Darwin's thought without having to disprove it. It enabled the humanist, intellectual, artist, or social scientist to go his autotelic way, untroubled by the deep past, his animal self, or rules that seemed given rather than made.

Today in the face of the evolutionary studies of culture, the intellectual dimensions of "primitive" thought, the profound biological adaptations to and through which culture is possible, and research on primates, that biological/cultural dichotomy cannot be articulated with a straight face. But society in general lags far behind. The misconception of social "evolution" replacing biological evolution will take many years to fade. The bogus homology of social customs or cultural forms and evolutionary adaptation remains a general feature of the modern intellect. In its own idiom this relativistic monism turns even our humanity and our ecological connections into an ideological choice.

Thus it can be argued that all views on the use of nature are in their way valid, or that all are at least legitimate claims in a democratic society. So, decisions will be made on the basis of "interest group" powers. "Environmental mediation" becomes the latest profession to spin off. A key phrase is "trade-offs." Economically we have become environmentally hip: we now know we must internalize environmental costs. Thus do we assimilate nature as one more variable.

There remains in the game no givens. The intractable nature of biogeochemical cycles and the requirements of the soil are but temporary obstacles in a world where every element of the ecosystem or of the biosphere, like every man, is regarded as having his price. Such an approach is not confined to a blatantly homocentric view of humanity, nor is it merely the spoilers view (the real-estaters and building industries). It is the prevailing mode in those governmental agencies and educational institutions which hire and train the professionals who deal with "land use": agronomists, hydrologists, foresters, and so on.

One could interpret Aldo Leopold's concept, the "ecological conscience," as social expediency: the obligation to conscientiously hear all claims to the control of the natural earth system. But that is not what Leopold meant. In effect, Leopold was rejecting the tenets of his own professionalism. In the preface to his book, *A Sand County Almanac*, he admitted to being one "who cannot live without wild things." Thus he seems at first merely eccentric, but in the end the reader is compelled to ask the same question of himself. To those who are assured that the Big Questions of our time have to do with

Peace, Race, Poverty, Economics, and Politics, the question may seem frivolous.

But the wild, taken to mean the whole community of species, is the prior question. In fact, it is not a question at all, for there is no alternative to living with wild things, only a world increasingly shaped after the desert regions of the Near and Middle East, where political wrangling and endless marauding are the tattered epilogues to a world goated to death, where people play out their roles like regressed primates, obsessed with the details of the social contract, the final inheritors of five millennia of ideological absolutism and ecological relativism.

It is not my intention, however, to enter into an ideological style in criticizing it: to argue a position and advocate that we relinquish one attitude for another. It seems unlikely to me that one can solve the dilemma by participating in its skirmishes. To insist that we adopt the view that our problems stem from the inconsistency of our views goes nowhere. I would suggest rather that the incapacity of the modern mind to find permanent environmental attachments is a consequence of defective ontogenesis.

The processes of establishing relationships vary enormously over the life span. The relativistic position is both a symptom and preoccupation with adult alienation. It neglects the identity-forming stages of early growth of which it is the defective outcome. Convinced that relatedness to the nonhuman as well as to others is made by the calculating consciousness of the adult, we have abused the needs of the child. Those needs and processes, given the opportunity, lead to a stable concept of selfhood which embraces the earth as firmly as it does the mother.

I cannot here elaborate on these processes which have been explored recently by Erik Erikson, Harold Searles, James Fernandez, Edith Cobb and others, but only remark that if the existential dilemmas of chronic relativism are indeed symptoms of inadequate nurturing then we have much reason to hope. For the child is predisposed to enter into the cultus in ways that are irreversible and subsequently undeniable. The total wisdom of humanity may not thereby be increased; its ecological effects will depend on just what the particular vision is. But the development of a mature identity inevitably reaches out to all things, to the growth of an organic relationship in thought as well as fact. In contrast, identity based on arbitrary and transient accretions to the selfhood is a kind of endless smorgasbord in which mature nausea follows adolescent appetite.

Sigmund Kvaloy

Touristic Lifestyles Versus Work in Nature

Among various points that are argued by Paul Shepard, I agree with his stress upon man's roots in the ecosystem as a pre-culturally given element, and his attack upon academic relativism. I am quite convinced that we will be forced to accept an ecophilosophy starting out from man's partnership with animals and plants as a fact.

I might disagree, however, on how much we will ever get to know about pre-cultural "human nature". I would not, for example, go along with the view that "man is really a hunter"—say, when speaking of man as a social being. As yet, we know too little about the past couple of million years to say that natural man is someone living like the few hunters that we can observe today. We do not even know whether there ever was a human social system that was not "homocentric", or whether there can ever be one. To agree with Shepard's way of thinking: we must also be sceptical of those who "choose models" to tackle this question! Furthermore, a hunter may organize his life in a multitude of manners—and some of these are—with respect to combined ecological and social stability—closer to some farmers that we know about than to hunters of other varieties. Norwegian farmers as I have known them in my own childhood are a good example here. The challenges they had to meet were extremely more complex in qualitative differentiation than what monoculture farmers, now or earlier, had to cope with. Likewise the Sherpas of Nepal-Himalaya today. Incidentally, these are both cultures where the goat, Shepard's great enemy, is an ecologically sound element.

The most important questions today are those pertaining to our contemporary eco-social crisis—a crisis that is different from earlier crises in that it is characterized by an exponentially self-strengthening increase in the number of *qualitatively* different attacks upon the ecosystem and the human organism, as a necessary consequence of the union of competition and applied science typical of the later stages of industrial society,—whereas earlier instances of man-made ecocrises were comparatively simple kinds of deteriorations along a few parameters—more meaningfully suited for quantification. A vivid confrontation with this situation should impress upon us that man is extremely flexible and adaptable—notably in his ability to construct "new ways out" that postpone any real understanding and solution to crisis developments that are part of the social system itself. With this in mind, it seems that searching for details as to man's species-specific, pre-cultural nature—even though it is there—will at best give us only a minor part of the solution.

One thing that we must continuously keep in mind is that what we are proposing is politically and socially viable in the present situation, or, in other words, it must be communicable to those who do not earn their living through intellectual activity. That man will function well only if he is organized in keeping with the hunter's way of life, as some ethnologists seem to claim, is a thought too far removed from the daily problems of most people or the present predicament of mankind etc. to be understandable to the broad public.

Rather than giving overriding priority to man's biological evolution (and to the troubles created or enhanced by his homocentric views), I would propose that we start off right away by asking what would lead man—given the probably social and political outcome of our present crisis—to regain the role of a complex, deft, and creative partaker in a complex eco-social system. How can he regain his courage to rely on himself instead of on complicated machinery and organizational expertise? How is ecological stability related to democracy?

I agree with Shepard that an important element in our strategy is the human child, in that what happens to the child is largely an irreversible social determinant. In my view, the technical gadgets of modern society surround the human being—children and adults—as a barrier that protects them from those challenges from nature that they need to develop in a sufficiently manysided manner. The most serious part of this is that natural challenges are lacking in modern man's *work*; leisure activities will never give him challenges that are real and serious enough to affect his personality in a deep way.

Worst of all: children are not allowed at all as partakers in responsible work.

I am stressing this because we have here to do with man's possibilities of finding and developing his own nature's bio-social rhythms which are Nature's rhythms as expressed through her human child. Without this basis, an integration with Nature and a dynamic and creative steady state ("homeorhesis" as the British geneticist C.F. Waddington calls it) is not possible.

Furthermore, the industrial way of doing work precludes a development of man's capacity for direct and loyal cooperation with his fellows. You have to join hands with your fellow sister and brother and your children in a concrete, literal sense, confronting the task of survival together, to build a stable social network and to live without harming the ecosystem!

It is at least conceivable that an *agrarian* society might materialize in this direction—after the inevitable breakdown of industrial society. There are many ways of doing agriculture and animal husbandry, and there have been many different social systems built upon them. I would say that there are still many more possible combinations and new solutions that have not been tried yet.

There are in the contemporary world hardly any more "wild things"—in the sense of "animals and plants and ecosystems unaffected by human manipulation", and we will be even further removed from that state in the future when, hopefully, the new society is built.

The only "objective value" basis that we are left with as regards man's relationship with nature is a few general principles that seem to offer a basis for ecological and social stability even in a world with no "pure" wilderness—-principles that we seem to be able to discern by studying a wide spectrum of different human cultures, but which have been given very different expressions in these cultures. Paleo-anthropology cannot help much here. I have above given reasons for stressing the role of work in building a stable society. I will here list four "objective" principles that have to do with human work:

1. Work should demand the unfolding of that rich complex of potentialities that every child is born with (which means work

should lead to high individual self-reliance and self-sufficiency
and ability to master changing conditions),

2. Work should demand the development of a human being's
   capacities for loyal, self-effacing cooperation,
3. The fruits of work should be such products and services that
   enhance human dignity, creativity, social participation, and the
   life strength of his ecosystem,
4. The economic basis of society should demand and appreciate
   children's and old people's participation in work.

These four requirements can be realized only in an economy based on "labor-intensive" work in close and manysided contact with
nature. My contention is, at the moment, that where these four principles are built in, you will have a society at peace with itself and its
Nature. With such a basis, the "conflict of ideology and ecology"
would no longer be a relevant one. We will get it—if ever—only after
the abundant industrial energy flows of the present Euro-American
societies have dried up, when the political power-pyramids built on
that—more than anything alienating man from nature—have consequently vanished,—in an eco-social situation where a touristic choice
of life-styles is no longer offered.—Until such a time, I think we will
have to live with "environmental relativism" in our—the affluent—part of the world.

Finally, after having tried various approaches, in meetings with
many very different groups of people, my experience is that these
four principles are something that most people understand and go
along with. They would, most of them, like to see their own work
built on those four requirements, while they also see that the
economic and organizational structure of our present society is incompatible with them. In other words, these principles seem to be a
good starting point for a campaign to prepare our societies for the
great transition ahead.

John R. Rodman

— A2 —

Theory and Practice
In the Environmental Movement:
Notes Towards An Ecology
Of Experience

Inquiries into the theories implicit in practice must be historical, since differences of principles tend to be overlaid by the stereotyped rationalizations that constitute the common rhetoric of any particular period. Differences within the environmental movement, traditionally confused by everyone's claim to be a Conservationist, are now obscured by the near-universality of the appeal to Survival.

Survival is one of those sloganistic arrests in the process of reflection, like Scarcity and Abundance, whereby a verb or an adjective is turned into an abstract noun and cast in the role of figure, while the real subject is relegated to the background of attention. When we try to make the subject of Survival explicit, we find that one writer seems to envisage the death of the biosphere, another the extinction of all organic life on the planet earth, another the passing of the human species, another the perishing of large numbers of humans and others in an ecological crash, and another the end of a form of civilization to which he has grown attached.

Why is the appeal to Survival so popular? It draws upon the popular Spencerian-Darwinian notion that life is "scientifically" seen to be a struggle for the survival of the fittest. It expresses an anxiety that our world-historical situation is extreme. And it revives the Hobbesian assumption that, whatever our varying notions of the good life, we all share some bedrock commitment to life itself, which makes possible such luxuries as arguing or fighting about the greatest good.

Yet it is one of the subtleties of the human condition that individuals and groups sometimes lose the will to live; sometimes commit suicide; and sometimes risk their lives to defend, or to try to establish, a particular way of life. Beneath Hobbes' own nightmare vision of the chaos brought on by warring fanatics lay a commitment to the ideal of an orderly, secure, tolerant prosperous, "civilized" way of life characterized by the flourishing of the arts and sciences and the amenities of commodious living. Now as then, the Hobbesian question of survival dissolves into the Aristotelian question of the good life or, as it is often phrased today, the quality of life. The basic proof of this is experimental: we can all imagine a world in which we should not care to live; some of us can even imagine risking our lives to prevent its coming to pass. Yet we suspect that it is easier to imagine this than to act when the time comes, especially since the time is apt to come upon us by degrees. Political events of this century have also brought home to us the extraordinary capacity of human beings in extreme situations to survive by adapting in unexpected ways. So the question becomes: when do adaptations amount to a significant change of character, or when does something survive by becoming something else?

This is not a linguistic or logical quibble, but a troubling existential question. Imagine a person whose honesty is fundamental both to his self-image and to his character as perceived by others, and suppose that conditions arise in which he can survive only by becoming an inveterate thief and liar, even to the point of self-deception. Imagine a hunting tribe that survives after being deprived of the land and the activity that were central to its way of life. Imagine a political system that has prided itself on its freedom and democracy surviving by gradually transforming itself into a totalitarian regime ruled by an elite of economic andecological planners. Or imagine that humanity can survive only by practicing a ruthless "lifeboat ethics" that leaves the survivors thoroughly inhumane. The appeal to Survival seems to presuppose some tacit notion, if not of the good life, then at least of a minimally acceptable way of life in which a subject can retain a sense of essential continuity—for example, a way of life in which human beings can remain recognizably human to themselves.

The remainder of this paper explores the images of humanity implicit in the human/nature relationships posited by four currents of thought discernible in the history of the contemporary environmental movement. My primary purpose is to clarify the kind of self we choose when we take up a particular posture towards the nonhuman environment. My secondary purpose is to suggest that the fourth of these alternatives may be the one most faithful to the integrity of experience. Throughout, the reader should keep in mind that I present ideal types which are seldom embodied in pure form; that limitations of space preclude any thorough discussion of the theoretical or practical problems entailed by any of the four views, as well as any documentation;* and that the present stage of analysis is based almost exclusively on American materials, so that the question of the typology's more general application is left open.

It frequently happens that people think they are engaged in a common action when they share only a common behavior. Their attention is still directed towards a common enemy, and the visions implicit in their acts have not yet become clearly differentiated. In the 1890's, for example, Theodore Roosevelt, Gifford Pinchot, and John Muir all supported the exercise of Presidential authority to set aside portions of the public domain as forest reserves. A shared hostility to the rapid destruction of land and trees by commercial interests aiming at short-term profits masked a diversity of visions. The principle of multiple-use made a good deal of accommodation possible, but disagreements, first over the use of the forest reserves for grazing and then over the future of Hetch Hetchy Valley, eventually made it clear that Pinchot envisioned a system of public lands scientifically managed for a sustained yield of timber, forage, water, and power, while Muir envisioned a system of wilderness parks where overcivilized people could repair to regenerate body and spirit, and the expansive Roosevelt envisaged all of the above together with bird sanctuaries for the ornithologists and game preserves to assure a sustained yield of sport for the Boone and Crockett Club. Specifically, Pinchot thought in terms of utilizing "natural resources" for

*For partial documentation, see my "Four Stages of Ecological Consciousness. Part One: Resource Conservation—Economics and After" (a paper presented at the annual meeting of the American Political Science Association, Sept. 1976); "The Liberation of Nature?" (Inquiry, Vol. 20, Spring 1977); "Ecological Resistance: John Stuart Mill and the Case of the Kentish Orchid" (a paper presented at the annual meeting of the American Political Science Association, Sept. 1977).

"the greatest good of the greatest number over the long run," and he judged the damming and flooding of Hetch Hetchy (to make a reservoir to supply water for the growing population of San Francisco) to be the highest and best use of the valley. Muir, on the other hand, thought of Hetch Hetchy as a holy place to be preserved from desecration because there a person could get in touch with his deeper self, his primordial roots, and the divine force still active in creating the evolving universe.

Resource Conservation in America has been an aspect of resource *development*. Frank Smith has admiringly written its history as a chronicle of the activities of the Forest Service, the Corps of Engineers, the Bureau of Reclamation, the Tennessee Valley Authority, and the Atomic Energy Commission. In the several years since the first "energy crisis" of 1973, the terms "conservation" and "development" have probably been more sharply distinguished than at any earlier time, as choices have been posed between conserving present energy resources and developing new ones. We are, of course, committed to both strategies, as is implied by agency titles such as the (California) Energy Conservation and Development Commission. Underlying the plurality of strategies is a common view of nonhuman nature as consisting of intrinsically worthless material which acquires instrumental value when appropriated for human use. (It is so evident to the Resource Conservationist that "the greatest number" refers only to humans that it seems superfluous to say it.) An important clue to the developmental ethos that underlies Resource Conservation can be found in the conception of Waste, which functions as an economic equivalent to Sin. Waste refers not only to excessive or inefficient utilization. It encompasses also John Wesley Powell's view of the arid lands of the American West as a wasteland until reclaimed by irrigation for agriculture, Lord Kelvin's view of Niagara Falls as a gigantic waste of water until harnessed to produce hydroelectric power, and a Southern California legislator's notion that the wild rivers of the North which flow into the ocean are wasted unless dammed and diverted to irrigate farmland, quench the thirst of cities, and support golf courses in the desert. There are, then, two ways to sin by wasting: to utilize inefficiently and not to utilize at all. Within this frame of reference, the process by which natural things go through their biological cycles has no value unless and until harnessed for human use, transformed into colonial processes within the expanding empire of technology and economics.

The Preservationist gospel, by contrast, became flesh in the Sierra Club, the Wilderness Society, to a limited extent in the National Park Service, and more in the Wilderness System authorized by Congress in 1964. Many of its vicissitudes are implicit in the tension between the esoteric appeal of re-creation and the mass appeal of recreation, others in the tension between the underlying religious need and the esthetic through which the satisfaction of that need is mediated.

The notion that "recreation" is a qualitatively differentiated and hierarchically structured experience of nonhuman otherness is accepted even by the Park Service and the Forest Service, although the variables they identify include only such items as the amount of skill required, the extent to which one must satisfy one's own "basic needs" (defined as food, shelter, and transport), the degree of administrative control, and the relative presence or absence of man-made "modifications for comfort and convenience." Just what it is that is supposed to happen in a condition of relative wilderness remains mysterious. A perusal of the literature of wilderness experience, however, yields the following model. Filtered through Muir's biblical/architectural imagery of Nature's cathedrals threatened with desecration are traces of the older notion of a sacred place where human beings can transcend the limitations of everyday experience and become renewed through contact with the power of creation. This process has two basic dimensions. On the level of depth psychology/mythology, the journey from the city or the farm into the wildernes is a journey out of the socialized self into the unconscious self, from which may emerge a new definition of personal identity, as when hitherto repressed traits become incorporated into the conscious self. On the cosmogonic level, Muir's imaginative reconstruction of the process whereby the Sierra valleys were—and are still—formed by glacial action over the course of geologic time functions as a vicarious re-enactment (within an evolutionary paradigm) of the creation of the world that environs the Self. While not every backpacker is born again, writers such as Muir articulate as well as guide the inchoate intuitions of larger numbers of people. The continuity of this tradition is demonstrated by Arthur St. George's sociological study of Sierra Club members in the early 1970's, which concluded that their values were (like those of their founder) primarily "religious and esthetic."

The relationship of the esthetic to the religious is essentially this: the experience of the holy is esthetically mediated. Nature experienced as beauty provides an external model of harmonious integration for the divided personality and arouses wonder at the "as if" possibility of an intelligent and benign cosmic order. Nature experienced as sublimity suggests depths and heights that transcend the flat landscape of everyday experience and evoke awe in the presence of overwhelming power or vastness. Hence a traditional commitment to saving the Sierras of life as the natural environments of peak experiences. It is not without some loss of intensity that this loyalty to special places is generalized to embrace the natural environment as a whole, as Sierra Club members become also Friends of the Earth.

Meanwhile, back at Yosemite, John Muir was complaining as early as 1912 about the crowds of people who came to fish and picnic, oblivious to the sermons sculptured in stone, as if they had not eyes with which to hear. The subsequent history of Wilderness Preservation has been an unending process of saving an area from private development by making it a National Park that gradually becomes administered for mass recreation, then further saving some special part of it by having it designated a Wilderness Area, to which access must eventually be limited by a system of bureaucratic permits. Wilderness Preservation and Resource Conservation thus tend to converge: wilderness becomes a type of land use, a scarce resource that can be conserved by being managed. For this convergence to be seen as more than an historical accident, however, it must be viewed from some perspective located outside either of these two traditions, so that Resource Conservation and Wilderness Preservation appear variations on the theme of wise use, the former oriented to the production of commodities for human consumption, the latter to providing human amenities.

One such alternative perspective is provided by the tradition growing out of the humane movement, recently radicalized by animal liberationists, and sometimes generalized to embrace non-animal beings as well. In contrast to the economic ethos of Resource Conservation and the religious/esthetic character of Wilderness Preservation, this perspective is strikingly moral in style. Its notion of human virtue is not prudence or reverence, but justice. In contrast to the caste-bound universe of the Resource Conservationist, the Nature Moralist affirms the democratic principle that all natural entities (or, more narrowly, all forms of life) have intrinsic value, and that wild animals, plants, rivers, and whole ecosystems have a right to exist, flourish, and reproduce—or at least that human beings have no right to exploit or unnecessarily harm or destroy other members of the biotic community. In contrast to the aristocratic universe of Wilderness Preservation, where some places (and some forms of recreation) are holier than others and certain types of natural entities (lofty mountains, grand canyons, redwoods, and whales) are traditionally more worthy of being saved than others (swamps, chaparral, and insects), the world of the Nature Moralist is characterized by an apparent egalitarianism. Pinchot and Muir once went on a camping trip to Grand Canyon, where Pinchot saw a tarantula and was about to kill it when Muir stopped him, saying that the tarantula had as much right to be there as they did. Pinchot was so struck with this curious notion that he not only let the tarantula live (perhaps out of respect for Muir) but recalled the incident a half-century later in his autobiography. (As for Muir, let this story serve to illustrate how ideal types overlap in the complexity of flesh-and-blood persons. The "rights" theme is nevertheless faint in comparison to the religious/esthetic theme in Muir's life and writings.)

It is easier to find isolated and anecdotal, rather than systematic and institutional, embodiment of the standpoint of Nature Moralism. Yet some limited notion of nonhuman rights would appear to be implicit in a century and a half of humane legislation, since it is only by the most tortuous rationalizing that cruelty to nonhuman animals can be punished on the ground of its being indirectly detrimental to human well-being. The U.S. Animal Welfare Act embodies a typical compromise between Nature Moralism and Resource Conservation, between the principle that at least warm-blooded vertebrates ought not to be made to suffer pain by humans with the principle that the "lower" animals are resources to be exploited in research carried on for the benefit of "humanity." (The animal liberationists who have picketed the American Museum of Natural History to protest federally-funded research on the effects of physical mutilation on the sex life of cats have testified, in effect, to the impending dissolution of this compromise.)

We can also speculate that Endangered Species Acts imply some recognition of a right to life on the part of certain nonhuman species, and indeed this notion was given official expression by the recent Assistant Secretary of the Interior for Fish, Wildlife, and Parks, Mr. Nathaniel Reed. Yet any species on the endangered list that is protected well enough to become fairly abundant (such as the *Alligator mississippiensis*) is apt to discover that the human coalition that made possible its protection contained not only Nature Moralists who believe that killing alligators to make handbags is morally wrong, but also sustained-yield Conservationists who want to resume hunting or "harvesting" it, and Preservationists who seem preoccupied with protecting instances of Nature's grandeur.

The fact that Nature Moralism is still more a dissident than an establishment viewpoint is typified in the decision of certain individuals (now under indictment for theft of private property) to commit their own Marine Mammal Protection Act by liberating captive dolphins, claiming that human beings had no right to imprison and exploit (even for academic research) beings that are by nature intelligent, wild, and free. Yet Nature Moralism may be in the process of being institutionalized in the Interior Department's Office of Endangered Species, as the movement to protect endangered species—initiated out of a variety of motives—gains momentum and becomes a kind of end in itself. Conflicts are inevitable, but as long as practical accommodations can be arranged—as in the case of the sandhill crane habitat that occasioned the redesign of some six miles of federally-funded interstate highway in Mississippi—a general confrontation between two fundamentally different standpoints can be avoided. However, the recent tendency to formulate issues in terms of protecting an endangered species versus completing some resource development project—the *Furbish lousewort* vs. the Dickey-Lincoln hydroelectric project in Maine, the snail darter vs. the Tellico Dam in Tennessee, a rare species of trailing pea plant vs. the Lafarge Dam project in Wisconsin—suggests the possibility of an emerging confrontation between Nature Moralism and Resource Conservation that is potentially as significant as the Hetch Hetchy conflict was for defining the difference between Conservation and Preservation.

There is probably something sound in our reluctance to let issues be defined in quite this way. It is not only that the theory of non-human rights is still inchoate both as to boundary (animals? plants? rocks?) and as to focus (individuals, populations, communities, species?); not only that if Congress intervenes to settle the Tellico Dam issue by amending the Endangered Species Act it will probably mean the end of the snail darter. Suppose only the TVA biologists succeed in breeding the snail darter in another river, so that the Little Tennessee can be dammed *and* the snail darter can be saved. At this point, it becomes evident that the preoccupation with saving species from extinction can become an absolute abstracted from the larger and more complex issue of defending a habitat that is shared by humans and nonhumans alike. To assume automatically that either snail darters or human beings can be artificially transplanted from one locale to another without being significantly changed presupposes a remarkably atomistic view of the world. Where this leads is shown by the proposal to "save" the California condor by breeding it in captivity.

As we begin to explore the notion of a shared habitat and the notion that an organism's relationship to its natural environment may be an important part of the organism's character, we drift away from the worlds adumbrated so far and enter a fourth world of perception and action that I call Ecological Resistance. This fourth world is implied by such considerations as the following. Ecologically disruptive projects (such as dams, highways, or power plants) are sometimes met with intense resistance on the ground that they would ruin a natural area, even though the area is relatively valueless as a material resource, contains no edifying scenery, is little used for recreation (in any sense), is no longer in virginal condition, and harbors no species known to be endangered. Such resistance nevertheless often involves a strong subjective identification between the persons resisting and the geographic area. *Some* of the persons resisting are also participants in campaigns of resistance to war, imperialism, racism, sexism, etc., and they feel that there is some among their activites.

A tentative sketch of Ecological Resistance includes the following features. (1) Ecological Resistance is not ideological action. Rather, action tends to precede theory, and theory emerges retrospectively as actors try to make their experience intelligible. (2) The central principle of Ecological Resistance is the conviction that diversity is natural, good, and threatened by the forces of monoculture. (3) The struggle between diversity and monoculture is perceived to occur in different spheres of experience ranging from the human/nature interaction, through the relations between races, nationalities, sexes, political parties, and individual temperaments, to the interaction between components of the intrapsychic ecosystem. It is characteristic of Ecological Resistance that it manifests itself in more than one realm. A good historical example is provided by John Stuart Mill, who defended biological diversity against the threat of a wholly humanized planet, West Indian blacks against European racists, women against the tyranny of a patriarchal tradition, and the many-sided personality against the totalitarian claims of economic/technological rationality. Thoreau, who once refused to pay taxes because the U.S. government made war on Mexico and required the return of fugitive slaves, would be a marginal case. John Mujir, who ignored almost every social issue of his time, starting with slavery and the Civil War and ending with female suffrage, would not qualify at all.

(4) The different levels of experience—*cosmos, polis, psyche*—mirror one another. It is no mere coincidence that Hitler envisioned an Aryan Europe purged of Jews *and* a totally humanized planet from which all micro-organisms had been eliminated, or that he depicted Jews as a "bacillus." It is no accident that Mill was involved in the struggle against the subjection of women *and* in an effort to liberate the "feminine" element within his own personality. (5) The relationship between levels of experience is one of metaphoric mirroring rather than one of superstructure and base, or effect and cause. *If* there is a base model it is that of an ecosystem; but the characteristics of this model are not so much extracted from biology and then imposed upon polity and personality as they are perceived

as a common *Gestalt* manifested in varying ways at different levels.

(8) Ecological Resistance involves a ritual affirmation of the Myth of Microcosm. Acts of Ecological Resistance are not undertaken primarily in the spirit of calculated, long-term self-interest (of the individual, the society, or the species), or in the spirit of obedience to a moral duty, or in the spirit of preventing profanation. One resists because the threat to the land, the river, or the biosphere is perceived *also* as a threat to the self, or rather to the principle of diversity and spontaneity that is the endangered side of the basic balance that defines and sustains the very nature of things. Purely humanistic accounts of resistance and rebellion postulate a human nature that mysteriously discovers its essential limits within an absurd or meaningless world. Ecological Resistance, by contrast, assumes a version of the theory of internal relations: the human personality discovers its structure through interaction with the nonhuman order. I am what I am at least partly in relation to my natural environment, and changes in that environment affect my own identity. If I stand idly by and let it be destroyed, a part of me is also destroyed or seriously deranged. An act of Ecological Resistance, then, is an affirmation of the integrity of a naturally diverse self-and-world. Its meaning is not exhausted by its success or failure in the linear sequence of events, since its meaning lies also in the multi-dimensional depth of an act in one realm that simultaneously affirms a principle valid in many realms. Ecological Resistance thus has something of the character of a ritual action whereby one aligns the self with the ultimate order of things.

Each of the four perspectives has theoretical problems. Resource Conservation provides no justification for its speciesism, its limitation of "the greatest number" to humans; and its notion of "the long run" appears quaint in the perspective of evolutionary time. Wilderness Preservation links the primordial experience of the encounter with the holy to a transient esthetic that is sometimes ecologically pernicious. Nature Moralism, in trying to give nonhumans their due, imposes upon interspecies relations an all too species-specific morality of rights and duties. Ecological Resistance has unresolved problems about the nature and status of the basic balance of which diversity is an essential aspect; and the implications of diversity as an organizing principle for society are unclear. The first three perspectives offer what are all too clearly abridgements of experience: an economic treatment of nature as resource, an esthetic view of nature as inspiring scenery, and a moralistic stance towards nature as something to which we have duties. The fourth perspective seems more comprehensive but needs exploration to see whether its comprehension is offset by vagueness.

Each perspective on nonhuman nature implies also a vision of humanity. We define ourselves in part by our choice of how to treat "nature." The image of humanity suggested by the stance of the Resource Conservationist is, in the first instance, a "masculine" image of Man the Master who maximizes value by managing and manipulating matter; man is the god-like creator of value. Seen through the lens of social history, Resource Conservation suggests a rather modern and very economic view of life in terms of trade-offs, costs, and benefits, and of character in terms of bourgeois avarice tempered by aristocratic self-restraint. From the Boone and Crockett Club to the Club of Rome, Resource Conservation is the creed of greed moderated by statesmanlike foresight and prudence. Finally, if we follow the hypothesis that our image of nonhuman nature mirrors our secret image of ourselves, we arrive at the paradoxical possibility that we feel ourselves not to be gods, and not even to embody intrinsic value, but to be so much raw material out of which value can be created through transformative labor. The counterpart of the natural resource is the human resource—material first for the self-made man, then for the socially useful person. It is a world in which none are saved by grace but some by work, a world in which the phrase "internal improvements" expresses not only a long-standing policy on public works but also an ethos of personal life.

The image of humanity implied in the vision of the Wilderness Preservationist is drawn like a landscape composed of valleys and mountains, where the valleys are wombs for rebirthing and the mountains are so many breasts through which a benevolent Mother Nature graciously dispenses nourishment to her wide-eyed children, this world wilderness is gentled by anthropomorphic metaphor, in-this world wilderness is gentled by enthropomorphic metaphor, inhabited by symbols of spiritual transcendence rather than by frightful demons or even by beasts of prey. We journey like pilgrims in search of we know not what, across a landscape whose depth is—like Walden Pond—all too measurable. In this sunlit realm of higher laws, ugly things like slavery, civil war, genocide, even predation, have no proper place. They occur outside the park.

The image of humanity implied in the vision of the Nature Moralist embodies all the ambiguity of the liberal civil rights worker who thinks that "we" can liberate "them." All beings (or animals, or whatever) have equal rights, except that only we humans have duties. By analogy, all parts of the self are equal, but some are more equal then others. The human/nature dichotomy is denied, only to be redrawn within the self as subjection to moral duty is pronounced "liberation."

The image of humanity implied in Ecological Resistance is more holistic and participatory. "Man" does not stand over against "his environment" as manager, sight-seer, or do-gooder; he is an integral part of the food chain, both predator and, if no longer prey, at least host to millions; an integral part of the organic cycle of birth, growth, decay, and death that unites all things; a microcosm of the cosmos who takes very personally the wounds inflicted on his/her androgynous body. By making the principle of diversity central, Ecological Resistance can incorporate the other three perspectives as moments within the dialectic of a larger whole. Economics, morality, and esthetic religiosity have niches in the ecology of our experience of nature, and each has its limits. Prudence, justice, and reverence may be essential parts of a good life, but a good life has also a kind of integrity by virtue of which the whole is greater than the sum of its parts.

Joseph W. Meeker

— A3 —
Fields of Danger and
The Wilderness of Wisdom

Like cows in the dairy advertisement, professional people like to be outstanding in their fields. Fields assure safety, comfort, nourishment, and identity to those who inhabit them, and they provide a familiar surrounding where large surprises or threats are unlikely to occur. They are artificial spaces designed and controlled for maximum efficiency, fencing out whatever is unwanted or too complicated, and encouraging whatever single crop the field is intended to produce. Fields are intentional distortions of reality in the interests of tidiness and efficiency.[1]

Left to its own devices, reality is neither tidy nor efficient, nor does it comfortably tolerate fences and fields. The real world is composed of astonishing patterns of complexity which shade and grade into one another in endless and random configurations. Its boundaries are fluid or permeable at all levels from the sub-atomic to the cerebral. Time, matter, energy, and mentality interact to create whatever exists with little regard for what is needed or appropriate. That is not to say that reality is necessarily chaotic, but merely that its processes are overwhelmingly complex and intricate. Reality is a wilderness.

Fields, we may assume, were invented as devices for taming reality and reducing natural complexity to more easily manageable proportions. Those Neolithic farmers who first hit upon the idea of raising single crops and enclosing their animals may not have realized the cultural importance of what they were doing, but they must surely have appreciated how easy it was to gather vegetable foods from a monocultural field and how gloriously simple hunting was when the animals could not run away. Farmer's fields became the enabling device which led to the domestication of plants and animals, permanent and elaborate human settlements, and stratified societies which allowed leisure to some people. Those gifted with leisure occupied themselves with philosophy and public affairs, but now these were divorced activities which bore little contact with the sensory and natural conditions of ordinary real life.

Such people as Plato and Aristotle fenced for themselves some very large fields of knowledge and praised the virtues of the contemplative life (cows in their fields appear to love contemplation, too). The benefits they gave to mankind have perhaps been enough justification for the labor of the many non-contemplatives who have always supported full-time thinkers like Plato and Aristotle, and like most of the people in this room. But of course everybody has a field, whether it be slavery or merchandizing or farming, or whether one is a woman whose field is assumed to include reproduction, housekeeping, and childrearing. The agricultural idea of field specialization proved easily applicable to social occupations and social structuring. It promptly replaced the ancient traditions of hunting and gathering, both of which, incidentally, are contemplative and philosophical activities which are fully in touch with a whole natural setting and which use the whole human being.[2] When agricultural and social specialization replaced hunting and gathering, mankind abandoned wholeness in favor of the fragmented but profitable way of life in the fields.

At the emergence of industrialized societies, a few centuries ago, the field metaphor was well established and ripe to be applied to the fencing of human activities into ever smaller and more intense specializations. Old fields were further subdivided (philosophy was transformed into a score or more of philosophical disciplines), new alliances among fields emerged(science formed a compact with a field called technology and they have been fussing over the boundaries ever since), and entire new fields were mapped out, such as advertising, insurance, social service, and a field called "education." Now virtually everyone can boast a field which is a part of personal identity more surely than one's gender, family, or personality traits. We have persuaded ourselves that specialization is a necessary condition of survival in an industrialized and overpopulated world. That may be so, but field specialization has also become one of the most dangerous threats to the healthy continuation of natural and human processes. Recognition of that danger is the best justification for holding this conference on the unity of the sciences.

Fragmentation and the failure to perceive context are necessary consequences of field specialization which have become serious threats to human well-being and to the stability of natural processes. The fencelines which define fields tell us not only what is within the fence, but what must be kept outside it. So scientists avoid ethics, artists abhor science, and engineers ignore esthetics as topics foreign to their chosen fields and probably threatening to their efficiency within their fields. Knowledge is thus circumscribed and shielded from the contexts which alone can give it depth and meaning. Habits of field thinking lead us to act imprudently and to misunderstand what we know. The intellectual and emotional myopia of field thinking have their consequences for all of us to see in the massive disruptions of environmental crisis, in the threats of destruction from nuclear warfare and nuclear peacefare, and in the mono-mental chaos that comes from the many minds locked in their compartments, failing to understand that there is a world out there that refuses to confine itself to the artificial boundaries imposed by field thinking. However efficient they may be in producing information, fields are necessarily crisis-laden, and they are incapable of producing what we most need: wisdom.

It may be argued that field specialization is not artificial at all, but is a normal human extension of the many tendencies toward specialization which are evident in natural evolutionary processes. There is a big difference, however, between an ecological niche achieved through evolutionary adaptation and a specialized field created by human judgment. Speciation is specialization, as plants and animals are modified over time to adapt to environmental changes and to ecological succession. The governing principle here is for the organism to modify its own structure and behavior to suit the ever-changing circumstances of its surroundings. Field specialization, as it has been applied since Neolithic times by human beings, goes in exactly the opposite direction. Its purpose is to restrain and to modify the existing world—whether it be a body of land or a body of knowledge—to accommodate human wishes and to serve human ends. If humans were to use their knowledge of the world as other animals do, to adapt to natural environments rather than to control them, then we, too would have niches rather than fields to live in, and we would be part of natural reality rather than at war with it.

Claude Levi-Strauss has given us the useful concept of "bricolage" as a major mode of human thought that is rooted deeply in our evolutionary history.[3] The *bricoleur* (a French term for an inspired handyman, with no good English equivalent) is the student, teacher, or craftsman who creates useful things from cast-off odds and ends which others have found to be useless. "The bricoleur," says Levi-Strauss, "is adept at performing a large number of diverse tasks; but, unlike the engineer, he does not subordinate each of them to the availability of raw materials and tools conceived and procured for the purpose of the project."[4] In bricolage, "it is always earlier ends which are called upon to play the part of means: the signified changes into the signifying and vice versa."[5] With what result? In bricolage, the result "will always be a compromise between the structure of the instrumental set and that of the project. Once it materializes, the project will therefore inevitably be at a remove from the initial aim."[6] Bricolage is the mentality of synthesis, a technique for creating, learning, and expressing human understanding, using whatever is present and what remains from the past to achieve an integrating form. That is what mythical thinking does, and it is what scientific and philosophical thought might do if they were freed from the manipulative purposiveness imposed by field specializations.

Evolutionary history is itself a long story of bricolage, according to Francois Jacob of the Pasteur Institute in Paris. Jacob argues provocatively that "Evolution behaves like a tinkerer (bricoleur) who, during eons upon eons, would slowly modify his work, unceasingly retouching it, cutting here, lengthening there, seizing the opportunities to adapt it progressively to its new use."[7] Unlike the engineer, the tinkerer or bricoleur does not have a grand plan or established criteria of excellence, but uses whatever is at hand to accomplish a creation that is likely to surprise even himself. The living forms that make up the natural world, including humanity, are the products of such tinkering. Jacob further applies the tinkerer's art to the evolution of the human brain: "the formation of a dominating neocortex coupled with the persistence of a nervous and hormonal system partially, but not totally under the rule of the neocortex— strongly resembles the tinkerer's procedure. It is somewhat like adding a jet engine to an old horse cart."[8] If that indeed is what our mental vehicle is like (mine usually feels that way), we had better drive with great care.

Bricolage and tinkering may seem like undignified methodologies for the conduct of evolution, science and philosophy. But consider the alternatives. What if there had been a conference of biologists at the beginning of creation to plan and implement the best possible strategies for the evolutionary development of life on the planet Earth? And of course there would have been a later conference of professional fields when it came time to introduce mankind, and another still when the development of human mentality was to be implemented. One can imagine gigantic trade-offs and compromises as engineers presented their cost/benefit analyses, as environmental impact studies were pursued, and as the professional societies and academic departments struggled with one another to assure that the needs of their respective fields were met by the new creation. I'll settle for our history of evolutionary bricolage, thank you.

What we have inherited from that history, our multi-leveled brain linked in many ways to our bodily functions and to our natural environments, is not a bad instrument for comprehending the world, providing we do not restrict its functions by the erection of artificial barriers. We are capable of perceiving clearly a many-dimensional world, of feeling deeply about it, of relating to one another and to other species in many ways, of analyzing logically our experiences and thoughts, and of bringing unlikely aspects of our awareness into creative new combinations. We are evidently designed for wholeness, or at least we are capable of it. That we have nevertheless elected our own fragmentation by arbitrarily building borders around parts of our lives is one of our saddest errors.

It is an avowed purpose of our present meeting to search for absolute values in a changing world. Although I confess to feeling awkward at the use of the adjective "absolute" to describe any values ("relatively absolute" would seem more comfortable if it were not a contradiction in terms), my reluctance is at a minimum when I consider wisdom as a value. Although absolute as a value, wisdom is by nature a perception of relativity and relationships, and thus provides a satisfactory resolution to the contradiction in terms. It is an awareness of the wholeness of things which does not lose sight of their particularity and concreteness or of the intricacies of the relationships among things. It is where left and right brains come together in a union of logic and poetry and sensation, and where self-awareness no longer is at odds with perceptions of the external world. Wisdom cannot be confined to a field, nor is it a discipline; it is the consciousness of wholeness and integrity which transcends both.

Fields make us smart and fat, but not wise. However useful and efficient it may seem to enforce boundaries of knowledge in the interest of high productivity, our great need now is for the unbounded insights of wisdom. It is possible to raise a crop of information in a field, and perhaps even to cultivate knowledge, but no one ever found wisdom there. Wisdom grows in a wilderness context. It is the state of complexity understood and relationships accepted.

The interdisciplinary movement of which this conference is a part is not an academic fad, but a response to the growing need among people everywhere to find a new sense of integrity for their own lives and for their understanding of the world around them. It is in part a corrective movement intended to combat the fragmentation that has resulted from centuries of field specialization. But it is also a creative effort directed toward greater wholeness and integration of human knowledge. The fences must come down to correct past errors and distortions, but at the same time we must learn new ways to live in the wilderness of wholeness where our best hope for the future lies.

The search for wisdom will require that we re-think many of our values, that we restructure some of our institutions, and that we revise our notions of personal and professional identity. As I have argued elsewhere,[9] a meaningful alliance among the value systems of science, art, and technology is now being created because of the new necessities faced by each of those "fields." Education, too, is ordering itself anew in response to recent discoveries about the nature of the human mind and its learning processes,[10] and as we increasingly discover that "training for a field" is not a sufficient purpose for education in a world where learning must be a lifelong process with many different stages and diverse focal points. And perhaps we are close to a breakthrough that will permit us to see our knowledge not as part of our personal identities, but as a common possession that links us to one another and to the world around us.

Synthesis is in the air—which is a good place for it, well above the fields where fenceposts are anchored.

Let me also suggest a small experiment that might be tried during this conference. As you meet and chat with people here, I can predict that you will be asked several times the same insidious question: "What is your field?" It would be interesting to see what would happen if we all avoided asking that question of others, and if we try not to answer when it is asked of us. It might feel a bit naked without a field at first, but perhaps it would be a step towards climbing over the fences that limit our imaginations. And, of course, if we really feel pressed to answer, we could always say, "Why, my speciality is bricolage."

NOTES

1. See Joseph Meeker, "Academic Fields and Other Polluted Environments", *Journal of Environmental Education*, (4:3, Spring 1973).
2. Excellent insight into the philosophical, scientific, and social depth of hunting-gathering life has been provided recently by a number of significant studies, notably: Claude Levi-Strauss' *The Savage Mind* (University of Chicago Press, 1962); Ortega y Gasset's *Meditations on Hunting* (New York: Scribner's, 1972); and Paul Shepard's *The Tender Carnivore and the Sacred Game* (New York: Scribner's 1973).
3. Claude Levi-Strauss, *The Savage Mind.* Chicago: The University of Chicago Press, 1966, pp. 16-30.
4. *Ibid.*, p. 17.
5. *Ibid.*, p.21.
6. *Ibid.*, p.21.
7. Francois Jacob, "Evolution and Tinkering". *Science*, 10 June 1977, p.1164.
8. *Ibid.*, p. 1166.
9. Joseph W. Meeker, "The Immiment Alliance: New Connections Among Art, Science and Technology", *Technology and Culture*, Spring, 1978.
10. Joseph W. Meeker, "Ambidextrous Education: How Universities can Come Unskewed and Learn to Live in the Wilderness", *North American Review*, Summer 1975.

Section B:

The "Legitimation Crisis" And The Quest For A New Consensus

— B1 —
Metaphors of Kinship
Mary Catherine Bateson

— B2 —
Authority in a Pluralistic World
Lonnie D. Kliever/Joseph D. Bettis/Gabriel Vahanian

— B3 —
Faith and the Multiversity
George P. Grant, Jr./Jean-Guy Le Marier
Herbert Richardson

Mary Catherine Bateson

— B1 —
Metaphors of Kinship

Introduction

Human beings tend to use a small number of ideas analogically to understand the very great complexity of the world around them. Thus, we tend to use the same forms of thought to understand our own bodies, our relationships to other people, our relationships to the rest of the natural world, and to the universe as a whole. Many people today, concerned at the dysfunctional and dangerous behavior of human groups in such areas as environmental degradation or international conflict, are exploring new kinds of metaphors drawn from other traditions (such as Buddhism in the United States) or from recent scientific insights (such as cybernetics or ecology).[1] However, it seems probable that key ideas are not usually embraced as a result of an intellectual process by adults, but are rooted in the basic experiences of infancy. Thus, handling a young child in a particular manner, embedded in a particular family constellation, presents him or her with an implicit pattern which will be generalized to the wider world.

These patterns differ from culture to culture. When Freud first recognized the fateful importance of Victorian family relationships in early childhood, he assumed he was discovering a human universal, and Malinowski, an anthropologist, was one of his sharpest early critics in showing that relationships assumed a very different pattern in a matrilineal system such as that of the Trobrianders.[2] Similarly, in discussions of ethics, the notion of brotherhood is often used as if it were a cross-cultural universal. This paper will be concerned with the ways in which relationships within the family have, through human history, served as an analogical basis for a variety of broader ethics.

The question of the basis for ethics provided by family structures is of great urgency today because of the changes taking place in family organization all over the world, especially in the gradual move towards a small nuclear family and in the greater equality of women. These changes will not only affect the position of particular family members or of women as sisters, wives, and daughters, but will have a general analogical effect on our thinking about relationship. It is important here to attend to differences between cultures and between traditional patterns and emerging ones. But we must also attend to similarities among all human groups. After all, the diverse human systems of kinship are all elaborations of the same biological algebra which decrees that procreation depends on a union of the two different sexes and that infants are small and dependent. This basic biological algebra can be emphasized or it can be played down or the two aspects can be superimposed (as when women are treated like children). It can be used analogically to foster both exploitation and wisdom. Thus, some may deplore the wish of some peoples for an autocratic leader to rule or care for them, but all of us need to be aware of our dependence on our earth and sun. Similarly, the same patterns are used to rigidify and embitter lines of conflict and to create concern and mutual support for the stranger and the disinherited.

This is an area of great and fateful variation, for when analogies from a particular family structure are projected out on the whole species or the natural world, patterns of cooperation or exploitation, love or rivalry, are projected as well.

Metaphors of Consanguinity

The commonest way in which kinship is elaborated is in terms of common descent, ties of blood. The basic human group is the kinship group. Many primitive peoples live in communities in which every member is related to every other, especially in small hunting and gathering bands which we may believe resemble the communities of our early ancestors.

When groups become larger and more complex, again and again the invention has been made of using the metaphor of consanguinity to establish relationship with those whose kinship is not known. Thus, larger tribal groups or confederations the world over tend to have legends of descent from a single ancestor. As political systems develop and groups with different myths coalesce, an institution such as kingship may express the same metaphorical relationship, as the ruler is regarded as the "father of his people," and similarly the land may be seen by a given community as a mother or father.

The universalistic religions have taken this a step farther, creating metaphorical kinship between all believers or even more widely. Thus, Christians are invited to call God Father, and are called to live in brotherhood, regardless of differences in nationality or race, "in one great brotherhood of love, throughout the whole wide earth." In Islam, which developed in tribal Arabia where kinship and lineage were all important, the kinship of believers created a new possibility for unity, intertribal peace, and joint action: "The believers are but brothers. So make peace between your two brothers and be pious toward God: perhaps he will have mercy on you." (*Qur'an* XLIX:10) There is a real sense in which we seem unable to sustain a recognition of others as meriting the kind of respect and concern we give to kin unless we actually use metaphors of kinship, so we have a vast number of institutions, from the ceremonial mingling of blood that makes comrades "blood brothers" to "National Brotherhood Week."

When the metaphor of consanguinity is extended outside of the "human family," it also carries an extension of respect and concern, proper treatment of the land which is a mother, the prohibition on killing a totem, or appreciation of "Brother Sun" and "Sister Moon" and all parts of nature in St. Francis' hymn. One of the traditional paths of meditation leading to compassion in Tibetan Buddhism is called "the recognition of the mother." One reflects that the world goes back to no moment of creation but has existed from all eternity. And in that infinity of time, all sentient beings have been ceaselessly reincarnated in different forms. Thus, in that infinity of possibilities, all sentient beings have been at some time and in some form the mother of all others. Realizing this, one comes to give to all sentient beings the same respect, love, and compassion that one owes to one's mother. It is probably only through the recognition of kinship of some kind not just with animals but with plants and even with whole ecosystems that we will learn to respect and care for the natural environment. But such metaphors must be rooted in experience. The Tibetan abbot, Nechung Rimpoche, who spoke on this meditation to the Lindisfarne Association, went on to comment that from what he had observed of American life, Americans simply don't feel that way about their mothers, and so perhaps they should try the meditation substituting their "best friends."

Today, living in a world of rapid change, it is important to choose metaphors that will not have built-in biases and exclusions and yet also not be rootless. The Tibetan metaphor includes all sentient beings. The Islamic metaphor developed in a society where "My brother and I will fight my cousin, my cousin and I will fight the stranger," and provided both unity within the Muslim community and a division of the world into two armed camps.[3] Feminist activists today no longer wish to speak only of brotherhood and are increasingly using the term sisterhood, yet they omit the fact that sisterhood, in the traditions of Western culture, cannot be a mirror image of brotherhood.

Furthermore, although the consanguineal metaphors of parenthood and siblinghood have been by far the most important, they carry with them the idea of a common past, a link with the familiar that looks out, perhaps defensively, toward the unknown. We are brothers and sisters because we come from the same origin. Yet there is a sense in which we should look out on the world in the expectation of creating ties which bring us closer as we face a common future.

Metaphors of Affinity

Consanguinity is kinship based on a common past, but human beings are also obliged to move, at least to some degree, out of the small group based on common descent, and to create new relationships. Human beings create kinship by marriage. Children born to a marriage will have blood ties to the families of both parents (although in the vast majority of human societies, the ties to the family of one parent are less important than to the other), but even before a child is born, affinal (marriage) ties are created between the members of both families. One of the commonest ways to cement relationships is by marriage: two brothers may exchange sisters, two tribes may exchange a number of women, two royal houses may celebrate a marriage between a prince and a princess. And when lovers belonging to warring factions marry, the newspapers carry the story as if a real step were being taken towards peace, as when a Christian girl and a Muslim boy married during the Lebanese conflict. Often, of course, the value of affinal relations is reinforced by consanguineal metaphors; as when we speak of brother-in-law, etc. or look ahead to the unborn child.

Every society includes rules requiring that marriage go beyond or outside of the existing consanguineal relationships, to deepen them or to create new ties, and this is done by the prohibition of incest.[4] No one (except in a few very rare ceremonial contexts) may marry their closest kin, their parents, children, and siblings, and in many societies the circle of kin who are too close to marry is a very large one. Outside of that circle, various patterns exist. In some societies there is a second circle inside of which it is required that one marry, outside of which marriage is taboo. The space between these two categories may be very small or very large: it may include only a small number of relatives on one side of the family, requiring for instance that one marry a father's brother's child (if there is one), or it may be very large, including all the members of a nation or a religion or a race. The circles may be very sharp or they may be fuzzy as they tend to be in American culture where marriage with a first cousin is frowned upon but not usually taboo and parents might prefer their child to marry someone from the same town but settle for someone from farther away—as long as it's not a real foreigner. When there is a relatively circumscribed group, with which numerous intermarriages have occurred in the past so that the groups are biologically quite interlocked, new relationships are not really being created but simply deepened and affirmed into a new generation. In such systems a child may grow up referring to the members of another group as "wive-givers" or, symmetrically, "spouse-givers" (here translations seem very clumsy).[5]

In many cases, the endogamous prohibition on marriage with outsiders who are members of a certain group is equivalent to a denial that they are really or fully human or deserving of the respect and concern due to full human beings. The impossibility of marrying a member of some group may accompany a whole set of other reservations—on eating together for instance, lest one be polluted, or on trusting them, or on praying together. The impossibility of fertile mating is indeed one way in which different species are recognized, as against different varieties, and treating a group as not eligible as marriage partners is one way of making them a different "pseudo-species." Those who are covered by the incest taboo (close kin) and those in groups with which marriage is permitted are clearly human. But those of whom we say, "I wouldn't want my daughter to marry one" have been defined out of a real possibility of relationship, however much we talk of brotherhood. This is not true for all cases however. For instance, there are ways of organizing societies into a number of lineages each of which is paired with one other lineage for marrying, or into complex patterns where the men of group A must marry women from another group while the women of group A must marry still a third group, until three or more groups are linked in a circle. Thus, the larger system clearly creates membership slots even for those with whom certain types of relationship are forbidden. In a similar way, although intermarriage is forbidden, the functional interdependence of groups with specialized activities in a caste system must have somewhat the same effect of creating common membership.

When we look at the effect of marriage on women we see that just as brotherhood and sisterhood are not usually symmetrical, so marriage has different effects on the kin status of men and women. Because no society lets its members marry their closest relatives, marriage usually involves a degree of separation: new obligations are taken on and some old ones weakened, a new relationship is established and some old ties are cut. American society is predominantly neolocal and bilateral—that is, ties with both sets of parents are more or less symmetrically weakened and a new household established. But much of our imagery goes back to societies like those depicted in the Old and New Testaments that followed the patrilineal pattern we still have in surnames whereby the woman gives up the name that links her to her family and the husband keeps his. In many such traditions, he brought his bride home with him and she became, physicially, a member of his parents' household. Thus, women have been called upon to bear the brunt of adjusting to new relationships, as the kinship created by marriage dominated their lives and they were surrounded by in-laws, while for men, in patrilineal societies, their relationships with their wives were the only really important relationships created by marriage. In such societies, "brotherhood" and "sisterhood" have completely different meanings and are not equivalent terms referring to different sexes. For brothers are forever members of the same family, sharing some of the same fortunes, and may even live under the same roof as they were supposed to do in traditional China. But sisters will be members of different families with different fortunes and few mutual obligations. Ties with maternal relatives may be maintained on the basis of affection and choice while paternal ties express significant obligations, and the maternal uncle is often a figure of play and indulgence.

There have been a considerable variety of other solutions to the dilemma of whose ties will be cut in order that new ties be bound. One can have a matrilineal society, where sisterhood really endures; or one can bring home a child bride and raise her at home so that her in-laws are virtually her parents; or, in the extreme case, one can alternate as the people of Dobu do, living alternate years in the village of each spouse. But these are minority solutions. Exciting as it is to look at these as possible variants on the human pattern, essentially we are building a world of people whose basic sense of kinship is patrilineal, either because of their present institutions or because of the myths that pervade their lives. Ethical systems concerned with extending the positive aspects of kinship to broader groups also need to wrestle with this element of separation in the need to move out of the limited consanguineal group. Thus, Jesus said, "Whosoever shall do the will of God, the same is my brother, and my sister, and mother." (Mark 3:35) But he also said, "Verily I say unto you, There is no man that hath left house, or brethren, or sisters, or father, or mother, or wife, or children, or lands, for my sake and the gospel's, But he shall receive an hundred-fold now in this time..."(Mark 10:29-30). A simple expansion of the consanguineal group is not sufficient. Creating new ties also involves departure, a degree of denial is involved, and a possible conflict of claims.

Prospects for the Future

As we struggle, in a world of increasing populations and increasing intercommunication and interdependence, for values that will support peace and mutual responsibility, kinship is changing. It is virtually everywhere changing in the same direction:[6] the kin group that lives together is becoming smaller and more mobile, and relationships with other blood kin are progressively weakening—that is, the nuclear family is replacing the extended family. The relationships with kin on both sides are becoming more symmetrical and more bilateral, and at the same time increasingly elective. One's spouse is becoming one's most important relative, rather than one's parents or siblings. For most people in the world, "Brother" is gradually coming to mean less. Even relationships with adult children and grand-children are becoming weaker, as each generation takes less responsibility for the previous one.

At the same time we are groping for affirmations of relationship. The term "brotherhood" carries a tremendous burden of hope, hope that the great invention of recognizing other communities, perhaps with different languages and physical features, as belonging to the same kind—which is really the same kin—may finally be made and stabilized, not repeatedly lost. Feminists use the term "sisterhood" with a meaning it never had in the past to symbolize a discovery of mutual respect and solidarity. "The brotherhood and sisterhood of humankind" is beginning to be current as a term for a broad metaphorical kinship to be built up with humanity.

However, although we cannot afford to reject any useful metaphor of relationship, especially one so hallowed by use as brotherhood is, we need to recognize that our increasing concern is with the world of the future—with creating a viable environment for all of our children, born and unborn. We are not concerned with diverging from a common point but with converging and with a convergence that will be fruitful in new life. In that sense, the most vivid metaphor of kinship for the modern world would be not blood but marriage, not consanguinity but affinity: I meet the stranger as someone to whom I might become progressively closer in shared responsibility, to whom I am linked by the future, not by the past, by choice and not by accident.

There are immediate reasons why the imagination recoils at the idea of using marriage as a basic metaphor for relationship. Perhaps the most important of these is the fact that whatever we may try to achieve in our own marriages, the background imagery of marriage is still one of inequality. Does the notion of brotherhood between two races propose equality? The notion of marriage suggests that one of them will be washing the dishes, will fill a servile role. During World War II, misunderstanding developed around the term partners, as the British used it to describe their relationship with the Americans, the Americans understanding it to mean an asymmetrical relationship in which one partner provided the effort and the other the cash, while the British used it for a symmetrical relationship of equality.[7] Even within the imagery of brotherhood, we have had to be very careful about echoes of older and younger brother, as in the case of the phrase "little brown brother" which used to be applied to the Filipino.

The relationship between men and women is used often in imagery, but almost always to emphasize the notion of fundamental asymmetry. Here it is that we meet up with a basic problem in imagery, the common failure ever, sincerely, to mean "different but equal." In Western civilization, every difference seems to acquire a positive and negative valence. Wherever we do want to affirm equal value and equal potency, we tend to affirm it by denying difference, by demanding similarity and symmetry. Thus the imagery of marriage has traditionally been asymmetrical. Those who do not think of the earth as their mother think of it as a spouse, to be dominated and made fertile, or possibly to be raped and exploited.

It is possible to compare the strengths and weaknesses of the two types of metaphor:[8]

The metaphors of consanguinity (especially brotherhood) refer to a common origin and a common inheritance from the past; they assert equality and similarity in fundamentally symmetrical relationships which may be competitive and may escalate into conflict.

The metaphors of affinity (espousal, etc.) refer to a common creative responsibility in the future; they assert difference and complementarity in fundamentally asymmetrical relationships which tend to be unequal and may lead to exploitation.

Once one considers the algebra of these two different systems of imagery, it becomes clear that, as a civilization, we are lacking a key image. We do not have, in the set of images that each of us brings to building and interpreting relationships, the key idea of a relationship that combines the two: a relationship that asserts both equality and difference, complementarity without exploitation, and which refers to a common future and a common responsibilty. Perhaps we could find it in the infinity of variants on the Tibetan meditation: all sentient beings have been my nurturing parent and my dependent child, my comrade and my lover. Alas, so far, where we assert difference, we tend to move towards exploitation, and where we demand equality we move towards a sterile denial of difference. Yet, just as the difference between the sexes is the basis of generativity, so all differences between human groups are to be affirmed and valued as leading to creativity.

From this point of view, the experiments being carried on in countless households around the world, newly isolated and fragile as they are, are of immense significance as models for human harmony. If these parents can truly demonstrate to their children that mothers and fathers are fundamentally different and yet fully equal, that they meet together in common commitment and creativity, they will be providing a new pivotal image to be extended to the world. They will be offering both their sons and their daughters a way of meeting others outside the home, men and women, with the affirmation "Together we will give birth to the future."

REFERENCES

1. For instance, Mary Catherine Bateson, *Our Own Metaphor: A Personal Account of A Conference on Conscious Purpose and Human Adaptation.* New York: Knopf, 1972, also *Earth's Answer: Explorations of Planetary Culture at the Lindisfarne Conferences*, ed. Katz, Thompson & Thompson. New York: Lindisfarne & Harper & Row, 1977, and many other sources.
2. Bronislaw Malinowski (1927), *The Sexual Life of Savages in North-Western Melanesia.* London: G. Routledge and Sons, Ltd., 1957.

3. For the well-documented tendency towards polarization in Arab communities, see Raphael Patai, *Golden River to Golden Road.* Philadelphia: University of Pennsylvania Press, 1967.

4. For a survey of the literature related to the incest taboo, see Margaret Mead, article "Incest" in the *International Encyclopedia of the Social Sciences.* David L. Sills, ed. MacMillan, 1968. V. 7.

5. The different types of marriage pattern referred to here would be reviewed in almost any anthropology textbook and are not referenced separately.

6. William J. Goode, *World Revolution and Family Patterns.* New York: Free Press of Glencoe, 1963.

7. Margaret Mead, "End-linkage: A tool for cross-cultural analysis" in Brockman, ed., *About Bateson: Essays on Gregory Bateson.* New York: E.P. Dutton, 1977.

8. For an interesting example of looking alternately at symmetrical and complementary relationships as more positive, see various essays in Gregory Bateson, *Steps to an Ecology of Mind.* New York: Chandler, 1972.

Lonnie D. Kliever

— B2 —
Authority in a Pluralistic World

Pluralism is in high vogue today but the ease and enthusiasm with which pluralism is embraced suggests a widespread misunderstanding or naivete about its meaning. Such blithe pluralists often simply equate pluralism with the diversity of interest groups and the toleration of religious differences in modern democratic societies. But such political and ecclesiastical pluriformity is not pluralism. The dispersion of political power and the freedom of religious assembly within non-hierarchical societies represent differences and disagreements *within* a shared commitment to one nation and one God. Pluralism by contrast assumes no such overarching unity or loyalty. Pluralism is the existence of multiple frames of reference, each with its own scheme of understanding and criteria of rationality. Pluralism is the co-existence of comparable and competing positions which are not to be reconciled. Pluralism is the recognition that different persons and different groups quite literally indwell irreducibly different worlds.

I. Assessing Pluralism—Peril or Promise?

Stated thus baldly, the peril of pluralism is obvious. What happens when these worlds collide? Can the relationships between contradictory visions of reality and schemes of meaning remain benign in a world of increasing population and decreasing resources? Can conflicts between such worlds be resolved in any way short of coercion or violence? What happens when the monopoly on world-definition is broken within a society? Can the common life survive without a common world-view and moral system? Can the individual form a stable identity without a single life-world that guarantees order and meaning? In other words, the situation of pluralism not only jeopardizes international order and social stability. It threatens the very possibility of being a self and having a world. In a pluralistic world there are no uncontested systems of reality definition, social integration and personality formation. Moreover, these tasks which are interlocking in the traditional society have been torn apart within the demythologized and historicized societies of the modern world.

Precisely this separation must be grasped if we are to understand the character and challenge of pluralism in our time. Traditional societies combined the practical task of securing identity with the theoretical task of interpreting reality in a single world-view.[1] Such interpretive systems dispelled chaos and guaranteed meaning by mastering the problems of survival in both nature and society. Of course, that mastery was always incomplete and thus explanations and consolations for failure were built into these "nominizing" systems. In primitive societies the problems of survival vis-a-vis nature were so drastic that human ignorance and impotence were counterbalanced by a heavy overlay of mythic order. But increased control over nature gradually freed secular knowledge from dependence upon and loyalty to sacral world-views, which in turn were increasingly restricted to functions of personality formation and social integration. The natural sciences eventually established a monopoly on the interpretation and control of nature through standardized procedures of verification and technological conquests of nature. But the later-emerging social sciences have developed no comparable methods of confirmation or conquests or contingency in the social world. Indeed, the social sciences have intensified these problems by relativizing or dissolving the traditional world-views which deal with human loneliness and guilt, suffering and death. Consequently the socio-cultural world, where fundamental questions of human worth and duty predominate, has been rendered problematic by the separation of traditional interpretive systems of the social world from the consensus interpretive system of the natural world.

This separation has triggered a radical "legitimation crisis" in the life-worlds of modern societies.[2] This crisis is felt on two levels. The *life-legitimating* systems, which nominize the chaos and terror that threaten personal and social existence, have been decimated by the scientific erosion of mythic explanations and relativized by the scientific discovery of multiple world-views. These disruptions have in turn generated a crisis at the level of *system-legitimating* arguments. Of course, "secondary legitimations" of a given life-world have always been required whenever challenges to the facticity or authority of that life-world have arisen. These arguments typically span a wide range of theoretical completeness and sophistication. Justificatory appeals range from the customary (historical narratives of origins) to the cosmic (metaphysical systems of reality). Such system-legitimating arguments were in the past thought to be universally compelling but today we recognize that they are system dependent. This is the heart of the contemporary legitimation crisis. Pluralism has put us in a situation where we do not know just which world we inhabit. To determine which world we are really in requires a means of arbitration that does not presuppose any of them. We have at hand, in scientific methods of verification, system-transcending criteria for adjudicating rival interpretations of the natural world. But appeals to publicly experiencable and repeatable evidence have not proven applicable to visions of human worth and duty in the sociocultural world. Thus we are confronted with a pluralism of life-worlds which are not legitimated by the cognitive content or criteria of scientific understanding. Shorn of demonstrably cognitive roots, religio-cultural forms of life are without authority for those not predisposed to believe them.

But what is the future of such systems of personality formation and social integration in a pluralistic world? There can be no doubt that the traditional religions have undergone a serious erosion of belief and authority in modern societies. These religions have lost their monopoly on world-definition and world-maintenance. But that loss has not signaled the end of religion. The massive debunking and dismantling of traditional world-view at the hands of modern criticism has only loosed a new rage for order and meaning.[3] The persistence of religion should not surprise us. Skepticism and nihilism are after all philospher's diseases and seldom if ever become epidemic among the populace. The human craving for meaning and order, which has the inexorable force of instinct, continues unabated despite the demystification and disenchantment of the natural world. Indeed the persistence of religion has fueled the pluralism of our time by multiplying the religious options present *within* modern societies. Herein lies the real question of the future of religion. Can human meaning and order survive in a world and in a society fragmented rather than united by religion?

Having thus clearly raised the problem of pluralism, I want to join the "blithe" pluralist in arguing that human meaning and order can not only survive but thrive in a pluralistic world. But the promise of pluralism will be reached only if the peril of pluralism can be avoided. And that will prove to be more difficult and costly than many enthusiasts for pluralism dare imagine. The promise of pluralism is a world and a society newly freed from diversity and even idiosyncrasy, newly flexible for change and experimentation. Out of pluralism's creative ambiguity and dissonance can come an enriched and enlarged sense of the possibilties of life here and now. Finally the promise of pluralism is the dream of allowing each life to be a distinctive work of art—each person fashioning the materials of his biological and cultural inheritance into a personal statement of reality. But this Nietzchean promise of a new man and a new world can be redeemed only if these diverse life-forms are not allowed to overcome, dominate or suppress one another. Pluralism permits different groups and persons to create worlds unto themselves but they dare not become laws unto themselves. We must admit that forms of life are logically and psychologically self-legitimating. There are no external or neutral vantage points from which to confirm or commend a given vision of human order and meaning. But pluralism will surely self-destruct if accepting pluralism means *carte blanche* endorsement for any and all forms of life. The sophomoric argument against moral relativism invoking the spectre of the maniac whose "world-view" licenses mayhem states the problem precisely if inelegantly because it recognizes the *social* solidarity of human existence and human value. Unfortunately that problem cannot be solved by the implied counterargument for moral absolutism. We can only solve the problem of pluralism from within, but solve it we must or whirl will truly become king.

In other words, the greatest peril of pluralism is that we will carry over into the pluralistic situation our centuries-old authoritarian habits of thinking and acting. These habits will not easily change because they are deeply rooted in *religious* craving for absolutes to fend off death and all its experiential counterparts—bafflement and impotence, suffering and evil, disorder and despair. Every religion and every sociocultural world is a pact with death. This pact takes the form of a system of death-defying and life-extending symbols and rituals, institutions and relationships which prescribe the patterns and dispense the assurances for heroic transcendence of death.[4] As such, these systems have traditionally claimed absolute devotion and exclusive deliverance for themselves alone. Such authoritarianism and exclusivism are highly effective instruments of integration and legitimation within a given group. But they are equally effective instruments of aggression and destruction against those beyond the group. This is doubly so when death is "fetishized"—located in special places, powers or persons.[5] Then the quest for heroic transcendence lays waste to those treasures and creatures, peoples and cultures which are isolated and identified as evil. This compulsive devotion and defense of social and personal "immortality ideologies" is understandable, given the stark terror and sheer chaos of existence deprived of some "sacred canopy." But just this compulsive power must be broken for a genuine pluralism to emerge and exist among us. Unless we can reshape the pretheoretical depths of religious fears and hopes pluralistically, we will not avoid the kaleidoscopic violence of a world or a culture of multiple absolutisms.

Unlearning old habits of reflective and religious expectations will not be easy or automatic. The mere presence of multiple frameworks in our midst will not dispel the propensity for groups to make absolute and exclusive claims for their own life-world. The human hunger and search for *absolute* religious and moral claims must be combatted and negated—absolutely! This means that pluralism requires an authority that transcends the authority of all systems of thought and life without becoming a system in turn. Pluralism is a possibility only if all frameworks are relativized by some absolutely iconoclastic principle or by some absolutely empty authority. The only absolute permitted and required in a pluralistic world is the absolute denial of all absolutes.

II. Protecting Pluralism—
Radical Transcendence or Radical Relativism?

How then can plural life-worlds be protected against all forms of absolutism? There seem to be two possibilities. We may place com-

peting and contradictory world-views within a context of radical
transcendence or of radical relativism. We may argue that human
order and meaning are grounded in a reality that radically
transcends every historic concretion or that human order and meaning are adjustive responses to individual and social needs without
grounds in any reality whether immanent or transcendent. Either of
these overviews of human value seems to offer a framework-tran-
scending authority which relativizes all sociocultural systems of
human order and meaning. As such both are iconoclastic or empty
principles of authority.

Radical transcendence as a normative overview of pluralism may
be expressed in either monotheistic or mystic terms. A radically
transcendent God can function as a permanent iconoclastic principle
which not only relativizes all concrete world-views and life-styles but
subjects them to perpetual revolution as well.[6] Such a "radical
monotheism" centers in the Transcendent One for whom alone there
is an ultimate good and from whom alone there are proximate
goods. This radically transcendent God permits the construction
and coexistence of many relative value systems—each of them tentative, experimental and objective. But these plural life-systems are
possible only because the Transcendent One prevents any one of
them from being erected into an absolute or even being elevated
above the others. In short, radical monotheism makes pluralism
possible by freeing the world from idolatry.

The long tradition of divine sovereignty has always recognized
that man is an idolater. Theologians of the sovereignty of God have
known that man left to his own designs seeks absolute security and
significance by absolutizing finite things and groups, ideals and
causes. To be sure, these theologians have not always perceived that
the pursuit of cosmic heroism and the escape from cosmic dread are
inseparable counterparts of the life-project of every human being.
Nor have they discerned the ambivalence and danger in their own
claims to absolute security and significance through their
understanding and relation to the Infinite God. But the wisdom of
this tradition can be carried over into a pluralistic situation by
translating sovereignty into radical transcendence. This move runs
counter to the reigning theologies of today which stress the pervasive immanence of God. But stressing the indwelling presence of

God too easily reinforces the human propensity to absolutize finite conditions and concerns. Only a God radically beyond yet universally related to the world can maintain the worth and well-being of all things. In a pluralistic world, the radically transcendent God is the experientially relevant God.

Despite its obvious prophetic power, such a monotheistic protection of pluralism may finally prove unsuccessful. For monotheism, God is the constructive principle as well as the iconoclastic principle of all systems of human order and meaning. As constructive principle, the symbol of God is vested with a content which militates against a genuine pluralism. Monotheistic conceptualities of ultimate reality as personal and eschatological will almost certainly reflect particular historical and ideological biases. This likelihood is increased by the centrality of historical revelations of God in the great monotheistic traditions. Thus the monotheistic concept of God, even though conceived of as radically transcendent, may be too ideologically particular to be genuinely iconoclastic.

Non dualistic mysticism offers an alternative conceptuality of radical transcendence. This type of mysticism conceives of the relationship between the everyday world and ultimate reality in a variety of ways. But all parties to the debate on the reality or unreality of the world agree that the ground of all reality is an all-inclusive, unitary Absolute which is empty of all distinctions, qualities and limits. This Undifferentiated Absolute relativizes the value of all things finite, shatters all attachments to particular things. Mysticism's Undifferentiated Absolute seems promising as an iconoclastic principle which continually breaks life open to variety and change. But this promise is compromised by the tendency in non-dualistic mysticism to lose all interest in the finite and particular world. The quest to achieve oneness with the Absolute need not but often does end in negation of the empirical and social world. Thus iconoclasm is itself turned into a belief-system that negates all order and meaning in historical existence.

The search for an iconoclastic principle that authorizes pluralism in a radically transcendent monotheism or mysticism runs into a common problem. The central principle in each is also the constructive principle of a concrete life-world. The iconoclasm of a Sovereign God or of an Undifferentiated Absolute is limited to keeping sym-

bolic and social expressions open and tentative *within* the general
world-view generated by each. This same iconoclasm serves as a
irenic principle of criticism and assimilation of alien world-views. In
other words, a radically transcendent monotheism or mysticism pro-
motes intramural ecumenism and unaggressive evangelism. But, as
welcome as all such retreats from absolutism and exclusivism are,
they do not legitimate pluralism.

What then of radical relativism as an authorization of pluralism?
Radical relativism differs from all notions of "objective relativism"
or "perspectival relativism." For objective or perspectival
relativism, symbolic and conceptual constructs are relative, but
they are relative *to* and relatived *by* an objective reality that in some
way stands apart and over against all human knowing, doing and
feeling. Systematic differences between human formulations of
understanding and value reflect the inescapable limitations of one's
standpoint. Relativism lies in the eye of the beholder rather than in
the beholded. By contrast, *radical* relativism assumes no such objective reality beyond our diverse interpretations of human order and
meaning. Can such radical relativism sustain co-existence and
cooperation between diverse and even contradictory life-worlds? If
so, how and why?

Once again there are broadly speaking two ways of articulating
radical relativism—mystic and naturalistic. Certain forms of
Tibetan, Chinese and Japanese Buddhism deny the reality of all unchanging absolutes, including the Absolute.[7] For these mystic traditions, the symbol of "emptiness" denies rather than describes the
eternal, self-sufficient, undifferentiated Absolute of non-dualistic
forms of mysticism. Indeed, the self-existent reality of any and all
entities is denied. Such denial does not involve the annihilation or
disconnection of all things but the discovery of the infinite
relatedness of all things in a continuous process of change. "Emptiness" is a symbol and a means of perceiving and participating in
the eternal relatedness and change of all thing. This new way of seeing the familiar world sees through the "fabricated" character of all
entities, qualities and distinctions in the phenomenal world. It
thereby diverts all religious craving for unchanging absolutes,
whether temporal or eternal. Awareness that all entities visible and
ideal are absolutely empty of self-sufficiency releases man from

thirsting after ultimates and its accompanying anxiety and defensiveness. Thus released from attachments to false ultimates, the enlightened can live without pain or peril in the ordinary structures of existence by participating in their mutual dependence and co-origination.

The iconoclastic power of this religious framework is obvious at a glance. The radical emptiness of all things offers a permanent check against all idolatrous attachments as well as the divisiveness and defensiveness that usually follow from such attachments. But considered in the round this mystic consciousness seems to radically undercut pluralism. Emptiness does not simply relativize the many solutions to the fundamental problems of human existence—it dissolves the problems themselves in a cosmology of non-self-existence and infinite relatedness. In short, the bottom line of this mystic way looks more like a processive monism than a radical relativism since the on-going process is "surrelative" to each fabricated 'moment' or 'part' of the process.[8] Perhaps this mystic version of radical relativism can be interpreted in such a way as to sanction diverse life-worlds. But I must leave that to those more competent and convinced than I that this is a genuine option for a pluralistic world.

We are left then with the radical relativism historically articulated in the philosophies of empiricism and materialism. These two traditions have typically argued that human values are relative to human needs—biological, psychological, sociological and cognitive. As such there are no objective and necessary structures of reality which predispose or compel one way of realizing these needs over another. Neither tradition of course denies that human values have the *air* of objectivity. The facticities of embodiment in a world, the conventions of language in a culture, the persistence of institutions in a society place severe limits on freedom and innovation in need-fulfillment at any given time and place. Nor do these traditions necessarily deny that actual value judgments are subject to reasoned argument. Ultimate principles of value lie beyond all argumentation but lower-level arguments about how and when these principles apply are certainly possible. But the objectivity of local standards and lower-level arguments do not overcome the *radical* relativism of values.

Such radical relativism clearly offers an iconoclastic perspective over against all value-systems and life-worlds. The categorical denial of universal objective standards deprives all human valuing of the sense of inevitability and necessity that so often sanctions defensiveness and exclusivism. By the same token this radical relativism is open to an endless variety of systems for giving human life order and meaning. But here, no less than in non-dualistic mysticism, the iconoclastic principle may be turned into a constructive principle which actively negates all historical order and meaning. Neither of these options is likely to prove attractive and workable for the masses. Radical world negation belongs to a madness or a saintliness that lies far beyond most of us. But thorough-going skepticism and nihilism is certainly a possible expression of this form of radical relativism.

We are left then with four distinct ways of protecting pluralism which divide in two over whether the grounds of value are radically transcendent or radically relative. Each of these ways offers an iconoclasm that relativizes all claims though perhaps not all cravings for the absolute. Yet there is a tendency in all, especially the monotheistic and mystic iconoclasms, to undercut a genuine pluralism of life-worlds. There are two reasons for this. First, a truly iconoclastic principle continually breaks the forms of life but it does not automatically remake those forms. Relativizing all options does not necessarily solve the inevitable problems of coexistence in a pluralistic world. In a densely pluralistic world or culture, some way to shape and sustain orderly change and conflict must be found. Each of these iconoclasms we have reviewed is drawn to this "other side" of iconoclasm. Second, each of these iconoclasms has historically been articulated as the critical principle of a constructive world-view. Thus, "buying into" one or another of these iconoclasms apparently involves assuming a distinctive tradition of human meaning and order. Little surprise that iconoclasm and evangelism are so closely interwoven.

Can iconoclasm avoid dependence upon some distinctive tradition? Certain monotheists and mystics have long sought a *philosophia perennis* but their programs never finally escape the shape and sounds of their own heritage. But naturalistic radical relativism can be separated from dependence upon any distinctive world-view.

Such a separation requires an important re-visioning of philosophical empiricism and materialism as well as of religious values. Much that is cherished if not central in religious systems of meaning and order will be lost or transformed in that re-visioning. But perhaps that is the price we have levied on ourselves to live in the modern world. Perhaps that is the final cost of legitimating a pluralistic world.

III. Legitimating Pluralism: Facts and Fictions

Empirical and materialistic accounts of man's value experience have in the past shown little resemblance or relevance to the actual value experiences of individuals and communities. Their emotive and epiphenomenal characterizations of values and value judgments have often obscured the role of factual knowledge in all value judgments, often minimized the function of value commitments in all human existence, and often ignored the centrality of value differences in all social conflict. Value judgments have been reduced to purely emotive or factual conditions and transactions which when recognized as such are thought to become harmlessly or harmoniously benign. But these accounts simply do not square with the urgency and ubiquity of values in all personal and social existence. Even if values are radically without grounds they remain present and powerful in human life—even in the lives of empiricists and materialists.

These traditions have failed to fully understand value because they have equated value's loss of ontological status with value's loss of existential function. This elimination or reduction of value is a consequence of philosophical literalism. Empiricism and materialism have typically been understood as explanations of the mechanisms of cognition and the stuff of reality (e.g., behavioral psychology and mechanistic metaphysics). But, as Ernest Gellner has persuasively argued, we must interpret these traditions not as descriptive accounts of knowing and being, but as *selectors* which establish the norms that "govern and limit our cognitive behavior."[9] These traditions gain enormously in plausibility and compatibility when they are read not as accounts of what knowledge and reality "really are" but as ways of sifting rival constructions and symbolizations of the "real world." As such, they operate independently of particular accounts of that world.

Gellner's "decoding" of the Western epistemological tradition throws valuable light on the entire question of pluralism. Gellner argues against "*cognitive* pluralism" by showing that the operative cognitive underpinnings of modern society support a "critical monism" of knowledgeable belief.[10] Though empiricism and materialism are at odds philosophically, they have come together in two decisive ways. They have carried out parallel programs of debunking all mystifying authorities and magic practices. They have also pervaded the structures of modern consciousness *and* modern culture with two different but reinforcing selectors of cognitive endeavor. Empiricism has trained us to accept evidence which is *experiential*—especially publicly available and empirically given data. Materialism has disposed our thinking to expect explanations which are in some sense *mechanistic*—especially publicly observable and universally reproducible structures. The normative demand for this kind of data and this type of explanation has transformed our cognitive style and thereby fatefully altered our life-worlds.

Our life-worlds have been split off from a universe which is mechanistically arranged, morally neutral and humanly indifferent.[11] Our cozy, comfortable and familiar life-worlds continue to exist because we cannot long inhabit the world we have discovered by means of our modern selectors. But as modern men we do not indwell these life-worlds in the same way as those who have gone before us. Our fateful choice of selectors has unmasked the "dirty secret" that we have so long hidden from ourselves—that the cold, heartless, impersonal universe *is* the real world. Precisely because modern science speaks of that world in an idiom which is discontinuous with everyday life yet still manifests a cognitive power greater than any available in everyday life, our life-worlds have become radically suspect and problematic.

Gellner uses the term "ironic cultures" to describe the character of modern man's life-worlds.

By this I do not mean that the individuals involved in them necessarily or indeed generally hold and internalize such cultures and their doctrinal content in a detached ironic spirit. The irony is not generally conscious, explicit or individual. It resides in the fact that the whole organization of such cultures, the way in which they are implemented and enforced in life, the limits within which they are enforced, works in a manner which tacitly presupposes and admits that they are not to be taken seriously, as knowledge. They contain claims, assertions which sound cognitive, and which in other, non-ironic cultures would indeed have been such; but here, it is somehow understood that they are not fully serious, not commensurate or continuous with real knowledge.[12]

In other words, human life-worlds are marginal elaborations on life in the real world. They are fictional transparencies projected on the factual world.

Speaking in this way of life-worlds as "fictions" involves more than the claim that they are imaginative fabrications or symbolic constructs. All reality claims, whether factual or fictional, are fabrications. All facts and fictions are constructions. 'Facts' are symbolic constructs which have been established as reliable representations of an external, objective world. 'Fictions' are not simply symbolic constructs which have yet to be verified. They are not hypotheses whose truth remains in doubt for the present. 'Fictions' are symbolic constructs which *cannot* be verified and hence *cannot* be true.[13] In the modern world, fictions are judged to be fictions (unreal and impossible cases) because they fail to pass the empiricist-mechanist selectors of knowledgeable belief. Why these selectors prove to be the final arbiters of reality-claims, the ultimate sifters of factual and fictional constructs, is the story of four centuries of theory of knowledge in modern philosophy and theology. The hidden God and the secular universe both pay homage to the emergence to dominance of empirical data and mechanical explanations. Only these selectors have produced a genuinely cross-cultural body of usable knowledge. Only these selectors have proven separable from any particular theory of how the world is. And in a world where all thinking proceeds by paradigm and all knowledge consists of constructions, the question of *how* we know is necessarily prior to the question of *what* we know and the assurance *that* we know.

These modern norms of cognitive belief and behavior have not brought an end to religion. The Enlightenment vision of nineteenth century rationalists and twentieth century secularists has proven vain. Reason does not produce a new closed naturalism, as gratifying to man as the old closed supernaturalism only upside down. Scientific reason generates no styles of life or systems of meaning. It succeeds only in depriving all of cognitive authority and universal necessity. But our scientific world does permit and facilitate an endless variety of styles and systems of human life and meaning. Emancipation from economic pressure, reduction of authoritarian education, dissolution of traditional institutions have encouraged an explosion of luxuriant and arduous, ecstatic and cerebral faiths both old and new. The religious and moral imagination has been gloriously freed for culturally-innovative meanings and freed from culturally-imposed guilt—in styles of dressing, eating, playing, schooling, working, mating, parenting and even dying. What Gellner calls "the meaning industry" is enjoying an unprecedented expansionist market.[14]

But despite our time's religious fecundity and exuberance, these modern life-worlds remain deeply ironic and inherently tragic. Gellner's comments about the revival of traditional faith equally applies to the survival of old faiths and the arrival of new faiths in the modern world.

> When a traditional faith was held in the full and literal sense it was wedded to the best available current forms of knowledge. When it is theatrically revived, in a kind of social inverted commas, it is revived, precisely, by disconnecting it from what is taken seriously as knowledge, and is kept alive only by this artificial insulation; by inventing special criteria and functions for it, which are carefully made distinct from serious cognition. But when serious issues are at stake, when the fate of individuals and communities are at risk, one will not fail to make use of the best available knowledge; so, in any crisis, men tend to ignore the revived 'tradition' and think in terms which they cognitively respect, rather than in terms of antiquarian conceptual furnishing. So, ironically, the traditional 'faith' is used when things go smoothly and no faith is really needed, but it is ignored when the situation is grave.[15]

For modern man, religion neither solves problems (monotheism) nor dissolves them (mysticism) but disguises them. Religious fictions dignify our daily round of problem-solving and distract our anxiety over insoluble problems by concealing both in a friendly and familiar universe. But the basic work of social-order and problem-solving has passed into secular hands. Everyday existence is based largely on a productive and administrative technology which is scientifically based and culturally indifferent. Religion remains decisive only in those areas of human need where genuine knowledge is still lacking or simply impossible. In short, religion is largely diversionary and decorative. Like play and art, religion is a way of forgetting the harsh limitations and necessities of our creatureliness. And like creative play and playful creation, religion is the triumph of illusion over reality—for a time. But modern man faces the special problem of remembering while he is forgetting. The separation of soluble and insoluble problems has deprived us of that innocent forgetfulness that lets us hope, even dare believe that all life's terrors and threats will be overcome. This is the tragic irony of modern religious consciousness.

But this same tragic irony is the special challenge to heroic transcendence—to seek an impossible beauty, to pursue an unattainable victory. Faced with the finality of death, we may respond in two ways. We may "rage, rage, rage against the dying of the light" or we may "play, play, play against the coming of the night." The first is the mandate for all science. The search for knowledge is the heroic quest for the extension of life—it is rage against the dying of the light. The second response is the heart of all religion. The venture of faith is the heroic quest for the enhancement of life—it is play against the coming of the night. Despite the radical separation of science and religion, the heroic quest still embraces both. Heroic transcendence is that rebellion and artistry which "contests reality while endowing it with unity."[16]

This situation *may* not be permanent. The cognitive norms of scientific knowledge are after all normative rather than descriptive. The modern world has in effect chosen to favor public, reproductive, impersonal and universal knowledge. It is at least possible that some post-modern and post-scientific world could select some other criteria of what counts as knowledge more amenable to sorting out visions of human order and meaning. Failing that incredible revolution in human thought, science may yet establish a demythologized and dehistoricized unity of the human world. Science will certainly

not take over all the functions of traditional world-views, particularly the compensatory ones promising ultimate fulfillment and death
deliverance. But some dynamic structure of reality which constrains
human cooperation and channels human activity toward the wellbe-
ing of one and all might yet be achieved through scientific argumentation. But neither of these eventualities are very likely. Our society
is deeply committed to empirically confirmed and technologically effective knowledge. Even latter-day returns to the agrarian society or
the magic universe are pseudocultures which rest on the scientific
and technological culture which they claim to reject. Moreover, a
scientifically founded social world which dispels life's chaos and terror and guarantees human order and meaning is scarcely conceivable, given the very nature of scientific explanation. The search
for impersonal and reproducible structures which are publicly and
empirically confirmable undercuts those values sought and sustained in the life-world—individual worth, freedom, responsibility, dignity and destiny. Indeed, scientific knowledge and technology
systematically and remorselessly eliminate the individual.[17] Thus
for the conceivable future the moral-practical task of fashioning a
human world that maintains meaningful personal identity and in-
timate community still falls to the religions, fictive though they are.

Thus, the modern world is pluralistic in a double sense—societies
and selves are a symbiosis of diverse conceptual and cultural styles.
The separation of cognitive imagination from other forms and functions of imagination places each of us in multiple worlds. Only the
cognitive imagination discovers and describes a single world. It is
an austere and impersonal world, but it contains and thus joins us
all. It requires and provides a fundamental order for personal and
social existence. But like the empty spaces and blank walls of a
spacious gallery, this world permits an endless variety of fur-
nishings and groupings to fill our lives with color and comfort, with
detail and delight. Moreover this world allows free exchange and
movement between such humanly designed and decorated sites. In
short, our scientific selectors legitimate a verdant pluralism of
meaning-systems and life-styles among groups and for selves. Indeed, "pluralism" may be the wrong word for a truly modern
religious consciousness. The right word may be "polytheism." But
that is a topic for another day.

There are other topics for another day which I have not addressed. Most have to do with the psychology and sociology of fictive
religions. How do fictive life-worlds maintain an intersubjectively
obligatory character? Can we intentionally create socially integrating fictions? Can the traditional religions be theatrically reviv-
ed? Can other fictive cultures (e.g., nationalistic, ethnic, avocational)
function religiously? To what extent can consummable values take
the place of scarce meaning values? Other questions have to do with
the politics and economics of knowledge. Must knowledge be concentrated in the hands of power elites to maintain social order? How
is knowledge to be deployed in the accumulation and distribution of
wealth? Still other problems have to do with the morality of
technological civilization. How can positive legal norms maintain
public order while allowing a maximal variety of private moral
systems? What is the educational system's role beyond socialization
in facilitating religio-cultural elaborations of life? That these problems trouble me I will not deny. But they are problems for the
point of view I have argued and not necessarily objections against
it.

IV.

I have argued a polemical thesis but I wish to close on an irenic
note. Without stepping back from the position that deserves and
surely will receive vigorous criticism from many here, I want to
reiterate the primary concern of this paper. That concern is to find a
way to make the world safe from value imperialism and safe for
value idiosyncrasy. Simply declaring a truce among competing and
contradictory life-worlds will not establish co-existence or avoid
disaster. We need some shared principle—either a principle of
overarching unity or of irreducible diversity—to legitimate such
pluralism. To that end, I enter a plea for advocates of all such principles to become party to the search for such a legitimation.

NOTES

1. See Peter Berger, *The Sacred Canopy* (1966), 3-104; Ernest Becker, *The Denial of Death* (1973), 1-66; Joseph Campbell, *The Masks of God: Creature Mythology* (1968), 573-624.

2. Ernest Gellner, *The Legitimation of Belief* (1974), 149-67; Berger, *op. cit.*, 29-51, 155-75. cf. Jurgen Habermas, *Legitimation Crisis* (1973), 97-143.

3. Andrew M. Greeley, *Unsecular Man* (1972).

4. I find Ernest Becker's discussion of religion as the quest for "cosmic heroism" very enlightening. See *The Birth and Death of Meaning* (1971), 65-129, 180-99. *The Denial of Death*, 1-8, 255-85; *Escape from Evil* (1975) 146-70. cf. Berger, *op. cit.*, 53-80.

5. Becker, *Escape from Evil*, 148-51. cf. H. Richard Niebuhr, *The Meaning of Revelation* (1942), viii-ix.

6. For prime examples, see H. Richard Niebuhr, *Radical Monotheism and Western Culture* (1962); Herbert Richardson, *Toward an American Theology* (1967); Gabriel Vahanian, *No Other God* (1966). Among Christian theologians, Vahanian has developed the iconoclastic theme most extensively. Of special importance to the present discussion, see his "Technology as an Ecclesiological Problem," *Union Seminary Quarterly Review*, XXX (1974), 261-70. There Vahanian argues that technological civilization presents liberating possibilities for human life when viewed iconoclastically.

7. The first patriarch of these traditions was the second century philosopher Nagarjuna. See Frederick J. Streng, *Emptiness: A Study in Religious Meaning* (1967), especially pp. 155-69.

8. Compare to the American process thinkers, especially Charles Hartshorne's *The Divine Relativity* (1948).

9. Gellner, *op, cit.*, 31.

10. *Ibid.*, 24-70.

11. Gellner speaks of this separation as "the big ditch" which divides traditional and modern socieites, the "savage" and the "scientific" mind. This cognitive division of labor has led to the autonomy of fact. *Op. cit.*, 149-67.

12. *Ibid.*, 193-94.

13. See Hans Vaihinger's distinction between hypotheses (constructs not yet proven), semi-fictions (unproven constructs which may or may not be verifiable) and fictions (constructs which are inherently unprovable and self-contradictory). *The Philosophy of 'As If'* (1935), 78-108.

14. Gellner, *op. cit.*, 191-95.

15. *Ibid.*, 147-48.

16. Albert Camus, *The Rebel* (1958), 296.

17. Habermas, *op. cit.*, 117-30.

Joseph Bettis

Commentary

In my response to Professor Kliever I want to do two things. First I want to acknowledge the validity of his analysis of the problem. He has asked the right question. Second, however, I want to disagree with the solution he proposes.

Professor Kliever poses one of the most fundamental and pervasive dilemmas of contemporary society. The question is, How can we maintain a commitment to the real and lasting value of the truths which give meaning and coherence to our lives, and at the same time acknowledge the genuine humanity and validity of essentially contradictory truths which other people hold? It is the question of finding a basis for sustaining confidence in the face of anxiety produced by the essential and disturbing precariousness of human life.

Professor Kliever's analysis of these options is essentially correct. Either we find ourselves inexorably drawn to an absolutism of our own values which denies the humanity of people who disagree with us, or we find ourselves inevitably slipping into a relativism in which our own values and meanings become suspect, fragmentary and ephemeral.

How are we to find a way between an intolerant absolutism and a vacuous relativism? Although we continually pretend we can avoid the embarrassment of the dilemma, it is not new. Lessing put it this way: "Accidental truths of history can never constitute the proof of necessary truths of reason. That, that is the ugly, broad ditch I can never cross over, no matter how often or earnestly I have attempted the leap. If anyone can help me over, let him do it!" And Goethe sent Faust on a quest among all the many relative events of life for the one moment which embodied the absolute; the moment to which he could say, tarry for thou art so fair.[1]

Professor Kliever points out that the modern crisis in legitimization is a result of the separation of the world of public fact from the world of private meaning. The scientific method, rooted in empiricism and materialism, has enjoyed unprecedented success as a means of validating factual knowledge. But although the scientific tradition has claimed to be an arbiter of all knowledge, it has proven ineffective in dealing with human meaning and value. The conventional role of religion, then, providing an understanding of nature and giving meaning and value to life, has been split in two.

Rather than trying to put Humpty-Dumpty together again, however, Professor Kliever accepts the division between the world of nature and the world of meaning. Science concerns itself with cognition and with the "real world" of facts. Religion concerns itself with meaning and the "life world" of values.[2] This division provides a basis for pluralism and satisfies the human need for confidence in a relativistic world. By debunking authority and magic and by establishing the two criteria of experience and explanation, the scientific method provides a verifiable common denominator which can provide the basis for universal human cooperation and understanding. But above and beyond the world of facts, there is a world of meaning and value which is the lived world and within which there is plenty of room for rich pluralism of meaning.

Professor Kliever does not espouse naive scienticism.[3] He recognizes that the world of scientific fact is a constructed world, as synthetic as the world of value and meaning and that the division between the world of fact and the world of meaning might be modified either through the emergence of criteria other than experience and explanation or through the successful growth of the scientific method. He also acknowledges that what he proposes would require the sacrifice of some of our most cherished beliefs about the reach and significance of value, meaning and religion. Nevertheless, in this "inbetween time" he argues that there is promise in the attempt to inject genuine significance into the world of meaning and value as a world of play, overlaying the no-stuff and-nonsense world of everyday factuality.

Professor Kliever has asked an important question, but I do not find his solution convincing. Most significant primitive mythological systems linked together three elements: understanding of nature, personal integration, *and social organization*. The classical mythological systems which emerged in conjunction with the evolution of the hieratic city-state in or around the fourth millennium B.C. all attempted to show the relationship between personal authenticity, cosmic order and social structure. The city-state was a meso-cosmic reproduction of the macro-cosmic solar system and the micro-cosmic individual. This three-part linkage appeared everywhere. The Navajo hogan was always built with its door to the east, symbolizing the relationship between the family unit and the circling orbs. The Inca and Mayan social order reflected the same intention, as does Stonehenge and all the other religious structures which were so carefully oriented to the position of the sun and moon at the time of the vernal or autumnal equinox.[4]

The social order is a third term standing between the publically verifiable world of experience and explanation and the private world of value and meaning.[5] At the point of actual concrete social organizations, institutions and systems, personal value and public fact are joined in an inextricable way that does not permit separation. A social system is not empty. It is comprised of individuals, and because these individuals define themselves in terms of their meanings and values, these idiosyncratic factors become inevitable parts of the system. And likewise, social systems are not merely fictive value-systems, they grow and operate in the world of experienced and explainable events. They are, therefore, constantly open to an assault from the facts.

For these reasons, Paul Tillich described individualization and participation as ontological elements which structure the world in an essential polar tension. And he showed how, when the tension is broken, the resulting extremes constitute the basis of estrangement, doubt and meaninglessness.[6] Both absolutism and relativism derive the power of their appeal from the power of the threat they embody in their pathological forms.

While absolutism and relativism appear to be incompatible alternatives, in actuality they have a common presupposition. Both are responses to threatening doubts about human efforts to give meaning and value to life; doubts which provoke anxiety, oppression and conflict. Absolutism is the attempt to impose one set of meanings and values on others, thus insuring the dominance and permanence of those values and reducing the threat of their failure. Relativism attempts to meet the threat by ascribing value to all systems of meaning and value. They are alternative answers to the same question. Behind them lies the search for a principle that can give confidence in the midst of the anxieties of human life.

The shared presupposition that confidence is to be found in a discursive principle constitutues the essential weakness and inadequacy of both absolutism and relativism. The entire mainstream of the Judeao-Christian tradition has tried to claim in one way or another that God is not a discursive principle. We should not forget that it was Mephistopheles who sent Faust on his search. And the search for a principle of meaning and value is doomed to failure, as that devil knew, because it is seeking confidence where confidence can never be found.

Genuine confidence is not to be found in any discursive principle. Confidence that can withstand all threat to life must come not from the absolutizing or relativising of any discursive principle of meaning and value, but as a gift through the presence of our fellow human beings. Confidence is not the possession of a principle but the gift of genuine shared life.

The question as it is posed by the enlightenment must be turned entirely around. The real question is not whether God is a valid constructive principle, but whether or not specific human projects are valuable in terms of the transcendent source of meaning. Each of us is not a possessor of truth, but a seeker for truth and the truth we seek cannot be obtained but can only be received and accepted. Such a gift provides a basis for genuine confidence not in principles but in compassion and love which we receive through the hands of our neighbors.[8]

NOTES

1. Heinrich Ott, "Language and Understanding," *New Theology*, No. 4, ed. Martin E. Marty and Dean G. Peerman (New York: The Macmillan Co., 1967), pp. 124-46. Cf. Joseph Dabney Bettis, "Theology in the Public Debate: Barth's Rejection of Natural Theology and the Hermeneutical Problem," *Scottish Journal of Theology*, Dec. 1969, pp. 385-403.

2. Cf. Bronislaw Malinowski, *Magic, Science and Religion*, (Garden City: Doubleday, 1948).

3. He does not, however, address the problem of the intentionality of the scientific method. John Dillenberger, *Protestant Thought and Natural Science*, (Garden City: Doubleday, 1960). David Stewart and Algis Mickunas, *Exploring Phenomenology*, (Chicago: American Library Association, 1974).

4. Joseph Campbell, *The Masks of God, Vol. I: Primitive Mythology*, (New York: Viking, 1959).

5. Gibson Winter, *Elements for a Social Ethic* (New York: Macmillan, 1966). On page 170 in the second paragraph Professor Kliever writes that, "...a scientifically founded social world which dispels life's chaos and terror and guarantees human order and meaning is scarcely conceivable, given the very nature of scientific explanation." But in the next paragraph he writes, "Only the cognitive imagination discovers and describes a single world. It is an austere and impersonal world, but it contains and thus joins us all. It requires and provides a fundamental order for personal and social existence."I think what Professor Kliever wants to say is that science can provide *order* in the social world and religion can provide *meaning*, thus providing unity on one hand and plurality on the other without falling either into absolutism or relativism.

6. Paul Tillich, *Systematic Theology*, 3 vols. (Chicago: University of Chicago Press, 1951-1963). Pp. Vol. I, 174-186, Vol. II, 59-75.

7. Professor Kliever correctly identifies the iconoclastic power of radical monotheism. "A radically transcendent God can function as a permanent iconoclastic principle which not only relativizes all concrete worldviews and life-styles but subjects them to perpetual revolution as well. Such a 'radical monotheism' centers in the Transcendent One for whom alone there is an ultimate good and from whom alone there are proximate goods. This radically transcendent God permits the construction and coexistence of many relative value systems—each of them tentative, experimental and objective. But these plural life-systems are possible only because the Transcendent One prevents any one of them from being erected into an absolute or even being elevated above the others. In short, radical monotheism makes pluralism possible by freeing the world from idolatry." (pp. 161ff). He goes on to point out that, while the obviously powerful prophetic element in monotheism is good, the problem with monotheism is that it becomes absolutistic when it turns to the constructive task of providing a meaning system. "Despite its obvious prophetic power, such a monotheistic protection of pluralism may finally prove unsuccessful. For monotheism, God is the constructive principle as well as the iconoclastic principle of all systems of human order and meaning. As constructive principle the symbol of God is vested with a content which militates against a genuine pluralism." (p.162)

8. Joseph Dabney Bettis, "Is Karl Barth a Universalist?" *Scottish Journal of Theology*, November, 1967, pp. 423-436. Cf. Calvin, *Institutes*, III. 1, 5.; III. xxiii. 4,5,11.; III.xxic.4. and Barth, *Church Dogmatics*, II/2.

Gabriel Vahanian

Commentary

God forbid that I should agree with Lonnie Kliever lest the pluralism he has so convincingly advocated should go radically uncontested. (It was a good paper, Lonnie. Thank you. And I mean it even if, as you and I have known, pluralism looks *OK* or rather sounds great so long as we all speak English.)

Pluralism, Professor Kliever argues, is not to be confused with diversity, although they both have one thing in common: iconoclasm. But diversity ultimately is not immune from self-idolatry—if only because in the end it must accommodate at least to *one* world. By contrast, pluralism alone can and does call for many worlds. Whereas diversity implies a common worldview, pluralism consists in the co-existence of contradictory frames of reference. Moreover, not only does pluralism imply worldviews that are different, it also holds them to be unreconcilable.

But we should not be led astray by Kliever's seemingly convincing argument. This argument boils down to this: the further we move away from diversity to pluralism, from *one* world to *many* worlds, the closer we come to iconoclasm. But then, *either* iconoclasm must finally yield to syncretism and one worldview melt into the other, *or* iconoclasm loses all meaning and turns into some kind of a justification for any and every type of conflictual situation. In the first case, we are back where we started from—syncretism being an alternative form of diversity. In the second case, iconoclasm is nothing but a device aimed at self-justification.

Kliever's first fallacy thus consists in pegging iconoclasm on the dualism of the one and the many. Instead, I would submit that iconoclasm has nothing to do with such a dualism, much less with the conversion of the one into the many, of one world in to many worlds, indifferent if not hostile to one another. Iconoclasm does not consist in converting the world into one or many but it consists in leaving open the possibility for *another* world, a new world. This utopian dimension of iconoclasm is precisely what Kliever overlooks when he forgets that man is man to the extent that he does not settle for less than a world radically other than either one common

105

world or many irreducibly different worlds.

Why does Kliever overlook that utopian dimension of iconoclasm? Because, I think, he tends to identify iconoclasm with
pluralism and—just as arbitrarily—pluralism with the rise of scientific knowledge and the concomitant process of secularization.
Whereas in the past myth compelled us into one common view of
reality, scientific knowledge—at least according to Kliever—calls for
a multiplicity of worldviews. Or, as Kliever would say, radical
monotheism has given way to a thoroughgoing polytheism. And
once again iconoclasm is subjected to a fallacy, Kliever's second: but
this time iconoclasm is understood in terms of a shift from one god
to many gods rather than being construed—as it should—in terms
of God's radical otherness.

As for Kliever's third fallacy, it occurs in relation to his dualism
of fact and fiction. Kliever readily admits to both fact and fiction being symbolic constructions. But it never occurs to him that if this is
so it is by virtue of man's verbal condition and its inherent utopian-
ism: language is neither monistic nor dualistic: no metaphor can obtain without transcending both monism and dualism. And whether
language subscribes to one world or to many, it never does so
without calling either of them into question. And the most radical
questioning of man surely lies in what makes it possible for him to
start *de novo*— as would and does a man who is the man without
precedent, neither male nor female, neither Greek nor Jew.

But I will conclude with a more concrete observation. The scientific revolution—Kliever contends and I agree—has brought about a
world barren of all meaning. Such a statement can mean nothing,
however, if it does not pull the rug from under our traditional,
religious perspectives and other worn out metaphors, until one can
come up with a metaphor that lies beyond fact and fiction, diversity
and pluralism, monism and dualism. The human lies not behind us
but ahead of us and is as radically different from where we stand
now as God is from man.

George P. Grant

— B3 —
Faith and the Multiversity

"Faith and the multiversity" is a subject which could be tackled from many angles, both practical and theoretical.

The essence of the question is, however the relation between faith and modern science. You may well say—not that terrible old chestnut once again! Hasn't there been so much discussion of that over the last centuries that there is nothing worthwhile left to be said about it? My answer is no. The relation between modern science and faith lies at the core of the relation between faith and the multiversity; and thought has not yet reached that core. Many Christians turn away from this relation because they want there to be no conflict here. Nevertheless it remains the fatefilled question of western intellectual life.

What is faith? "Faith is the experience that the intelligence is illuminated by love."[1] What is given in that definition of course requires a careful analysis of each of its terms:—experience, intelligence, illumination, love. As that analysis is not possible here, let me quickly make four comments, particularly about the use of the word 'love'. This word has lost its clarity in contemporary language, particularly in theological usage.

(1) 'Love' is attention to otherness, receptivity of otherness, consent to otherness. Such an account sounds abstract until we give it content through all the occasions of life, from elementary human relations to the very Trinity itself. When we love other human beings, we know those human beings because we have paid attention to them, have received something of what they are, and consented to what they are as good. Indeed in this example, consent is easily joy, because of our obvious need of people close to us; whereas consent may not easily be joy in the more difficult reaches of love. The interdependence of love and knowledge is most clearly manifest when we try to understand what it is to love justice—(and it must be remembered that the love of justice is what all human beings are primarily called to). We can only grow in our knowledge of justice insofar as we love what we already know of it and any new knowledge of justice then opens

up the possibility of further love which in turn makes possible fuller knowledge. The road to this perfecting is what we mean by the lives of the saints. Most of us are at the most elementary level in this process, but we have to start where we are, paying attention, receiving, consenting to justice as it is required of us in daily life. In our daily attempts to be just the central fact about human love is made plain. Love is only love insofar as it has passed through the flesh by means of actions, movements, attitudes which correspond to it. If this has not happened, it is not love, but a phantasy of the imagination by which we coddle ourselves. As far as love is concerned, and particularly love of justice, "matter is our infallible judge."

(2) As the definition "faith is the experience that the intelligence is illuminated by love" is difficult to fathom, I will mention two writings, one a novel, one philosophy in which the sentence is clarified. In Simenon's account of one of Chief Inspector Maigret's criminal investigations in Paris (which in English has the title "Maigret's Mistake") the meaning of this definition is beautifully illustrated. The definition is philosophically clarified at the centre of Plato's Republic. In Plato's account of the movement of the soul to perfection he speaks metaphorically in three images, known as the Sun, the Line and the Cave. In his account of knowledge he uses the metaphor of sight. What he is describing through that metaphor is what I mean by love. As would be expected from our highest philosophic authority, Plato hits the perfect not perfectly. Love and intellect must be in unity if we are to gain the most important knowledge. If we are ever to get near to understanding the Republic, we must recognize what is given in that metaphor. This is extremely difficult for us moderns because most German and English scholars have, for the last two centuries, read it through Kantian eyes (a great darkening) and Catholics through Aristotelian eyes (better, but still a darkening).

(3) Such an account clearly makes faith something open to all human beings at many levels and does not reserve faith to describe our responses to certain Christian teachings. The only claim of those of us who are Christians is that the unity between love and intellect can be seen in Christ. If I may speak technically for a moment as a theologian to those who study theology, it is well to remember the universality implied in that definition of faith. We are bombarded

by the works of German historical theologians, who have been defeated by the philosophers of their own country without even knowing it, and are trying to rescue themselves from that defeat by making Christianity dependent on the particularities of 'history'. Faith properly defined is necessary both for philosphy and theology, whether they are practised in east or west.

(4) If faith is an experience, it is clearly not a matter of will or of choice or of merit. Experience is always something given us. Faith is a matter of luck or, if you prefer a slightly different language, a matter of providence. I prefer luck, Luther was often misguided, but he hit the nail on the head in his blunt way when he said that Christ had nailed merit to the cross. It is necessary to state this for the following reason. When a theologian such as myself defines faith as the experience that the intelligence is illuminated by love, I am making no claim for my own ability to love. To be quite particular, I spend a lot of my life in meetings with colleagues and to put it mildly, my intellect is not lit up by love. This side of the truth concerning the dangers of the intellectual life is very beautifully expressed in St. Francis' writings about the philosophers. When one says that faith is an experience, it is essential to emphasize that the possession of it, however limited, is in no sense dependent on willing. This is particularly necessary to say because nearly all western human beings are impregnated (whether they know it or not) by that account of will which was ennucleated by Leibniz and Kant and Nietzsche. When one says that faith is the experience that the intelligence is illuminated by love, it must be made clear that we are talking about something concerning human beings at a higher level than that at which will as activity properly operates. It is essential to insist that love and will are different. Love knows itself as needing; will now thinks itself as creating. As has been beautifully said: "One degrades the mysteries of faith in making them a matter for affirmation or for negation, when they ought to be matters for contemplation."[2]

Now to turn from Christianity to the multiversity. It is very important to be clear what is meant by the multiversity particularly because it is an institution which has only realized itself recently in Europe and the U.S., during this century—although its coming to be was a slow emergence over the last four centuries. In Canada it has only been realized in the last thirty years. I often meet people of my generation who went to university in the 1930s, and who speak as if the institutions their children or grandchildren are now attending are really the same as those they went to. But this is simply an illusion. The names for these places are the same, but they are such different places that they should have different names. To say what they now are, it is necessary to describe the dominating paradigm of knowledge which rules in them and is determinative of what they are. Different civilisations and differing periods within the same civilization have differing paradigms of knowledge, and such paradigms shape every part of the society and particularly its institutions of learning. The principle of any paradigm in any civilization is always the relation between an aspiration of human thought and the effective conditions for its realization.

The question then is what is given in the modern use of the word 'science'. This is the paradigm which has slowly reached definition over the last centuries, and has since 1945 reached its apogee of determining power over our institutions of higher learning. Of course, it would be folly to attempt to summarize in a paragraph that brilliant progress of self-definition by philosophic scientists as to their activity over the last centuries. Suffice it simply to say that what is given in the modern word 'science' is the project of reason to gain objective knowledge. What is meant by objective? Object means literally some thing that we have thrown over against us. *Jacio* I throw, *ob* over against, therefore 'the thrown against'. The German word for object is *Gegenstand*—that which stands against. Reason as project, (that is, reason as thrown forth) is the summonizing of something before us and the putting of questions to it, so that it is forced to give us its reasons for being the way it is as an object. Our paradigm is that we have knowledge when we represent anything to ourselves as object, and question it, so that it will give us its reasons. That summonizing and questioning requires well defined procedures. These procedures are what we call in English 'research', although what is entailed in these is more clearly given in the German word 'forschung'. Often people in the university like to use about themselves the more traditional word 'scholar' but that word means now those who carry on 'research'. Those procedures started with such experiments as balls running down an inclined plane, but now the project of reason applies them to everything: stones, plants, animals, human beings, societies. Thus in North America we have divided our institutions of higher learning into faculties of natural science, social science and humanities, depending on the object which is being researched. But the project of reason is largely the same, to summons different things to questioning. In the case of the humanities the object is the past, and these procedures are applied to the relics of the past. For example, I live in a department of religion in which much work is done to summons the Bible before the researchers to give them its reasons.

This paradigm makes it accurate to use the ugly neologism 'multiversity'. Each department of these institutions, indeed almost each individual researcher, carries on the project of reason by approaching different objects. The limitations of the human mind in synthesizing facts necessitates the growing division of research into differing departments and further subdivision. "[However] much use is made of algebra and instruments, science (as a synthetic activity) will always largely depend on man's intelligence and physique, which are limited, and do not become less so with the passing of centuries."[3] This paradigm of knowledge makes it therefore appropriate to speak of the multiversity.

The achievements of the modern project are of course a source of wonder. The objects have indeed given forth their reasons, since they have been summonsed forth to do so over the last centuries. The necessities that we can know about stones or societies surely produce in us astonishment in its beautiful sense. These achievements are not simply practical, but also have theoretical consequences. All of us in our everyday lives are so taken up with certain practical achievements, in medicine, in production, in the making of human beings and the making of war, that we are apt to forget the sheer theoretical interest of what has been revealed about necessity in Einsteinian physics or in Darwinian biology. It is not my business here to speak of the appropriateness of these procedures in giving us knowledge of the human things through the social sciences and the humanities, or to raise such difficulties as that we cannot use experiment when the past is summonsed before us as object to be put to the question.

The purpose of this paper is to ask what is the relation of science to faith. The question is now defined as: what is the relation between this paradigm of knowledge and the experience that the intelligence is illuminated by love? Or to put the matter practically: how do those who know that the second statement is true live in institutions dominated by the paradigm?

The relation between the modern scientific project and what I have called love can only be clarified in terms of certain distinctions. For example, it is clear that from the earliest days of the modern experiment, the motive for mastering nature was often the desire to alleviate the human condition—that is, it was undertaken from love of human beings. This was often the motive for the attempt to overcome chance by knowing the reasons why objects behaved the ways they did, because chance, whether in the form of hunger or disease or the necessity of labor, produced such agonies. Those who worked for the development of the new arts and sciences and their union (which we call technology) were spurred to their work by their hope of better human conditions. How can we not wish to interfere with chance in nature, when chance is the cause of so much suffering? The new science was the intellectual underpinning of intelligent interference, and as such was motivated by love. This is, of course, true to this day. However much there may be good cause to fear certain researches, which are possible because of the discovery of the structure of DNA, there is no doubt that many who advocate the pursuit of such researches are doing so, not because of pure curiosity, but also because they think that such researches will lead to the overcoming of certain chances which have up to now plagued the researches which are at the heart of modern psychology. The consequent sufferings of the dogs or rats or pigeons are justified by what may result to limit human suffering. Within a utilitarian calculus, experiment on human beings may be justified in terms of the greatest good of the greatest number. But it is clear that the love involved in the modern project here is not given to or received from the objects of the research, but to other beings who will be the recipients of the goods which result.

To go further: it is also clear that many people who have given their lives to the pursuit of the modern project have been held by the beauty of what they were studying and discovering. Beauty is the cause of love, and therefore one can say that their intellects were illu-

minated by love in what they studied. Can one read Heisenberg's
books about his studies without becoming aware of that? There is a
dear account of Charles Darwin by a friend who walked with him in
the country. "Nothing escaped him. No object in nature, whether
Flower, or Bird, or Insect of any kind, could avoid his loving recognition." But the very dearness of the description must not prevent us
from seeing its ambiguity, which lies in the use of the words 'objects' and 'loving recognition' in the same sentence. Darwin's loving
recognition of the flowers, birds, insects, means that he was receiving them as more than objects. However, Darwin's most general
scientific truths concerning animals are statements about them as
objects, and are true whether or not animals are greeted or not
greeted with loving recognition.

Indeed it is clear that the modern project of reason as projected
towards objects summonsed before us to answer our questions is
not an activity which depends on the love of the objects studied. Objects can be summonsed before us without love for the things summonsed. This is true, whether the object is a tree, a beast, a human
being, a society or the past; that is, whether our researches fall
under the natural sciences, the social sciences or the humanities.
Therefore as this paradigm of knowledge becomes increasingly all
pervasive, faith as the experience that the intelligence is illuminated
by love, must have less and less significance in the central work of
the multiversity. Indeed, what has happened in modern society as a
whole is that knowledge qua knowledge is detached from love qua
love. In this context it is impossible to avoid mentioning the "fact-
value" distinction. Facts are now identified with objects and are
abstracted from things in their wholeness. The rest is labelled
'values' and is tucked away as part of one's own subjectivity. Values
are detached from 'objective' being. But justice and beauty are not
values which we subjectively 'create'. Nor are stones, plants,
animals and human beings simply objects. They only become objects when they are placed in a certain relation to us—that of being
at our disposal.

This is luckily not the place to discuss the disunity between love
and intelligence, as it affects the destiny of western civilization as a
whole. It must be remembered also, that those who partake in the
truth of the Vedanta have not dissimilar problems in relating to that

paradigm as those who would partake in the truth of Christianity. My task is confined to Christians in the North American multiversity. For many generations youngsters have been coming into the universities which were fast becoming multiversities, and those who came from one or other established religious traditions have faced the complexities of that relation. There was no escape from the multiversities, for those institutions were made to serve the social purpose of imposing the standards of professionalism and professionalism is the very fabric of our American society. (Fabric in the sense that there is no successful life outside its borders. Successful in the sense that what is deemed successful by the dominating classes is just that professionalism.) If I were going to describe that past history as comedy one could start from that description of the personnel of the YMCA: "People went into it to do good and then used it to make good." The problem of working through the relation between faith and modern knowledge at an earlier time was easier, because the established Protestant churches were still socially powerful, and the institutions of higher learning had not been thoroughly integrated into the new paradigm of knowledge. But it seems to me more useful to forego history and to talk about today. It is always easier to be more certain about the past because we have had time to contemplate it, while the present is difficult to fathom, particularly in a quick changing technological society like ours, in which the unchanging is hard to apprehend.

The difference between my generation and the young people today is that the latter come to institutions of higher learning from schools which are already integrated into the modern paradigm of knowledge. They have been taught at school by people who have themselves been taught within that paradigm. The teachers may not have been taught well within that paradigm, but they have been taught within it. Those youngsters who wish to go on with higher education come to the multiversity not to learn some new paradigm but to become professionals within the same. Most of such students have practically no relation to any religious tradition, and the relation of the intelligence to love is not a question which will ever arise for them, except perhaps at some half conscious level of remembrance. If they are clever and ambitious, most of them will become professionals in the outside world, and some within the multiversity itself. These days of course the possibility of that professionalism presents problems for many, because of the diminished North American position in the world. This is particularly pressing in Canada since, because of our strange relation to the North American economy, we are integrated to it as very, very, very junior partners. There is a minority of students who have passed through school with a continuing relation to some religious tradition. The members of this minority vary very greatly according to what tradition they come from, and its degree of religious and/or theological vigor. From those who come from a tradition of some religious vigor, (often Catholicism or some form of fundamentalism), the relation between faith and the technological paradigm may continue to be an issue of intensity. The question is more often practical, rather than theoretical. For example, one of the great agonies which is going on today is among those young people who want to be gynecologists; and who cannot be admitted for such training unless they are willing to take part in the full work of their teachers. As the full work requires that they take part in a steady program of fetuscide, they are not in a position to gain admission to the training which they desire. That agony and exclusion is not much publicized by the medical profession. As to be expected in such a situation, many give way to the demands of professionalism. [A distinguished neuro-surgeon has alerted me to this situation.]

There have been, there are and there will be attempts within the fabric of the multiversity to live in ways of learning that are outside this paradigm of knowledge. These appear particularly in those areas we call the humanities and the social sciences, because in studies which deal with the human things the project of objectivity most obviously shows its limitations. Some of these minority voices in the multiversity, which stand outside the dominating stream, have their roots in the continuance of the truths of religion, others come forth from the radical tradition in politics. But it is clear that these minority voices will not turn the multiversities from their determined end. Civilizations are destinies, and the destiny of western civilisation, as far as learning is concerned, is the project of researched objectivity. The possibilities of living outside it within the multiversity are limited. If I may be allowed an example of those limitations from my own life, I will speak of the attempt to build a department of religion within a secular multiversity. The original intuition from which that attempt came was the recognition that the theological colleges had been forced out of the mainstream of the multiversity by their secularized colleagues, and by the secular governments. There was therefore need for an institutional framework in which people could think carefully and freely about religious questions which are part of the western tradition, and could think about these questions not simply in a western context, but with all the stimulus which could be thrown into them from the truths that had been received and thought about in other great civilizations. As these truths are not by definition objective, nor for that matter subjective, (the opposite side of the modern coin), the hope was to make a situation in which the study would be made neither of technical skill nor an exploration of personal eccentricity. The attempt to do that has been beset by one overwhelming failure. It is caused by the fact that the spirit of the multiversity is just too strong to allow the study of religion to transcend the modern project of reason, as producing objective knowledge. Our modern institutions have their carefully worked out reward systems for professors and students; they also have their particular prestige granting systems. The reward system is geared towards the production of objective scholarship; the prestige system is geared to the international market, and international in Canadian terms means chiefly the big American multiversities. There is no alternative for any department but to live within these reward and prestige systems. The result is that the study of religion increasingly tends to become objectified into antiquarianism. The religions become like flies caught in amber, worthy objects for libraries and museums, but not living realities in a living culture.

At a time when knowledge is not known as related to love, and when the official churches seem complicit in the civilization that has brought about the disunity, it is bound to happen that many young people seek that unification in new forms outside formal education. The desire that there be something eternal which is loveable belongs too deeply to human beings for it to be put aside, just because it has been put aside in the multiversity. People seek the fulfillment of that desire outside the established forms. This can be seen in the strength of Christian pietism and fundamentalism in North America, and in the strength of new religious organizations, some of which have their origins in Asia. The response of the multiversity to these happenings is the following. At the level of study they will be objectified under the sociology of religion; in general they will be ridiculed as outside the stream of established western rationality. I will not speak here of the more brutal public response of deprogramming. I think those of us who are Christians should be very suspicious of this hostility by the established bastions of western rationality to the new forms of religion or the revival of old forms. The recognition that the intelligence is illuminated by love is the recognition (however dim) that there is a loveable eternal. And in the light of that recognition by ourselves, we should turn with the greatest sympathy to young people, who finding that the official organisations have become oblivious of eternity, seek to partake in that eternity in ways that are unexpected to us. Let me put the matter in a cold light. I often find myself rather alien intellectually when I meet members of some of the new religions or some fundamentalist Christians. But then when I talk to them about such matters as mass fetuscide for convenience, I find myself at home in a way which is rarely the case concerning such matters with most of my colleagues in the multiversity, or as far as that goes with members of the larger official Protestant bodies. Not to be close concerning questions as to the way faith is formulated is a small thing compared to the absence of faith itself. To repeat: when the eternal is concerned, matter is our infallible judge.

Finally—In saying a strong word of praise for those who try to live faith outside the paradigm of the multiversity, I do not want in any way to downgrade the intellect. What has been learnt through our paradigm of knowledge—in its mathematics, its physics, its biology, its anthropology, etc.—is a great achievement of the intellect. It is always the job of the intellect to teach us of the order of necessity, and the details of that order given us in modern science are amazing to contemplate. To speak of faith as the experience that the intelligence is illuminated by love is in no way to imply that love could try to bypass the full knowledge of the order of necessity reached by intelligence. The reason why love knows that such a bypassing is futile is of course that only the intelligence, by the exercise of that means that are proper to it, can recognize its own dependence on love for the highest knowledge.

Indeed it may be the case that the enormous web of necessity given in the discoveries of modern science will be just the cause of some human beings rediscovering what was given in the word 'love'. Both the divine love and our consent to it has under any conditions to cross that order of necessity which separates them from each other. Is not the crucifixion the crossing of the implacable distance? I do not much like to criticize Christianity in public these days when evevery Tom, Dick and Harry makes cracks at it. Nevertheless it seems true that western Christianity—both in its Protestant and Catholic forms—became, as it established civilization in the West, a religion which simplified the divine love by identifying it with power, in a way which failed to recognise the distance between the order of good and the order of necessity. Western Christianity became exclusivist and imperialist, arrogant and dynamic by the loss of this recognition. It is now facing the public results of that failure. Perhaps, the scientists by placing before us the seemingly seamless web of necessity, which itself excludes the loveable, will help to reteach us the truth that the orders of good and necessity are different. One of Nietzsche's superb accounts of the modern world was that Christianity had produced its own gravediggers. It was out of the seedbed of western Christianity that modern scientists had come, and the discoveries of science showed that God is dead. In that sense, Christianity had produced its own gravediggers. Perhaps we may say that that formulation gets close to the truth of history, but is nevertheless not true. The web of necessity which the modern paradigm of knowledge lays before us does not show us that God is dead, but rather reminds us of what western Christianity seemed to forget in its moment of pride: that necessity through which love must cross. Christianity did not produce its own gravediggers, but the means to its own purification.

NOTES

1. S. Weil, *La Plesanteur et la Grace*. Plon, Paris. 1948. p. 148. My translation.
2. *ibid.* p. 149
3. S. Weil, *Sur la Science*. See "La science et nous".

Jean-Guy LeMarier

Commentary

In the general context of values and the unity of sciences, and especially of the contribution of religion or faith to the scientific understanding of man and the universe, Professor Grant has selected to focus our attention on the importance of love in a thorough grasp of reality, on the contribution of faith and religion to that aspect of love and on the suspicions of the university communities towards the distorting effect of love upon the objective requirements of truth and research, and therefore towards the dangers of religion for the academic endeavor.

My observations should start with an acknowledgment of my general agreement with the fundamental points of Professor Grant's contention. It is, I suppose, my duty—I should hasten to say, a pleasant one—to thank him for sharing with us his experience and his knowledge, and that with love—and for contributing a well-thought and provocative paper for our discussion and reflections.

The points I want to raise now should not be construed as disagreements, but they are, I believe, fields of possible further investigations and also of some qualifications which a short paper does not necessarily have to make.

I. The Definition of Faith.

Professor Grant has proposed an interesting definition of faith as the "experience that the intelligence is illumined by love". This definition underlines one of the important components of faith: namely the interplay of knowledge and love in a profoundly human experience.

As Professor Grant explicity indicates, such an account of faith makes it "something open to all human beings at many levels". And he concludes that "faith properly defined is necessary both for philosophy and theology". I fully agree. I would even venture to say that such an inclusive definition of faith makes it a fundamental requirement of all forms of knowledge, threfore of all scientific endeavors. Trust and confidence, Professor Grant would say "attention to otherness, receptivity of otherness and consent to otherness", are necessary steps in the whole process of human knowledge: as a starting point for it, also as an accompanying factor for its whole development. If I understand him correctly, Professor Bernard Lonergan has precisely attempted in his Method of Theology, to show that faith constitutes the basis not only for theology but for all sciences.

But at this point I think it is important to introduce the distinction between a human faith, it would be more exact to say faith in man (for man and to man), and a religious faith. While these two types of faith are similar, there are also important differences. Christian faith for example is not simply a "response to certain Christian teachings". The religious dimension brings forth radically the aspect of transcendence: man's relation to it and its influence upon the whole human reality.

Before pursuing this line of thought, I want to go back briefly to the definition of faith as the "experience that the intelligence is illuminated by love" and to propose that other realities could also be very conveniently so described. I am thinking of *the artistic intuition* and of *the moral decision*. I could not develop here the parallel of this suggestion. If I may at this point resort to Aristotelian categories, I will propose that we are confronted with the three fields of human activities where the speculative and the practical are radically intertwined, where knowledge and love are perfectly interdependent.

After this aside, I want to conclude this point with the suggestion that faith as the "experience that the intelligence is illuminated by love" present us with an important characteristic of the reality of faith, that the religious faith encompasses other dimensions, mainly that attention to otherness (love) illuminating the intelligence is definitely attention to the others, radically attention to the Other (with a capital O): transcendence.

II. The Neologism "Multiversity".

The neologism "multiversity" used by Professor Grant did slightly surprise me. I must confess that while I share his concern for the contemporary university scene, I would personally be inclined to read and stress positive signs of interesting development on that scene. I shall limit my comments on this section to two brief observations.

1. Multiversity-University.

If I understood correctly Professor Grant, he felt compelled to change from unity to multiplicity, the characteristic of our institutions of high learning. It is one intersting facet of the age-old problem of the one and the many.

Universities, if I read well history, came into existence for the sake of both *universality* and *unity*. Professor Grant's assessment indicates that in the last century, and for Canada in the last thirty years, universality has claimed a primacy over unity to the point of disappearance of the goal of unity, possibly to the point of deafness to true otherness. Is that the price one must pay for the sake of specialization?

If I beg to differ with Professor Grant's evaluation, it is not simply because of conferences like the one we are presently attending (It could be an argument for Professor Grant's thesis: this conference is not organized, so far as I know, by a university), but because of the promises of interdisciplinarity.

I acknowledge that these promises have still to produce important fruits (they still are simply promises), but I hope that the students' unrest of the late sixties was not all in vain.

2. Reason-Intelligence.

This leads me to my second observation. It would be the place to investigate the contemporary meanings of science, paradigm of knowledge, objectivity and research. I have already been too long. So I will limit myself to underline that while dealing with the reality of faith, the ability to know has been presented in terms of *intelligence*, in this section about universities, it becomes *reason*.

Now I have great respect for rationality: it is one normal human way of knowing (to reason is a function of knowledge). I dictated this modification of language simply to evoke the possibility of long-range effect of extended rationalism (the primacy, self-sufficiency of reason, the Goddess Reason). Universities, I agree with Professor Grant, are slow in escaping the tentacles of rationalism. I, for one, read promising signs on the university scene: thanks to the efforts of wholeness in health sciences and psychology, in sociology, in arts, in philosophy, in religion, and even in theology.

III. Faith and Science.

We come now to the central part of Professor Grant's expose. After all my previous remarks and questions, one may expect that I will quarrel with his thesis on the relation of science to faith. On the contrary, I fully concur with Professor Grant's plea for attempts to make room—and an extensive one—for religion and theology on the university scene and for the possible fecundation of faith by the contribution of sciences.

This goes simply to prove that my comments intended to underline the validity of Professor Grant's considerations and to express hope for further develoments and clarification of his thoughts. Again, I want to thank Professor Grant for a stimulating presentation.

Herbert Richardson

Commentary

It would be inappropriate for me to speak without first acknowledging my great debt to Professor Grant who has been, for the last four or five years of my life, my mentor and teacher. I'm sure we've all had the experience of having mentors and teachers in our earlier years. But when one, much later in life, encounters someone who restores light and life to the mind, then what a blessing it is. Professor Grant has been that blessing for me.

A right interpretation of Professor Grant requires that we pay attention to what he does *not* say. Convinced that the most important realities are beyond speech, he practices silence. His references to Simone Weil remind us that holiness is always more important than learning. Hence, we scholars are not saints; we play a secondary role. We acknowledge this role, and the reality of a holiness that transcends speech, by not seeking to speak about and thereby objectify everything in the world.

Today, says Professor Grant, human reason seeks to speak about and inquire into everything. It does not acknowledge that anything is beyond it. It summons all things before it, requiring that they "give their reasons." This inquiry is carried on most effectively through academic specialties. They create the modern pluriversity, and in that pluriversity the unity of knowledge is lost. Also lost is that understanding of knowledge as an activity motivated by love of the good.

Professor Grant is attempting to restore to reason its spiritual character when he speaks of our intelligence as properly illuminated by love. Love for what? Love for truth as the good of the human person and the world. This is a Platonic idea, and Professor Grant's reference to Plato as his teacher is correct. Grant is a Platonist, but a Platonist who has made revisions that might help us today.

Plato spoke about the mind as animated by an intellectual eros or love for the good. The good, said Plato (Professor Grant agreeing), is justice. A person gives us evidence of his intelligence by seeking justice, rather than seeking mere information and the organization of data. A person who seeks these alone is "technology reasonable," but not an intelligent man. This "technical reasonableness," the characteristic of modern science, is what Christian theologians call "fallen or sinful" reason. Technical reasonableness is no longer using our reason as God intended us to use our reason, namely to search for and to unite with God and his purposes for our lives and the world. In technical reasonableness, the spirituality of reason has been lost. Having lost the spirituality of our reason, we're delivered into that autonomy through which we're busy destroying ourselves, namely into an autonomy governed by a desire for ever-increased power.

Here, now, is Grant's philosophical innovation. Whereas Plato spoke about the mind animated by love, and understood that love to be towards God, Grant says that the love which animates our reason towards God, and that good which is justice, realizes itself *in the world*. Plato points us to a justice which is above and beyond the world. But Grant says our love of justice seeks realization by turning towards the world so that we see about us not "objects" and "things," but fellow creatures. Brother Moon, Brother Sun—says Saint Francis. Fellow creatures. The world is our family and our true home. On the basis of the "redirected" interpretation of the Platonic idea of intelligence, Grant suggests that a scientific reason illuminated by love for world (now perceived as co-creature) would seek the just structure of goodness appropriate to things. It would seek the justice of the world. In so doing, it would affirm that the world is our place to live, to know, to grow spiritually. (Here are overtones of Professor Shepard's earlier paper.)

I think Professor Grant's proposal is a significant and relevant innovation in the Platonic tradition and its understanding of reason. But I want to end just with one question. Why did Plato believe that one could not and should not love co-creatures as ultimately valuable? That is, why did Plato think that one could not find justice *in the world?* The answer is that Plato believed that there wasn't justice in the world, and that the truth of this statement is proved by our experience of the world. If there is no justice in the world, then reason cannot, according to Plato, be directed *towards the world.*

The world, from Plato's point of view, is fallen. Plato doesn't use this expression, but Plato believes one cannot find the good in the world. That is why, according to Plato, a person who loves the good searches for God and finally leaves the world. On the other hand, what Professor Grant has advocated can only be true if there is a God whose purpose for the world is to restore justice to it so that the world might eventually become just. Then justice would be the intended order of this world even though this world is not yet just. If this were true, then we could acknowledge all beings as our brothers and our sisters.

In conclusion, we can see that Profesor Grant's understanding of the task of philosophy is not classical and traditional at all, but is somewhat Marxist. Like Marx, Grant suggests that our task as philosophers and as theologians is to transform the world. But, Grant is not a Marxist; he is a Biblical millenialist. He believes our striving for justice in the world originates not in hatred of evil (the class enemy), but in love of good. The love of God's purpose for this world and the spiritualization of reason so that it seeks this-worldly justice, is Grant's fundamental vision. It is also, the basis for his innovation within, and renewal of, the Platonic tradition.

Section C:
The Individual and the Political Order

— C1 —
The Reciprocity of Liberty and Authority
Andrew J. Reck

— C2 —
Freedom and Authority
Gerald McCool

— C3 —
From Authority to Absolute Dominion in our Administered World
Klaus Rohman

— C4 —
The Elect and the Preterite
Richard L. Rubenstein

Andrew J. Reck

— C1 —
The Reciprocity of Liberty and Authority

The most ancient sense of liberty has been attached to political communities. A *polis* was deemed free when it was not subjugated by an alien *polis* or subordinated to an imperial system. This ancient sense of freedom has its contemporary analogue in the widely acknowledged right of people to self-determination. It is operative today in the emergence of new nation states in the Third World, usually achieved after arduous revolutionary struggles against entrenched imperial powers. Freedom in this ancient sense has often been thought to filter down to the people themselves. But as Jacques Juillard recently pointed out, the establishment of a national state does not guarantee the freedom of a nation, a people. "The peoples of the Third World may be free as long as they are fighting for national independence, but as soon as this is won they tend to fall into the hands of pitiless dictators who use ideology essentially as an instrument of power." Julliard calls for a new *"Internationale"*—*"an 'Internationale* of human rights'—the only response to the *'Internationale* of sovereign states.' "[1]

Julliard's call is one which we Americans instinctively heed. Our nation is founded not on ethnic groups bound to the past but on the commitment of individuals to the ideology of human rights—the rights of individuals to life, liberty, and the pursuit of happiness. The "American Way of Life" fulfills, at least rhetorically, the promise of the Western liberal tradition, whose core consists in the primacy of the value of the individual. Western liberalism was born from the all too often mortal conflicts between individuals, on the one hand, and ecclesiastical and governmental authorities, on the other.

As the West has evolved into a secular, technological, and democratic civilization, the concept of freedom has assumed siginificance independently of metaphysical meanings. In the

opening sentence of his celebrated essay *On Liberty* (1859), John
Stuart Mill declares that his subject is *not* the topic of freedom
and determinism, "But Civil, or Social Liberty: the nature and
the limits of the power which can be exercised over the
individual."[2] Mill's use of the term "liberty" in place of
"freedom" lends support to the view that "liberty" has a
specifically legal and/or political meaning and that "freedom"
bears a metaphysical connotation. However, by attending to ordinary usage one meticulous scholar has concluded that the two
words are interchangeable.[3] And in this paper I shall accept the
synonymy of "liberty" and "freedom," not only because my
usage is ordinary, but also because the meaning of liberty or
freedom cannot be plumbed without consideration of its
metaphysics. Mill exemplifies what has been fundamental to the
West since the late eighteenth century—namely, that liberty
belongs to the individual standing against external power.
Freedom in this sense is freedom *from* external restraints and encroachments; its sense is fundamentally negative. Its targets
have been Church and State. The cries for liberty were raised
against ecclesiastical and political authorities which coerced
modes of religious worship and repressed thought, speech, and
publication. They still sound today against governmental interference in the affairs of business and in the social and political
associations men form. Sometimes this sense of liberty is expanded to include what is properly called license—the privilege to do
whatever we want. In this broadened sense liberty has come to
mean, for example, the commerce in pornography without censorship or police suppression.[4] It is difficult, if not impossible, to
deny the utilities of negative freedom. Since the eighteenth century it has liberated the creative energies of men to make a new
world of science, technology, industry, and political democracy.
It has released the vast reserves of human initiative to fuel the
remarkable progress of the past two centuries. And it has
fostered the rich diversity, the multicolored variety, the intellectual, religious, and aesthetic pluralism, the moral experimentalism, the universal vitality and spontaneity, the openness and
dynamism, of contemporary civilization.

But it has also exacted an exorbitant price. It has ripped the fabric of the social cohesion indispensable to the survival of the human race. An inhabitable environment, to cite a well-known example, has been the birth right of all mankind; but after a century of industrial exploitation, mainly for private profit, our birth right to an inhabitable environment is no longer to be taken for granted. Man himself is an endangered species. The disutilities of freedom in an exclusively negative form cannot be ignored. Social groups require not only the cooperative pooling of individaul efforts to realize common goals; they also need to restrain and repress individual deviations detrimental to the realization of these goals. The Great Depression of the 1930's shook the foundations of traditional liberalism. The western democracies, solicitous of the rights of individuals, were for a while overwhelmed by economic paralysis, while totalitarian states of the right and of the left mobilized their peoples. The outcome of course, was the devastation of World War II. But within the crucible of historical experience new concepts of liberalism were forged. John Dewey, the philosopher of American democracy for the first half of the twentieth century, articulated the issue neatly when, in *Liberalism and Social Action*, he declared that, in order to attain the ends of traditional liberalism—the fullest development or growth of individuals, it was necessary, in an urbanized, technological, industrial society, to alter the means.[5] Freedom could no longer be esteemed as freedom from government, for government itself, when democratically responsive to its citizenry, can be an important instrument for the realization of human values.

Thus negative freedom, freedom *from* . . . . is complemented by positive freedom, freedom *to* . . . . When freedom signifies the removal of restraints exclusively, it often lacks the purpose for which restraints are removed—to be, to have, or to act in ways which the restraints prohibited or restricted. If there are neither positive projects for choice and action, nor objective and social instrumentalities for the realization of these projects, the removal of restraints falls short of total freedom. Jean-Paul Sartre describes the riot of the workers at Croix-Rousse in 1830.[6] The rioters had the power to overthrow the local police and proprietors, but after their successful revolt, they withdrew to their homes. Military reinforcements came in and beat them down. Sartre imputes the failure of the rioters to their lack of a project; they did not have a conception of what to do when free from their opposition. Without a positive concept of freedom, they had nothing to be free *to*. . . .

We recognize in our own social situation that it is relatively empty to guarantee large masses of our citizens the right to think, speak, and write without fear of governmental suppression, unless they are also provided an education which enables them to think, speak, and write. It is futile to claim that men and women are free to choose any job or career they want—a cardinal claim of the free enterprise system—unless the economy is rich with opportunities for jobs and careers. Positive freedom is therefore often linked to the welfare functions of the modern state. Whereas liberty in its negative mode often proves to be incompatible with the twin democratic ideal—equality,[7] positive freedom and equality are reciprocally supportive. Nevertheless, the concept of positive freedom has been embattled by the critics, foremost among whom in recent decades has been Isaiah Berlin.

Berlin argues that, while different philosophers have defined the concept of positive freedom in various ways, it nonetheless yields a basic, common import.

> (Positive freedom). . . derives from the wish on the part of the individual to be his own master. I wish my life and decisions to depend on myself, not on external forces of whatever kind. I wish to be the instrument of my own, not of other men's, acts of will. I wish to be a subject, not an object; to be moved by reasons, by conscious purposes which are my own, not by causes which affect me, as it were, from the outside. I wish to be somebody, not nobody; a doer deciding, not a being decided for. . .[8]

Negative freedom, by contrast, denotes the absence of external interference by other persons within an area of choice and action which is mine. In this sense, "I am normally said to be free to the degree to which no being interferes with my activity."[9] Proponents of negative freedom "want to curb authority as such," while advocates of positive freedom "want it placed in their own hands."[10] Sensitive to the shortcomings of both concepts, yet especially critical of the positive concept of freedom, which is invoked to justify the suppression of men's actual desires to realize an allegedly, inherent, non-empirical, essential self, Berlin acknowledges that each concept has "an equal right to be classed among the deepest interests of mankind."[11] But he contends that they "are not two different interpretations of a single concept, but two profoundly divergent and irreconcilable attitudes to the ends of life,"[12] and he repudiates monistic final solutions to the problem of choosing between incompatible human values. Therefore, he contends that " 'negative' liberty . . . seems . . . a truer and more humane ideal than the goals of those who seek in the great, disciplined, authoritarian structures the ideal of 'positive' self-mastery by classes, or people, or the whole of mankind. It is truer, because it recognizes the fact that human goals are many, not all of them commensurable, and in perpetual rivalry with one another."[13]

Berlin's viewpoint is most appealing. He values the individual, cautions against authority which leads to totalitarianism, unmasks the deceptions and mistakes which disguise enslavement as self-mastery. Yet, in the last analysis, he is incorrect in his derogation of positive freedom. Negative freedom and positive freedom are not two separate kinds of freedom, nor do they express two disparate concepts which denote separate things. Rather the concepts of negative freedom and positive freedom represent distinguishable aspects of the same liberty. For liberty is, as I have argued elsewhere,[14] a complex triadic relation. This complex relation incorporates the ordinary relations of *from*, *to*, and *of*. Specific historical situations supply the concrete terms of this relations. Particular liberties are vectors of historical change. In philosophy we can, by means of speculation and analysis, grasp the universals which history conceals in its particulars. The universals which we uncover in the case of liberty are, I suggest, what Paul Weiss has aptly called "modes of being." Hence liberty may be defined metaphysically as the freedom *of* substantial actualities *from* situational existence *to* an ideal state of possibility.

To oppose the concept of liberty to the concept of authority, as Berlin does, is in accord with much that is thought and said within the Western liberal tradition. Yet the conviction that liberty and authority are necessarily incompatible is a causative factor in the social malaise spreading throughout contemporary

civilization. As many astute social critics testify, ours is an epoch
in which authority is crumbling or has already collapsed. The
philosopher Maynard Adams has examined what he calls "the
present crisis of authority;" he argues that "the structure of
authority is crumbling in our society not so much because of injustice and repression as because of the erosion of its intellectual
foundations."[15] The sociologist Robert Nisbet has employed the
striking phrase "twilight of authority" to characterize our age,
an age marked by the major stigmata of "cultural and social
decay, celebration of war and power, and intense, often morbid,
subjectivism."[16] Although following different lines of reasoning,
neither Adams nor Nisbet find liberty and authority incompatible. On the contrary, they maintain that freedom is genuine
within a framework of authority. I wish to re-enforce their argument by showing that fundamentally liberty and authority are
reciprocally supportive.

What is authority? Always arresting and provocative, Hannah
Arendt has claimed that authority has vanished in the modern
world.[17] Thus she has put the question in the past tense: What
was authority? Since, according to Arendt, we lack common,
authentic, and indisputable experiences to furnish content for the
concept of authority, we must go to the ancients to discover its
meaning. Her focus is on the concept of political authority.
Elucidating and interpreting the texts of Plato and Aristotle, she
has found that the Greek philosophers, mixing such models as
parent/child and shepherd/sheep from the agricultural household
with the model of ruler/subject from the *polis*, failed to formulate
an adequate concept of authority. Extending the theoretical considerations of the philosophers to have a direct bearing on
political practice, she has propounded a sophisticated interpretation which judges that the Greek philosophers did not "find a
concept of authority which would prevent deterioration of the
polis and safeguard the life of the philosopher" because "in the
realm of Greek political life there was no awareness of authority
based on immediate political experience."[18] Turning from the
Greeks, Arendt uncovered in the Romans the first and perhaps
the best record of the fundamental experience which grounds the
concept of authority. She subjected the term *auctoritas* to

etymological analysis, and correlated her findings with a penetrating interpretation of Roman civilization. It was the founding of Rome which "became to the Roman the central, decisive, unrepeatable beginning of his whole history, a unique event."[19] To this singular founding the Romans constantly referred, and fit all living authority was derived, augmenting the past which remained vibrant as their indisputable, common experience. Further, the Roman Catholic Church continued to render the Roman concept of authority meaningful after the fall of the Roman Empire, but in its rationale replaced the historical founding of the earthly city of Rome with the supernatural advent of Jesus Christ. And even the founding of the American nation, completed with the establishment of the Constitution, is represented as an expression of authority in the classical Roman sense.

Arendt's insistence that authority does not now exist is too extreme; and it is compromised by her interpretations of the American Revolution and Constitution. Her theory is an idiosyncratic concoction of classical scholarship and imaginative speculation which, nonetheless, provides several of the essential elements requisite to an adequate concept of authority. She has rightly shown that authority involves two essential ingredients—reference to a singular past event and a hierarchy of agent/patient. Ideally, the agent commands, and the patient obeys. She is wrong to suggest that in its fundamental meaning authority, while demanding obedience, precludes the external means of coercion by force or persuasion through arguments.[20]

Building upon Arendt's insights, I wish to advance the thesis that authority is a triadic relation of agent over patient by reference to some past event which is somehow their common experience. Metaphysically, authority consists in a hierarchical relation between actual, substantial men justified by reference to some past event, usually idealized. I shall illustrate my thesis by attending to some social institutions in which authority is presumed to be present. Since my major thesis is that liberty and authority are compatible and even reciprocally supportive, I shall also point to the signs of liberty in these institutions.

The family is the oldest institution in which authority is

manifest. Traditionally it evinces the hierarchical relations between husband and wife and between parent and child, although,
as the anthropologists have shown, the distribution of roles in the
familial hierarchy is not always determined as in the West where
women have historically been treated by men as inferiors.
Matriarchy or patriarchy, polygamy or polyandry as well as
monogamy are diverse patterns of familial hierarchy. But hierarchy there is. The determination of agent and patient, superior and
inferior, furthermore, is grounded in the past fact which
established the marriage, just as the children born therein submit
to their parents by virtue of the founding of the family. For most
of us our first able experience of authority is as infants within the
family. Sometimes the experience engenders a distaste of authority, perhaps because of the habit, cited by Bertrand Russell, of unwise parents who are "always saying 'don't do that,' without
stopping to think whether 'that' does any harm."[21] This leads to
the obverse portrayed in the teen-ager's lament: boy likes girl,
and girl likes boy, until she finds out that her parents like him,
too. The moralization of men as children in the family has been
fundamental to civilization; and liberty is a root of the founding
of the family—if not in the choice of mates or the date and ritual
of matrimony, which may be regulated by custom and anterior
agents—yet at least in the spontaneous natural impulses for sexual expression and affection. Because the family is for most men
the paramount and sometimes the only experience of liberty and
authority, weakening of the family has devasting effects upon
society at large, as we are learning painfully in the United States
today.

Analysis of the family brings to light a characteristic feature
of authority. The agent in the hierarchy establishes the moral
rule which dominates the patient; and he may do so by mere position as well as by persuasion, by force, or by a mixture thereof.
This is troubling to those who, influenced by Kant, are persuaded
that a man cannot yield his freedom to choose and to act to
another and yet remain moral. Of course, this argument has less
cogency against the familial hierarchy than against hierarchies in
other social institutions. In the case of the family the child is not
fully mature and knowledgeable, so that the parents find justifi-

cation for their authority not only, though mainly, by their role in the founding and the provisioning of the family which produced the child, but also by their longer experience and more comprehensive knowledge by means of which they can assist and guide the child.

At this juncture, it is pertinent to note that a sort of authority distinct from moral authority is involved—what Richard T. De George has called "epistemic authority."[22] Evident in such social groupings as lawyer/client, doctor/patient, teacher/pupil and so on, the hierarchy expressing epistemic authority is founded on the certification of the expert. This certification proclaims that the expert has the special knowledge to do for the client, patient, pupil, and so on, what the patient wants done but lacks the knowledge to do for himself. Liberty is a root of epistemic authority when the expert chooses his career, selects his school, and so forth; and also when the client or patient chooses his expert. Let us remark that if parental authority is reduced to epistemic authority, as in the cliche "Father knows best," it runs the risk of being upset by junior as soon as his school certifies him at a higher grade than his parents ever attained.

It is unnecessary here to enter into the long-standing quarrel between Plato and Aristotle on the role of the family in political society, although it is useful to observe that Aristotle seems to have the better side of the argument. The family has been and is an indispensable institution which prepares men for citizenship in political society. Still it should be conceded that sometimes the family has been obstructive of public policy, corrupting and subverting the state. At least since John Locke,[23] it has been clear that familial authority (in his words, "parental power") is not the same as political authority, no matter how often the two have been confounded in the history of thought.

Many other institutions in civil society besides the family display forms of authority as we traverse the route to the political state. Voluntary associations, private corporations, labor unions, non-profit foundations, churches. etc., all exhibit hierarchical structures with gradations of authority and responsibility. Those in authority command, and even enforce their commands by persuasion or varieties of coercion from monetary fines

fines to expulsion. To legitimate their existence and operations, these institutions hark back to a past event, whether the issuance of a charter or a letter of appointment. Members of such institutions, moreover, may be related to them voluntarily. Theoretically they can choose to depart, although financial and other considerations may compel them to remain.

It is the source of the authority of the political state which constitutes the major problem in modern times. We cannot easily opt out of political society, without falling under the governance of some other political society. The legitimacy of the rulers in a political state may be traced to different sources: the fact of conquest, the dynastic proprietorship of the territory, the history and customs of a people, the fact of revolution, the settlement of newly discovered lands, the presumption of divine grace, the establishment of a constitution, and so on.[24] Power, while necessary, is never sufficient *to* justifiy authority. For authority is, in the words of the musical *Camelot*, might for right. And it has been the considered judgment of the Western liberal philosophers that political authority must be justified.

The problem is grave and almost insuperable. On the one hand, modern liberal political theory rests on the proposition that men are naturally or morally equal. On the other hand, political authority, like all authority, is hierarchical; it draws a distinction between ruler and ruled, governor and governed, bureaucrat and citizen. The solution which the political thinkers of the seventeenth and eighteenth centuries gave to the problem is the well-known social contract theory of political society. The essence of this theory, however, variant the versions of different authors were, is that men, naturally equal, joined together and entered into a compact which established a government over them, deriving its powers from them, and in turn securing them in their lives, liberties, and properties. The theory legitimates political authority by referring back to a putative contract into which men originally entered freely and to which their successors now tacitly consent. It is a theory which became historical fact in the establishment of the United States. In implementing the theory, the American people invented a new mechanism, omitted by the philosophers but indispensable if they were to wield their sovereign power—namely, the constitutional convention.[25]

The Western liberal theory of the social contract underscores the reciprocity of liberty and authority. The contract is presumed to be voluntary and therefore rooted in human freedom. And the authority it establishes has as its paramount objective the securing of liberty and the blessings of liberty for the people it embraces. The American national state rests in fact upon such a contract, visible in the document of the constitution of the United States.

The theory has been challenged not only by those who base authority on events and principles indifferent and even inimical to freedom, but also by those who have prized liberty above all. The former do not care whether the regimes they support are legitimate, so long as they are powerful; they consequently fall outside the scope of political theory. The latter deny that any political authority is legitimate. According to a well-known recent formulation of this position,[26] the moral autonomy of the individual precludes his obedience to the laws of the state. Otherwise he would sacrifice his moral autonomy which he is obliged to preserve. Therefore, he is not obliged to obey the laws of the state. But if political power or authority lacks obligatoriness, it is morally illegitimate. The argument assumes that the moral autonomy of the individual is the paramount moral value, overriding all others. This assumption is the weak premise from which the argument proceeds. In the last analysis, the defense of anarchism assumes what it must prove, and is consequently reducible simply to an assertion of anarchism. I wish to suggest that anarchism is to social practice as solipsism is to knowledge. Solipsism can be believed, but it cannot be said, for to state it is to assume another with whom to communicate. Anarchism may be believed, but it cannot be practiced, because to act is to relate to at least one other whose existence makes moral demands and imposes non-moral pressures that erode the agent's autonomy. Authority, I have argued, is a feature of human institutions, including the state, so that in belonging to institutions—family, church, corporation, etc.—an individual enters into hierarchical relations which, unless he is a god and not a man, cannot always place him in the superior position. The authentic anarchist must perforce be a recluse or a hermit. Then he cannot state his doctrine, because there would be no one present to hear him. Nor can he publish it, because he would have to submit to the procedures of publication. He would dwell alone in utter silence, wrapped in the pure mantle of his precious moral autonomy.

A more serious threat to authority comes not from the anarchist but from the state itself. The legitimacy of the Western liberal state rests on the proposition affirming human equality and the presumption of a contract into which men, naturally equal, entered freely. It is tempting to endeavor to reconstruct all institutions in conformity with this attractive democratic model employed in politics. To a considerable extent the Western liberal state has undertaken such a mission, intruding into institutions which antedate it and undermining the hierarchies intrinsic to them. Family, church, private school, industrial corporation, medicine, science, art, etc., have all been invaded by government. As the authoritativeness of these institutions is sapped by governmental regulation and regimentation, they wither, and their functions must be assumed by the government itself. Political authoritarianism stands on the backs of institutions the state has trampled under. And while the state has grasped more power than was ever had by all the institutions it has trod upon, the society as a whole suffers a deficit of authority, palpable in the pervasive licentiousness of the present. The decay of Western liberal civilization is redolent with the cloying fragrances of both authoritarianism and libertarianism.

Yet philosophy is perennial. The metaphysics of authority, like that of liberty, involves distinguishable modes of being: an existential past which is customarily idealized, on the one hand, and actual, substantial men who are hierarchically related as agent to patient, on the other. The ontological link of liberty and authority is mankind existing in space and time as actual substances. By referring to a past, though ideal, authority is a stabilizing principle which endows social groups with the cohesion indispensable to the realization of their goals and ultimately to the survival of the race. As a vector of activity from a present existential situation to a future, possible ideal, liberty is the dynamic principle of social progress. Since a living civilization requires both social cohesion and progress, it depends upon the reciprocity of liberty and authority. Without authority a society eventually loses the efficacy of positive freedom.

Although philosophy is perennial, practice is shifting. Herein lies the message of Solzhenitsyn for our times, crying for liberty in Russia, and for authority in America.

NOTES

1. Jacques Julliard, "For a New 'Internationale,' " The New York Review of Books, XXV (July 20, 1978),p.3.
2. John Stuart Mill, On Liberty, ed. by Alburey Castell (New York: Appleton-Century-Crofts, Inc., 1947), p.1.
3. Maurice Cranston, Freedom, A New Analysis (London: Longmans, Green and Co., 1953), p. 45.
4. On the liberty/license distinction, see Ronald Dworkin, Taking Rights Seriously (Cambridge, Mass.: Harvard University Press, 1977), pp. 262 ff.
5. John Dewey, Liberalism and Social Action, (1935; New York: Capricorn Books, 1963), pp. 54-55.
6. Jean-Paul Sartre, Being and Nothingness, trans. by Hazel E. Barnes (New York: Philosophical Library, 1956), p. 435.
7. See my "The Metaphysics of Equality," The New Scholasticism, XXXIV (1960), p. 337 f.
8. Isaiah Berlin, Two Concepts of Liberty (Oxford: Clarendon Press, 1958), p. 17.
9. Ibid., p. 6.
10. Ibid., p. 51.
11. Ibid., p. 52.
12. Ibid., pp. 51-52.
13. Ibid., p. 56.
14. See my "Metaphysics of Liberty" in Irwin C. Lieb, ed., Experience, Existence, and the Good; Essays in Honor of Paul Weiss (Carbondale: Southern Illinois University Press, 1961), pp. 285-294.
15. E.M. Adams, "The Philosophical Grounds of the Present Crisis of Authority," in R. Baine Harris, ed., Authority: A Philosophical Analysis (University of Alabama Press, 1976), pp. 3-4.
16. Robert Nisbet, Twilight of Authority (New York: Oxford University Press, 1975), p. vi.
17. Hannah Arendt, "Authority in the Twentieth Century," Review of Politics, XVIII (1956), pp. 403-417.
18. Hannah Arendth, "What Was Authority?" in Carl J. Friedrich,

ed., *Authority, Nomos I* (Cambridge, Mass.: Harvard University Press, 1958), pp. 97-98.

19. *Ibid.*, p. 99.
20. *Ibid.*, p. 82. Not all scholars agree with Arendt's judgment that the Greeks lacked a concept of authority. See Robert S. Brumbaugh, "Metaphysics and the Justification of Authority," (1978), 7 pages off-print.
21. Bertrand Russell, *Authority and the Individual* (New York: Simon and Schuster, 1949), p. 21.
22. Richard T. De George, "The Nature and Function of Epistemic Authority," in Harris, *op. cit.*, pp. 76-93.
23. See John Locke, *The Second Treatise of Civil Government*, Ch. VI.
24. See Charles W. Hendel, ed., *David Hume's Political Essays* (New York: The Liberal Arts Press, 1953), especially VI, "Of the Original Contract," pp. 43-61.
25. See my "The American Revolution, A Philosophical Interpretation," *The Southwestern Journal of Philosophy*, VIII (1977), pp. 102-103.
26. R. P. Wolff, *In Defense of Anarchism* (New York: Harper Torchbooks, 1970).

Gerald McCool

— C2 —
Freedom and Authority

It is over thirty years since Max Horheimer and Theodore Adorno brought out their *Dialectic of Enlightenment.*[1] Much more recently the distinguished German theologian, Wolfhart Pannenberg, published two important books, *Theology and The Kingdom of God*[2] and *The Idea of God and Human Freedom.*[3] All three books have made a significant contribution to our growing awareness of the crisis between freedom and authority in our liberal technocratic Western society. They have also called attention to the dangerous weakening of Western democracy through its failure to resolve this crisis. As the failure of individualistic Western democracy to solve the ethical and social problems of our age becomes increasingly apparent, Marxism's vigorous use of collective authority to achieve its social goals becomes increasingly attractive. To the idealistic youth of the Third World and of the technically developed West as well Marxism is more than a brutally effective technique for getting things done. Marxism proposes a philosophy of nature, man and society whose human and social goals give a meaning to dedicated work and personal sacrifice. It holds up personal and social ideals which the hedonistic individualism which characterizes much of our Western culture can no longer furnish. Marxism is even more attractive to idealistic young men and women who no longer derive the meaning of their life and work from religious faith but must find that meaning through natural reason in the finite, historical world of human experience.

Atomic individualism and Marxist collectivism confront each other today at the culmination of a long historical evolution.[4] That evolution of ethical and social thought stretches from ancient Greece through the Middle Ages, the Renaissance, the Reformation, the Enlightenment up to the present day. The tension between individual freedom and collective social authority has been a constant element in that long evolution. At different times different solutions have been proposed for it. For the purposes of this paper, however, we can divide the evolution of Western ethical and social thought into three significant historical stages. These are: (1) the dominance of the organic tradition in ethical and social thought in ancient Greece and the Middle Ages; (2) the dominance of the individualistic mechanist tradition from Descartes through the Enlightenment; (3) the re-assertion of the organic tradition in our modern Post-Enlightenment world.[5] In the organic tradition the interpretative model for the relation is the relation of a living whole to its organic members. The social whole owes its origin to nature. The whole is prior to the parts. The individual is related to the natural social whole as a subordinate organ with an in-built natural function to perform and therefore final causality provides the key for the understanding of social relations. In the mechanist tradition wholes are constructed mechanically from atoms as a machine is built from its non-living parts. The part is prior to the whole. Society owes its origin and nature to human convention. It is an artifact. Mechanics and human convention rather than final causality are the key to the understanding of social relations.

I will now consider the relation of freedom to authority in both of these traditions as they have influenced our Western social thought. From this historical consideration a number of practical conclusions may follow.

I. The Organic Tradition

In the organic tradition, which has its roots in classical Greece and the Middle Ages, freedom had three major meanings. The first meaning was psychological. In the psychological sense freedom signified the human agent's intrinsic power to make his own free choices. Choices were free because they were neither determined by physical forces from outside the agent nor from ir-resistible psychological drives from within the agent. This psychological power of intelligent free choice was the famous *liberium arbitrium* of the medieval philosophers and theologians. Medieval defenders of *liberium arbitrium* did not claim that every human act of the will was free. They were agreed, however, that,

even in sinful man's fallen state, the acts of the will which followed upon rational reflection and deliberate choice were indeed free.
These were the truly human acts (*actua humani*) which Thomas
Aquinas contrasted to the acts of the human agent which were
not truly free (*actus hominis*).[6]

Moreover, man's intellectual and moral growth was accompanied by a corresponding growth in his psychological freedom.
Growth in psychological freedom entailed an increase in man's intellectual ability to judge correctly for himself and the growing
power of his free will to dominate man's irrational passions with
ever increasing completeness and consistency. Medieval
educators in fact considered that a growth in what they called the
habit of freedom was one of the major aims of their theoretical
and practical education. Once Aristotelianism had become the
reigning metaphysics of man in the Universities of the High Middle Ages, man's growth in freedom was explained through his ac-
quisition of the requisite intellectual and moral habits (the intellectual and moral virtues). In Aristotle's metaphysics of man
every human agent possessed the fundamental power of free
choice in virtue of his human nature. By acquiring good or bad
moral habits, however, each individual agent either increased or
diminished his power to act freely.[7] Virtuous and well-educated
men were freer than infants and profligates. That point of view
has consequences for politics as well as for education. Plato had
already made that clear in his *Republic*. Who is free and adult
enough to be able to govern himself and to govern others? Who
are the free and adult citizens in a given society and what type of
intellectual and moral education is required to enable them to acquire the habit of psychological freedom?

Moral Freedom

The second principal meaning given to freedom in the Greek
and medieval tradition was a moral one. Freedom in the moral
sense was the necessary condition for moral responsibility. The
individual moral agent was held responsible for those actions
alone which proceeded from his conscious and deliberate free

choice (*actus humani*). In other words moral freedom presupposed psychological freedom. Moreover since the praise or blame expressed by a community implied the common admission of an objective norm in virtue of which actions could be judged good or
bad, praise or blame had a moral character. More was implied in
the assignment of moral culpability than bad calculation or bad
taste. The presence of an absolute moral "thou shalt" or "thou
shalt not" in human experience was also implied. Long before
Kant had done so the medieval philosophers had already pointed
to the categorical imperative of duty in moral experience and to
psychological freedom as the prerequisite for moral obligation.
Medieval ethics was unabashedly normative.[8]

Political Freedom

The third sense given to freedom in the organic tradition was a
political or social sense. Freedom in the political sense implied the
inalienable right to the individual citizen, the member of a family
or of a subordinate society to exercise his freedom and not to be
impeded therein by the holders of political authority. This is the
sense in which freedom even today is associated with civil or
human rights. It is the immediate context in which civil conflicts
between freedom and authority arise. In the organic tradition the
meaning and scope of political freedom was defined by the positions already held concerning psychological and moral freedom.

The notion of duty or moral obligation as the ground of moral
responsibility was the foundation stone of the medieval defense
of individual freedom against the abuse of social authority.
Man's moral duty toward God and his fellow men (in a family
context, for example) was the basis of his inviolable right both to
freedom and to the means required for the exercise of freedom.
For, if a man had the moral duty to perform a given act or a given
series of acts, he had a moral claim on his fellow men to be permitted to do so. Consequently in medieval ethical and social
theory the moral duty of the free responsible individual was the
basis of his inviolable right to social, political and economic
freedom or, to use the word of Locke echoing this tradition, to

life, liberty and property. Since these rights were based on duties which no man was morally free to disregard, these rights were inalienable. This followed necessarily, if one held, as the medievals did, that politics was part of ethics.[9]

The notion of duty or moral obligation as the ground of moral responsibility became the foundation stone of the medieval defense of individual freedom against the abuse of social authority. Man's moral duty toward God and his fellow men was the basis of his individual right to freedom of action and to the means required for its unimpeded exercise. For if man had a moral duty to perform a given act he had a moral claim on his fellow men to be allowed to do so. This moral claim in fact was what medievals understood by a right. Man's duty to God as an individual, a parent and a member of a family were the basis of his right to political and religious freedom and to his right to the private property which he had acquired by labor, occupation or legitimate purchase.[10]

In the line of ethical and political thought which runs from Augustine and Aquinas through Bellarmine, Suarez, Hooker to John Courtney Murray and Jacques Maritain the individual's moral duty was taken to be an unconditioned categorical imperative. To fail morally was to fail as a human being. Social action could not be divorced from individual ethics. One and the same moral law governed both; and the demand of this moral law manifested themselves in the judgment of reason and the absolute claim of moral duty. And in this tradition, whose father is Saint Augustine, both reason and duty were ultimately grounded in the intellect and will of the world's free and provident creator. Morals and politics were both derived from God's eternal law.[11]

The intelligibility of the moral order, in its individual and social dimensions, was derived from the divine ideas which served as the supreme exemplar for all created reality. But the specific absoluteness of the moral ought was grounded in God's will. A wise and provident creator could not fail to will that the human agent should conform his free activity to the intelligible order grounded upon the divine ideas. In Augustine's ethics and in his social philosophy love, reason and duty went hand in hand. His political theory could fairly be called a philosophical transposition of the Pauline "doing the truth in love" and the Johannine, "if you love me, keep my commandments".[12]

Therefore Augustine's ethics could not be reduced to an ethics of self-development, intelligence and aesthetic fitness as classical Greek ethics has been. Greek ethics was founded upon intelligible form, intelligence, finality and happiness as the necessary consequence of human self-development. Augustine's ethics was grounded on personal freedom in the divine creator and the human moral agent. Consequently it was an ethics of loving self-surrender to God and to the order of values grounded upon God's being, intellect and will. Surrender to value and to the divine authority in the fulfillment of moral duty in Augustine's ethics constituted the fulfillment of freedom; and in Augustine's universe there could be no fundamental conflict between true freedom and true authority.

Freedom and Authority

In Augustine's political philosophy, the divine ideas grounded the set of intelligible reactions which constitute the peace and order of political society and determined the common good toward which society tended by its very nature.[13] Man's duty toward God and his fellow men grounded the authority or the moral claim of society's rulers to the obedience of the individual members. Reason can establish that political society cannot achieve its common good unless the actions of the individual members receive the direction which government alone can supply. God wills therefore that the governor direct the society toward its common good. Therefore the governor has a duty to direct society and, if he has the duty, he has a moral claim upon the obedience of the individual members. Legitimate authority therefore is derived from God's eternal law. Its derivation, however, immediately establishes its limits. Authority extends only as far as the duty of the ruler, i.e. to the achievement of society's common good. Furthermore, since every individual has the duty to obey God as an individual, when the illegitimate commands of political authority interfere with its execution, the individual has the duty to disobey the civil government and, at times, to resist it. For illegitimate authority is not authority at all.[14] Thus in Augustine's ethics although there is no conflict between true freedom and legitimate authority, reason can discover the principles in terms of which conflicts between freedom and illegitimate authority can be resolved.

In the High Middle Ages Thomas Aquinas codified this tradition of freedom and authority and gave it the form in which it came down to Locke through Hooker. Unlike Augustine, who was basically a Platonist, Thomas Aquinas built his theory of freedom and authority, on the Aristotelian philosophy of the natural society. Aristotelian man was inserted by the in-built drives and exigencies of his human nature into a number of inter-related societies. Two of the most important of these were the natural family and the *polis* or political society. Man was a political animal by nature, not by convention. The individual human being could no more live outside the total living being of which it was a part. Cells come and go but the living organism lives on. Men are born and die but society endures. Living parts define themselves through the function which they serve in achieving the common good of the living whole. In an analogous manner, individuals must subordinate their personal interests to the good of the whole society. Every given individual needs society but society needs no given individual.

For Aristotle this organic philosophy of society required that the good of the social whole must always take precedence over the individual good of the citizen. Thomas, however, was not a pure Aristotelian. He linked his Aristotelian philosophy of society to the Augustinian metaphysics of God's eternal law and to the Augustinian ethics of the individual agent's moral duty toward God. This entailed a radical revision of Aristotelian politics. The common good might require the subordination of individual interests to the good of the community. It could never require total subordination however. As a free moral person each individual confronted God directly and that meant that in the divine plan society was for men. Men did not exist for society. Since the individual was ordered directly to God as his personal end, he had an inalienable right to personal freedom of choice upon which the community could never legitimately infringe. Aristotle, and more so Plato, could be accused of totalitarianism. Thomas Aquinas could never be.[15]

Society and Authority

A natural society of free agents could not achieve its common goal unless a ruler or a group of rulers were able to direct the activity of its individual members by law. Laws in turn could not be effective unless the rules or a community had the power to enforce them by punitive sanction. Reason demands therefore that there be a legislative authority in every *polis* to determine its laws and a legislative and judicial authority to execute them and punish their violation by punitive sanction. Reason also can see that God, as the provident orderer of nature and society, must have conferred in the holders of legislative, executive and judicial office the moral authority to make and enforce the laws which are required for the common good.

Reason can also see that this authority is not unlimited in its scope. Both the nature of political society and the individual member's duty toward God and his fellow men place limits on the restraints which political authority may legitimately impose upon him. The ruler's right to command, like every other right in the medieval philosophy of society, was grounded in his prior duty to direct the society to its common good.[16] In the Augustinian philosophy of society, rulers might indeed claim divine authority. But in Thomistic political philosophy that right was clearly defined and limited by a common goal determined by the intrinsic finality of a natural society. Authority employed in the personal interests of a ruler or a ruling class contrary to the common good ceased to be legitimate authority. This in short was the Thomistic "natural law" philosophy of freedom and authority which came down the seventeenth century Catholic Europe through Bellarmine and Suarez and came down to Locke and the Anglo-Saxon world through Hooker and the seventeenth century Anglican divines.

II. The Individualistic Mechanistic Tradition

By the seventeenth century, however, the unity of Christendom, which Thomas and Augustine had taken for granted, had been shattered by the Reformation and the savage wars of religion which followed in its wake. Francis Bacon's experimental science, built upon his mechanistic physics, displaced Aristotelian philosophy of nature as the key to the understanding of organic and inorganic reality. Descartes' combination of "angelism" and mechanism transformed man from a dynamic unified Aristotelian nature to a dualistic "ghost in the machine." Platonic and Aristotelian final causality, the metaphysical foundation of the medieval philosophy of individual freedom and social authority, was rejected as a valid category in physics and metaphysics.

In England Hobbes was fascinated by Descartes' machine, i.e. Cartesian mechanistic physics. Hobbes was less impressed, however, by the Cartesian "ghost" or "angel", i.e. the metaphysics of the mind as a spiritual substance whose defining attribute was thought. For Hobbes there was no such thing as a spiritual substance. Atomic matter, mechanical motion and sheer brute chance explained every natural event. Human life and human history were no exceptions. They too could be explained exhaustively in terms of atoms and mechanical motion. A number of consequences for freedom and authority followed immediately. The psychological freedom of medieval *liberum arbitrium* was an illusion. Where there was no psychological freedom there could be no moral obligation or duty in the Augustinian sense. If there was neither freedom nor obligation, Augustine's argument for political and social freedom could not be defenced philosophically and Hobbes never attempted to do so.

Mechanists or not, all believing Christians in the seventeenth century still accepted the Augustinian dictum that the Creator's will still imposed the duty of obedience upon the created will. As Christians, they continued to draw the political conclusion that no worldly authority had the right to impede the individual Christian from obeying God's divine command. As long as Christianity retained its social and cultural dominance in Western Europe, Augustine's defense of freedom would continue to be a powerful influence in support of individual liberty. However, the distrust of philosophical reason in much of Reformed theology reduced the Augustinian defense of freedom to the status of a conviction based on Christian faith alone. In principle its evidence was unavailable to non-believers; and, once believing Christians became a minority, the Augustinian defense of freedom could be considered a special interest claim of a religious group.[17]

Seventeenth century England was torn by the civil war between Puritan defenders of parliamentary rule and the Stuart defenders of the divine right of kings. The Puritan's rejection of the hierarchical, sacramental established Church and its episcopal authority was linked to their rejection of the medieval theology of religious and political authority. In seventeenth century England Puritanism and mechanism had a psychological affinity. Both were focussed on an atomic individual who was no longer metaphysically inserted into a natural or ecclesial society understood in terms of Aristotelian metaphysics. Puritanism, and German pietism, retained their belief in the inviolability of the individual's political freedom based upon his duty to God. That belief, however, no longer rested on philosophical reason and it was no longer related to a natural law theory of social authority. Puritan religious individualism could rest its defense of political freedom on transcendent spiritual grounds. Mechanistic philosophical individualism could not. The Puritan triumph in the Civil War and the influence of Puritan ideas after the Glorious Revolution of 1688 had profound consequences for English history and for English and American political theory. One of the major consequences was the eclipse of the Augustinian and Thomistic philosophy of social authority in the English speaking lands. Another major consequence was the triumph of economic and political individualism and the blurring of the profound difference between Puritan religious individualism and mechanistic philosophical individualism.[18]

Thomas Hobbes

The abandonment of Aristotelian metaphysics and physics undermined the medieval philosophy of the origin and intrinsic limits of political authority. The medieval philosophy of freedom and authority presupposed both psychological freedom and the intrinsic finality of human nature. Mechanistic physics and anthropology cut the ground from under both. Consequently a new philosophy of freedom and authority had to be devised.

By the middle of the seventeenth century Hobbes had proposed it in his *Leviathan*. The corner-stone of Hobbes' political society was the hypothesis of an implicit social contract that derived its authority through the cession of rights which isolated individuals had previously possessed as individuals.

The social contract philosophy of freedom and authority differed from medieval political philosophy not only through its mechanistic rejection of final causality. Even more importantly the social contract theory was individualistic, whereas the medieval natural law theory of society was organic. In the social contract theory individuals, as atomic agents, were the primordial possessors of all rights. Society was not a work of nature. It was the work of man.

In Hobbes' political philosophy, the ethical order with its moral duties did not come into existence until social authority had been constituted by the social contract. Moral duty was not grounded upon a command of God but on a command of society itself. Politics was no longer a part of ethics. On the contrary political power constituted ethics by its purely human authority.[19]

This meant, of course, that the rights of the individuals prior to the social contract were not moral claims in the medieval sense. They were claims of power and self-interest. The legal order established by the social contract was not a demand of an ethical order derived from the natural order of God's creation and ultimately from the intelligibility of the divine being itself. The factitious legal order was its own foundation and the legal contact through which the political order was established would become the unique model through which social relations could be understood. This conclusion would have significant consequences for social and political life and thought, especially in America.

John Locke

It is understandable therefore that John Locke, the great philosophical defender of the Glorious Revolution of 1688, was unwilling to break completely, as Hobbes had done, with the medieval natural law tradition which had come down to him from Hooker and the great Anglican divines of the seventeenth century. Locke's original state of nature was not Hobbes' original state of universal warfare in which every man's hand was raised against his neighbor until the social contract established political authority and, with political authority, the moral order. Enough of Aristotelian nature remained in Locke's metaphysics of action and substance for him to argue, in a manner reminiscent of Thomas Aquinas, that each individual man had, in virtue of his human nature and the duties which it imposed upon him, the inalienable right to life, liberty and property.[20] God could be known by reason as well as revelation; and God's existence was required to ground the specific claim of the moral ought. That is the reason why Locke, in his *Letter Concerning Toleration*, refused to extend civil toleration to atheists.[21] In the Augustinian tradition Locke derives civil authority from God. He had no need to recur to the social contract as Hobbes had done in order to ground the moral order through the command of political authority. In his system morality was not identical with legality. Like Thomas Aquinas Locke believed that men were compelled to enter society by the demands of their human nature. There is some similarity too between Locke's theory of the "original compact" in determining the form of civil society and Bellarmine's conception of the role of consent in determining the legitimate possessor of authority and the legitimate form of government. For in Locke's philosophy of society by the "original compact" through which men enter society men yield to civil authority the power to make and enforce the laws required to direct society to the attainment of its common good.

Thus in Locke's philosophy of society man's duty toward God and the end of civil society still limit the authority of its ruler. Nevertheless the free consent of individual men in the "original compact" is given a more important role than in the Thomistic natural law theory of society. Furthermore it is taken as evident that implicit in the "original compact" is the tacit understanding that civil authority will be exercised in a lawful manner in accordance with the will of the majority and not through the unchallengeable decree of an absolute monarch.

Although Locke was later in time than Hobbes, his philosophy is older in its content. It is also less coherent since it is a melange of Aristotelian naturalism and seventeenth century mechanism. Locke's theory of liberty and authority presupposes a philosophical justification of psychological freedom which his metaphysics of man cannot provide. It also presupposes a fair amount of Aristotelian naturalism and requires the existence of God as the source of morality and authority. Unfortunately neither Locke's epistemology nor his metaphysics of man and nature could establish these claims to the satisfaction of his successors in England and on the Continent. Thus, although Locke's semi-empiricism would be very influential on the Continent during the eighteenth century, the remnants of the medieval natural law tradition which he had taken over from the Anglican theologians would not survive.[22]

The sensism and mechanism of continental Enlightenment philosophy could provide no speculative defense for human freedom. Neither could it build a speculative bridge between the metaphysics of man and nature and the moral demands of the ethical and social order. Social authority was defended through the theory of an implicit social contract by which atomic individuals surrendered their rights to the authority of the state. Mechanistic metaphysics of man and nature could not justify the existence of any natural societies between the atomic individual and the all-powerful state. The agnostic stance toward God of Enlightenment philosophy reduced religious assertions to the status of purely personal claims. Thus neither human nature, subordinate societies, nor the authority of God could be advanced, as they had been in the natural law tradition, in a philosophical defense of individual liberty against the encroachments of the state.[23]

III. The Reaction Against the Mechanistic Tradition

Three centuries after Hobbes and Locke the evolution of the movement with which their names are linked has led to the conflict between unrestricted individualism and unrestricted totalitarianism which has destabilized the social order of the Post-Enlightenment West. That is why the Enlightenment is now being blamed for the alienation of modern Western man from the impersonal technical society in which no intrinsic natural values claim his reverence. Through a supreme irony, Enlightenment mechanism and individualism, with its social contract theory of society, has led to the modern bureaucratic omnipotent state which the isolated individual regards as a threatening restraint upon his individual freedom.[24] The unity of man with nature and society which characterized the medieval natural law syntheses has been broken. The speculative link betwen nature and freedom, ethical demand and social authority has been severed. The old medieval synthesis led to the self-fulfillment of man, through his natural insertion into a series of inter-related socieites. The mechanistic philosophy of Descartes, Hobbes and the Enlightenment has led to the alienation of man from a mechanized society and an omnipotent bureaucratic state.

This is the phenomenon to which Pannenberg, Horkheimer and Adorno have pointed in their remarkable books. Even after he had abandoned the Aristotelian natural law theory of society, the individual German pietist or Anglo-Saxon non-Conformist could still point to his individual duty to God as the sacred ground of his freedom and personal inviolability. But once religious faith had died, as it has in the West, Pannenberg points out, the individual had no more ground for his inviolable claim for freedom. Freedom never exists for itself alone. Freedom's meaning and dignity comes to it as a human response to a value which transcends the individual; and if that value is not the transcendent God of the great religions, it must be, as Plato thought, the commonwealth. Hence the invincible attraction of Marxism to idealistic non-believing youth. Totalitarianism is better than meaninglessness, and, after all, in all realms, the highest life is the life of sacrifice. Self-fullfillment, as Augustine saw, comes through self-giving. Achievement is response to transcendent demand.[25]

Individual freedom was the ideal of the Enlightenment. But in the mechanistic world of the Enlightenment every social structure had to be an artificial construction. Culture, society and its institutions in the theory of the social contract, had their origin in pure individual human freedom. Hence, say Horkheimer and Adorno, by an inevitable dialectic, the absolute position of society by atomic individual freedom must end in the alienation of that very freedom. For individuals need structures and, in the breakneck growth of scientific society, isolated individuals can no longer understand or control the operation of the institutions which they have themselves constructed. Therefore these artificial institutions and bureaucracies take on a cancerous life of their own and in their mindless operation crush out individual initiative.[26]

The alienation of modern man then becomes an irrefutable proof of the bankruptcy of Enlightenment mechanism and its theory of society. The hope of salvation of the alienated individual lies in a return to the old organic philosophy of man, nature and society as it once existed in Plato and it exists today in Marx.

I am no advocate of Marxist totalitarianism. Yet, if we do not establish a satisfactory philosophy of freedom and authority grounded upon the reality of psychological freedom and man's duty toward a transcendent God, it is hard to see how its attraction can be overcome. Neither Plato nor Aristotle were able to escape the temptation to totalitarianism. They liberated the individual from meaningless individualism but, in doing so, they subordinated him to the good of the natural whole of which he was a living part.

The empiricism and mechanism of the Enlightenment can establish neither psychological freedom nor moral obligation. They can neither protect the individual from totalitarianism nor give an intrinsic value to society and the commonwealth as the finalistic metaphyscis of Plato, Aristotle and Marx can do.

It is understandable therefore that in contemporary Continental philosophy a powerful movement has sprung up whose aim is to go back not only beyond the Enlightenment but also beyond the "presuppositionless" deductive scientific method of Rene Descartes. Descartes' philosophy of clear and distinct ideas forgets both the human subject and the basic intentionality of the free conscious subject to his world. The phenomenological movement which began with Husserl has redirected our attention to the role of the subject's intentionality in constituting or responding to his world. Since Heidegger the role of freedom in that reponse has received even greater stress. America has not given sufficient attention to the contribution of the phenomenological movement to our understanding of society. It has largely ignored the telling critique of Enlightenment empiricism by Horkheimer and Adorno. An objective linguistic philosophy of abstract ideas, a metalogic of the empirical sciences, cannot grasp the intelligiblity of freedom, finality and value, and, failing to grasp these, it will fail to understand the nature of freedom, value response and moral obligation.

The Heideggerian and Post-Heideggerian critique of the Enlightenment has a lot to tell us. Nevertheless, to really confront the crisis of freedom of authority I am convinced that we must return to the full metaphysics of the old organic tradition. One can still do so and remain faithful to contemporary philosophy. Whitehead's philosophy of God and society has a lot to offer and so, I am convinced, has the Thomistic tradition in the hands of its contemporary representatives.

NOTES

1. Max Horkheimer and Theodore W. Adorno, *Dialectic of Enlightenment*. New York: Seabury Press, 1972. Original edition *Dialektik Der Aufklarung*. New York: Social Studies Association, Inc., 1944.
2. Wolfhart Pannenberg, *Theology and the Kingdom of God*. Philadelphia: The Westminster Press, 1969.
3. Wolfhart Pannenberg, *The Idea of God and Human Freedom*.

Philadelphia: The Westminster Press, 1973.

4. This is also the opinion of Jacques Maritain. See *Integral Humanisn*: Notre Dame, Ind.: University of Notre Dame Press, 1973, pp. 228-234.

5. Associated with this movement is the epistemological critique of Cartesian and Enlightenment "presuppositionless" scientific method. See Hans Georg Gademer, *Truth and Method*. New York: Seabury Press, 1975, pp. 235-274. See also Richard E. Palmer, *hermeneutics*. Evanston, Ill.: Northwestern University Press, 1969, pp. 181-193. For a defense of the organic tradition by a contemporary political philosopher see Leo Strauss, *Natural Right and History*. Chicago: The University of Chicago Press, 1950.

6. For an excellent collection of St. Thomas' texts dealing with free "human acts" see Anton C. Pegis, *Introduction to St. Thomas Aquinas*. New York: Modern Library, 1941, pp. 478-543.

7. Pegis, *op. cit.*, pp. 578-596. See also Joseph de Finance *Existence et Liberte*. Paris: Vitte, 1955, pp. 325-355. Also Bernard J.F. Lonergan. Insight. New York: Philosophical Library, 1957, pp. 619-624.

8. See Dietrich von Hildebrand, *Christian Ethics*. New York: David McKay Company, 1953, pp. 180-190. Also A.D. Sertillanges, *La Philosophie de S. Thomas D'Aquin*, 1940, v. 1, pp. 230-237. The great Jesuit scholastic moralist and political philosopher linked the absolute character of the moral demand explicity to man's knowledge of God. See Frederick Copleston, A *History of Philosophy*. Westminster, Md.: The Newman Press, 1953, v.3, pp. 383-388.

9. *Summa Theologiae*, II-II, qq. 57-62. See also Gilson, *op. cit.*, pp. 424-461.

10. *Summa Theologiae*, II-II, q.66,a. 2. *Summa Contra Gentiles*, III, c. 129. See also Etienne Gilson, *The Christian Philosophy of St. Augustine*. New York: Random House, 1960, pp. 176-177.

11. Augustine, *De Libero Arbitrio*, I, 6, 15. See also Gilson *The Christian Philosophy of St. Augustine*, pp. 165-177.

12. *Ephesians*, 4:15; *John*, 14:15.

13. Augustine, *City of God*, XIX, 11-13.

14. For a brief summary of the philosophy of authority in Augustine and Thomas see Frederick Copleston, *A History of Philosophy*, v. 2, pp. 87-90; 413-414.

15. For a penetrating treatment of the Thomistic philosophy of the common good see Jacques Maritain, *The Person and the Common Good*. New York: Charles Scribner's Sons, I, q. 96, a. 4, I-II, q. 95, a. 2.

16. *Summa Theologiae*, I, IIae, q. 90, a. 3, c. and I, IIae, q. 96, a. 4, c. For a concise and accurate account of St. Thomas' political theory, see F.C. Copleston, *A History of Philosophy. Westminster, Md.,*

Newman, v.2, pp. 412-422.

17. Wolfhart Pannenberg, *The Idea of God and Human Freedom*, pp. 99-115.

18. Leo Strauss, *Natural Right and History*, pp. 165-177. See also the excellent introduction by C.B. MacPherson to Hobbes' *Leviathan* in Thomas Hobbes, *Leviathan*. New York: Penguin Books, 1968, pp. 9-61.

19. Hobbes *Leviathan*, II, c. 13, pp. 183-188.

20. Frederick Copleston, *History of Philosophy*, v.5, p. 143

21. Locke, *Letter Concerning Toleration in Sterling p. Lamprecht (ed.)*, *Locke, Selections*. New York: Charles Scribner's Son, 1956, pp. 50-51.

22. Leo Strauss, *Natural Right and History*, pp. 203-251. Strauss brings out clearly the inconsistency in Locke's philosophy of individual and society. This inconsistence arises from the blending of Aristotelianism and seventeenth century mechanism in Locke's ethics and his social contract thinkng in his theory of government. Locke looked to the past and the future. He was both a traditionalist and a revolutionary in his political philosophy.

23. See Roger D. Masters in his editor's preface to Jean Jacques Rousseau, *On the Social Contract*. New York: St. Martin's Press, 1978, pp. 13-27.

24. See Walter Kasper, *Jesus the Christ*. New York: Paulist Press, 1977, pp. 52-58.

25. Pannenberg, *The Idea of God and Human Freedom*, pp. 116-143.

26. Horkheimer and Adorno, *Dialectic of Enlightenment*, pp. 240-242.

Klaus A. Rohmann

— C3 —

From Authority
To Absolute Dominion
In Our Administered World

Authority has traditionally been understood as the dialectical opposite of freedom. Acccording to Anselm of Canterbury, e.g. commitment to faith requires freedom of reason to acquire belief. He asserts that unaided reason cannot succeed in solving questions of ultimate concern. He also asserts that by itself faith is insufficient, since human nature requires both faith and understanding. Essentially, there is a polarity of authority and freedom, as e.g. Karl Jaspers put it. According to Jaspers, freedom can exist only by means of authority: by authority freedom obtains substantiality and thereby is distinguished from arbitrariness. Genuine authority in turn exists only through free commitment; otherwise it is perverted into mere power demanding total obedience. This does not mean that power must be absent from true authority. By power authority gains general validity and temporal duration. Were authority not linked to power, it would oblige only a small elite and this only in rare moments. Power lurks in the background of authority and, if necessary, urges by internal or even by external force. As power in itself is incompatible with freedom, authority and freedom are not simply complementary, but are in tension with each other. Nevertheless, when power has been separated from genuine authority, it tends to deteriorate into despotism, since it no longer requires free consent. Although there is a tension between freedom and authority, as the latter is necessarily linked to power, there is not or should not be an antagonism, because the very essence of authority is to bring about freedom and in so doing to make itself superfluous. True authority encourages initiative and releases creative forces in those subjected to it.

According to Kant, a human being is free in measure that his will is not ruled by external or internal, i.e. instinctive, forces, but only by pure reason. The more a man has insight into the necessity of that which concerns his actions, the more he is free; and in the same measure he no longer needs authority. Freedom, therefore, is only possible, insofar as man has insight. Thus, for a single individual freedom cannot be perfectly achieved in all spheres of his existence. If man does not have insight or does not understand the meaning of freedom, he runs the risk of confusing freedom with arbitrariness. Because of this risk freedom always needs essentially limitations, namely limits set by authorities. Nevertheless, authority must essentially withdraw and bring about freedom, as already said. Nevertheless, it remains in some sense still present, even after freedom has been achieved. Not infrequently, it remains present as a resisting force, namely, in those instances when insight has come to oppose its contents. But even when man sets his face against it, authority supports freedom by preventing it from slipping into arbitrariness.

Authority, however, is not present in always the same shape. Human existence and intellectual insight may change and, in fact, have constantly changed it. In other words, authority is historical. It bears the mark of the experiences and beliefs of past generations and, thus, is identical with traditions and institutions, transmitting the tradition of a people or a religious community. Transmitting the past, authority is related to the present in a dialectical way: it will be developed, modified or changed by contemporary experience; which for its part has been brought about by it.

One has to notice that not only authority itself and the realization of freedom, but also the relationship between them, is changing within history. And, this relationship has, indeed, shifted enormously since the end of the Middle Ages. As we know, the Middle Ages were to a great degree bound to authorities. Medieval man had an absolute footing, namely, the divine revelation as transmitted by the church. When he wanted to get insight in his belief he did not try to replace it more and more by reason. Instead, he used his reason to build up an imposing system of faith by means of a distinguishing and comparing logic. With regard to the natural sciences, the Middle Ages were completely bound to ancient literature, especially to Aristotle; there was nearly no autonomous scientific investigation of the world. Arguments were resolved by quotations from ancient authorities. However, since the second part of the fourteenth century, the quest for knowledge has been directed to the actual world of things. Now man wanted to see with his own eyes, to establish proof by his own reason, and to attain critically-founded judgements, independently of inherited models. This resulted in the rise of modern experiment and natural sciences, historical research into source material, modern political theory and jurisprudence. Science, now detached from the unity of life and work which formerly had been determined by religion, became an autonomous cultural sphere. Policy appeared more and more to have its norms in itself, norms which were only for the purpose of enhancing domination and administering power. Injustices committed in the attainment of this goal now did not even elicit a bad conscience, but rather seemed to express a sense of duty and honor. The new freedom to use one's own intellect instead of seeking answers in past authorities, was nevertheless, made possible by authority itself, namely by the authority of the Judaeo-Christian tradition. It has often been observed that modern scientists dared to explore nature only because of their belief in creation: A creator who, in an act of free sovereignty, called the world into being is independent of the world. He does not belong to it as e.g. did Aristotle's unmoved mover. Thus, there was nothing divine in the world itself, and the impetus to acquire knowledge was no longer impeded from pressing nature to give answers by experiments. Biblical belief in creation was without doubt a very important precondition for the rise of modern sciences.

One has, however, to inquire why this rise did not occur before the end of the Middle Ages. It would appear that nothing would have happened if the Arabs had not transmitted their mathematical knowledge to the west. An exact exploration of the world thereby became possible. In particular, it became possible to construct telescopes and to observe the planets with greater precision than ever before. The discovery of new worlds of stars initiated the belief in the infinity of the world. This belief, was, however, reinforced by the acceptance of mathematics in general, for in the world of numbers infinity is not impossible. When man regarded the world as infinite and the earth ceased to be the center of the universe, man lost his anchorage. If there were no limitations of space, it followed that there also were no limitations of time. Without beginning or final goal, there was no longer a centre where man could find orientation. So he became important to himself, and modern subjectivity arose. One has only to look at the human *grandezza*, expressed in the tall sculptures of the Renaissance! A self-confidence of a new kind had come to birth: Man himself became infinite. Although we can observe a pervasive yearning for infinitude already in the Middle Ages, medieval man was conscious of being finite. There was, however, a compensation available to him: He believed that he could transcend the finite reality of this world and reach the absolute. And he conceived of himself as the representative image of the original Absolute. Thus, he could consider himself as being relatively absolute. The term "relatively" is taken to mean "in relation", namely to the Absolute. This was entirely new. The Greek philosophers thought that there was a non-personal, all-pervasive absolute *in* the finite human being which departed from the more or less meaningless individual when he died. Medieval man thought of himself as being absolute *as* a relative and finite individual by participation insolutely absolute. Now, at the end of the middle ages the exaggerated idea that the individual is absolute without qualifications was enunciated. As we have noted, this was, for a great part the result of the discoveries of astronomy. Being apparently lost in an endless universe, man became important to himself.

Whereas in medieval scholasticism, following Greek metaphysics, thought was infinite and absolute in regard to its validity, now the thinker becomes absolute by thinking. Absoluteness in the realm of logic was changed into absoluteness in the domain of human reality. The absolute human being is the quintessence of modern subjectivity. It was Kant who gave the sharpest definition of modern subjectivity. According to him, the subject is the primary ground where all philosophical questioning begins and ends; and no question can be beyond subjectivity. Subjectivity stands in itself and establishes the meaning of life.

It is self-reliant and autonomous.

Whereas Kant himself understood the absolute subjectivity as transcending the individual, the general mood in the period since the Renaissance can be characterized by the desire of the individual to become absolutely autonomous. Such thinkers as Goethe gave witness to this. Man attempted to take over the attributes of God. Formerly servant and adorer, he now attempts to become creator, and most of all the creator himself. As a self-created being he wanted to unfold himself out of his own disposition by his own will.

It is, however, obvious that this kind of autonomy is unavailable for single individuals,—save perhaps in the case of the great personality of the Renaissance. But once the idea of autonomy was brought to birth, it became ineradicable. Unavailable for the individual, autonomy was taken over by such forces as science, economics, politics, and arts. Each of these realms itself builds up out of its own substance and sets forth its own autonomous norms. Ethical norms are restricted in their validity to the individual alone. The idea that man is the creator, thus determined the impetus to modern science. The scientist does not simply listen to the reality and watch natural processes, he rather urges nature to give answers which are relevant to a system created by human mind. Science, thus, reveals itself as a means of dominion. In accordance with this the outcome of modern science, technology, does not have primarily the aim of being helpful or useful to mankind. Technology pretends to bestow prosperity, but it achieves dominion, dominion over man as well as nature. In the case of technology it is obvious that autonomy and dominion have become intertwined. However, the state having become the most powerful of all human enterprises, tends to subordinate such fields as science, art, and education which on their past had previously claimed autonomy. Annulling their claim to autonomy, the state uses them for its own goals. Moreover, the state is no longer understood to exist by the grace of God and to represent his divine authority; instead it is understood as the result of the self-organization of a people. And the individual with all he is and has is now regarded as at the disposal of this dominion.

About two weeks ago, we commemorated the fortieth anniversary of *Reichskristallnacht*, when the destruction of European Judaism was started. Richard Rubenstein has pointed out in his book *The Cunning of History* "That the Holocaust was something very different than an outburst of monumental violence and hatred such as the massacres that have all too frequently punctuated human history" (78). "At Auschwitz, the Germans," he asserts, "revealed new potentialities in the human ability to dominate, enslave, and exterminate"(79).

And he continues to say that

> it was the organizational skill of the Nazis rather than their new weapons that made the society of total domination a reality. And, most of the organizational tools with which such a society can be set up have been greatly improved since World War II. Of supreme importance as a weapon of bureaucratic domination is the modern computer. Few weapons were as indispensable to the Gestapo as its files (79).

Rubenstein maintains that

> once a system of domination has been demonstrated to be a capability of government, it invites repetition. There are a number of circumstances in which a future ruler of a modern state might be tempted to install his own version of such a system (79).

According to Rubenstein, in a bureaucratic society

> men are and perhaps cannot be in control of their own destiny, but . . . their grim, consuming destiny unfolds beyond their intentions and behind their back (87).

If power nowadays is no more essentially related to a particular person, it is evident that dominion has become a reality in and for itself and has slipped out of man's hands.

The general mood of our time is the feeling of being powerless and delivered to an anonymous dominion. When the German Chancellor, Helmut Schmidt, admitted before Parliament that he is unable to read his private computerized bills he expressed the feeling of many people. At present, German politicians are solicitous about the fact that the younger generation not only does not trust the established political parties because of this sense of impotence, but are wary of the state in general. The term *"Staatsverdrossenheit"* weariness of the state, has become a political slogan in Germany. In reality, it is a wariness of all kinds of administration, including the administration of the state, have lost or are losing its authority.

To sum up, the very essence of authority is to achieve and to support freedom. Freedom can only be realized by insight into the contents which the authority of a certain tradition and its institution offers. This process of liberation is constantly happening in the life of individuals as well as in the history of people. The biblical tradition of creation in particular released the world to free investigation, and thus, initiated a turning-point in the history of mankind, as soon as the conditions of its realization were given. The result was that man achieved power, first over nature and then over man himself. On the other hand, he felt lost in an immense universe and retreated into himself so that he thought of himself as autonomous. Autonomy, in a full sense unrealizable by the individual, however, was soon taken over by science and other domains of human enterprise. At last the state claimed autonomy exclusively for itself and seemingly achieved total dominion by means of technology and bureaucracy. Yet, technology and bureaucracy, as well as economics, which were woven into a complex unity, tended from the very beginning to become self-sufficient. They became like a machine which had, previously been an instrument in the hands of man, but had become an autonomous, self-regulating system.

Today, however, the individual increasingly feels powerless and exposed to absolute dominion, that is to say, to a dominion which is unrelated to identifiable persons. Unlike authority absolute dominion does not result in freedom at all, but becomes radical constraint. Thus, our society is characterized by the demand of standardization and its fundamental units are correlated to the functioning of machines. Man has to take the ready-made consumer goods and life styles as they are offered to him. The fact that in most of the Western countries police suppression, censorship or the like does not exist and even libertinage if possible is deceiving. People who suppose that they have privilege of doing whatever they like, are but reflecting general tendencies and reproducing prefabricated life styles, which they mistakenly presume to be their own.

One has only to listen to people in the street discussing political subjects; very often they are reproducing TV-casting without being aware of it. We all depend on information filtration by news reporters, who for their part are not free in making their selection. They must e.g. satisfy the thirst of exciting sensations of people who because of the redundancy of information grow unable to have true sentiments outlasting the present moment. So TV must be taken as an example of technology which has attained independent power. Even if people presume to have license to think and do whatever they want, they are in reality delivered to a system of absolute dominion. Certainly, some people feel at ease with the fact that they are relieved of making their own decisions. This is particularly true of young people who sometimes seek for firm guidance in new communities in which they can dispense with their own will. The quest for dependence and guidance may be engendered by the fact that freedom has become worldlessness and has been perverted to license. Nevertheless, the sense of being delivered to an absolute dominion continues to grow all the more as man has largely dispensed with the traditions which previously gave him security and shelter, in the measure that our consciousness has become enlightened and our knowledge enlarged. In this lecture, we have traced the historical development from freedom which was supported by authority to a kind of autonomy that progressively eliminated authority and tradition, and which, after having been taken over by anonymous, complex social unities, finally developed into absolute dominion. This dominion not only involves restraint on individual freedom, but also carries with it the possibility of unanticipated destruction of the human world, since dominion has slipped out of man's hand. The possibility that dominion, having become independent of individual men, will lead into catastrophe, is no longer merely a frightening nightmare. We have already witnessed the ways in which technology and bureaucracy had together already been

fully put to use in the Holocaust. *Ours, therefore, is the task of
getting dominion over dominion.*

What can we do? Or can we do anything at all? Is the process
we have traced perhaps a necessary process driven by interior
forces beyond the influence of man? Though the process does not
lack inner logic, its necessity is unrecognizable. If however, its
necessity were recognizable, we would know its structure and
could predict its final outcome. But, this is impossible. What we
can see, however, is the fact that the process leading to absolute
dominion has been initiated by man's freedom to get power over
nature. Why should he, then, not become able once to manage
dominion? We can nevertheless, not effectively improve our condition apart from the tendencies of the historical process. So we
must carefully detect already existing tendencies pointing to
possible futural improvements and encourage their realization.

What kind of tendencies are already visible? Our generation
contrasting with previous generations is apparently gaining a
new sense of finitude. The immense spaces of the universe no
longer matter. What matters is the fact that the resources of our
earth are not inexhaustible. This engenders the feeling of responsibility which is not directed to atomistic parts of reality, but
regards the wholeness.

The sense of finitude, then, has brought forth an appreciation
of asceticism, as Romano Guardini perceived already 26 years
ago. Asceticism must not be understood as a kind of obsolete
hostility to life, but is taken to mean a renunciation of the inferior
for the benefit of the superior. It means self-education to gain
freedom from possession "as though" we possessed not; freedom
to a reduction of one's claims; freedom to fight against the
automatism of advertisement, against the inundation of sensations; freedom to independence of one's judgement, to resistance
against what one says, one does. . . Asceticism means self-education for distance.

By proclaiming asceticism I do not want to support a retreat
into the private sphere. It rather revolves about strengthening
observable tendencies in our public opinion in order to create a
new general consciousness by which dominion over dominion

might be achieved. Nobody knows whether we will succeed or not, and we have to reckon also with the possibilty of failure. Nevertheless, nothing of greatness has been achieved without asceticism. What is at stake today is something very great, nay definitive: the issue, whether dominion becomes total or will be mastered by man, who thereby, regains creative freedom which may make again possible genuine authority.

Indeed, dominion seems no longer to be exercised in a completely controlled way by people who can be clearly identified. Dominion has developed an autonomous existence which operates anonymously. Man on his part has been degraded to the status of an object. This is evident in all kinds of bureaucratic registrations, not to speak of the unexpected violence against individuals, groups, and even whole peoples. Moreover, such treatment of human beings including violence, did not occur only in times of extreme emergencies or in the paroxysms of war, but often appears to be a normal contemporary method of governing.

To stress the point once again: Domination no longer seems to be a means employed by an identifiable political elite, even in the case of dictatorship. The supreme political instance has to be conceived of as an executive instrument of the will of a complex unity, in spite of the seeming independence of its actions. If the executive of the anonymous will of the totality does not succeed, the political leader, even a dictator, cannot maintain his domination. The situation of the political leader is not unlike that of the subordinated official who will be removed, if he does not function properly within the system. This is to say that even a dictator is but the complement of the multitude he rules and has in some sense been brought forth by it. Certainly, his function differs from that of other people; nevertheless, he remains within the same framework as the multitude and depends on the complex unity of economical, social, and ideological realities.

BIBLIOGRAPHY

The author is very much indebted to:

R. Guardini, *Das Ende der Neuzeit, Ein Versuch zur Orientierung*, Basel:
Heb Verlag, 1950.
Die Macht. Versuch einer Wegweisung, Wurzburg: Werkbund Verlag,
1965.
K. Jaspers, *Von der Wahrheit, Philosophische Logik*, vol. 1, Munchen:
Piper Verlag, 1947.
Philosophie und Welt, Reden und Aufsatze, Munchen: Piper
Verlag, 1958.
Der Philosophische Glaube Angesichtgs der Offenbarung,
Munchen: Piper Verlag, 1962.
R.L. Rubenstein, *The Cunning of History. Mass Death and the American
Future*, New York: Harper & Row Publishers, 1975.
W. Schultz, *Philosophie in der veranderten Welt*, Pfullingen: Neske
Verlag, 1974.

Richard L. Rubenstein

— C4 —
The Elect and the Preterite*

This essay is in large measure an effort to think about the unthinkable. In setting forth its thesis I have no desire to indulge in unwarranted sensationalism or apocalypticism. Yet so much that is catastrophic has already taken place in our century that it is no longer prudent to avoid reflection on the possibility that further misfortune may await us in the foreseeable future.

As we enter the final quarter of the twentieth century, an air of foreboding concerning mankind's future can be discerned in many circles. A large body of popular and scholarly literature has addressed itself to the darkening aspects of the human prospect.[1] We need not review that literature here, but it is important that we understand the social reality that has given a measure of plausibility to these pessimistic projections. I refer to the rise of a mammoth, world-wide *superfluous population* that can no longer emigrate to underpopulated regions of the globe that await exploitation.

In considering the notion of a superfluous population, it is well to bear in mind that there is nothing absolute about the concept. A surplus population need not be a function of a society's numerical strength. It is, however, a function of a society's capacity to utilize its human resources. A person or a group becomes superfluous only when excluded from a meaningful role within his or her society. This was the condition of the Jews in Nazi Germany. In a less severe way, this is the condition of America's unemployed millions today. There is, of course, a profound difference between bureaucratically-imposed total superfluity such as was experienced by the Jews, and economic superfluity, such as currently afflicts America's unemployed. Unfortunately, one of the hazards confronting an economically redundant population is that, under extreme circumstances, it

---

*Preterition: The passing over of the non-elect; non-election to salvation.

may be dealt with by strategies of population riddance such as large-scale war or even those employed in the Holocaust.[2]

Although Americans tend to regard technology as a means of solving problems, the problem of surplus people in contemporary America is as much the "product" of technological rationality as are the automobile, the computer and the nuclear bomb. One of the most important elements in the "production" of a massive, economically redundant population has been the rationalization of agricultural production. Since the New Deal, government policy has favored the absorption of small farms into large agri-business enterprises. Inefficient producers have been displaced by highly efficient corporations that require only a fraction of the old work force to produce a far greater output. Between 1940 and 1970 over 4,000,000 agricultural workers lost their jobs, were compelled to leave the land and migrate to an unfamiliar urban world.[3]

As is well known, a large proportion of the displaced workers were black. The physically enforced migration of blacks to the New World brought them into a society where they were *needed*. Their economically enforced migration to the urban centers during the twentieth century began when they were *no longer needed* in the agrarian South. A large proportion of the migrants found it difficult or impossible to gain new roles in the cities and became permanently unemployed.

The final chapter in the story of the migration of millions of technologically displaced workers to the urban centers has yet to unfold. The bulk of the migrants came to the metropolitan regions at a time when America was either at war or enjoying a period of prolonged economic growth. At the time, it was possible to absorb many into the industrial economy. That era appears to have come to an end. It now appears that the displaced workers who failed to find employment in the cities have become the unhappy vanguard of millions of others. According to some economists, the problem has been further aggravated by those multi-national corporations that have transferred manufacturing operations from the United States to foreign centers where labor costs are only a fraction of what they are at home.[4] Thus, the threat of permanent economic superfluity now confronts millions of American workers.

Every day the number of people condemned to live beyond the margins of a viable economic system continues to increase and, to repeat, there is no longer any "new world" to which the problem can be exported. Furthermore, there is little evidence that either political party is prepared to deal with the accelerating impact of job-destroying rationalization of business enterprise upon American life. For the moment, decision-makers do not seem to regard the phenomenon of mass unemployment as intractable or as having reached crisis proportions, in spite of the spreading social pathology that is all too visible in America's cities. Nevertheless, unless there is a reversal of the apparently long-range trend towards ever-increasing numbers of unemployed persons in our society, government leaders may some day be compelled to reconsider the ways in which the problem is to be managed. Should that time ever come, the following are the most likely scenarios to which a frightened or a desperate government might resort: (a) The decision might be taken that millions of people are to be condemned to more or less permanent reliance on public assistance, with little hope that they or their descendants could escape the cycle of poverty and its socio-cultural entailments. This is, I believe, the least likely long-term scenario. (b) The permanently unemployed might be compelled to submit to compulsory sterilization in a program resembling the one the Nazis were trying to perfect in their death-camp medical experiments. On a small scale, efforts in that direction have already been attempted by some "welfare" officials.[5] This would be a "clean" way of handling the problem. Its disadvantage would be the length of time required before the desired results could be achieved. Conceivably, such a program might be attempted experimentally as an initial step, only to be discarded because of the need to accelerate the process. (c) Millions might perish through what Malthus called "some species of misery" such as famine, epidemic or nuclear war. Such disasters might actually be welcomed by a government that despairs of its own capacity to manage the nation's social and economic problems, (d) In an extreme economic crisis, I stress the word "extreme," a frightened or desperate government might deliberately resort to a program

of large-scale, bureaucratically-administered population riddance.

Unfortunately, one of the most harrowing lessons of both the
Nazi and Bolshevik experience is that for a dominant elite, the
most "rational" and "economical" method of dealing with
surplus people is to dispose of them. For such an elite, planned
disposal might be regarded as preferable to nuclear conflict
because it can be limited to strictly defined and controllable
groups, whereas it would not be possible to predict the outcome
of a nuclear war or to specify its victims. Population-riddance
might some day be regarded as preferable to tolerating a growing
mass of permanently workless people whose behavior cannot be
motivated by the same incentives and penalties as the normal
population. Living under radically different conditions, the
hopelessly unemployed would constitute an outlaw underclass
and, as such, an abiding threat to the stability and security of the
social order from which they have been excluded. This
phenomenon is already visible in America's metropolitan areas.
In all probability, in a time of economic extremity, such a decision might also be regarded as preferable to permitting large
numbers of people to languish without public assistance. The un-
fortunates might be seen as a source of physical and even moral
contagion. Their very presence might be regarded as having a
brutalizing effect upon those who participate in the normal socio-
economic system.

Should dehumanized arguments of efficiency and cost-effec-
tiveness continue to outweigh humanitarian sentiment in government and business decision-making, the arguments favoring a
bureaucratically-administered population-riddance program
might someday become irresistible, especially if the victims are
of a different racial or ethnic derivation than the elite. In the light
of twentieth-century experience in disposing of unwanted populations, there is little reason to believe that a moral barrier, once
crossed, cannot again be crossed in the future.

It is hardly likely that the question of doing away with permanently superfluous people would ever surface in any kind of
popular referendum. Such a decision is more likely to be taken *in
secret* by a ruling elite and conveyed only to the relevant sections

of the police and civil service bureaucracy. In addition, such a decision is precisely the sort that carries its own legitimation. Humility has seldom, if ever, been a dominant characteristic of elites. Few things can reinforce an elite's sense of class pride as the knowledge that its members have the god-like power secretly to decide the fate of millions of ordinary men, yet are themselves exempt from the consequences of the awesome judgements they mete out.

Furthermore, there are convergent structural and religio-mythic elements in American society that could conceivably affect the way a permanently superfluous population might be dealt with in especially hard times. One of the most important structural consequences of the bureaucratic organization of political and economic enterprise in the modern era has been the dichotomous division of the world into a secret-bearing elite and a largely inarticulate mass of outsiders.[6] Unfortunately, such a division can be a recipe for political and social mischief on a vast scale. Those who possess the secrets—the insiders—are likely to regard the mass of outsiders with suspicion, distrust, contempt, and even downright hostility. In the case of governing elites, there is often the fear that the elite's ability to govern can be seriously compromised should even innocuous "official secrets" fall into alien hands. The very possession of inside knowledge—one of an elite's most prized prerogatives—can engender a paranoid posture towards outsiders that can easily be transformed into hostile acts. In America this phenomenon was by no means restricted to the Nixon presidency. On the contrary, Max Weber's observations concerning secrecy and bureaucracy are, as usual, extremely prescient:

> Every bureaucracy seeks to increase the superiority of the professionally informed by keeping their knowledge and intentions secret. . . . The conception of the "official secret" is the specific invention of bureaucracy and nothing is so fantastically defended by the bureaucracy as this attitude. . . .[7]

Although this dichotomous division is a structural consequence of modern social organization, it bears a strong resemblance to the Biblical division of the world into the elect and the damned, especially its Calvinist variant. Moreover, the resemblance between structure and doctrine may not be entirely fortuitous. One student of the American elite, Richard Barnet, has estimated that between 1940 and 1967, "all of the first and second level posts in the national security bureaucracy were held by fewer than four hundred men who rotate through a variety of key posts."[8] According to Barnet, most of these "public servants" never held elective office. They were in reality a self-perpetuating elite whose power remained unchanged during both Republican and Democratic administrations, save perhaps for the Nixon interlude. According to Barnet, the religious and educational background of the elite, as well as their lifestyle and social status reflected a remarkable homogeneity. Of especial interest is the Calvinist background and upbringing of almost all of these men.[9] Other observers have noted a certain tendency on the part of these men to interpret their status as almost divinely certified. Just as there was a tendency among earlier Calvinists to interpret worldly success as evidence of divine election, so observers have noted a tendency on the part of members of the American elite to regard their ability to excel in a fiercely competitive mass society as a sign of their own election and an almost "divine right" to govern the most powerful nation on earth.[10] It would, of course, be bad taste to express such sentiments publicly. Nevertheless, there has been enough evidence of class pride, if not arrogance, to justify such observations.

In a culture in which worldly success may certify divine election, worldly failure is likely to attest to a double rejection.[11] The poor are likely to be regarded as both social outcasts and, what is far worse, as objects of divine rejection. Their plight is likely to be seen as deserved. It reflects God's justice, for the poor are seen as having failed life's supreme test.

In the past, the ideology of elite election and mass condemnation, especially of the indigent, has had the effect of adding a measure of harshness to the way the disinherited have been dealt with, especially in the administration of poor relief.[12] However, were a ruling elite ever faced with the question of whether to preside over the elimination of the permanently poor in a time of extreme scarcity, the likelihood that a "hard," "objective" solution might be favored would be strongly reinforced by the elite's Calvinist inheritance. In such a crisis of decision, the controlling images would probably be the secularized equivalent of the division of mankind into the elect and the reprobate. An elite of Calvinist background would find it exceedingly difficult to squander scarce resources on the impoverished, who have so obviously become the objects of God's wrath.

Lest I be misunderstood, when I refer to a Calvinist elite, I do not restrict that designation to members of Presbyterian or Reformed churches. On the contrary, the Calvinism I discuss long ago left the confines of the sanctuary and entered the worldliest precincts of secular society. One need not be formally a Protestant to be a secularized Calvinist. Any American be he Protestant, Catholic or Jewish, who has achieved elite status is likely to conduct the business of life in accordance with the Puritan work ethic and the Calvinist division of mankind into the elect and the preterite.

Should a secularized Calvinist elite ever be compelled to consider the need for draconian measures in a time of national or world crisis, those favoring a "hard" solution would in all likelihood resort to the same Social Darwinist ideology that the Nazis used when they argued that the "survival of the fittest" was the universal law of nature and that both the preservation of "superior" elements and the radical elimination of "inferior" elements in the population were justified by a people seeking to prevail in the universal "struggle for existence."[12a] Let us recall the full title of Darwin's great work, *The Origins of the Species by Means of Natural Selection, or the preservation of Favored Races in the Struggle for Life* (1859). Admittedly, Darwin never contemplated a Nazi-type program for the "preservation of favored races." Nevertheless, as Hans-Gunter Zmarzlik has pointed out, the core of Darwin's theory is the postulation of "a process of selection in which value judgments play no part."[13] In Darwinism, the survival of the species is not dependent upon virtues such as humility and Christ-like *agape* but upon characteristics that had been previously regarded as sinful in Christianity, such as aggresion and avarice.

According to Zmarzlik, European Social Darwinism became in-creasingly popular with the rise of the new imperialism and the Second Industrial Revolution in the last quarter of the nine-teenth century. There was at the time a tendency towards "the naturalization of political thinking" and "the brutalization of political methods." The ideology of a universal "struggle for ex-istence" became dominant among the bourgeoisie at a time when imperialist and capitalist expansion become the order of the day.[14] Nowhere was Social Darwinism as influential at the time as in the United States. The expanding American economy gave successful Americans the conviction that they were truly winn-ing the harsh struggle and were in fact the world's most favored race. Richard Hofstadter has noted that, while England gave Darwin to the world, Darwinism received its most sympathetic hearing in the United States during the last three decades of the nineteenth and the beginning of the twentieth century.[15] Herbert Spencer was far more popular in the United States than in his native England.[16] Darwinist ideas were especially appealing to success-oriented men who had taken their chances in a highly competitive, industrial society in which all honor went to the vic-tors and the losers were relegated to economic and social obscur-ity.

The winners in the bitter struggle regarded their victory as "merely the working-out of a law of nature and a law of God." This was a judgment offered by John D. Rockefeller in a Sunday school address.[17] Another magnate, James J. Hill, argued that the absorption of small railroads by the larger ones was determin-ed by "the law of the survival of the fittest." The very men whom Max Weber regarded as incarnating the Protestant ethic in their success as business entrepreneurs looked upon Darwinism, especially as expounded by Herbert Spencer, as fully congruent with their own experience.

On the surface, Darwin's theories appeared to be anti-Christian and were so regarded by religious conservatives. Dar-win contradicted the scriptural account of human origins when the Bible is taken literally. Far more serious was Darwin's rejec-tion of conventional moral judgments in describing the evolu-tionary process. Yet, as both David Bakan and Richard Hofstadter have observed, Social Darwinism can be seen as a secularized form of Calvinism in which the "survival of the fittest" is the Darwinian equivalent of the Calvinist "salvation of the elect."[18] The parallelism seems closer when we remember that in the title of the *Origin of the Species*, it is "favored races" who survive. Darwin could hardly have come closer to the Judaeo-Christian term, "the elect" without abandoning his posture of scientific neutrality altogether.

In Darwin's sytem, while the "fittest" survive, there is little, if any, reason to regret the passing of those who fall by the wayside:

> When we reflect on this struggle, we may console ourselves with the full belief, that the war of nature is not incessant, that no fear is felt, that the vigorous, the healthy and the happy survive and multiply.[19]

Darwin's vision resembles a Biblical theology of history: The plight of those who suffer must be viewed from the larger perspective of the Great Plan. In the Bible, God is the Author of the Plan; in Darwin it is "Nature." In both, history derives its meaning from the fate of the fortunate few. *Of greatest importance is the fact that both Calvinism and Darwinism provide a cosmic justification for the felicity of the few and the misery of the many.* It is precisely this feature of both that may prove so dangerous in the years ahead.

There are other important links between Darwin and Protestantism, if not Calvinism directly. As an undergraduate at Christ's College, Cambridge, from 1828-31, Darwin was a student of divinity who intended to become a clergyman. In 1838, Darwin read Thomas Malthus's *Essay on Population*, and was deeply influenced by it. Darwin credited Malthus with being the source of the idea of natural selection:

> . . . I saw on reading Malthus on Population that natural selection was the inevitable result of the rapid increase of all organic beings; for I was prepared to appreciate the struggle for existence having long studied the habits of animals.[20]

If Darwin's idea of natural selection came from Malthus's

reflections on population, *Malthus saw the process by which unchecked population increased geometrically while the food supply increased arithmetically as an expression of the wise and providential design of the Creator.* Thus, Malthus's *Essay on Population* is a theodicy!

Like Darwin, Malthus studied divinity at Cambridge. Unlike Darwin, he took Holy Orders and served as an Anglican parson for part of his career. Malthus never felt under any constraint to avoid theological argument or terminology in his writing. On the contrary, it was important for him to set his bleak drama of overabundant population within the context of God's providence. Malthus attempted to do this in the last two chapters (XVIII and XIX) of his *Essay on Population*, in which he argued that it was Providence that ordained "that population should increase much faster than food." Malthus conceded that this arrangement "produces much evil," but he argued that if we

> ...consider man as he really is, inert, sluggish and averse from labour unless compelled by necessity...we may pronounce with certainty that the world would not have been peopled but for the superiority of the "power" of population to the means of subsistence.[21]

For Malthus, mankind's original sin is "torpor." Were men not goaded by necessity to overcome their natural inertia, they would never have emerged from "the savage state."[22] Both the imbalance between population and subsistence and "the species of misery" required to keep population in check are part of God's plan. In his wisdom, God has inflicted the goad of necessity and scarcity upon mankind.

Having demonstrated the operation of God's plan in the natural order, Malthus concluded the *Essay* with his own version of the Biblical doctrine of election: "Nothing can appear more consonant to our own reason than that those beings which come out of the world in lovely and beautiful forms should be crowned with immortality." He also offered his justification of the fate of those whom Providence rejects:

> ...those which come out misshapen, those whose minds are not suited to a purer and a happier state of existence, should perish and be condemned to mix again with their original clay. Eternal condemnation may be considered as a species of punishment.[23]

Thus, Malthus agrees with both the Calvinist and the Social Darwinist position that those who survive are those chosen to survive, as well as its bleak corollary. One of the many reasons why Malthus is a crucial figure is that he anticipates the Social Darwinist position and reveals the powerful convergence of religious and scientific themes in that overwhelmingly important philosophy of life. Not only are his ideas on population still the indispensable starting point of the contemporary population debate, but his views on the support of the indigent are among the earliest serious expressions of the point of view that favors cutting adrift those who do not have the resources to feed themselves. Malthus argued that, in spite of the good intentions of its advocates, public relief for the indigent only aggravates the problem of a surplus population. He opposed all forms of public assistance. To feed the indigent, he argued, would only increase their numbers. Eventually, this would lead to general scarcity and misery.[24]

Opposition to public assistance for the poor has remained a consistent theme in Social Darwinist theory to this day. Herbert Spencer was particularly harsh in his opposition. He argued that "The whole effort of nature is to get rid of such (i.e., the poor), to clear the world of them, and make room for better." Nature is the final arbiter of who shall live and who shall die. Those who do not pass nature's test of survival die "and it is best that they should die."[25]

The last example of the link between Protestant elitism and Social Darwinism we will consider is the famous Yale sociologist, William Graham Sumner (1840-1910). Sumner believed that untrammeled competition for property and status had the beneficient effect of eliminating the unfit and of preserving both racial soundness and cultural vigor. According to Hofstadter, Sumner was brought up "to respect the traditional Protestant economic virtues."[26] In his later life, Sumner once wrote that the holder of a savings bank account was a "hero of civilization."[27] Like Darwin and Malthus, Sumner studied theology as a university student. Upon graduation from Yale, wealthy friends supplied the funds that made it possible for him to secure a substitute to take his place in the Union Army. We do not know the fate of the soldier who took his place, but while the Civil War raged, Sumner studied theology at Geneva, Gottingen, and Oxford. When he returned to America after the war, he was ordained a priest of the Episcopal Church. Although Sumner spent most of his professional career as a Yale professor, he served as rector of the Episcopal Church in Morristown, New Jersey, for a number of years.[28]

Like Darwin and Spencer, Sumner was strongly influenced by Thomas Malthus. He was also an unwavering supporter of free enterprise capitalism, as were most of the American Social Darwinists of the period. He regarded the system of unbridled economic competition that was regnant in post-Civil War America as a social expression of the process of natural selection and, as such, Nature's providential means of advancing the progress of civilization. Sumner had no doubt that millionaires are Nature's elect:

> The millionaires are a product of natural selection, acting on the whole body of men to pick out those who can meet the requirements of certain work to be done.[29]

As in other variants of both Biblical and Social Darwinist theology, Sumner invoked the dichotomous division of mankind. He was utterly devoid of sympathy for those who faltered in the competitive struggle. Their misfortune was further evidence of the wisdom and beneficence of Nature's ways. The damned receive their just deserts:

> Many . . . are frightened at liberty, especially under the form of competition. . . . They do not perceive that here "the strong" and "the weak" are terms which admit of no definition unless they are made equivalent to the industrious idle, the frugal and the extravagant. They do not perceive, furthermore, that if we do not like the survival of the fittest, we have only one possible alternative, and that is the survival of the unfittest. The former is the law of civilization; the latter is the law of anti-civilization.[30]

The only kind of "civilization" Sumner could envisage is one in which the happy few prosper and the "idle" and "extravagant" perish as omnipotent Nature separated the wheat from the chaff.

Writing during World War II, Richard Hofstadter concluded his book on Social Darwinism in America with the observation that the Darwinian apotheosis of tooth and claw competition no longer reflected the mood of the social class that had been its most enthusiastic advocates, the middle class. Nevertheless, Hofstadter warned that the resurgence of Social Darwinism was always possible as long as the predatory element is strong in society.[31] Hofstadter did not reflect upon the possibility that a "survival of the fittest" philosophy could influence policy-making in both government and business as the fundamental ideology of the decision-making elites, no matter how it was received among the general population.

Thirty years after Hofstadter set down his concluding reflections, Social Darwinism or secular Calvinism has not been discredited as a governing ideology of the elites. On the contrary, it gains in apparent plausibility every day the world economy worsens. The decision-making elites are precisely the groups to whom an ideology of dividing mankind into the fortunate chosen few and the damned majority is most appealing. As H. Richard Niehbuhr has observed, Calvinism *"repelled"* the poor and gave "religious sanction to the enterprise of the business man and the industrialist by regarding it as a divine calling."[32] What the Calvinists do in the name of God, the Social Darwinists do in the name of a strangely providential "Nature." Social Darwinism or secular Calvinism fulfills the most fundamental function of a viable religion. It provides an overarching structure of meaning in which a group's experiences and values can be comprehended. It enables its adherents to believe that their social location, way of life and fundamental values are cosmically grounded rather than the accidental product of precarious human invention.[33] Should the world become ever more endangered by the sort of population problems we have discussed, Social Darwinism or some version of secular Calvinism is likely further to gain in plausibility to the dominant elites. Should such men then be faced with the kind of decisions that could easily lead to the death of millions of their fellows, Social Darwinism could provide them with the requisite legitimating ideology. Furthermore, the plausibility of Social Darwinism is enormously enhanced by the fact that its roots are to be found in both the predominant religious and scientific traditions of our culture. Social Darwinism is not merely one ideology among many. It is a conceptualization of the pre-theoretical foundations of the ways in which the American middle and upper classes structure social reality. H. Richard Niehbuhr has observed that really poor people seldom became Calvinists.[34] It is a theology for the elite or for those who have some expectations, however, remote, that they or their offspring might become members of the elite.

The dreary scenarios we project are admittedly based on an assumption that many will regard as highly questionable. Each scenario presupposes that the abstract rationalization of the political and economic spheres will continue to multiply the number of men and women whom our society cannot productively utilize. Regrettably, the wars and other social catastrophes of the twentieth century serve as reminders of the folly of facile optimism as we consider the prospect before us. Nevertheless, our reflections inevitably raise the question: What is to be done? In response, I would stress that it is not my intention to discuss large-scale public planning in this essay. I have a more modest aim. I have attempted to raise some questions about the pretheoretical foundations of our legitimating ideologies as well as the possible public consequences of these ideologies in a future crisis.

It is my conviction that the human costs of a job-destroying technological rationality and its Social Darwinist legitimations are far too high. Unfortunately, it is easier to count the costs of our social values than to alter them. No matter how destructive Social Darwinism may be as a legitimating ideology, it carries to their logical conclusion values that are everywhere operative in a highly competitive society. An obvious alternative would be to adopt some less competitive set of public values. In any event, before we could bring about fundamental economic and/or political changes, we would have to alter profoundly the hierarchy of values that informs our decision-making and our conceptions of human worth. Yet, one wonders whether such a transformation is possible, especially where it counts most, that is, among those who prize their elite status and seek to perpetuate it for their heirs. Few insiders, whether in government, business, the academy, or even religion would willingly abandon the exclusive character of their standing. Indeed, the very size and complexity of society make a high degree of stratification and structural differentiation unavoidable. Furthermore, value-formation is not a rational process. It is not at all certain that an individual or a community will desist from patterns of response simply because they perceive the consequences of their behavior to be "injurious to health."

Perhaps the real question confronting us is whether it is possible to transform the structures of consciousness that have brought us to our present hazard simply by comprehending them. If comprehension is transformative, we may not be fated helplessly to live out a bitter destiny. There is both hope and despair in Hegel's oft-quoted reflection concerning the power of philosophical comprehension at the close of the Preface to his *Philosophy of Right*:

> One word more about giving instructions as to what the world ought to be. Philosophy in any case always comes on the scene too late to give it. As the thought of the world, it appears only when actuality is already there cut and dried after its process of formation has been completed... When philosophy paints its grey in grey, then has a shape of life grown old. By philosophy's grey it cannot be rejuvenated but only understood. The owl of Minerva spreads its wings only with the falling of the dusk.[35]

If philosophy is in the words of Shlomo Avineri "the wisdom of ripeness," to the extent that we have understood the processes currently at work upon us, we announce the demise of the world we comprehend. Unfortunately, there is no way of accurately forecasting the human costs of the dissolution, and history offers few examples of decisive political and social transformations that have not been accompanied by collective trauma. Lest we be tempted to an optimism which our situation hardly warrants, let us recall another observation by Hegel:

> (history is) the slaughter-bench at which the happiness of peoples, the wisdom of states, and the virtue of individuals have been sacrificed...[36]

A principal reason for my emphasis on Calvinism and Social Darwinism as the legitimating ideologies of greatest utility to decision-making elites, especially in times of massive dislocation, has been my desire to make manifest the depth of the psychic, cultural and religious resistances to an effective social and political transformation, at least on the part of those with the greatest decision-making power. The path to a more equitable society is blocked by far more effective impediments than mere avarice. Much that is central to our ancestral religious and cultural heritage would probably work against such a transformation. As we have seen, from an elite perspective, the intensification of mass misery throughout the world would tend to *confirm* rather than discredit the ideologies discussed in this essay. Although I earnestly hope that I have erred on the side of pessimism, I must confess that there are times when I wonder whether we may yet be destined to render full account for having accepted a religious ideology that denies the mystery and magic of the natural order and divides the human order into the elect and the damned.

NOTES

1. Out of a voluminous literature, I cite Garrett Hardin's essay, "The Tragedy of the Commons," *Science,* Vol. 162, pp. 1243-1248, December 13, 1968; Hardin, *Population, Evolution and Birth Control* (San Francisco: Freeman and Co., 1969); Robert Heilbroner, *An Inquiry into the Human Prospect* (New York: W.W. Norton, 1975).
2. This issue is discussed in detail in Richard L. Rubenstein, *The Cunning of History* (New York: Harper and Row, 1975).
3. Frances Fox Piven and Richard Cloward, *Regulating the Poor* (New York: Vintage, 1973) pp. 201ff.
4. Cf. Richard J. Barnet and Ronald E. Muller, *Global Reach: The Power of the Multinational Corporations* (New York: Simon and Schuster, 1974), cf. especially pp. 303-333.
5. Cf. "Sterilization: Coercing Consent," *Nation,* January 12, 1974 and "Sterilization: Newest Threat to the Poor," *Ebony,* October 1973, pp. 10ff. This issue is discussed in Rubenstein, *The Cunning of History,* pp. 53f.

6. This is discussed by Max Weber in his essay, "Bureaucracy" in *From Max Weber: Essays in Sociology*, trans. H.H. Gerth and C. Wright Mills (New York: Oxford University Press, 1946) pp. 231-235; cf. Hannah Arendt, *The Origins of Totalitarianism* (New York: Harcourt, Brace and World, 1966) pp. 376ff. On the sociology of secrecy and the secret society, cf. *The Sociology of Georg Simmel*, ed. Kurt H. Wolff (New York: Free Press of Glencoe, 1964) pp. 307-374.

7. Weber, *op. cit.*, p. 233.

8. Richard J. Barnet, *Roots of War* (Baltimore: Penguin Books, 1973) p.48.

9. Barnet, *op. cit.*, pp. 68ff.

10. Barnet, *op. cit.*, p. 70.

11. Among the many observers who have made this point, cf. H. Richard Niehbuhr, *The Social Sources of Denominationalism*, (Hamden, Conn.: The Shoestring Press, 1954), p. 96 and Sydney Ahlstrom, *A Religious History of the American People* (New Haven: Yale University Press, 1972) pp. 789f.

12. According to Andrew Carnegie, "neither the individual nor the race is improved by alms-giving" in "Wealth," *The North American Review*, Vol. 39, (June 1889), p. 663 cited by George Bedell, Leo Sandon, Jr. and Charles J. Wellborn, *Religion in America* (New York: McMillan and Co., 1975), p. 320; cf. Walter I. Trattner, *From Poor Law to Welfare State: A History of Social Welfare in America* (New York: Free Press, 1974) pp. 50-55.

12a. Cf. Helmut Krausnick, "The Persecution of the Jews" in *Anatomy of the SS State* by Krausnick, Hans Buchheim, Martin Broszat and Hans-Adolf Jacobsen (New York: Walker and Company, 1968) pp. 10-18 and Hans-Gunter Zmarzlik, "Social Darwinism in Germany, Seen as a Historical Problem" in *Republic to Reich*, ed. Hajo Holborn (New York: Pantheon, 1972) pp. 435-474.

13. Zmarzlik, *op. cit.*, p. 440.

14. Zmarzlik, *.op. cit.*, pp. 442ff. Although England's leading nineteenth century Social Darwinist, Herbert Spencer, was strongly opposed to his nation's imperialist policies, the imperialism of the period "was most widely justified by an appeal to Social Darwinism." Cf. J.D.Y. Peel, *Herbert Spencer: The Evolution of a Sociologist* (New York: Basic Books, 1973) pp. 234ff.

15. Richard Hofstadter, *Social Darwinism in American Thought* (Boston: Beacon Press, 1955) p. 44.

16. According to Peel, Spencer was "in no way the apologist of capitalist interests." However Spencer's "misgivings about industrial capitalism" were ignored by his busines admirers. Cf. Peel, *op. cit.*, pp. 214f.

17. Cited by Hofstader, *op. cit.*, p. 45.

18. David Bakan, *The Duality of Human Existence* (Chicago: Rand McNally, 1966) p. 35.
19. Charles Darwin, *The Origin of the Species* (New York: Modern Library, 1936) p. 62.
20. Charles Darwin, *The Variations of Animals and Plants Under Domestication* (London: John Murray, 1868), Vol. I., p. 10 cited by Anthony Flew, in his introduction to Thomas Malthus, *An Essay on the Principle of Population* (Harmonsworth: Penguin Books, 1970), p. 50.
21. Malthus, *op. cit.*, p. 205.
22. Malthus, *op. cit.*, p. 202.
23. Malthus, *op. cit.*, p. 215.
24. Malthus, *op. cit.*, pp. 193ff.
25. Herbert Spencer, *Social Statics* (New York: D. Appleton, 1864) pp. 414f.
26. Hofstadter, *op. cit.*, p. 52.
27. A.G. Keller and M.R. Davie, ed., *Essays of William Graham Sumner* (New Haven: Yale University Press, 1934) Vol. II, pp. 22ff. and William Graham Sumner, *The Challenge of Facts and Other Essays* (New Haven: Yale University Press, 1914) p. 52.
28. Hofstadter, *op. cit.*, p. 53.
29. Sumner, "The Concentration of Wealth" in *Social Darwinism: Selected Essays of William Graham Sumner*, ed. Stow Person (Englewood Cliffs, N.J., Prentice Hall, 1963).
30. A.G. Keller and M.R. Davies, *op. cit*, Vol. II, p. 56.
31. Hofstadter, *op. cit.*, p. 201.
32. H. Richard Niehbuhr, *op. cit.*, p. 96.
33. Cf. Peter Berger, *The Sacred Canopy* (Garden City: Anchor, 1967) pp. 29-51.
34. Niehbuhr, *op. cit.* p. 105.
35. G.W.F. Hegel, *The Philosophy of Right*, trans. T.M. Knox (Oxford: Oxford University Press, 1942) pp. 12f.
36. G.W.F. Hegel, *Reason in History*, (Indianapolis: Bobbs, Merrill, 1972.).

Section D:
Contemporary Images of Death

— D1 —
The Anatomy of Death
Ninian Smart/Alfred Alvarez

— D2 —
Death as a Source of Philosophy
Ben-Ami Scharfstein

— D3 —
The Art of Suicide
Joyce Carol Oates

Ninian Smart

— D1 —
The Anatomy of Death

The bones of death can be mapped by philosophical analysis, but since in a certain sense they are bones that live one needs too to explore their meaning through a theory of individual life and substance. I shall take these two paths in this essay. In doing so I shall be developing conceptions which I worked out in previous writings, including contributions to *Man's Concern with Death*[1] by Arnold Toynbee and others, and *Six Approaches to the Person*.[2] I shall begin by reflecting upon individual identity in its living context, in relation to death; and I shall deal second with the analytic conclusions one may extract from a consideration of the language of death.

I

The question of personal identity—"Who and what am I?" with which we puzzle over ourselves—is not for most people at all the problem of identity as pursued by the philosophers. I leave the latter question here on one side: it concerns how we know that a person at one time is the same person as he was at a previous time, and the roles of the body and the memory in identity. Rather the existential question is to do with value and purpose. The very fact that we can sometimes see ourselves utterly from within, and independently of our social and historical context, implies our capacity for a kind of vertigo in which all the value assumptions which permeate daily existence are suspended. Such an inner shock, derived from the feeling that everything that we have been and are is somehow adventitious, is repeated in the contemplation of death.

It is true that when I die there will yet linger on something of my social and historical substance. I may attract an obituary or two. What I have done will have its effects in the future. And memories of me, friendly or the reverse, will linger on in a few people's minds. Some think by being famous to increase this substance: many will still harbor the famous in their memories. Yet it is a thin kind of immortality, as also is that which is found in progeny. What am I to my greatgrandfather? I do not know who he was, and even with dear parents—well, how should I want to live their lives? Proud as I am of my children, I can scarcely expect much more in them, after my death, than fond memories of me, and may they keep tidy and cheerful my grave.

Since the question of identity sometimes takes a philosophical form and sometimes an existential one, it is perhaps useful to signal the distinction by the use of differing words. For this and for some other reasons I shall refer to the non-philosophical, existential question as being about my personal substance. Because in so much of living I identify with groups, and draw my substance from their substance by a kind of mystical participation (to use Levy-Bruhl's old language); and because my status is so to speak ritually enacted by others in daily converse and transactions—because of such factors the who and what I am from at least a worldly point of view has to do with the social colorations and grandness or otherwise of my substance.

The figure of Father Time, and the image of Death, therefore mock us because they threaten our substance. Even the groups that sustain me, and will sustain me in ghostly form after my death, will fade and shift. For by process of death and time the sources of substance will be cut off. In my death, my substance virtually vanishes, save for those shreds which linger in other folks' minds, and what is that to me?

Leaving aside for the present the possibility of immortality or rebirth or resurrection, possibilities, that is, of my existing after my death in some form or other—any substance I draw from what people do or say about me after my death comes essentially as a contribution to (or diminution from) my present substance. I now derive perhaps satisfaction from contemplating my good repute after my death. But there is no such satisfaction, clearly, once I am dead. In so far, then, as it is natural for a person to hope and even work for the maintenance and aggrandizement also of his substance, death mocks, for it destroys such social identity, and is as we know the ultimate threat to status.

Substance one might regard as being mediated by performative and ritual acts: the esteem which I hope to have in the eyes of my friends and community is something which they communicate in words and gestures. To be praised, ignored, despised, flattered, humiliated, loved: such acts and attitudes are the power which I draw upon, in so far as I am a social being. Indirectly also what I do—my job, primarily—can be a channel of substance, for its value to the community, or rather its perceived and communicated usefulness and importance, will confer value on me.

What counts as the relevant community, of course, shifts. For some cultures the family and clan remain crucial. In more modern society it is increasingly identified with the nation state. For this reason it is the nation which feels entitled to call for the greatest of sacrifices, for a man to lay down his life for his country. This tendency towards the dominance of the national group even occurs when the ideology may be internationalist—as in socialist countries like those of Eastern Europe, where "the people" necessarily becomes defined as the Romanian people, Bulgarian people or whatever, and when the very process of centration involved in socialism as commonly understood conduces to national identity. It is national socialism, however much it may be tempered by the slogan "Workers of the world unite!" Here in a most marked fashion a person's worth is tied to his role in the life of the nation and the class struggle within the nation.

The individualism of much Western democracy and social democracy yields a more complex equation concerning substance. The thrust of personalism is towards valuing the idiosyncratic. Thus the individual is made to feel a tension: on the one hand his value to society rests upon his doing a job (which others in principle might do instead of him), but in himself his value is held to lie in his uniqueness. Yet it is unwise here to calculate that eccentricity is a virtue, for the same logic of the ritual and performative aspect of social life obtains: it is through the transactions of esteem and disesteem a person's substance is enhanced or diminished, and this implies a considerable pressure towards conformism. It is true that modern society often produces the phenomenon of the lonely crowd, and solitude often spells a kind of freedom, since nonconformist conduct need not attract much disesteem. But by the same token, there is not much in the way of a supportive society around one—a group whose transactions of esteem give one a sense of importance, and thus meaning.

The individual, in participating in a network of ends or purposes, through his job and other institutional activities, can be said to have teleological value: he derives teleological substance from the groups to which he belongs. He also can be said to have attributive substance in possessing attributes that are esteemed—such as beauty, wealth, creativity, seniority or whatever. The two varieties of substance can attract differing forms of self-satisfaction and despair. Thus when an institutional framework of purposes is threatened, there is too a threat to meaning. For instance, what happens when a whole way of life is coming to an end? This can breed the sort of despair which afflicts communities such as American Indian and Aboriginal groups where the old purposes and customs are being overwhelmed by the alien forces of White culture. Sometimes social change brings with it radical changes in attributive substance: thus being old, from being a prized attribute and sign of wisdom, can become a liability—the final loss of pretensions to youthfulness, which is the prized attribute. Since both teleological and attributive substance depend upon the continuance of a given society, it is natural that eschatologies of doom themselves provide a similar vertigo to that found in the contemplation of one's own death. Present acts draw substance from the past, for it is the past which is the matrix of the group and through which it celebrates its identity; but also from the future, which is mediated to us by hope or foreboding. It is no surprise that religious symbolism should embrace both first and last things. Because of our typical dependence, for substance, upon the esteem which only a group can provide, the specter of collective death is peculiarly emptying. The vertigo it produces feels like an assault on meaning.

It is worth noting here that in the pregnant sense of the word in which we speak of "the meaning of life", meaning has to do not with sense of significance, but rather with value. That is, to say that something or other is meaningless or pointless is to say that it has lost its value. The meaningful is that which has the power to move us. Thus collective death is peculiarly threatening, because it renders our teleological values empty and our attributive values without social basis. And in our own age, this is no idle speculation. The specter of collective death has a certain reality about it, because a nuclear war between the major powers could well end life in the northern hemisphere, and perhaps life altogether on the planet. It is easy to be discouraged about building a better world, when the military planners talk with ease about megadeaths. But the psychological mechanisms which serve to conserve and expand our personal substance continue to operate, and they tell us to believe that really the next war is just a bad dream: our leaders would not be so foolish as to start a nuclear holocaust.

In view of the teleological and continuing social life of attributive substance, it is not surprising that we are attracted to theories of history which see it ending successfully. The upward rhythms of the Marxist dialectic, Hitler's vision of the thousand year Reich, the hope of the convergence to the Omega point in the thought of Teilhard de Chardin, the vision of the millennium in Christianity—these are different expressions of hope in a kind of justification by the future.

Nevertheless, there is often ambiguity and vagueness about these culminations of the future: this world is transformed into a new heaven and a new earth, and the millennium is only a figure for an uncalculated length of time, somehow between time measured and eternity. To this point I shall return.

How does religion essentially relate to the meaning of life? If I am right in seeing the latter as to do with the maintenance of value, then Christianity (for example) can be seen as involving a kind of communication of substance which should make the individual immune to meaninglessness. It will be instructive to consider the approach of Buddhism, which is diametrically opposite, in appearance at least, because it involves evacuating the individual of all permanence and substance. Let me expand on these remarks.

The logic of the doctrine of the special creation of man by God is that man has a unique capacity for communication with God. There is some sense in which he can participate in the divine substance. Now it so happens that the monotheism of Christianity implies that there is only one holy being, and so only one source of holy substance. Consequently, the capacity for holiness is not something intrinsic to man, and so the soul itself is a gift of God. Still, in effect the transactional situation is this—that if man puts himself in right relationship to God he will gain something of the divine and deathless substance of God. As Christianity sees it, Christ is the channel of communication, so individual Christians have to go through Christ to gain that access through which the immortal substance flows.

The logic of this in turn is that the Christian really has all that he could possibly want: for to partake of the substance of God is to participate in the infinite. There is no one with more power and substance than God: in having access to that power the Christian has more than the kingdoms of this world. And yet there turn out to be certain paradoxes about this power, in the light of which the Christian has the capacity for deathlessness. For one thing, in participating in God's being the Christian participates in the career of Christ. For God's nature is not just a static affair, but is stamped with a character derived from his incarnation: is stamped indeed by the story of salvation, or as one might say, the myth of salvation. Thus God is not just an essence, but contains so to speak a moving myth, so that the Christian as well as taking a share in God's substance in general takes part in the myth. Indeed the central rites of Christianity re-enact the myth and in doing so convey its character to the Christian, so that through the rituals he is assured of participation in the divine substance. But it turns out, of course, that Christ in his life and death has emptied himself of power. The Christian then has all the power he could possibly wish for, since he has the power of God communicated to him; and yet that power turns out to be self-emptying. This dialectic between the pomp of power and the humility of Christ runs through much of the Christian liturgy and should run through the Church's life.

Thus the Christian idea of the conquest of death is that of the capacity of the person to share in the power of God, which is, however, communicated to him under the form of the myth of Christ's life, death and resurrection.

I may add here in parenthesis two things: the triumphal sense of sharing in God's power and substance reached its apogee in the Western Church, through the almost magical mediation of that power through Host, monstrance, hierarchy and indulgences. Yet through all that, and through the numinous glory of the Orthodox Liturgy and the transforming energy of the Protestant preacher there is sounded the note of the Suffering Servant. There is a hint of desolation in the midst of the divine substance. And this leads me to the second observation. Who knows? The Christian may picture himself as crowned with the saints in glory in the hereafter, but the existence of that hereafter is not literal, and heaven is not a literal place: the Christian is in effect gambling on the existence of God, who inscrutably provides a resting place for the faithful. Since God of his nature is unprovable, save by "proofs" themselves in doubt, the Christian, in so far as he feels the power of God's substance in his own life, is yet making an ontological gamble. This is not Pascal's wager, but the gamble of faith, seen in modern times as involving more than moral commitment or a decision for Christ but as an ontological gamble too. The Christian's certitude, therefore, in the face of death is not a certainty.

Nevertheless, because of the nature of God as having eternal substance, in action however through the myth of salvation, the Christian concept of the person always contains what may be called a "transcendantal footnote". It always has built in to it some reference to transcendent destiny. In this sense, death no longer has its sting, because my personal substance in the last resort is not based upon merely this-worldly teleological and attributive evaluation. On the other hand, this cannot give the Christian this-worldly certainty: the assurance of sharing in God's deathless substance is an assurance contained within faith which is necessarily both an existential and ontological gamble, a fact both symbolized by and accentuated by Christ's self-empty.

Since the theme of Suffering Servant is central in Judaism, it would be possible to rewrite the above description with a different "transcendental footnote", for a similar structure of gambling is to be found in Judaism, though expressed in terms of a national identity and destiny.

I now turn to an opposite way of looking upon death, and on individual substance: the Buddhist. At the heart of the Buddha's analysis of the nature of the world and of salvation there lies the so-called *anatmayada* or theory of non-self. The individual is de-substantialized, and this in two ways. On the one hand the forward continuance of the individual and his past and present are chopped up minutely into instants of time; he becomes an ongoing swarm of events. Second, the individual is broken up into different factors or *skandhas*—the states of consciousness, perceptions, feelings, dispositions, bodily states. (Alternatively, for the purposes of meditation one may contemplate the individual as made up of bone, marrow, pus, urine, synovic fluid, liver, etc., etc.). The destruction of the unitary person by his dissolution into events and factors and the absence of any identifiable eternal self "behind" all these, means that the whole exercise of the maintenance of my individual substance is pointless. In the last resort there is no substance. It is true that by skillfulness in means the Buddhist religion develop an apparatus of god-like Bodhisattvas and the celestial Buddhas: assurance of rebirth in the Pure Land, for instance, is much like the Christian promise of heaven. But ultimately these dreams dissolve—the Pure Land is a kind of prelude to the disappearance of the individual into the ineffable plane of nirvana.

It should be noted that not only is the dissolution of substance a different way of dealing with it than the divine other-worldly enhancement of substance which the Church could mediate through Christ's sacrifice, but it is also predicated on the natural continuance of the individual through an endless round of rebirth (endless, that is, unless liberation is attained). The problem remains that the Buddhist dissolution of substance has to be done without inducing despair and humiliation: it is easy for the sense that there is no ego, that I am after all nothing, worthless, to be a danger to true serenity, for in feeling all that the individual is still playing in the "worldly league". Thus the rituals and festivals of Buddhism and the figures of celestial Buddhas are means of assurance. One must feel that the Buddha is a sure refuge even if in the end he is no refuge, just as one must reign with Christ even though Christ is the servant after all. For all their differences there is a certain congruence between the opposite paths of Christianity and Buddhism. Incidentally the doctrine of rebirth has its own vertigo: by accepting the yearning for continued existence it shows forth an ultimate ennui.

The fact of impermanence, so much emphasized in Buddhism, and the vertiginous threat posed to individual and society when one's death or the death of one' society is contemplated, account perhaps for the vagueness and ambiguity which we earlier noticed in the pictures of future consummations. Very often end-time shares a characteristic with primordial time, of being in a sort of timeless time. They are to time what sometimes uncharted outer regions were to map-makers, places that were non-places, and hence "Here be dragons".

One may of course reject both the Buddhist and Christian pictures and other religious ways of understanding death. Western tradition in bifurcating into two main ideologies beyond Christianity, namely scientific humanism and Marxism pursued the analytic and mythic modes found respectively in Buddhism and Christianity. Perhaps something of the appeal of Buddhism in the modern Western world lies in the fact that it combines compassion with a de-mystification of the person; while Marxism's appeal lies in its powerful recreation of the mythic, substantive mode in a modern age when the anthropomorphisms of Eden and *Revelation* are less serious-sounding than the dialectical ballet of economic and cultural forces. But perhaps it is nationalism above all that has an ideology in the modern world sublimated death most spectacularly. Millions and millions have gone willingly, if nervously, to their deaths out of an attitude that death for one's country is a meaningful act; and refusal to do so is sinful cowardice in which a life is truly thrown away for it has recoiled from the glorious sacrifice that endows the flower of youth with the greatest and most sublime substance.

II

If the question of the meaning of death is at one level bound up with substance, there are also things to be said at the linguistic level. I want to show that only in a metaphorical sense do we face death daily (save exceptionally) and so the bringing of death to bear as a focus of existence (as with Heidegger) represents more a method of meditation.

Though it may be said that we are all dying, since we are moving onwards toward death, which is inevitable at some time or other, it is not so in a more literal sense: for if I were to say that a friend of mine is dying, I would be taken to mean that he or she is now reaching the end of his or her life, through some mortal sickness or the final tiredness of old age. Of course I may turn out to be wrong—what appeared to be the final stage of life may in fact not have been so: the patient was dying it seemed, but recovered. Moreover it is proper to say that a person died fast or slowly, over a long or a short time. Thus dying is a process. Consequently, when people say they fear death, they may in fact have in mind that they may fear the process of dying, which can of course be painful.

But it is possible to undergo death without the process of dying as when a person dies in her sleep. Such a death may be described as peaceful or merciful, but not agonizing, or heroic or otherwise.

Indeed it only makes sense to talk of (for instance) an heroic death in the case of those who in some sense face death: but though facing death may take the form of dying—as someone on a sickbed or on a stretcher during battle—it need not do so, for the soldier may face death throughout a battle without at any time being in process of dying. Of course, someone can face death in an heroic manner without actually dying: only if he dies does he die in an heroic manner, because he faced death in an heroic manner.

Dying, incidentally, is not the same as being in a situation where there is a high probability of death: in some battles there is for each participant such a high probability of dying, but each participant is not dying. Of course, if one is dying there is a high probability of death, since one can only truly say of someone that he is dying if he does indeed end up actually dying or if alternatively he would certainly have died had it not been for some intervention. Thus one might say: "X is dying" means "X is in such a state that if the natural process continues he will actually die".

Since not everyone undergoes the process of dying, either because of dying in one's sleep or being suddenly struck down, and since some people are in process of dying without knowing it, questions of courage, serenity, etc., in the face of death do not always arise, as we have seen. Moreover, though we can continuously take death into account, e.g. by paying insurance premiums, it is not accurate to say, as far as ordinary usage goes, that we are continuously faced with death. This might be true of someone in a peculiarly hazardous occupation, say a motor racing driver; but scarcely of a university professor, even in the riotous sixties.

What then of Heidegger's *Das Freidein fur den Tod?* I think the imperative to reflect upon death, as if we face it daily does represent a kind of meditation. The vertigo which it induces, because it reminds us of the perishing of our social substance and of this-worldly meaning, can be used constructively, in that freedom may accrue upon the willingness to assert a kind of independence—that is, independence of the social rituals and the performatives through which our substance continuously is fed. It may, somewhat paradoxically, form the basis for a new kind of personalism, in that the very emptiness of substance which the vertigo induces can be seen everywhere else—in other persons. We thus begin to see them afresh, not as having status, ability to help or harm us, bewitching beauty, curmudgeonliness or whatever: but rather to see them in themselves. It is in this direction also that a certain rapprochement is possible between Christian and Buddhist models of the human being.

There is, of course, a lot of interest at the present time, through the Hospice movement and in other ways, in helping people who are in process of dying. I do not need to expatiate on this front, beyond saying that while some folk may be prepared for solitude they are liable to suffer through loneliness, for the ebbing of life almost demands an increase in the closeness of friends and relatives.

Death itself is a passage from one state to another: at any rate the dead one leaves society, and it is worth saying something briefly about the concept of mourning. It is in fact an affirmation of the value of the mourner that one expresses sorrow, for sorrow is proportionate to loss, or at least perceived loss. It is thus in its own way a celebration of the individual who has passed away. But the loss is not just related to the individual—but also to the state of his achievements. The death of an old man who has led a full life, mostly happy, attracts some grief, but it is much tempered by the reflection that he has had a goodly ration of life's blessings. The loss of someone very close who is cut off in youth or prime is more insufferable and intensely felt, for there is a loss both of the individual as he actually was and as he would continue to be. We mourn an unfulfilled future. And that sense of loss can easily turn to anger, as if we expect justice in this world.

Perhaps I conclude with a feature of some funerals which may illustrate something of my discussion. It is not uncommon for those who return from the funeral and the burying or cremation of the dead one to have a meal together. It is not uncheerful. Why? The reason lies in the fact that it itself is a kind of ritual, though not fully perceived as such. It is a rite of passage too, during which the relatives and friends return to normal life again. They have previously been in close ritual and emotional contact with death. That itself is disturbing. The cold corpse is symbolically powerful, simultaneously peaceful and charged with a certain fearfulness. Return to normality demands a kind of shaking off of the grief and seriousness.

The more perfunctory it is, the shallower our grasp of death, and the less we have honored the dead one with our grief. Modern technology supplies methods of hurrying the dead on their way, unseen, cosmetic, here today and gone tomorrow. It is a paradox of society which claims to honor the rights of individuals that it often does so little to honor the individuals themselves. Thus from another angle again we see that the dignity of the person can be seen in death. Death causes vertigo in life.

NOTES

1. Arnold Toynbee and others *Man's Concern with Death*(London: Hodder and Stoughton, 1968).
2. R. Ruddock, ed. *Six Approaches to the Person* (London: Routledge and Kegan Paul, 1972): "Creation, persons and the meaning of life."

Alfred Alvarez

Commentary

I want to pick up a couple of central points from the wealth of interesting ones which Professor Smart made in his paper. The comments I am going to make, I realize, since arriving here, are going to be blindingly simple and self-evident to this distinguishsed audience, but you must bear with me.

The first concerns personal death; the second, in a sense concerns general death. I'm worried by a phrase that Professor Smart uses in his paper, but very much avoided in his comments on his paper just now, and that is "substance": the psychological and social accretions which give us some sort of sense of identity and validity. And also about death appearing basically in the process of dying. Now, there's an old saying which comes up continually in Hollywood movies—very vividly, for instance, in that movie "Hud", which was on BBC TV recently—and that is that "Nobody gets out of this life alive." In youth, none of us really believe that. For young people death is not their concern, but later on—and I assume this takes in most of the audience here—in mid-thirties, and mid-forties, etc., it becomes a prime concern. I also think it becomes a prime element in one's emotional, intellectual and creative life. I'm talking really about a phrase invented by the psychoanalyst Elliot Jacques, that is, the "mid-life crisis." By that Professor Jacques meant a period of intense depression which sets in sometime when you are half-way around the tract, when your children tend to be grown up, or growing up, and your parents die. Now, the thing about parents is that they stand, as it were, between you and the ticket office, and once they die there is no one ahead of you in the line. Now, what the mid-life crisis is about is having to accept the fact not only that one's youth is over and won't return, however fervently you jog or press-up or whatever, but also having to accept the emotional reality, not just the theoretical reality, of the inevitability of one's own death.

Now, I think this is probably one of the most difficult things anybody has to do, and it's notable in the arts that there are, relatively speaking, few great artists who manage to negotiate the mid-life crisis, and the ones who do tend to be the very greatest of them. I'm thinking of someone like Beethoven or Shakespeare or Dante or Bach or Donatello. That is, their work, in the later stages, moves into a new dimension. Their later work is richer and better than their earlier work. It's more profound, it's more tragic, it's more reflective, it's more serene. This serenity doesn't come, as Professor Smart suggests somewhere in his paper, from the process of dying, either heroically or through sickness, but from an earlier, a prior acceptance of *the fact of mortality.*

Now, in this context, I think to talk of "substance" is not a way of facing death, it's a way simply of cheering yourself up—that is, of avoiding death. One of the functions of religion, presumably, is to redeem death, as well as to redeem life, but not to have religion does not absolve one from thinking about the subject, and from bringing it into one's life. I think rather the reverse: if you can die with all the consolations of the church, it becomes easier. Those of us who do not have any taste for these consolations are not thereby exempted from having to face actually what has happened, or the reality of what is happening.

What I think I'm saying is that death, either your own or someone else's is basically only meaningful for the living—i.e., for yourself when you are alive—and it is, in a sense, an essential aspect of living.

The second point I want to make is based on a phrase Professor Smart uses, "The vertigo of collective death." The simple fact of the matter is that what Durkheim would have called "altruistic suicide"—that is, heroic death for a cause—is being made obsolete by modern technology, by modern collective society. We now have reached the point where war is more dangerous for the women and the children and the old, who are not fighting, than it is for those who are at the battle front. And the awareness of ubiquitous and arbitrary death, which descends very much like the Black Plague descended on medieval communities—that is, on the unjust and the just, without discrimination, without warning and without reason—is, I think, central to our experience of this century. We've had two world wars to show it, we've had extermination camps, we've had genocide, we've had nuclear and biological weapons, and we have also something we don't automatically think of: we have the fact of the earth itself being shadowed by nuclear weapons, orbiting out there in outer space.

Now what has happened, this vertigo of collective death, which is a phrase of Profesor Smart's I admire very much, means that death itself has become not only another aspect of the omnipresent technology, but it's also become absurd. It's become random, it's become totally disconnected with any personal rhythms or reasons or subtance. The whole psychoanalytic attitude which asserts that somehow or other even a dreadful disease like cancer, for instance, is part of a personality—saints get cancer, they say—that has been removed from us, given the fact of total destruction. I think we haven't really faced this problem. A Hiroshima survivor said, in a phrase I quote several times in my book, *The Savage God*, "There exist no words in any human language which can give comfort to guinea pigs who do not know the cause of their death."

Now I suspect that this is a problem which the arts have been trying to face in this century, and very few of the other disciplines have. And I also suspect that that sense of strain which is common to all the best in modern art of any type, comes from this need to forge, as it were, a language of mourning to cope for the possibility of this collective death.

Ben-Ami Scharfstein

— D2 —
Death as a Source of Philosophy

While we live, we live irremediably, and when we die, we die irremediably too. Of course, not all of us are equally convinced that death is irremediable; but the great variety of escapes from death, none very plausible, that men have conceived, shows that they take the danger to be great, for only a great danger could stimulate the creation of so many intellectually desperate remedies. Desperate or not, the most intellectually interesting of these remedies, or, to speak more neutrally, of these reactions, have of course been those proposed by the philosophers. Who that has studied philosophy does not remember how Plato tried, in the *Phaedo*, to prove the implausibility and even the impossibility of death? Who does not remember how the Stoics hardened themselve against the fear of death and the abhorrence of suicide.

I will not go on and recall the reactions of subsequent philosophers to the fear of death. To do so would be to repeat too much of the entire history of philosophy. I have, in any case, been more interested in the philosophers' subtler, more concealed responses to the fear. In trying to understand how such more concealed responses affect philosophy, I have studied the lives of twenty-two philosophers, beginning with Montaigne. Let me name them, in historical order, not because I hope to discuss them all here, but simply to indicate the range of evidence I have tried to use. The philosophers are Montaigne, Hobbes, Descartes, Pascal, Spinoza, Locke, Leibniz, Berkeley, Voltaire, Hume, Rousseau, Kant, Hegel, Schopenhauer, Mill, Kierkegaard, James, Nietzsche, Santayana, Russell, Wittgenstein, and Sartre. Before I end, I will summarize something of what I have discovered of the reactions of these philosophers to death, which I mean to include the death of those, notably their parents, whose life has sustained and has therefore, in a sense, been synonymous with their own.* To make what I will then say more plausible, I will describe

---

Complete references will be found in my book, The Philosophers; Life and Thought, published by Oxford University Press in 1978.

in what detail I now can, the instance of Friedrich Nietzsche. I choose him because he is interesting in himself and because the evidence relating to him is relatively clear, but not because I suppose his life to be representative of those of the other philosophers except in the very general point I am trying to make.

Nietzsche's father, a country parson, died of what was called "softening of the brain" when Nietzsche was four years old. A few months later, Nietzsche's younger brother, Joseph, died, and Nietzsche was left in a family composed of himself and five women, his mother, his younger sister, Elisabeth, a grandmother, and two maiden aunts.

To judge from Nietzsche's autobiographical writings, the death of his father was a catastrophe that cast its shadow over the whole of his subsequent life, which it divided, as Nietzsche remembered it, into a brief demi-paradise followed by a long period of sorrow and affliction, affliction that became physical no less than spiritual. I will not describe his physical suffering, which he himself describes to his friends with grim eloquence, but concentrate, as my purpose makes necessary, on his suffering from human isolation. "If only I could give you an idea," he wrote to a friend, "of my feeling of *loneliness!* No more among the living than among the *dead* do I have anyone I've felt related to."

As his thought shows, Nietzsche's loneliness expresses his need for his long-dead father and, though he came at times to hate them, for his still living mother and sister. It also shows his constant struggle to gain independence of all of them and of all they represented. When young he had written, "In everything God has led me securely, as a father his weak little child . . . I have firmly decided to dedicate myself forever to his service." His extended and violent attack on this decision shows that he never got emotionally free of it, and his contrary aims were, as he sometimes recognized, analogous and, it seems to me, compensatory. As he once explained, in 1881, to a friend, he had never despised Christianity in his heart. When Zarathustra said of Christ, "He died too early; he himself would have recanted his teaching, had he reached my age," Nietzsche, I think was expressing a fantasy in which his father was Christ who, as such, had come to learn that his son, Nietzsche, was right. But such a fantasy was not an easy one to sustain because it required an identification with suffering and ostracism, and, even beyond this, with the suffering that was caused, not only to the Christians but by them. It was in an access, I think, of such masochism that Nietzsche said, "I do not read but *love* Pascal." The reason he gave was that Pascal had been murdered, body and mind, by Christianity. This means, I take it, that Nietzsche felt that his father, the representative of Christianity that he had been closest to, might somehow have been responsible for his, Nietzsche's suffering. In the face of the death, the pain, and the emotional bondage Nietzsche had endured, he could retain the security of his childhood ideas only as they continued to exist in their opposites. He therefore blamed his troubles on "that damned 'idealism' " that reminded him, it appears to me, of his father and his father's death, for Nietzsche identified pity and self-sacrifice with "the *turning against* life, the ender and sorrowful signs of the ultimate illness."

I have made many assertions in the last paragraph. Let me attempt to cite more of the evidence in their favor, especially in favor of the assertion that the relationship with the father was decisive for Nietzsche's pshilosophy no less than for his life.

First, let me recall some of Nietzsche's aphorisms on father in his early books. These show an ambivalence toward the father, that is, *his* father, not even hinted at his early autobiographical accounts. The aphorism, "If one had no good father, one should then invent one," means that Nietzsche may have understood that he had idealized his dead father, that is, invented him better than he had really been. But the aphorism, "Fathers have a great deal to make up for having sons," says that simply to be a son is painful, and that a father, that is, *his* father, is for that reason guilty. "In the ripeness of life and understanding a man is overcome by the feeling that his father was wrong to beget him," is surely the same attack on the same father (and on himself, the son who ought not to have been born.) Two further, later aphorisms have a perhaps more complex meaning. The first of these is, "Often the son already betrays the father—and the father understands himself better after he has a son." In context, this aphorism means no more than that later generations reveal the potentialities of the earlier ones. Perhaps, however, the words, "der Verrater seines Vaters," carry the associations of betrayal. If such is the case, the aphorism implies the father's self-discovery in the antagonism of the son, who, despite this antagonism, fulfills the father.

The second aphorism says, similarly, "What was silent in the father speaks in the son; and often I have found the son the unveiled secret of the father," meaning that the father, in spite of appearances, could know and come to effective expression only in the son. Here context is unambiguously negative, for the immediately preceding sentence in Nietzsche's text is, "Aggrieved conceit, repressed envy—perhaps the conceit and envy of the fathers erupt from you as a flame and as the frenzy of revenge."

In *Zarathustra* and the *Genealogy of Morals* Nietzsche insists on the blood relationship between himself, or the person or persons in whose name he is speaking, and the priests. Zarathustra, for example, proclaims that the priests are evil enemies. "Yet," he proclaims, "my book is related to theirs, and I want to know that my book is honored even in theirs." Then, significantly for Nietzsche, Zarathustra adds that the priests are meant to live as corpses, that their speech smells of death chambers, and that "whoever lives near them lives near black ponds out of which an ominous frog sings its song with sweet melancholy." I think that this passage reflects the scene of the burial of Nietzsche's father, which he more than once described in the most heartfelt words. The *Genealogy of Morals* lays down that priests are ill and neurasthenic, and that the ascetic priest opposes the healthy person because "the priest is the first form of the *delicate* animal. . ." Then, in the *Antichrist*, Nietzsche complains that "philosophy has been corrupted by theologian's blood. The Protestant parson is the grandfather of German philosophy," as Protestant parsons had been the father and grandfathers of his own philosophy. In the *Will to Power* he again insists on the closeness of philosopher and priest and states that the philosopher aspires to take authority into his own hands. In the abrupt words of his probably unrevised text:

"The *philosopher* is a further development of the priestly

type:—has the heritage of the priest in his blood; is compelled, even as a rival, to struggle for the same ends with the same means as the priest of his time; he aspires to supreme authority."

Ecce Homo records Nietzsche's claim to be defined and set apart from all the rest of humanity by the fact that he has exposed Christian morality. He says, "Blindness to Christianity is the crime *par excellence*—the crime against life." What is most terrible of all, he says, is that "the concept of the *good* man signifies that one sides with all that is weak, sick, failure—suffering of itself," and he immediately exclaims, "Ecrasez l'infame!"

It is in *Ecce Homo*, I believe, that Nietzsche reveals what he has against the father he is never tired of praising, and what he has, therefore, against Christianity and conventional goodness. Here, in *Ecce Homo*, Nietzsche makes the last of the review of his life, still referring with great feeling to the death of his father. In almost the same words he used to characterize the ascetic priest in the *Genealogy of Morals*, he calls him "delicate, kind, and morbid." He then adds, "In the same year in which his life went downward, mine, too, went downward: at thirty-six I reached the lowest point of my vitality . . ." He himself, he tells the reader, is a decadent, but also the opposite, for he has turned his will "to health, to *life*, into a philosophy." He states, "I consider it a great privilege to have had such a father," and he concedes that any other privileges he may enjoy stem from this one. But he adds the fatal qualification, "Not including life, the great Yes to life." He recalls, on the one hand, that his father was responsible for his involuntary entrance "into a world of lofty and delicate things," and, on the other, that there had been a heavy though fair price to pay. He says, "That I have almost paid with my life for this privilege is certainly no unfair trade." He praises the "Incomparable father" who passed on the inability to predispose people against even himself. Soon thereafter, he says, most revealingly, "At another point as well, I am merely my father once more and, as it were, his continued life after an all-too-early death." The open identification with his father is here joined with the sense of recurrence that plays so crucial a role in his thought. Then, further on in the text, there is an astonishing sentence, as if he had suddenly forgotten the paradise of his early childhood, "Altogether, I have no welcome memories whatsoever from my whole childhood and youth." Finally, in the last passage I will cite in this connection, Nietzsche speaks of his admiration for the fact that "precisely at the right time, my father's *wicked* heritage came to my aid—at bottom, predestination to an early death."

The evidence seems to me to be strong. Nietzsche was, in effect, accusing his father of passing on to him his weakness and the possibility of an early, similar death, for which reason he, Nietzsche, would denounce and surpass nationalism, Christianity, and conventional truth and goodness, everything connected with the father he felt so close to. For all these signified the death whose threat to him he had painfully learned to oppose with life and life's values. His father, he had come to feel, had been drawing him, as in a dream he had drawn Joseph, his brother, down to the grave. This feeling, I think, is the nerve of the emotion that animates Nietzsche's philosophy—the simultaneous longing for the father and rejection of him.

It is possible that even the relativity or murkiness of the truth that Nietzsche stresses reflects to complexity of his love in antagonism. The criterion of truth, Nietzsche prefers to believe, may be, not the usual objectivity, but the arousal of feeling, the imparting to thought of the feeling of strength, the feeling of strength being exerted against resistance. In brief, "The criterion of truth resides in the enhancement of the feeling of power." Given his loneliness, his illness, and his fear, Nietzsche was willing to accept as truth whatever restored his pleasure, creative accomplishment, self-esteem, and feeling of power. Truth in this sense often meant the feeling of power given to him by his ability to see sharply and state sharply what he had seen. This power to see and state sharply, this surgical mind and tongue, was largely the gift of his painful, conscious or near-conscious ambivalence. As person and thinker, he loved, moved, and had his being in intelligently and painfully formulated ambivalence. To say this is of course not to give a magic key to his individuality, but it is to stress the degree to which death, his father's catastrophic death and his fear that he might inherit a like death from his father, was a source of his whole philosophy.

At this point I should like to remind the reader that I have dwelt on Nietzsche primarily as an example of how death may serve as a source of philosophy. I should further like to recall the names of the philosophers, beginning with Montaigne and ending with Sartre, that I cited on an earlier page. It is needless to emphasize that each of them is an individual, and that the pattern of Nietzsche's life fits Nietzsche alone. As in the case of Nietzsche, however, it can be shown that death was a source of their thought. Perhaps I should say, death and its antecedents, sequels, and psychological analogues, which include anything felt or perceived to be a threat to life. Consider, for example, the ages at which the philosophers I have named lost their parents. Of the twenty-two philosophers, two had lost both parents and eleven at least one by the age of six. In only six cases both parents survive until the philosopher was fifteen. But the mere survival of parents may not shield children from experiences that are psychologically threatening to life. Schopenhauer was seventeen when his father died; but although he was no longer a child, the circumstances of his life made the blow particularly devastating; and it was the more devastating because his father had appeared to be losing his mind and had, it was believed, committed suicide. Mill was given an unbearable education by a domineering, apparently cold father, and he came almost to despise his mother. James's father had been tragically mutilated and ended his life in a strange form of suicide. Wittgenstein's father could be extremely harsh to his sons—enough, perhaps, to provoke the suicide of two of them and raise the specter of suicide in Wittgenstein's own mind. If these are the facts, only the families of Locke and Berkeley are left to qualify as good in the conventional psychological sense; and Berkeley, it may be recalled, was, for unknown reasons, suspicious as a child, while Locke was at first rigidly disciplined by his father. Death and other painful psychological separations are no doubt common in early life, but it seems nevertheless notable that at least twenty of the twenty-two philosophers may be supposed to have experienced them. They certainly fit the generalization proposed by psychologists that persons of exceptional accomplishment have suffered exceptionally heavy parental loss in childhood.

If I go beyond the philosophers I have listed, I may name

Jaspers as an apparent exception to the generalization I have just made. He praised both his parents, who survived late into their fifties; but Jaspers was cut off from much of life by illness. The once famous philosopher, Hans Vaihinger, is an example of how a sensory defect, like the death of parents, or like severe illness, may affect a philosopher's experience and so his philosophy as well. Vaihinger "wanted to be a man of action," but his extreme nearsightedness forced him into scholarly pursuits. He regarded the contrast between his physical constitution and the way he would like to live as irrational and his defective vision made him sensitive to other frustrating aspects of existence. It seems likely to me that his desire to modify the Kantian categories into something more empirical may have depended on his experience of near-blindness, as may his whole "as-if" theory of life-serving fictions.

Two more summary comments can be made on the philosopher's relations with their parents as threats to life. The first is that a parent's death might leave the philosopher in fear that he had inherited some vulnerability or even death itself from the parents. Descartes feared that he had inherited pallor, weak lungs, and a probably early death from his mother; Kant assumed he had inherited a narrow chest and consequent weakness and hypochondria from his mother; Schopenhauer was preoccupied with the problems of insanity and suicide as the result of his father's strange behavior and presumed suicide; Kierkegaard was convinced that he would die young because of punishment visited on his father; James may have felt his breakdown to be a repetition of his father's; Nietzsche believed that he had inherited madness, perhaps, and an early death from his father; and Russell was haunted by the fear of hereditary madness. The least result of such, usually concealed fear or resentment was a powerful ambivalence, for the parent, the source and support of life, was also felt to be the direct source of weakness and death.

The second comment I have to make on parents as threats to life concerns the philosopher's acceptance or rejection of the idea of God. In my accounts of individual philosophers I have adopted the psychoanalytic view that a child's idea of God is likely to be modelled on its father. That is, it may combine elements taken in any proportion from both parents, but the predominant image in our culture of God as masculine and the formal and often practical dominance of the man in family life has made the association of God with father more natural than with mother. However that may be, it strikes me as significant that the four philosophers, Hume, Nietzsche, Russell and Sartre, who lost their fathers earliest in life are all atheistic or close to it. Hume, to be accurate, seems to have believed in some very remote creator, but his discussion of God is more marked by carefully expressed skepticism than by faith, while Nietzsche, Russell and Sartre are all explicit atheists, but such as miss God badly and say so. The remaining atheists among the philosophers are Mill and Santayana. However, Mill, who considers the possibility of God's existence calmly, and who takes Jesus as the ideal guide for humanity, is an atheist, as he says, out of identification with his atheistic father. The instance of Santayana is more complex, for he was attracted, with his sister, to Catholicism, but both his parents were disbelievers, so that even if they were gods in his childish imagination, they taught him the atheism to which he remained faithful in the end.

About mothers and gods I have only a brief word to say. If we except Russell, because he lost his father, too, quite early, the three who lost their mothers earliest are Descartes, Pascal, and Rousseau. Granted Descartes' strong rationalistic leanings, his choice of what I take to be an irrationalistic God is surprising and may have something to do with the early death of his mother. Pascal's belief in God is so basically irrationalistic that it for the most part excludes itself from the realm of philosophical discussion. Rousseau does argue metaphysically for the existence of a God. But his "Profession of Faith of the Vicar of Savoy," which contains his major attempt to argue so, is not really typical of him, and may have been prompted by a temporary desire to argue like a *philosophe*. What seems more natural to Rousseau is more obviously related to his lack of a mother: an ecstatic identification with the whole of nature, a belief in immortality that allows him the hope to be completely himself, without contradiction, division, or need, and a faith that he is fundamentally a spiritual and moral being. It is possible, then, that the early loss of a mother biases philosophers in the direction of an irrationalistic or more emotionally apprehended God. I raise this possibility hesitantly, but I do not think that the instance of Kierkegaard contradicts it, for reasons that I cannot go into here.

I do not want to be dogmatic in my biographical interpretations; but though I have often felt hesitant in making them, I do not hesitate to conclude that death is directly and indirectly a source of philosophy. Death is often the challenge to which philosophy is the response, sometimes quite openly so. Like sportsmen, philosophers may be of the sort that need to experience great stress. The explanation of the need may be that the mastery of external stress wards off old anxieties, perhaps because in returning from danger to safety one's feeling of safety is renewed. Alternatively, the explanation may be that, to overcome fear, one coordinates one's powers and arrives at an experience so intense that one becomes addicted to it, for it creates a self that at moments measures up to one's fantasies. Both mountain climbers and philosophers may be engaged in exploring their reactions to new exacting experiences and use their sport or occupation in order to explore their own potentialities.

Philosophers are like mountaineers. At least one daring philosopher, Berkeley, had been a daring mountaineer; and I have been told that both Wittgenstein and Popper were mountaineers. It is true that literal mountaineers are rare among the abstraction-prone men we are concerned with; but more than one of them would agree with Husserl when he said that the philosopher's radical search for truth requires him to risk his life in its behalf. For philosophers and other intellectuals, especially the great ones, take deliberate intellectual risks and endanger themselves sometimes even physically in order to arrive at intellectual power and self-mastery that is also, as in the mountain climber, a mastery of the world; and, like the climber, they are often impelled by the fantasy that they will climb a Himalayan peak and survey all existence. The risks they undergo and the price they pay add to their satisfaction when, they feel, they accomplish something intellectual. Wittgenstein therefore respected Russell for having exclaimed, "Logic is hell!" He himself "thought that the measure of a man's greatness would be in terms of what his work *cost* him."

There is much more that I should like to say on death as a source of philosophy, but life (the philosophers say) is short, and I must end. I have tried to be relatively empirical in my remarks. I have used psychology, but without any intention to maintain a psychological determinism. Perhaps I have done little more than repeat in my own factual, prosaic way the moral of an Amerindian legend. According to this legend, the first human pair in existence were granted the possibility of renewing their youth year after year. However, an insidious trickster-like figure persuaded them that to be immortal would be to give up the experience of falling in love, of having and bringing up children, and of growing old in mutuality and wisdom—of everything that gave human life its value. The human pair agreed with the trickster's reasoning and gave up their chance to keep renewing their youth. Later, however, when it was too late, they thought the matter over. "He was right," the man said, "but all the same, I'm sorry." The woman concurred, for he was not only the primal philosopher, but a good, and an honest one. I certainly respect him, as, I think, having heard him, you do. It's wonderful to be alive, but we resist paying the price; and so, among other things, we philosophize.

Joyce Carol Oates

— D3 —

The Art of Suicide

In the morning of life the son tears himself loose from the mother, from the domestic hearth, to rise through battle to his destined heights. Always he imagines his worst enemy in front of him, yet he carries the enemy within himself—a deadly longing for the abyss, a longing to drown in his own source, to be sucked down to the realm of the Mothers. His life is a constant struggle against extinction, a violent yet fleeting deliverance from everlurking night. This death is no external enemy, it is his own inner longing for the stillness and profound peace of all-knowing non-existence, for all-seeing sleep in the ocean of coming-to-be and passing away. . .

Jung, *SYMBOLS OF TRANSFORMATION*

Not only the artist, that most deliberate of persons, but all human beings employ metaphor: the conscious or unconscious creation of concrete, literal terms that seek to express the abstract, the not-at-hand, the ineffable. Is the suicide an artist? Is Death-by-Suicide an art-form, the employment of a metaphor so vast, so final, that it obliterates and sweeps into silence all opposition? But there are many suicides, there are many deaths, some highly conscious and others, groping, perplexed, perhaps murderous, hardly conscious at all: a succumbing to the gravitational pull of which Jung speaks in the quotation above, which he envisions in terms of the hero and his quest, which takes him away from the "realm of the Mothers"—but only for a while, until his life's-energy runs its course, and he is drawn down into what Jung calls, in metaphorical language that is beautiful, even seductive, the "profound peace of all-knowing non-existence." Yet if we were to push aside metaphor, if we were no longer even to speak in a reverential tone of Death, but instead of Deadness—mere, brute, blunt, flat, distinctly unseductive Deadness—how artistic a venture is it, how meaningfully can it engage our deepest attention?

For the "artistic" suicide—in contrast to the suicide who acts in order to hasten an inevitable end, perhaps even to alleviate terrible pain—is always mesmerized by the imaginative act of self-destruction, *as if it were a kind of creation.* It is a supreme gesture of the will, an insistence upon one's absolute freedom; that it is "contrary to nature", a dramatic violation of the life-force, makes the gesture all the more unique. One can   determine one's-self, one's identity, by choosing to put an end to that identity—which is to say, an end to finitude itself. The suicide who deliberates over his act, who very likely has centered much of his life around the possibility of the act, rejects our human condition of finitude (all that we are not, as well as all that we are); his self-destruction is a disavowal, in a sense, of what it means to *be* human. Does the suicide who is transfixed by metaphor suffer a serious derangement of perception, so that he contemplates the serene, transcendental, Platonic "all-knowing non-existence" while what awaits him is merely a biological death—that is, deadness? One thinks of Simone Weil, taking inspiration from an early Christian teaching (later banished as heretical): one may hasten the "decreation" of his or her life by refusing nourishment, and God will not be offended. In fact, "decreating" oneself, in Weil's extraordinary imagination, is a mystic act; it brings one back to God. To Weil the body and its appetites and inclinations were vile, lived out "here below" (to use her phrase), so that any activity that hastened the decreation of the body would necessarily be good. The puritanical consciousness errs initially by imagining a tragic split between the physical self and the spiritual self—as if the spirit were not a function of the organic being in its entirety; the error is complicated by the invention of a metaphorical combat between the two, so that the body and the soul are locked in warfare. *Why*, if the body is God's creation, if its impulses are clearly part of God's design, should the body be treated as if it were a dangerous beast, a creation of the Devil? The "art" of the puritan's suicide is an art badly confused by metaphors taken from inappropriate sources.

In Sylvia Plath's famous poem "Lady Lazarus" the young woman poet boasts of her most recent suicide attempt in language that, though carefully restrained by the rigorous formal discipline of the poem, strikes us as very close to hysteria. She is a "smiling woman", only thirty; and like the cat she has nine times to die. (Though in fact Plath's next attempt, an attempt said not to have been altogether serious, was to be her last.) She is clearly proud of herself, though self-mocking as well, and her angry contempt for the voyeurs crowding around is beautifully expressed:

What a million filaments.
The peanut-crunching crowd
Shoves in to see

Them unwind me hand and foot—
The big strip tease.
Gentlemen, ladies

These are my hands
My knees
I may be skin and bone,

Nevertheless I am the same, identical woman.

. . . .

Dying
Is an art, like everything else.
I do it exceptionally well.

I do it so it feels like hell.
I do it so it feels real.
I guess you could say I've a call.

In this poem and in numerous others from the collections *Ariel* and *Winter Trees* the poet creates vivid images of self-loathing, frequently projected onto other people or onto nature, and consequently onto life itself. It is Sylvia Plath whom Sylvia Plath despises, and by confusing her personality with the deepest layer of being, her own soul, she makes self-destruction inevitable. It is not *life* that has become contaminated, and requires a radical exorcism; it is the temporal personality, the smiling thirty-year old woman trapped in a failing marriage and overburdened with the responsibilities of motherhood, in one of the coldest winters in England's recorded history. Unable to strike out at her ostensible enemies (her husband Ted Huges, who had left her for another woman; her father, long dead, who had "betrayed" her by dying when she was a small child) Plath strikes out at the enemy within, and murders herself in her final shrill poems before she actually turns on the gas oven and commits suicide. If her death, and even many of her poems, strike us as adolescent gestures it is perhaps because she demonstrated so little self-knowledge; her anguish was sheer emotion, never translated into coherent images. Quite apart from the surreal figures of speech Plath employs with such frenzied power, her work exhibits a curious deficiency of imagination, most evident in the autobiographical novel, *The Bell-Jar*, in which the suicidal narrator speaks of her consciousness as trapped inside a bell-jar, forced to breathe again and again the same stale air.

"There is but one truly serious philosophical question," Camus has said, in a statement now famous, "and that is suicide." Camus exaggerates, certainly, and it is doubtful whether, strictly speaking, suicide is a "philosophical" problem at all. It may be social, moral, even economic, even political—especially political; but is it "philosophical"? Marcus Aurelius noted in his typically prudent manner: "In all that you do or say or think, recollect that at any time the power of withdrawal from life is in your hands," and Nietzsche said, perhaps less sombrely, "The thought of suicide is a strong consolation; one can get through many a bad night with it." But these are *problems*, these are *thoughts*; that they are so clearly conceptualized suggests their detachment from the kind of anguish, raw and undifferentiated, that drove Sylvia Plath to her premature death. The poet Anne Sexton liked to claim that suicides were a special people. "Talking death" for suicides is "life." In Sexton's third collection of poems, *Live or Die*, she included a poem characterized by remarkable restraint and dignity, one of the most intelligent (and despairing) works of what is loosely called the "confessional mode." Is suicide a philosophical problem? Is it intellectual, abstract, cerebral? Hardly:

Since you ask, most days I cannot remember.
I walk in my clothing, unmarked by that voyage.

Then the almost unnameable lust returns.

Even then I have nothing against life.
I know well the grass blades you mention,
the furniture you have placed under the sun.

But suicides have a special language.
Like carpenters they want to know *which tools*.
They never ask *why build*.

In Sexton the gravitational pull toward death seems to preclude, or exclude, such imaginative speculations as those of Camus, *that* death is desirable is never questioned. There is a certain mad, perverse, rather wonderful logic to Dostoyevsky's Kirilov as he reasons through the necessity for his suicide (for, by defeating the life-instinct, he will become God—he will be the first man in history to become God), but Kirilov's reasons would be incomprehensible to someone with the temperament of a Plath or a Sexton—"born" suicides, we might say, because their myth-making propensities are so narrowly circumscribed as to exclude the larger social, political, historical world which so intrigued Camus and Kirilov. (Indeed, Kirilov hints in one of his long speeches that his suicide may be a consequence of his realization that Jesus Christ was *not* the Son of God, but only a mortal human being like himself, doomed to extinction.)

Of course there are the famous suicides, the noble suicides, who do not appear to have been acting blindly, out of a confused emotional state: there is Socrates who acquiesced courteously, who did not choose to flee his execution; there is Cato; Petronius; Jesus of Nazareth. In literature there are, famously, Shakespeare's Othello, who *rises* to his death, and Shakespeare's Antony and Cleopatra, both of whom outwit their conquerors by dying, the latter an "easy" death, the former an awkward, ghastly Roman death, poorly executed. Macbeth's ferocious struggle with Macduff is a suicidal gesture, and a perfect one, as is Hamlet's final combat with the enemy most like himself in age and spirit. The Hamlet-like Stavrogin of Dostoyevsky's monumental *The Possessed* worries that he may lack the "magnanimity" to kill himself, and to rid the world of such a loathsome creature as he (and he *is* loathsome, even in the context of the *The Possessed)*; but he acquires the necessary strength and manages to hang himself, a symbolic gesture tied up clearly with Dostoyevsky's instinct for the logic of self-destruction as a consequence of modern man's "freedom" (i.e alienation) from his nation. (Stavrogin does not love Russia. He does not know Russia. The idle son of a wealthy landowner, he has not had to work; he has travelled in Europe, and elsewhere in the world, as a curiosity-seeker; so detached from common life is he that in order to feel anything at all, even so ordinary an emotion as fear or disgust, he must experiment along debased, sadistic lines. His suicide is a political act far more significantly than it is a private, subjective act: it is clearly paradigmatic and prophetic.)

Is the subjective act, then, nursed and groomed and made to bring forth its own sort of sickly fruit, really a public, political act? "Many die too late, and a few die too early," Nietzsche says boldly. "The doctrine still sounds strange: *Die at the right time!*" Nietzsche does not address himself to the less-than-noble; he is speaking, perhaps, not to individuals at all but to trans-individual values that, once healthy, are now fallen into decay, and must be hastened to their inevitable historical end. The fascination with Death in its romantic aspect, stimulated, if we are to believe the early novel *Confessions of a Mask*, by an obsessive contemplation of certain morbidly rendered illustrations of the martyrdom of St. Sebastian and other Western, Christian, comely martyrs, emerges into a rather flamboyantly public and political guise in the work and life of that extraordinary Japanese writer Yukio Mishima, who committed ritual suicide as a gesture of his despair over and his contempt for the "degenerate" spiritual condition of contemporary Japan. Faulkner's Quentin Compson, his father's son in a number of respects, appears to insist upon his sister's loss of honor in order that his suicide be justified: *The Sound and the Fury* must rank with *Moby Dick* in terms of its tragic scope, its exploration of the doomed linkage between a society given over to marketplace values and its most sensitive protagonists, but Quentin's powerful section, which details with fastidious attentiveness the young man's last day of life, is a rhapsody of Death itself, Death quite apart from social or even familiar implications, Death as sheer lyric metaphor.

If until recent times death has been a taboo subject in our culture, suicide has been nothing short of an obscenity: a sudden raucous jeering shout in a genteel gathering. The suicide does not play the game, does not observe the rules; he leaves the party too soon, and leaves the other guests painfully uncomfortable. The world which has struck them as tolerable, or even enjoyable, is perhaps to a more discerning temperament, simply impossible: like Dostoyevsky's Ivan Karamozov, he respectively returns his ticket to his creator. The private gesture becomes violently and unmistakably public, which accounts for the harsh measures taken to punish suicides—or the bodies of suicides—over the centuries. It is possible to reject society's extreme judgment, I think, without taking up an unqualified cause for the "freedom" of suicide, particularly if one makes sharp distinctions between kinds of suicides—the altruistic, the pathological, the metaphorical self-murder in which what is murdered is an aspect of the self, and what is attained is a fictitious "transcendence" of physical circumstance.

For instance, can one freely choose a condition, a state of being, that has never been experienced except in the imagination and, there, *only in metaphor?* The wish "I want to die" might be a confused statement masking any number of unarticulated wishes: "I want to punish you, and you, and you"; "I want to punish the loathsome creature that appears to be myself"; "I want to be taken up by my Creator, and returned to the bliss of my first home"; "I want to alter my life because it is so disappointing, or painful, or boring"; "I want to silence the voices that are always shouting instructions"; "I want—I know not what." Rationally one cannot "choose" death because Death is an unknown experience; and perhaps it isn't even an "experience"—perhaps it is simply nothing; and one cannot imagine nothing. The brain simply cannot fathom it, however glibly its thought-clusters may verbalize *non-existence, negation of being, death,* and other non-referential terms. There is a curious heckling logic to the suicide's case but his initial premise may be totally unfounded. *I want to die* may in fact be an empty statement expressing merely an emotion: *I am terribly unhappy at the present time.*

Still, people commit suicide because it is their deepest, most secret wish, and if the wish is too secret to be consciously admitted it will manifest itself in any number of metaphorical ways. No need to list them—alcoholism, accidents, self-induced malnutrition, wretched life-choices, a cultivation of melancholy. The world is there, the world *is* not awaiting our interpretations but unresisting when we compose them, and it may be that the mere semblance of the world's acquiescence to our metaphor-making brains leads us deeper and deeper into illusion. Because passion, even misdirected and self-pitying and claustrophobic, is always appealing, and has the power to drown out quieter, more reasonable voices, we will always be confronted by the fascination an intelligent public will feel for the most skillfully articulated of death-wishes. Listen:

> Life, friends, is boring. We must not say so.
> After all, the sky flashes, the great sea yearns,
> we ourselves flash and yearn,
> and moreover my mother told me as a boy
> (repeatingly) "Ever to confess you're bored
> means you have no
>
> Inner Resources." I conclude now I have no
> inner resources, because I am heavy bored.
> Peoples bore me,
> literature bores me, especially great literature,
> Henry bores me, with his plights & gripes
> as bad as achilles,
>
> who loves people and valiant art, which bores me.
> And the tranquil hills, & gin, look like a drag
> and somehow a dog
> has taken itself & its tail, considerably away
> into mountains or sea or sky, leaving
> behind: me, wag.
>
> (John Berryman, Dream Songs, #14)

My thesis is a simple one: apart from circumstances which insist upon self-destruction as the inevitable next move, the necessary next move that will preserve one's dignity, the act of suicide itself is a consequence of the employment of false metaphors. It is, as the quotations from Berryman, Sexton, and Plath indicate, a consequence of the atrophying of the creative imagination: the failure of the imagination: not to be confused with gestures of freedom, or rebellion, or originality, or transcendence. To so desperately confuse the terms of our finite contract as to invent a liberating Death when it is really brute, inarticulate Deadness that awaits—the "artist" of suicide is a groping, blundering, failed artist, and his artwork a mockery of genuine achievement.

Section E:
Contemporary Images of Salvation

— E1 —
Redemption Today: Back to the New Testament?
Etienne Trocme

— E2 —
Marx and the Question of Salvation
Maurice Boutin

Etienne Trocme

— E1 —
Redemption Today:
Back to the New Testament?

It is sometimes claimed that the idea of redemption is old-fashioned and should be discarded as a useless relic of the Dark Ages. This is a rather naive view of things as they are today. As a matter of fact, contemporary thinking is familiar with the idea that men must and can be redeemed from this or that form of slavery or, if one prefers, alienation. Whether we like it or not, many doctrines of Redemption hold a powerful sway over the minds of the men of our time.

To take but a few examples, Marxism may be a scientific approach to social problems, as Marxists are prone to say and as is at least partly true. But its emphasis on alienation of the proletariat and on the price to pay in order to achieve a classless society in which all will be free makes it at core a doctrine of Redemption. Freudian psychoanalysis is about in-built alienation of the individual and the freedom that can be regained through long and costly efforts. The ideology of Progress, in its various forms, is based on the painful discovery that mankind is a slave to ignorance, bigotry, poverty or illness, combined with the faith that education, science, development or hygiene will redeem it ere long.

The struggle against colonialism or racial discrimination or dictatorships of all types aims at ending slavery and bringing about at all costs a future of freedom. Anarchism considers all forms of power as evil because they deprive men of their birthright as free agents and enslave them. It provides a doctrine of liberation under which the sacrificial violence of a few brave ones is the way of redemption for the masses. As for all the "back to Nature" movements which attract widespread support in Western Europe, they consider society as a victim of industrial growth and the slave of technocrats. Redemption will be achieved when zero growth restores freedom.

All these doctrines of Redemption have some common features, although they diverge widely on many points. First of all, they are *doctrines*, that is systematic theories which are expressed in speech and made to be taught. The redemptive process begins with the teaching of the doctrine or of some elements of it to the alienated slaves. Of course, action is often part of this process, as the Marxist emphasis on *praxis* shows. But this action is based on the doctrine and has to be constantly explained and commented upon, which means that it is really an occasion for making the doctrine known. A terrorist's act, a strike, an anti-nuclear demonstration contribute nothing to the redemption of man unless the spoken or written word gives it meaning for those to be freed.

Once these people realize that they are alienated and that redemption is on its way, it is the common belief of the supporters of the various doctrines that they will change. Instead of accepting their fate, they are expected to start fighting toward liberation, thus making a contribution to the redemption of themselves and of others. Conscientization opens the way to freedom or revolution.

The final goal of the redemptive process varies of course. But it can be described in all cases as reconciliation. The inner tensions and contradictions of man will be totally overcome in the end. The conflicts and misunderstandings which beset social life will disappear. The struggle for physical survival and the careless destruction of nature which for so long meant war between Man and the Universe will give way to Peace.

It comes as no surprise, against this back-drop of popular doctrines of Redemption, that many religious thinkers and leaders of our day have their own brand of Redemption to offer to an alienated mankind which longs for freedom. This is of course not new, but has become more noticeable with the coming of mass migration, air travel and the mass media. The new religions of the nineteenth and twentieth centuries, each in its own way, all aim at redeeming men from some form of slavery or alienation, which is sometimes seen in the life of individuals and sometimes as the fate of a whole people or even of mankind. From Mormons to Christian Science, from the Baha'i faith to Kimbanguism, from the Cargo cults of Melanesia to the Black Muslims of North America, in spite of all the differences between the various groups, the basic pattern is the same: alienation, redemptive doctrine, a new freedom, the hope of final reconciliation in this world or the next.

When religion is borrowed from an exotic culture in which it has had deep roots for a long time, the idea of Redemption often comes to the foreground rather more than it did in the country where this religion has its home. South American Protestant sects and African Christianity are good examples of this striking change of emphasis. So are the various brands of Hinduism and Buddhism established in the West, although they preserve their identity: meditation and the techniques that lead to it are welcomed as ways of liberation from the bustle of industrial civilization and from Western over-preoccupation with the self. Instead of redemption from the slavery of sin, it is redemption from the prison of an oppressive culture.

Other religious movements that place the doctrine of Redemption at the heart of their teaching are to be found among groups which try to bring back the past splendor of their religion as they imagine it. Revivalism, with its strong emphasis on personal salvation, is the best example of that tendency. On the Catholic side, some reactionary splinter groups like that of Bishop Lefebvre in France and some conservative movements combine extreme respect for tradition with an understanding of the church as a redemptive institution that gives its full strength to the famous saying: *Extra Ecclesiam nulla salus.*

Is there a basic difference between these religious doctrines of redemption and the philosophical and political ideologies which we discussed earlier? Of course, metaphysical premises are in most cases less visible in political theories and the eschatological bliss announced by religious leaders tends to be more boldly mythical than the far future promised by secular thinkers. But both categories of doctrines are made up of widely diverging theories and in each group many a doctrine of Redemption is closely akin to this or that theory of the other group: no one denies that Marxism is related to Jewish Messianic hope and to Christian Millenarism; there is a narrow connection between the struggle against racial discrimination in the United States and the movement of the Black Muslims; etc. . . . In other words, all the doctrines of Redemption we have been discussing are structurally similar and are answers to the same feeling of alienation and to the same longing for liberation.

Some people, particularly among Christians, may feel uneasy about this conclusion, "What," they might say, "about the doctrine of

Redemption of mainstream Christianity? The tradition of the churches, whether Eastern or Western, whether Protestant or Catholic, has a lot to say about this basic tenet of the Christian faith. Can all that be reduced to a mere variant of a vast body of contemporary ideas about the liberation of mankind from every form of slavery?" True enough, Christian tradition has given much attention to the question of man's Redemption. Far-reaching divergences between Churches and between theologians arose throughout the centuries on that difficult point. Extensive and frequently heated debates were held at various stages and led to growingly complex conclusions. It was unanimously agreed, among Church leaders and theologians, that a correct interpretation of Redemption was one of the keys to orthodoxy, even though they could not agree on what that was.

This is not the place to give an account of these debates and of the results they reached. A few examples will be enough. At the end of the Dark Ages, when all the subtle debates of the fourth and fifth centuries had been forgotten, theologians tended to equate the Redemption of men by Christ with the payment of a ransom to the Devil. This highly mythological understanding of the Crucifixion was subjected to searching criticism by eleventh and twelfth century thinkers like Anselm of Canterbury, Abelard and Bernard of Clarvaux. After much debate, Peter Lombard attempted a synthesis which accounted for the redemptive effect of the Cross of Christ in sacrificial, juridical and moral terms. This rather shapeless compromise became the basis of later orthodoxy, but theologians tried again and again in the following centuries to reach a clearer definition of Redemption. In spite of their efforts, the doctrine of the Atonement retains to this day a number of mythological features borrowed from past civilizations: quasi-magic effect of sacrifice, sacredness of blood, etc.... This makes is difficult to use in our scientific age.

But if we leave aside these antiquated elements, which do not belong to the core of the Christian doctrine of Redemption, there is a striking similarity between this doctrine and the other religious, philosophical and political teachings discussed earlier. Alienated man, enslaved by sin, can be redeemed if he hears a message; his life will then be changed and the hope of final reconciliation will give meaning to his daily behavior. The only substantial difference is that the Christian Gospel refers to an historical event, the life and death of Jesus of Nazareth, and insists that this even comes to life every time the redeeming message is preached. Is this a minor oddity, which leaves Christianity a part of the numerous army of the redemptive doctrines? Or is it more significant?

*　*　*

It might seem at first that the similarities are weightier than this difference. The Christian doctrine of Redemption appears so central in the Christian religion that it could easily be said to be its core. If it is, Christianity is basically a redemptive teaching, like Marxism or Buddhism, and the unusual feature we discovered in its Gospel means little. But what if the Christian doctrine of Redemption is a late outgrowth that followed the pattern of other redemptive teachings for the most part? Could it then be that when it refers to the life and death of Jesus it lets something of an older structure show through later accretions?

These questions may seem strange. But if we go back to the classical age of the Ancient Church, before the Dark Ages, we find that Christian theology had not really room for a doctrine of Redemption. Of course, the idea of the Atonement is present occasionally in Athanasius and Gregory of Nyssa. But the Greek Fathers from the fourth to the eighth century emphasize far more the doctrine of the Incarnation of the Son of God, which restores human nature and leads to its divinisation. As to the Latin Fathers, they make no real attempt at systematization of the various concepts and metaphors (Salvation, liberation, resurrection, redemption, ransom, atonement, etc. . . .) used in early Christian tradition to describe the work of Christ. Augustine is the best example of this eclectic and haphazard use of earlier materials. Neither the Greeks nor the Latins feel the need for a coherent doctrine of Redemption, whereas they make great efforts to build a well-balanced body of teachings on the person of Christ and the Trinity. To the Christian thinkers of that age, Christianity is first and foremost an account of the Jesus event.

The same is true of their predecessors of the first three centuries. The struggle against Gnosticism, that perfect example of a
religious movement centered around a doctrine of Redemption, led
some of them to stress very strongly the importance of the Cross
of Christ as a redemptive act (Origen, for, instance). But their
writings deal with Redemption in bits, when an occasion arises.
They use the word and the concept along with a number of others
as a description of what they consider to be absolutely central: the
historical achievement of Jesus Christ, seen as part of God's plan
for mankind (Irenaeus).

In the New Testament, none of the writers gives pride of place
to the idea of Redemption, whereas Justification is central in
Paul's interpretation of the work of Jesus Christ (See Romans,
chap. 1 to 5) and the concepts of Priesthood and Sacrifice are the
core of the understanding of Christ's mission in the Epistle to the
Hebrews. Of course, words like *lytron lytosis, apolytrosis* occur a
fair number of times in various books of the New Testament. But
their meaning is very pliable and depends greatly upon the context
(For instance, *apolytrosis* applies to different things in Romans
3/24 and Romans 8/23.) What is even more striking is that their occurrences are scattered and isolated: the best example of this is the
lonely use of *lytron* in Mark 10/45. In other terms, the theme of
Redemption is a minor one in early Christian thought, although it
has deep roots in the Old Testament. None of the other concepts
used to interpret the work of Christ or his death and resurrection
can be said to be central in the writings of the New Testament.
They are all attempts at accounting for a set of events which the
kerygma narrates without an interpretation. Apart from the
repetitive assertion that it all happened "for us," this narrative is
the whole Christian message as preached by the apostles and
evangelists of the first century.

Having reached this conclusion, we are driven to admit that
later Christian doctrine differs greatly from its early form. Instead
of a narrative, a theological theme has become central. The Jesus
event has receded into the background and the doctrine of
Redemption has come to the forefront. This *theologoumenon* has
grown so large that it is the tree that hides the forest of genuine,
original Christianity. If so, Christianity is basically different from

the doctrines of Redemption alluded to earlier. But then, has it anything to offer to modern man, who is attracted toward these doctrines by his longing for a better, freer life? In order to answer that difficult question, let us try to state in contemporary terms, but as accurately as possible, what the early Christian *kerygma* is about.

As it is not possible at this time to engage in full-scale research on that topic, a well-chosen example will be enough. Rather than trying to reconstruct the *kerygma* from what is left of it in the various New Testament writings, we shall start from the four Passion Narratives as we find them in the Gospels. This can be done because, in spite of some later accretions, these narratives have close similarities between them and all go back to a very early common archetype. The wording of this archetype is beyond our reach, but its outline is visible and is enough to perceive its meaning.

The Passion Narratives emphasize very strongly the fact that the events they relate are entirely according to God's will, as announced by the prophets and stated by Jesus himself. What is happening is the fulfillment of God's eternal plan, both as a whole and in every detail. God's action in history, as illustrated in the Old Testament, reached its apex in the life and mission of Jesus, whose sufferings, death and resurrection are part of his God-given mission. Thus, God's action ends in complete failure on the Cross, out of the Creator's own decision. This bold paradox is at the heart of the early Christian *kerygma* and must be kept in mind as we proceed.

The disciples of Jesus, constantly his companions and co-workers so far, are progressively pushed aside as the narrative goes on: still present at the Last Supper, they recede in the background in Gethsemane, run away when their Master is arrested and play no part in the events that follow, apart from Peter who denies his Lord. This may be due to the weaknesses of these men, but it is also part of God's plan: Christ goes to his death alone and his disciples are spared. They resent it, but it cannot be helped, because they are not destined to share in their Master's Passion. They have to attend the awful destruction of the one who carried all their hopes and cannot even die with him.

Worse still, they are compelled by their Master to accept responsibility for his death. This is the meaning of the story of the Last Supper, if we look at it squarely. What the disciples do when they eat bread and drink wine on that occasion as commanded by their Master is a symbolic action similar to those of the Old Testament prophets. For instance, Hosea or Jeremiah make strange gestures or take strange attitudes at times, because God instructs them to do so in order to illustrate their message and prefigure the future events they announce in their preaching. As a matter of fact, the prophet's actions are a proleptic part of the acts of God he has to predict. They get the process started and vouch for the fulfillment of what has been prophesied.

By calling the bread his body and the wine cup his blood at the same time as he tells his disciples to eat and drink it, Jesus turns a most straight-forward act into a deed of cannibalism. As the disciples proceed to do as they are told, their behaviour takes an ominous meaning. The death of their Master is no longer a future event they have just heard about. It becomes a divine action which they are implicated in and contribute to bring about. No guilt is attached to their acts, as in the case of Judas, but they are certainly responsible for the Cross.

This would be crushing if the death of Jesus was the end of the story. As is well known, it is not. The failure of God's action in history is complete, but it is made good by the Resurrection of Christ, which turns boundless disaster into an unexpected and paradoxical triumph. This is not the place for studying what early Christianity meant by the Resurrection. It will be enough to say that when Christ rises from the dead, this does not concern him alone. This event is part of the general resurrection of all believers and has both immediate and delayed consequences for all men.

For the disciples of Jesus, the four Passion Narratives stress that their life was transformed when they were confronted with their Risen Lord. Whereas they were weak and had to be dragged into action before their Master's death, they became at once brave witnesses who were not afraid of facing death and thus achieved great things (see the Book of Acts). As was the case with God himself and with Jesus, they had plunged deep into failure before taking the path to a victory which was a radically new type—humble triumph. These changed men had accepted the death of the One who carried all their hopes and had sealed his fate by their symbolic action. Now, they enjoyed a new life as a result of their being closely associated with the Risen Lord.

This story of failure and triumph was meant as a narrative. As such, it was dated and localised in a precise way: under Pontius Pilate, in Jerusalem. But the Resurrection and its consequences ensured that this distant event had an echo in the life of men of all times and all places. A sign of this was the outpouring of the Holy Spirit on many Christian gatherings and congregations. An even more convincing sign of the permanent value of the Passion narrative was the constant repetition of the Last Supper in Church meetings. The apostle Paul gives us a most interesting clue when he quotes the narrative of that meal in the Upper Chamber as a norm for the common meals of the Corinthian Church (I Corinthians 11/23-26). Even in a distant congregation which cared little about what was done in Palestine, the Eucharist could be described as a commemoration and repetition of the Last Supper. In other words, just as the Jews throughout the ages are taken back to the days of the Exodus each time they celebrate Passover, Christians celebrating the Eucharist were taken back to the eve of Christ's Passion and found themselves placed in the same situation as the disciples of old; by their symbolic action of eating the body and drinking the blood of the Lord, they accepted his death and contributed to its taking place.

This understanding of the Eucharist may have been largely forgotten in later ages. It was never completely lost sight of. The same would be true of the outpouring of the Holy Spirit. As a result, Christianity always retained its nature as an historical religion. Of course, the doctrine of Redemption came to the forefront. But, largely thanks to the presence of the four Gospels in the New Testament, some room was left for the theme of Christian life as a closely-knit union with Christ Jesus. If Christianity is to make its distinctive contribution today, might it not go back to its origin and restore this favorite idea of Paul (*en Christo i*) to its central position? It would thus avoid being just one more doctrine of Redemption struggling to look different from the many others. It would be itself. And it would offer to the men of our time the key to a changed and fruitful life, which is what they need and long for.

Maurice Boutin

— E2 —
Marx and the
Question of Salvation

It is commonplace to state that man's salvation is central for Karl Marx, though the topism of salvation, i.e. the locating of it within a given system, Christian or Marxist or whatever, is at least with regard to Marx himself, a matter of discussion and dissent. On the other hand, it is commonly agreed that salvation belongs to the religious dimension of man and relates directly to redemption as well, as the decisive issue in both parts of the biblical tradition. Accordingly, it is spontaneously taken for granted that the Marxian view of man's salvation focuses on the classless society predicted by Marx and Marxism, once have taken place the radical transformation of industrial capitalism and the disappearing of the dictatorship of the proletariat that should characterize the period of transition towards communism. We should then understand Marxism as a peculiar, yet crucial, version of a secularized christianity.

This approach to Marxism does not avoid cliches according to which Marxism gives up the reference to the Kingdom of God expected for the future and dreams of the "great evening" when communism will be celebrated as the end of man's bestial prehistory, i.e. our present history, and the dawn of an age really human. While maintaining biblical teleology, Marxism opposes biblical religion precisely because it brings an inversion of prospects within the same topism of salvation, of course without any obligatory mediation of the biblical God.

Thus Marxism is viewed mainly from its atheistic angle which should not be minimized. Yet, the overemphasis on Marxist atheism often copes with a mere repetition of what biblical religion claims to be. It gives rise to the strengthening statement that Marxism is able to give what religion only promises. Such an alternative soon turns out to be nothing but sterile; it gives no opportunity for a sound self-criticism, and furthermore it stands aloft from what is at stake when the question of salvation arises:

neither the pledge for or the denial of an ideal of God, nor the "criticism of heaven" (which Marx considered globally achieved), but reconciliation of men with themselves and with reality as the very core of human salvation.

Salvation demands a severance from the present order of things. It requires therefore a critical analysis, not merely a global rejection, of industrial capitalism in its beginning period (for Marx) or in its later form (for us). This does not mean that criticism is the key issue here; obviously, it wasn't for Marx either. But it means that "what now is" cannot be presumed as already known simply because it is experienced in daily life. Likewise, the search for absolute values cannot be determined by "what should be," and ignore "what now is." The quest for values could lose some of its ambiguity only if the predominant value in industrial capitalism providing a world-wide shaping of human reality today is re-evaluated. Otherwise this predominant value would be reinforced by the absolute values searched for, which would stand in glaring contradiction with the very search for them.

If the search for absolute values is considered nowadays necessary, in my view it is because industrial capitalism hinders man's achievement. At the same time we cannot simply withdraw from it. In any case, it would be useless to keep declaring that industrial capitalism is going to go bankrupt in the near future. This is not primarily a reference to the historical development in the West over the last two centuries in which period industrial capitalism overcame various crises. Industrial capitalism, as we well understand now, broadens indeed its encroachment on men more and more *qualitatively*; in fact, it extends measurement on qualitative matters according to an increasing tendency towards higher quantification. Living on its own crises, industrial capitalism generates them in a kind of permanent revolution that adds to its inner complexity. Naturally the question of salvation is set aside, and at the same time it is made more provoking.

My approach to the Marxian question of salvation tries first of all to situate the topism of salvation in such a way as to avoid that the discussion on Marx ends before it really begins. Man's

salvation must be located, it seems to me, in the most fundamental contradiction, where useful value (Gebrauchswert) and exchange value (Tauschwert) constitute a polar but contradictory unity. In this way, the very tension between human activity and men's
being, which is characteristic of industrial capitalism according to
Marx, is brought out.

The following step stresses the production process, with reference
to Marx' "Critique of Political Economy" published in 1859, and to
"The Capital" the first book of which was published in German in
1867. It is a well known fact that the opening part of "The Capital"
is not easy to understand and that it is largely responsible for the
misunderstanding of the method used by Marx, as he himself points
out in the "Postface" of the second German edition in 1873; for instance in 1868 the French "Revue Positiviste" objects to Marx' too
metaphysical treatment of economics, and in 1872 Illarion I. Kaufmann points out in the "Europaischer Bote" (published in St.
Petersburg) the clinching differences between Marx' "realistic"
research method and his exposition that would be unfortunately
"German-dialectical"— In this second part of my paper, I cannot
present an overall analysis both of the various distinctions of labor
worked out by Marx, and of useful value as a major reference for
him, though useful value, according to the French sociologist Jan
Baudrillard, did not draw Marx' attention sufficiently. We could indeed take Marx' own judgement on Aristotle as he formulates it,
and say: Marx' genius lies precisely in stressing the fundamental
importance of the production process; however, the historical limitation of industrial capitalism of his time prevents him from making a
thorough analysis of useful value, an urgent task for us today.

As a third step, I refer to a statement on religion in the first book
of "The Capital," chapter 13 on "Machinery and Big Industry." As
far as I know, this statement has been almost completely ignored in
debates on Marx' understanding and critical evaluation of religion,
until quite recently. There are two main reasons for the still rare interest in this statement. First, in his earlier period Marx deals with
criticism of religion more explicitly than he does later on. Second, in
his first works Marx expresses himself more directly in
philosophical terms and therefore stays closer to categories familiar
to philosophers, theologians, and scholars interested in religion. Yet,

a greater emphasis on this statement could free us from simply repeating the Marxist criticism of religion or the refutations of it. Perhaps discussions on Marx' understanding of religion would be then more fruitful as they are now.

I

I suggest that Marx' dialectical understanding of human reality moves within three circles closely related to one another. One must stress the first circle in order to get a deeper insight into what salvation is all about. In other words: the dialectical view of historical development towards communism, i.e. the third circle, though important in itself, can no longer be in the forefront *in this question.* As already referred to, the reason is that it does not help to tackle the question of salvation directly enough; it even draws away from it quite often.

The third circle has to be based on the second circle referring to the gap between reality as experienced by men and reality itself. It is therefore necessary to question interpretations and experiences of the process in which we are involved today. This questioning makes out the very essence of science, for the possibility—and necessity—of science is only given because of such a gap.

For sure, this second circle is so familiar to us that mentioning it appears rather like running against an open door. Moreover, referring to it does not make Marx' complex analysis of reality easier to handle. Marx himself pays careful attention indeed to this second circle insofar as he repeatedly urges criticizing of any attempt to substitute one's own ideas and representations to reality itself. One example of this, out of many others found in Marx' works, helps to get to the core of his main concern. It is taken from the chapter on "The Trinitarian Formula" (i.e. capital-profit, soil-ground rent, labor-salary) in "The Capital." Here once again, Marx blames political economy for doing most of the time nothing else than translate in a doctrinarian way, systematize and defend apologetically what men, caught in the capitalist production process as they are, spontaneously stand for. On this occasion he has the remark that all science would be indeed superfluous if the appearing form and the very essence of things would coincide directly.

The question is then the following: what lies beyond or beneath industrial capitalism *as it appears* in exchange value predominant in it? For there is no way of identifying truly relevant values for men of today unless we consider why industrial capitalism gives place to ideal values and relates them to generalized exchange value. But in doing so, industrial capitalism covers up its very essence, so that men are doing things without really knowing what they are doing, so that men do not know what they do, but nevertheless do it, as Marx keeps on saying in "The Capital."

This leads to the first circle in which values, either economical or ideal, must be situated: the dialectical relationship between men's being and human activity. Here, special emphasis must be placed on the production process which, in industrial capitalism, is radically subservient to generalized exchange process. What does it all mean for men's own being in terms of salvation?

II

The answer to that question, we may think, depends on what kind of values we acknowledge *besides* exchange value. However, the distinctions within the realm of predominant exchange value itself is more important here than taking for granted that economic values are of course different from other values, idealistic or religious or whatever, and that we should worry only about the latter and let economists take care of the former to the best of their ability under the present circumstances.

Even if we agree to consider more closely the influence of exchange value, we should not forget that exchange value itself is something "ideal" (Marx says "ideell") and that the distinctions exchange value generates are *not mere reflexive ones.* We may of course distinguish useful value from exchange value and consider, as Marx does, useful value as the support for exchange value. We may notice that Marx refers here explicitly to Aristotle who said that there is a twofold way of using things: in their natural property—and hence as necessary, useful or enjoyable things, and as exchangeable things. We may even recall that English writers of the seventeenth century often spoke of "worth" when they meant useful value, and used the world "value" for exchange value. This would correspond, according to Marx, to the proper spirit of the

English language which likes to express the *immediate* thing in a germanic way and the *reflected thing* in a romanic way.

But all this is not the core of the question. The distinctions we have to look at pertain mainly to production process as the basis for exchange process in its other principal elements: distribution, circulation and consumption. These elements are also parts of production process itself, for they all are differences within a unity that has, as Marx says, an organic character, i.e. in which the different moments interact. Consumption for instance is not only necessary for men to keep themselves alive; it is also considered by Marx as an important aspect in production process, since human activity does not create out of nothing, but only through transformation, which implies the consumption of materials and instruments in working activity itself. Capitalists consume the work power of workers by letting them consume, i.e. transform materials into products presented as necessary, useful or enjoyable. According to Marx, the production process must be viewed, however, as prevailing over distribution, circulation and consumption because it specifies to the last extent their mutual relationship, and because it is the only way for analysis to reveal the real contradictions and hence to achieve more than a mere dialectical balance of concepts.

For our purposes, it may be useful to pay attention to the qualitative and quantitative aspects of the whole process in which men's being and activity are involved, for it is a distinction that Marx oftens refers to in his analysis of industrial capitalism.

What does Marx understand here by quality? Quality does not refer primarily to the inherent specificities of exchangeable products at the final station of exchange process: consumption, but which products fall out of the process and satisfy what is really felt, or only considered, as human needs. If the possible loss of quality on the extensible line of equivalencies within exchange process has to be denounced, it is not in the way consumers would do and it is not because it could be a paying business to produce and sell things that are more perishable, and that consequently keep up and intensify the dynamism of exchange process. Of course, we are reminded of the quality of products especially when quality is missing. For instance when our car is eaten away by rust more and sooner than normally expected. But this is not the way Marx looks primarily at quality. He understands it in terms of what the production process requires from workers involved in it: not only useful things to be produced, but also how workers produce them, the circumstances and the specific conditions in which workers do perform their work. Quality pertains therefore to the very relation of working activity to the workers' being itself. The word "quality" will be used in this sense in the following.

Marx does not take quality "in se" as the direct object of his analysis of exchange process. He concentrates on the intricate ways by which quality gets a contradictory, and yet real existence, by which it is hidden, easily forgotten and thrown out of the various metamorphoses of products and of work itself within exchange process.

Exchange process needs for its functioning a "comparability" of exchangeable products that is at least conventionally accepted. It calls for equivalency and measurement, for a quantification of quality, for quantity as a *common quality* of what is going to be exchanged. Thus exchange process presupposes not only a diversity of products and a diversity of working activities. The mere existence of such a diversity had to be given forms by which products will be represented: more and more developed and flexible forms, up to the stage where these forms get enough autonomy as to give the illusion they would move all by themselves, thus making out of exchange process a goal in itself, out of exchange a processual, self-propelling value. This is for Marx no timeless possibility. The conditions for this high development are historically given only in industrial capitalism, though this development involves—and deeply transforms—the previous forms of trade capitalism and of usurer capitalism, and of course an adequate development of circulation process, especially of money as the *first* appearing form of capital, but by no means its very substance that it is to be seen rather in "plus-value" process.

Exchange process as it goes on does not reveal directly and explicitly its contradictory forms. It does not reveal that it cannot be separated from what is not immediately exchangeable, from quality in production process for instance. Quantification as the fundamental or basic requirement for the functioning of exchange, as the intricate process of making up a common quality, a fictive but nevertheless commonly accepted equality, as a precondition for exchangeability, has to reduce quality into quantity, to represent abstractively quality through quantity. Quantification at all stages of exchange process is essentially a *reduction and abstraction* process. With special consideration of working acitivty, the English language allows a useful distinction here, as Friedrich Engels says in a marginal note to the fourth German edition of the first book of "The Capital" in 1890: human activity that creates useful values and is qualitatively determined can be called "work" in opposition to "labor," whereas human activity creating value, i.e. exchange value, and measured only quantitatively can be called "labor," in opposition to "work."

This marginal note is not a superficial remark made by Marx' closest friend and cooperator whose clarification of Marx' thought and exegesis of Marx' works are sometimes questionable and are also more explicitly put into question occasionally in recent years. Marx himself acknowledges that even Ricardo's analysis of value, which he considers as the best one available in his time, and of course political economy in general, never distinguish explicitly and with clear consciousness between human activity as it expresses itself in exchange value, and human activity as it expresses itself in the useful values of its products. Political economy, he says, does of course consider human activity sometimes quantitatively, sometimes qualitatively; but it does not care about the fact that the mere quantitative distinction between various working activities presupposes their qualitative unity or equality hence their *reduction* to abstract human activity, to quantity as a common quality. Political economy, he adds, cannot succeed in finding out the very form of value giving products an exchange value. The main reason, according to Marx, is that the value-form of products is the most abstract, and still the most general form of the capitalist way of producing and is therefore a particular or specific way—consequently a historical and not eternal and natural way—of social production as it develops in money form, capital form etc., in the final form of generalized equivalency: money.

Work as intrinsic part of production process geared to exchange process builds up value, but it is no value in itself. It has value only as quantified work, i.e. if it is reduced to labor, like products which must have not only a useful value, but also be exchangeable in order to enter into exchange process. Labor, therefore, makes abstraction of quality inherent to working activity which cannot be expressed, or is not considered as being presentable, in quantity as the common quality necessary for exchange process.

This should not mean, however, that quality does not exist at all within working activity! It simply means that quality is at least considered as falling out of the scope of value elements in exchange process. Yet, the shifting of quality out of exchange process must be accepted, and even interiorized, by men involved in this process, if the increasing of mediating elements occurring in the historical development of exchange process is going to be tolerated by them. This happens through a shift of the very relation to man's own being, to their being as consumers. While products are more and more diversified and all kinds of sophisticated services are offered to men, men have to be convinced that use of these is for them the most adequate way for reaching self-achievement. They have to be convinced that consuming activity is for them the best way of relating to their own being and that working activity is not, though it is still necessary for exchange process. Working activity is looked at not as relating to men's own being, but as a means to provide the possibility of consuming as the necessary link to one's own self-achievement.

This is the answer to the question how quality in working activity is going to be saved (!) while set aside from the scope of exchange value: the reduction and abstract transformation of quality into the common quality of quantity leads to a radical change in men's relation to their own being, to a shift of this relation from working activity to consuming activity. In consumption as the final station of exchange process where products fall out of this process in order to satisfy needs, be they real needs or be they felt as needs because of stirred up desires, men are going to achieve their own being.

Consuming activity is presented as the ultimate goal for men. But it is *not* the final goal of exchange process itself. The final goal of exchange process is—itself, i.e. exchange for exchange's sake through the activating of consumption as self-fulfillment of men's being. In order to be its own final goal, in order to keep up and activate its process, exchange has to give men consumption as their ultimate goal. Exchange process becomes a kind of automatic subject, a value in itself and for itself. We may call it with Marx a *processual value*.

Marx agrees to the statement saying that in affluent society there is nothing superfluous. This statement is true and false at the same time, i.e. in different respects. With regard to consuming activity it is false. But with regard to exchange as a processual value it is true. Nothing, in fact, should exceed the self-activating goal of exchange process, even if on the one side exchange process presupposes an equality between exchangeable products, and on the other side this equality is properly a nonsense when exchange process becomes a processual value. For where equality is, there is no profit, and hence no self-activating of exchange. As a processual value exchange lives on its own contradiction that makes out its very reality.

If we do not accept the statement on the non-superfluity in affluent society *in its truth*, if we only have in mind the visible conditions of affluence in our present society, we will never get to the processual value that rules our own existence. How can we then go on searching for absolute values, if we cannot re-evaluate the processual value by which exchange value and useful value undergo an inner transformation within the development of industrial capitalism? Will then the absolute values we are searching for really exceed processual value that causes the shift of men's relation to their own being, if working activity is not coming at the same time to the fore? Can we forget that most of the consumers have also to work, besides consuming, and that working activity is not simply a means for providing exchanges of products and for integration within exchange process through consuming? Can we forget that working activity not only implies the transformation of other elements belonging to production process, but also brings about a transformation of men's own being, as Marx points out?

These questions may easily come up when we accept Marx' invitation to have a look at the hidden place of production on whose door is stated: "No admittance except on business"—of production that hides even more than its very place. If we do accept this invitation, it is not because we dream of a romantic going back to a natural stage in which, like Defoe's Robinson, one is happily reduced to consume only what he directly produces; it is because arguing *from* the objective and self-evident situation of affluence does not help seeing what exceeds it in another way than a mere idealistic one.

III

Man's salvation must be located today in the twofold shift I already spoke of. For sure, biblical tradition focussing on redemption as the very clue to man's salvation gives us *no program* of whatever kind for a radical transformation of the fundamental contradiction causing this shift. It also gives us *no adequate instrument* for analyzing this contradiction. The Bible does not give either the *answer* to the question of salvation *as it arises today,* for it cannot be *identified* with the Word of God as salvation event.

Marx also does not give the answer to the question of salvation, and even "The Capital" cannot be handled as a recipe-book for the cooking of the future. At times, the young Marx did describe the stage of classless society in the future, for instance in "The German Ideology" (1845/46): but he refrains from it in his later works.

However, Marx' dialectical analysis of human reality brings a deeper understanding of industrial capitalism and helps situate the topism of salvation. Marx shows how today's situation should be analyzed, at least in terms of a re-evaluation of exchange as a processual value, and he indicates in "The Capital" what the scientific method, as he understands it, should be with regard to religion:

Technology, he says, reveals the active behavior of man towards nature, the immediate production process of his life, of his vital relations in society and of the intellectual representations coming out of them. Even a history of religion that makes abstraction of this material basis is—uncritical. For sure, it is easier to find through analysis the terrestrial core of the religious fogginess, than to do the contrary: to develop out of the specific and real vital relations their heavenly forms. The latter is only materialistic, and hence scientific method.

If I understand correctly what Marx says here, this means at least three things. First, a scientific method with regard to religion has to deal with the immediate production process of life in specific and real situations *as revealed* through technology. This should not be understood as if one has to take technology as the starting point; shortly before the text I have quoted, Marx says that the critical history of technology he regards as necessary does not yet exist. Second, the immediate production process of life cannot be merely referred to as that one which makes possible a critical analysis of religion; this would be too easy, Marx ironically remarks. Third, the immediate production process of life has to be considered as the starting point within which religion could develop. Neither religion, nor the "material basis" itself should be considered as laying out of—and thus giving sense to—an approach to religion that could be deduced from them. One has to take as an object of investigation *the developing itself* or its move within the "material basis," and be recalled at the same time that the vital relations he investigates do not coincide directly with their appearing forms.

If religion emerges from within the specific and real vital relations between men, then the important thing is not, according to Marx, what men think of themselves or how they feel about it, but what these vital relations are—and should be, in order that man's salvation becomes an always new reality.

PART II:

Religious Responses to Modernization

F The Persistence of Religious Aspects of Experience

G Comparative Religious Responses to Modernization

H Religion and Science: Convergent or Divergent Definitions of Reality

Section F:

The Persistence of Religious Aspects of Experience

— F1 —
Aspects of Religious Consciousness
Edward A. Robinson

— F2 —
Introduction to Eugene P. Wigner's 'The Existence of Consciousness'
Eileen W. Barker

— F3 —
The Existence of Consciousness
Eugene P. Wigner

Commentary
R.J. Zwi Werblowsky

Edward Robinson

— F1 —

Aspects of the Religious Consciousness

What do we mean by "the religious consciousness"? The question should not be hard to answer. After all, we speak of 'political consciousness', 'racial consciousness', even 'aesthetic consciousness' without leaving serious doubts as to what we are talking about. Those, for instance, who are 'politically conscious' are aware of current political issues. Unlike many of us, they don't go about in a state of indifference amounting almost to unconsciousness where political questions, which may in fact affect us deeply are concerned. So perhaps with the religious consciousness. Maybe we should think of it as a particular direction of awareness, that of those who turn their attention, take a particular interest in religious questions. Thus common usage seems to endorse the idea that different forms of consciousness can be distinguished by the different areas of human concern that they are directed to. A well-known educational psychologist once declared that religious thinking was really no different from any other kind of thinking; it was simply 'thinking directed towards religion'. Can we not simply define the religious consciousness in this way?

It would save a lot of trouble. And this method may work in establishing boundaries, e.g. between the various sciences which for practical purposes are differentiated by their subject matter. With the religious consciousness, however, the process must be reversed. The whole area of thought and feeling that goes by the name of religion is in fact no more than the expression of, the product of, the religious consciousness. This is the irreducible datum. and all religion is derived from it. Religion may in fact be a universal phenomenon in all human societies. But even more universal in every individual human being is this consciousness, this capacity for experiencing life which is properly to be called religious.

Recent advances in physiology and psychology have revealed the apparently simple notion of consciousness to be as complex and many-layered as a Danish sandwich. The investigation of its various levels and the study of the techniques and formulas which enable us to move from one to another now occupy the attention of whole university faculties devoted to this single subject. The kind of gear-change that was once automatic can now, it seems, be controlled by anyone who has mastered the system. States of ecstatic contemplation that were once thought to be the gift of God are now apparently, thanks to our new technology, found to be at the disposal of man. Somewhere here, then, we can surely find the key to the nature of the religious consciousness.

Silence is necessary to music, both in its composition and in its performance. Silence may indeed be most significant in music, but it is the music itself that gives it that significance. I have a friend who practices the traditional art of Batik. In this she must start with a plain white piece of fabric. The purity of the cloth is as necessary to the subsequent picture as the silence is to the music: each is a necessary condition, not a sufficient one. This cloth she then throws onto the table, seemingly at random. In the patterns made by its fall she often finds the source of her ideas or, to use an old-fashioned word, her inspiration. But again, the throwing of the cloth is not by itself sufficient. Chance is in fact much cultivated by some modern artists. But the nature of chance is a much more mysterious subject than at first appears. Luck favors the prepared mind, not the evacuated consciousness. Christianity is not the only religious tradition that warns us against clearing the mind of distractions without having any positive purposes to put in their place. Among our modern technicians of altered states of consciousness too the bad trip is a well-authenticated phenomenon. So we must receive with great caution the suggestion that any particular condition of mind or level of awareness is more closely related to the religious than any other. Nor can we exempt from the charge of irresponsibility those who claim that by following their formula, whether psychological or chemical, we shall ipso facto come any nearer to the attainment of enlightenment, the Kingdom of Heaven or any other spiritual goal whatever.

We shall not, then, gain any better understanding of the religious consciousness either by trying to define its objects or by analyzing the mental or physical circumstances with which it may be associated. Let us try another approach.

To be conscious means to be aware of one's surroundings, to know what is going on. It means to be capable of *response*. Response is a word much used by psychologists; it is correlated with *stimulus*. This often leads to an abuse of language. Worms for example do not respond to a stimulus; they react. Response is a specifically *personal* form of reaction. Human consciousness includes the capacity in us to respond to our experience. A great deal of the time of course we do no more than react. And any human lives rise little above the animal level for long periods. Material comfort can make us insensitive. Yet to those who have eyes to see and ears to hear life is continually putting questions. Our experience again and again demands a response of us. Some experiences in particular seem to *address* us in a peculiarly direct way: in them we encounter a demand to which we are required to respond, though being at the same time free to reject it; a demand which we find it most natural to describe in the language of personal relationships.

It may seem at this point that I am using language that implies a theistic interpretation of religious experience. But I am not trying to smuggle in a surreptitious theology. I am just observing the way people describe their experience. People like this, for example:

> After this experience I knew, as Walt Whitman expressed it, that there was more to me than was found between my hat and my shoes. It was up to me to find out more about that MORE; and so, as I see it, my miniscule will was linked up with the will that our forefathers called God. I don't know what that power is, nor do I call it God. But by it I live, and in my slow, often frustrated effort to learn means of communication with it I grow inch by inch into a person more nearly resembling a human being than was ever imagined by me to be possible.

This could, I suppose, be described as representing no more than a kind of elevated humanism. Others might see it as leading a good deal further. Accounts such as these, and I could give countless parallels from our files, are admittedly open to criticism on the charge of vagueness; also they are highly personal. Sooner or later someone is going to use that specious word 'subjective'.

It cannot here be emphasized too strongly that the habit of thinking in terms of the opposition between subjective and objective is the source of nothing but muddled thinking and psuedo-scientific prejudice. All our experience, without exception, has elements of both the subjective and the objective. It is particularly unfortunate to describe religious experience as subjective if by this it is implied that it is 'all in the mind' or has no reference to any external reality, because this is exactly what those whose spiritual experience is most obviously authentic will most explicity deny. If we want to learn, we have got to learn to listen. Here is a girl of twenty:

> I remember moments of utmost depression when I felt completely alone and useless, wondering why on earth I was alive. . . . About a year ago I suddenfly felt as if I'd had my answer. It was an overpowering feeling of joy and strength. Hell, I didn't *want* to believe in anything; it was against all my intellectual convictions, and yet it satisfied my aspirations. For the past year I've doubted, I've searched, but my attempts to deny it have on-ly led to a realization that for me this power is the only thing that matters. I have a growing sense of reality, and personal identity, which comes from being united to something more powerful than myself, something that is helping me to be what I want to be, what I think I should be like. It's as though I'm at the beginning of my true development; it's like an evolution in the individual life of man.

As to the quality of imprecision or vagueness that seems inseparable from these accounts, this may be given a more positive value if we adopt a less rigidly Cartesian approach. "The sum total of religion," wrote Schleiermacher, "is to feel that, in its highest unity, all that moves us in feeling is one; to feel that aught singular or particular is only possible by means of this one." One of the things that makes it peculiarly difficult to speak with precision about the religious consciousness is just this *universal* quality in it: there is no aspect of life that can be excluded from it, or from which it can be excluded. There are no experiences, however apparently trivial (and I shall come back to that point later) which may not, for a particular person at a particular moment in time, be felt to be of "religious" significance. Furthermore, if a religious experience is meaningful, it is the *whole* of life that it gives meaning to—the whole or nothing. And this is why, in those dark moments when belief is no longer possible and all light is drained away, it is the whole of life that becomes dead and pointless, and nothing, literally nothing, seems worth doing any more.

Another way of describing this absolute aspect of the religious consciousness is to say that it is concerned with the transcendent. This word is much overworked these days, since it is one of the few remaining concepts that can serve without embarrassment to describe that mysterious side of life that lies beyond our finite horizons. And this is literally just what it means: that which lies beyond. But it is more important that this word should not be appropriated by those whose experience takes them far beyond the reach of our common everyday consciousness, to plunge them straight into the heart of eternity, the presence of God or however they may describe it. I myself lived for many years in Central Africa, one of those tribes, the Bemba, has a rich store of traditional wisdom embodied in proverbs, often homely, almost always poetic. One of these makes my point here aptly. "The arrow flying through the sky," they say, "is only hunting: when it falls to earth it has come home." So with ourselves: however lofty the flight of our speculations, our visionary aspirations, this earth of ours remains our home, for the present at least. So this word transcendent, for all its sublime connotations, is also the word for the humdrum (but no less vital) awareness that the horizon is not just the limit of what you can see; it is also the beginning of the unseen; for the sense that today is not just another day soon to be added to the long line of the past; it is "the first day of the rest of your life."

It is not, however, my intention, as I hope will soon become clear, to reduce the religious consciousness to something explicable entirely in terms of everyday common sense, or to evacuate it of all mystery. Very much the opposite. For if we feel that the world as we know it in our everyday lives does on the whole make sense, what need is there for religion? Religious questions do not begin to arise until people start feeling that *life does not by itself make sense,* until they have some sense of its (and their own) incompleteness, until they feel that there is a larger whole of which their own mundane experience is only a part, and that that whole has another dimension of which most of the time our normal human consciousness remains unaware. This is why, to anyone with a wholly secular outlook (which means most people these days, at least in the West) there is something nonsensical in any sincere account of religious feeling or experience. But we should not be surprised at this. One of the most genuinely characteristic elements in any profound religious experience is *paradox*. In fact many of the most penetrating spiritual insights seem to involve quite impossible contradictions, anomalies of logic that have led mystical writers again and again to describe their experiences as ineffable. Yet it is this *coincidentia oppositorum* as Nicholas of Cusa described it, that is one of the surest guarantees of spiritual authenticity.

And not only of authenticity but also, absurd though it must seem, of practicality, because, to those who have once experienced it, *this is what life itself is like*. Insist above all on logic, and all sorts of things become quite impossible. But learn to *live* with unanswerable questions, with seemingly insoluble problems, and they emerge in the end as the very key to the whole mystery. You may remember how in *The Brothers Karamazov* Dostoevsky contrasts the intellectual Ivan who cannot accept life without first finding consistent meaning in it with his brother Alyosha who simply believes in "loving life above everything in the world." "Love life more than the meaning of it?" asks Ivan. "Certainly," Aloyshal replies "Love life regardless of logic, and only then will one understand the meaning of it."

So I propose in the rest of this paper to consider some of the many ways in which this element of paradox emerges in human experience as we open ourselves up to a religious view of the world, or, to use another of Schleiermacher's telling phrases, to "a life in the infinite nature of the whole." Of course these various anomalies and contradictions are themselves only consequences of the central paradox, which is man himself—that curious creature whose life is at all points subject to the finitude of space and time, of birth and death, yet who can at the same time both conceive and experience infinity. I am also aware that there is nothing new under the sun, and that much of what I say will be familiar to those who are at home with the mystical traditions of any religion. Yet these are not truths which, once established, can be passed on from one generation to another. They are truths that must be perpetually rediscovered.

"To feel that all that moves us in feeling is one". This is apt enough as a description of the final state or goal of the religious quest. It does not tell us so much about the means by which we are to achieve it, or the ways in which the individual may relate to that unity. Schleiermacher was, of course, well aware of these questions, but rather than describe his own analysis (which is, in fact, at least as acute and profound as those of many more fashionable psychologists of religion) I should like to quote briefly from the accounts of one or two of the large number of our correspondents who have themselves reflected on that feeling of oneness and their own response to it. In certain traditions that unity is commonly sensed as so overwhelming that the total absorption of the individual is the only possible result. In the West, however, this surrender, this merging with the Whole, is more commonly accompanied by an enhanced awareness of individuality rather than a loss of it.

> For the first time in my life I felt completely and vitally conscious of everything that was going on about me. I seemed to be pulsing with a new and hitherto unexperienced vitality, and to feel completely effective and master not only of my own destiny but of the entire destiny of the universe. Yet I, as an individual ego, no longer had any substance: I was part of the process of creation. I felt a sense of complete fulfillment and yet of complete security, and the only way I can describe it is to say that I felt I was part of God, part of His purpose and His eternal creative activity.

By mundane standards, of course, this sort of thing makes no sense at all; yet it is common for our correspondents to insist that experiences such as these have been the most meaningful of their lives. Here I should like to make a distinction between "sense" and "meaning" which I hope you will not feel stretches the natural use of these words too much. If a thing makes *sense*, I take it that it is internally consistent, or that it relates satisfactorily and intelligibly to other things at its own level so that they all as a whole make sense together. If we are speaking of an activity, it will be one that has a visible end which in turn determines the means by which is to be achieved; means and end will be parts of a single process which once completed leaves no loose ends. To say that something has a *meaning*, on the other hand, is to say rather more than this, because meaning is always related to something *beyond* the meaningful object, concept, activity or whatever. Adopting this distinction one may say that life does not make sense but may still be meaningful. This would further imply that what makes it meaningful is some factor not to be found in life itself but in some way lying beyond it, i.e. transcending it. Now we have a special word for activities that make sense on their own terms but have no meaning external to themselves; we call them *"games."* To the question, then, "Is life a game?" the religious man will answer "no." (The secular man may also want to answer "No," but can he then give a good reason for his answer?) Here I think of Pascal's remark about the last step of reason being to recognize that there are many things that lie beyond it.

Here is another correspondent who describes in similarly paradoxical language another such "timeless moment", a "glimmer of understanding" in which "the door of eternity stood open". She concludes:

> My own part, however limited it might be, became in that moment a reality and must be included in the whole. In fact, the whole could not be complete without my own particular contribution. I was at the same time so significant as to be almost non-existent and so important that without me the whole could not reach fulfillment.

Absorption of the ego into the whole and at the same time the intensification of the sense of individuality—this particular paradox sheds light not only on the nature of any close human encounter but also on the question of the responsibility of the individual not to abdicate his own judgement in relation to the demands of any religious organization that demands his or her loyalty. Like all paradoxes it cannot be solved in general terms but only held in suspension in the life of each one of us, its two seemingly incompatible elements as mutually essential as the positive and negative leads of an electric battery for the production of light and energy.

There is one further point of interest about these two accounts which I have just quoted. The essence of the experience described in each (as fuller quotation would bring out) is remarkably similar. Yet the circumstances in which each occurred could hardly have been more different. The second writer is recounting an experience she had as a child, sitting in the grass outside her home and watching a colony of ants; while the first is describing an episode in his late adolescence when he lay in a coma after a car accident, when he had been driving off in an alcoholic haze to visit his girlfriend. A study of the various triggers or conditions that may set off or give rise to moments of religious insight shows that there is no circumstance however slight or seemingly trivial that may not touch off an experience of the most profound significance to the person concerned.

And this brings me to William James, a writer whom no student of the religious consciousness, at least in the English speaking world, can long ignore. Let me say at once that he is a man for whom I still have enormous admiration, and affection too. The sheer gusto of his writing, his irreverence for established ideas and his psychological penetration never fail to delight me. All the same, I feel a considerable ambivalence about his overall influence. One of the things that makes him so compulsively readable is the richness of his illustrative material. But it is just here that we must be on our guard. When one studies the whole range of experience which men and women have at one or another in their lives found most significant, the moments they look back on as having made most difference to them, the things that really set them thinking, doubting, questioning—these often have little or nothing of the dramatic or sensational quality that you find again and again in James' examples. Not that his material is inauthentic; but is it typical? He himself never makes such a claim.

"I sought my documents," he says, "among the extravagances of the subject." He believed, that is, that religious experience could best be understood by the study of its extreme forms. And so he deliberately selected cases that were most one-sided, exaggerated and intense. So I think it is largely due to James that religious experience is often thought of as being something striking, something clearly distinguishable from the common run of everyday experience; there must be in it some unmistakable confrontation with Reality, an encounter loaded with a powerful emotional charge. Thus people talk of "a religious experience"; it is quite an event.

Of course there are people whose life-patterns are like this, like a staircase with its treads and riser: progress is either horizontal or vertical, with nothing in between. For others, perhaps the majority of us, no such clear-cut model applies. Typical of these is the man who writes, "I have never had anything that I could call a religious

experience, but throughout my life I have been increasingly
aware. . ." and he goes on to tell a story that at first sight seems
quite lacking in episodes of any special interest. But the significance
of the seemingly insignificant is a common theme in the teaching of
all religions. The Bible is full of telling examples: the still small
voice, the one coin lost, the single sparrow that falls to the ground.
That great French writer, Jean-Pierre De Caussade, comes back
again and again to this thought:

> The marvels of God's activity which delight us when we read about them
> only serve to make us bored with small happenings around us. Yet it is
> these trivialities, as we consider them, which would do marvels for us if on-
> ly we did not despise them. We are so stupid!

Here, then, is another paradox. Not only do our most important
insights often seem to have no direct relation to the circumstances
that gave rise to them, but these circumstances may often be, I
would say generally are quite commonplace, part of the
unremarkable and sometimes even degraded fabric of our daily
lives. This is why any truly religious view of life calls for a reversal, a
metanoia. We are here in this conference concerned with "The Re-
evaluation of Existing Values". Our secular culture encourages us
to impose our own estimate, our own pattern instead of learning to
listen, to watch and to wait, to learn what each of us has it in him or
her to become, to discover the shape given to each life, a gift that
can be accepted but is so often just not recognized; a shape within a
unity which ultimately confirms the significance of each individual
component.

This is the seventh annual Conference on the Unity of the
Sciences. What unity is this? One which we believe in some sense
already to exist, or one which we hope by these discussions to bring
nearer? In Europe in the Middle Ages such a unity did indeed exist
under the authority, freely accepted, of Christendom. I do not
myself look back with nostalgia to a culture in which theology was
queen of the sciences. But I do believe that reality can be seen as
one; and that that vision of unity is always going to have about it
something of this paradoxical quality that I have noted as a distinguishing element in the religious consciousness. That is to say, it

will be a harmony achieved out of conflicting opposites. And this surely is true to our experience. I am not thinking of the often opposing views of reality presented by different branches of science. Even within one single discipline the real breakthroughs are always made by people who recognize and even welcome anomalies, not by those who find them a source of irritation because they upset some pivotal conviction. A distinguished scientist once said to me, "All my discoveries were disappointments at the time."

But whereas the sciences these anomalies are resolved in the discovery of a larger unity in which each conflicting element is found to have its essential place, it is a characteristic feature of the religious consciousness that no permanently satisfying resolution of the paradoxes can ever be established. It is, after all, a presupposition of all science that the universe does make sense, or will ultimately be found to do so. But to the religious view, man's reach will always exceed his grasp. There will always be moments of vision in which all questions fall away. But these, it seems, are a gift; a gift, furthermore, that is not transferable. And this brings me to my final point.

I start by suggesting that any attempt to define the religious consciousness, to confine it to a particular area of human experience for convenience of study, will always break down because of its universal and essentially unpredictable nature, which may often emerge in highly paradoxical forms. One such anomaly, I said, was the need for each generation to rediscover for itself the truths of its own tradition. I should like to end by reflecting a little further on this point.

It is my conviction, for which I can offer no precise evidence, that the processes of human history, perhaps of all evolution, are subject to a pattern of ever-accelerating change. Consider the almost motionless stability of ancient Egyptian culture in the second and third millenium before Christ. Since then each succeeding civilization has run its course a little more quickly, until now, like an asymptotic curve which starting from the horizontal is now approaching the vertical, the pace of change in human affairs becomes increasingly bewildering each successive year. You may know the riddle of the water-weed which for hundreds of years has been slowly growing over the surface of a lake, doubling its area each day. It now covers half the water; how long will it be before it covers the whole?

The conflicts of age and youth, of experience with inherited tradition, have always been with us. They provide the most familiar theme in human history. What is so special about those of today? Simply this: this intensified rate of change has also enormously increased the distance that must now be spanned, the conflicts that must be reconciled.

Men do not just need religion, they need *a* religion. More precisely, they need *their* religion. There is a growing feeling in the West that if you don't like the religion you have got, well, you can always try another. The resulting welter of experimentalism is familiar to us all. This is a tragic delusion. The religious tradition of any culture is as integral to it as the chemical composition of the bloodstream is to the life that it sustains. To change the metaphor, the roots of all our language, our art, of all our values, are to be found in our religion. Most of the time we may be unaware of this. We may even be tempted at times to think that those roots are lifeless. If this were so our situation would be even more desperate than it is.

To this extent I am a traditionalist. But what is it that keeps a tradition alive? One thing alone: its capacity for growth, for change. Unless it is ready in every generation to be refashioned, more than that, to be broken up, to be atomized beyond recognition (in its outward forms at least) no tradition can pass on its inheritance alive. This is the age-old truth, the supreme spiritual paradox, that to live you must die. And never, in these dizzying times, have the demands of this paradox, to find new life out of the ruins of the old, been more daunting, or the need to face them more urgent.

There are two tragic alternatives: that in the search for new forms of life the tradition will be recklessly cast aside, the old wisdom lost, or, that faced with a chaos that seems only destructive, the keepers of tradition will seek to preserve the forms at the expense of the spirit, so disinheriting the present in the name of the past, and this in the name of external truths which are only eternal in so far as they are delivered from the process of time, not embalmed, or imprisoned, within it.

These are two alternatives; there is a third.

We meet here as guests of an organization that has taken "Unification" as its distinctive aspiration, its password. It is not for me, a stranger, to suggest what is meant by this. But I know what it could mean: "to feel that in its highest unity, all that moves us in feeling is one; to feel that aught single or particular is only possible by means of this one." It is because I share this hope that I have been glad to accept the hospitality of the Unification Church; and it has been in this hope that I have drawn your attention to these particular aspects of the religious consciousness.

Eileen Barker

— F2 —
Introduction to
Eugene P. Wigner's
'The Existence of Consciousness'

Professor Wigner, Doctor twenty-one times, needs, to use a well-worn phrase, no introduction. I am however going to spend a couple of minutes introducing his paper. As this has not yet been written out, I asked him last night what he was going to talk about and he was dismayed at my inability to make sense of what he was telling me. It soon however appeared obvious that most of my misunderstanding stemmed from our having different presuppositions (he the physicist and Nobel Laureate and I a sociologist and social philospher) about the meaning and scope of certain key concepts. But by now Professor Wigner had become worried lest there be others as uncomprehending as I, and he suggested that I should break into his talk whenever I became confused. This I do not want to do as I feel certain that we all want to hear what Professor Wigner has to say in its entirety, without interruption. I have however agreed to introduce his talk with a brief summary of how he resolved my initial difficulties last night.

The problem arose when Professor Wigner told me that he wished to say that physics should cover all that the life sciences cover at the moment, and that the study of human action itself should eventually become part of physics. But, he also insisted, he was not a reductionist.

This, it seemed to me, was invoking his famous Hungarian bird—which is capable of being in two places at once. *Either* one accepted that there were properties (potentialities and constraints) that emerged as one reached the more complex phenomena studied by the biological and social sciences *or* one thought these could be translated or reduced to a lower level of description. While such phenomena would certainly have to be *"allowed"* by physics, I could not, as a sociologist, accept that they could be described by physics alone without the use of variables which would help us to differentiate the world which physics allowed and which *did* occur, and the world which physics allowed and apparently did *not* occur. In the study of social phenomena, I argued, one either believed that one had to take into account such variables as historical contingencies, cultural beliefs and institutionalised structures—or one believed that these could be reduced to the world of physics. I could not see how physics could describe social phenomena *without* recourse to reductionism.

Now let me try to trace Professor Wigner's answers to my confusion.

To begin with, he told me, he was not a reductionist because he did not believe that subjective feelings and things like happiness could be reduced to physics. Here I supposed that he was referring to the kind of subjective phenomena that Sir John Eccles, following Popper, would refer to as World II. I took it that Professor Wigner shares with Sir John a dualistic perspective in which there are two kinds of reality—(1) that belonging to World II which could not be reduced to physics, and (2) the rest of the natural world, which could be so reduced. In other words, Professor Wigner's denial of reductionism meant that one cannot translate subjective feelings into physics—a proposition with which I heartily concurred.

But even if we accepted the dualism (which I was not sure I did, but which I had no difficulty in understanding) I was still left with a problem. How did Professor Wigner feel physics would help us in a study of, say, the Boer War, or the ICUS?

Professor Wigner next explained that I was making a mistake in assuming the physics that he was talking about was physics as it is now. Perhaps, he added, he should not be talking about physics but about science in general. That science in general (so long as it was not tautologically defined in terms of physical science) should cover what the life sciences are now studying seemed to me entirely acceptable, involving no necessary problem of illegitimate reductionism. There was only one question that remained. What was science? Science, Professor Wigner told me, was not a body of explanations. It was a body of descriptions, of regularities and generalizations. At last we had reached a point where not only did I understand, I agreed. What I now understood Professor Wigner to be contending was that the science of the future ought to contain more links between the natural, the life and the social sciences.

Eugene P. Wigner

— F3 —
The Existence of Consciousness

Thank you very much both for your introduction and also for your participation in the discussion yesterday. It pointed to a number of questions which I should clarify and it also gave me an opportunity to voice my conviction on the questions discussed: my conviction that life and consciousness cannot be described in terms of the concepts of *present-day* physics. I hope that science will eventually develop concepts which give interesting and highly significant information not only about inanimate objects—as does present-day physics—but also about life and consciousness. Whether the so encompassing science will be called physics or will have another name, I do not know. Perhaps it will be called scisif. But that is not important. What is important is whether the three basic principles which physics obeys will be maintained. For this reason, I would like to discuss these principles, the discussion of the second one of which will contain again the demonstration that we are as yet far from a unification of physics and the life sciences.

Before starting on that discussion, I wish to apologize to the physicists among you. You know the principles I will present at least instinctively, even though you may not have heard them presented before. Basically, what I will say will not be really new to you. However, I cannot help because right now I do not talk principally to physicists. And I apologize also to some of the others who attend this meeting because what I'll say has very little to do directly with religion. I also realize that it is very difficult to accept principles on first hearing. If I were giving a class, I would talk about one and a half of the principles one hour, again so much at the next class, and summarize all of them at the third meeting. Because we are not inclined to accept, nor even to ingest, general principles just because someone pronounces them. —Let me now go over to the discussion of the first characteristic of present-day physics which I wish to present.

The Limitation of Physics—Separation of
Initial Conditions and Laws of Nature

The distinction between initial conditions and laws of nature is implicit in Newton's *Philosophiae Naturalis Principia Mathematica* of 1687. Among other accomplishments, this contains the law of gravitation. This permits the calculation of the position and velocity of the planets at all times if the position and velocity at one single time is given. These latter are called initial conditions and the laws of physics give no information about them. In fact, in many parts of physics, in particular in the theory of heat, it is assumed that these are entirely irregular—the positions of the atoms in a gas are as irregular as possible and the same holds of their velocities. The laws of nature, which determine the changes of these quantities as functions of time are, on the contrary, in the words of Einstein, simple and mathematically beautiful.

Let me give a couple of examples. Newton's theory of gravitation says that any two bodies are attracted to each other, the force of attraction being proportional to the product of the masses of the two objects and inversely proportional to the square of the distance between them. And the direction of the force is toward the attracting body. Thus, if one lets loose a body such as this key here, it will fall in the direction of the heaviest body nearby, which is the Earth. If the initial position of the key and its initial velocity—which was zero —are given, the time at which it reaches the table underneath can be calculated. It can also be demonstrated that two objects, even entirely different ones, will fall equally fast—as long as we can neglect other forces, different from the gravitational one, such as air resistance. More than that: the motion of the moon, the existence of its circular orbit, can be demonstrated, and fully calculated, given, of course, its position and velocity at one time. Similarly, Kepler's three regularities of the motion of the planets follow from Newton's laws. It is truly wonderful that regularities of such a great diversity of phenomena can be summarized in a law as simple as Newton's gravitational theory.

I do not know whether I should mention that when Newton first thought of his principle, it did not check. The moon moved too fast. But when the radius of the Earth was remeasured, it suddenly checked. And when the new measurement of the Earth's size was presented to the Royal Society, he at once knew—now my theory is confirmed.

It may be good to reemphasize the point that Newton's theory describes the motion of the moon and of the sun's planets, but does *not explain* their initial states and velocities, not even the existence of the moon or of the planets. These are outside the area of the laws of physics, they are initial conditions. It is also good to realize that Newton's theory has only limited validity—there are forces different from the gravitational one—the air resistance was mentioned before. It is, however, wonderful that we are given situations in which only the gravitational forces play a significant role—such as the motion of the sun's planets. I call these situations "limiting cases." However, in the course of time, physics has expanded greatly, and we can now deal with many situations in which, for instance, other forces, not gravitational ones, also play a significant role. This will be my next subject which will also show that the expansion is, as yet, far from complete and that, in particular, it does not extend to the phenomenon of life.

The Expansion of the Area of Physics

The first enormous extension of the area of physics occurred more than a hundred years ago; it was due principally to Faraday and Maxwell. Their theory describes the regularities of electromagnetic phenomena, the behavior of electric charges and of magnets, their interactions, and even more importantly, the phenomena of radiation, that is in particular of light. It is also based on a simple set of equations called Maxwell's equations, but the distinction of initial conditions and laws of nature remains.

Yet, the whole description of the physical situation is very different from that used by Newton. Newton's description of the "state" of the system consisted in giving the position and velocity of each object; Maxwell's equations describe the electromagnetic field by giving the values of its components at every point of space. The former consisted of a set of numbers, the latter of functions of the three space-coordinates, usually denoted by x, y, and z. I will admit that there was an almost continuous transition between Newton's "classical dynamics" and the electromangnetic field theory, yet the difference remains very great. Even the reformulations of classical dynamics referred to position densities and velocities—very different concepts from field strengths. As all of us know, Einstein fundamentally reformulated Newton's gravitational theory and he made a great effort to give this theory, and that of electromagnetism, a common basis. There is quite general agreement among physicists, including Einstein, that he was not fully successful. It is true, nevertheless, that the perhaps artificial union of the two theories extended the area of physics tremendously. The theory of light describes the way we obtain information about the positions of the planets and the union gives a description of the insides of stars where both gravitational forces and electromagnetic ones, in particular light pressure, play a decisive role.

Neither of the two theories mentioned—that of the essentially gravitational of Newton or the electromagnetic of Maxwell—considered the atomic structure of matter seriously. The extension of the area of physics to this domain is due to a third "revolution," that of quantum theory and quantum mechanics. When I started to be interested in physics, if you wanted to know the density of aluminum, there was a thick book in which you could look it up—it was 2.7. You do the same now but, just the same, the properties of materials are part of present-day physics. They *can* be derived from the atomic structure of the materials, from the interaction of the atoms contained in those which can be derived with the aid of the quantum mechanical theory. All chemistry also, we believe, could be derived on the basis of our understanding of the molecules' atomic structure. This is again a tremendous change—an extension of the area of physics which was just impossible to think of when I first learned about this subject. But, of course, it is still far from describing correlations between all kinds of events—it says nothing about my thought, emotions, desires, etc.

As matter of fact, there is a degree of similarity between the relation of the theory of light to the study of planetary motion and the relation of the hoped-for theory of life and consciousness to quantum mechanics. The theory of light describes our obtaining information about the motions of the planets—their consistency with the theory of gravitation. Similarly, a theory of our consciousness would provide the description of our observation process and the now mysterious "collapse of the state vector," i.e., it would tell us about the "measurement process" which permits us to verify the probabilistic statements of quantum mechanics on the outcomes of observations or statements of quantum mechanics on the outcomes of observations or statements of quantum mechanics on the outcomes of observations or measurements.

Before going to the third characteristic of physics, let me apologize for the gross incompleteness of the present one. In particular, it gave credit for the development of physics only to a very few people when, actually, many dozens of physicists contributed to it decisively. In particular, Einstein's contributions' mention was badly neglected. I did not find it possible to give an even superficially valid description of the many contributions to the expansion of the area of physics.

Physics Deals Best with Limiting Cases

This is a very obvious remark. It is that practically all laws of physics were discovered, and also verified, under conditions when these laws manifest themselves in particularly simple ways. Thus, the law of gravitation was discovered and verified under conditions in which no other but gravitational forces play a significant role. This applies, for instance, to the motion of the planets—there is, of course, a light pressure from the sun's radiation but this has practically no effect. If we verify the law by dropping an object here on the Earth, we choose one of high weight and small size so that the air resistance remains negligible. Where we verify the conclusions of quantum mechanics, we use microscopic objects, that is atoms, because the quantum effects manifest themselves most clearly on these. The skill of the experimental physicist consists in large part in creating circumstances in which the law of nature to be tested manifests itself in a simple way, that is, the effects of which he has no full mastery are very small.

The question then arises: is present-day physics always dealing with a limiting case? Do we carry out all our experiments, and do we do all our theoretical thinking, using circumstances in which some phenomenon is absent or at least plays no significant role? The answer is "yes," we experiment almost always under circumstances in which life and consciousness play no role. As was pointed out before, the mere idea of these is foreign to present-day physics, it does not even ask the question whether I think of my grand-daughter or of prime numbers, whether I am experiencing pain or pleasure. There is, for practically all effects a continuous transition from the situation in which it has virtually no effect, to the situation in which it has a decisive one. Is there such a continuous transition between the situation in which the role of life on consciousness is negligible to one in which it plays a decisive role? The answer is, I believe again "yes": the properties and behavior of viruses and microbes could probably be well described by our physics—and our biologists had considerable success in this regard—the behavior of higher organisms, with clear consciousness I do not really believe follow all laws of physics. Is there some evidence for this? I believe there is. First of all, in every case, except that of heat, when the area of physics was extended, the basic laws, in fact their subjects, have changed. But there is some more mathematical proof for this to which I have alluded before: according to quantum mechanics, I could be put into a state in which I have neither seen, nor not seen, a flash—in which I am in a "superposition" of these states. Yet, the fact is that my mind is never in such a superposition. I realize that this last statement is difficult to swallow for a non-physicist but I wanted to mention it just the same.

Will all this change, are we going to have a science which encompasses life, so that its validity is not restricted to inanimate nature? We have seen that the area of science has greatly extended in the past and we can hope, and I do, that it will be extended further, to cover the phenomena of life and consciousness. But we can not be sure of this—after all, according to Darwin, we are animals and our ability to "understand," that is to discover important and interesting correlations between events, may be limited. I often tell the story that I wanted to explain the associative law of multiplication to a very nice dog but got nowhere—similarly our understanding may also be limited. But I think we should strive to acquire such an understanding and I hope that some day somebody will have a very bright idea, similar to those of Maxwell, of Planck, or Heisenberg, and get us closer to such an explanation or at least to the description of the regularities of events involving life.

With this I should stop and let the commentator tell us where I am wrong.

R.J. Swi Werblowsky

Commentary

Madam Chairman Sir, Persons and Gentlemen,

I apologize for choosing this kind of address to the audience, but I have been assured by experts in the field of local Lib Folklore that there are no more Ladies left in this progressive and liberated society.

But facetiousness aside, permit me before responding to Professor Wigner's paper to take up—by way of introduction as it were—some of the issues raised in an earlier session, before our coffee-break. Two of the speakers referred to themselves (and/or were referred to by others) as Protestant and Catholic respectively. Since this element of denominational identification has crept into our deliberations, I feel in private duty bound to present myself to this public as what I am: my religion is Comparative Religion. The term, I admit, is an ugly and un-English neo-barbarian neologism, but in a world in which neo-barbarianese has become the norm this violation of language will, I surmise, not be considered as too disturbing.

Comparative Religionalists (another barbarian neologism?) are often accused of looking at religion through a macroscope (if I may borrow Professor Wigner's term, albeit in a way he had not intended) instead of behaving like decent scholars and concentrating on microscopic research. I confess to my professional sins and weaknesses, especially as I shall not be able to offer reasoned arguments but—obeying the instructions of our chairman—only considerations and reflections. Considerations rather than arguments also happen to be the only possible type of response to Professor Wigner's paper which has not been circulated in print. None of us has seen, let alone read it, and all we can do is to attempt improvised reactions after having listened to it.

In order to clear the ground for my improvised response, permit me to return once again to the earlier part of today's proceedings. Although I am a macro-comparatist, I have unbounded admiration for the kind of narrow and specialized research that modestly refrains from lodging big claims. Macro-comparatists, whether in the fields of sociology, anthropology or history of religions, know only too well how easily one trips up as a result of inadequate knowledge and insufficient competence. It is also precisely for this reason that some of the discussions in our "Religion and Philosophy" section left me rather dissatisfied and even unhappy. Either *expressis verbis* or surreptitiously the word religion, whenever it was uttered, seemed to have Christian (or Judeo-Christian, or Biblical) resonances. Almost nothing of what was said here about securlarization made sense to me as long as I thought in terms of Buddhist (Ashokan) paradigm. I was struck by the absence of even the Islamic dimension although Islam is often lumped together, as the youngest "daughter religion", with the other western monotheistic or "Abrahamic" faiths. But surely its specific spirituality is very different fom that generated in the course of western history. And if much that was said here is inapplicable to Islam, it is so *a forteriori* when we try to step into the shoes of a Hindu or Buddhist. This situation vitiates a great deal of what has been solemnly pronounced as characteristic of "religion". If the speakers had said "Christianity" this would have been fair enough and occasionally even correct. But you must not say "religion" when you really mean the Christian shadow lurking behind it. But we have also been given to understand that the term Christianity may be too wide, and personally I have immense respect for my more learned and specialized colleagues who even refuse to speak of *Religionsoziologie*, preferring to deal with *Kirchensoziologie*. They seem to suggest that unless you are an all-out macro-comparatist you cannot even speak of Christianity as such, but only the Lutheran Church in Wurtenberg or the Anglican Church in Lancashire. This narrowness of research is not a symptom of narrow-mindedness but, on the contrary, of an extremely conscientious and responsible scientific mentality. The accusation of lack of scientific spirit should be levelled at those who talk about religion in general but really have one particular religion in mind (or at the back of their minds). This also holds true of the writings of Aldous Huxley or R.C. Saehner which have been mentioned in these sessions. No doubt both Huxley and Saehner were eminent men and scholars. But to me, as a Comparative Religionist, their contributions are not to my academic discipline. Huxley's work is a contribution to a certain type of twentieth century semi-syncretistic Hindu-inspired type of religiosity. Zaehner's work, in spite of the impressive scholarly apparatus accompanying it, belongs to the category of modern Catholic apologetics.

The above preliminary and somewhat polemical remarks are not as irrelevant as they may appear when turning to the issues raised in Professor Wigner's address. Our explicit theme for today was "Aspects of Religious Consciousness". I for one am not sure at all that such a thing really exists, and even if it did it would seem to me that the far more interesting and important problem is that of "The Religious Aspects of Consciousness". In fact, Professor Wigner addressed himself precisely to the problem of consciousness as such. This of course is a problem which a physicist cannot tackle alone. He needs the help and collaboration of chemists, molecular biologists, geneticists, and above all neurologists. For reasons of professional incompetence in all these areas, the whole subject of the emergence, evolution, development and functioning of consciousness is, of course, out of bounds to me. But as a student of religion I find the *fact* of consciousness to be of overriding interest. What does it mean that we are conscious human beings? What is it that we are conscious of? And does this fact have religious implications (i.e. if only in the Marxist sense that without consciousness there could be no alienation)? Professor Wigner has very much stressed the obvious fact that animals too have consciousness. This commonplace was of course known to every ethologist, and even many phenomenolgists (e.g., the Dutchman Buytendijk) and psychologists have written on it long before ethology became so widely popular through the work of K. Lorentz, Tinbergen and others. We now have descriptions and analyses galore of the phenomenology viz. structure and morphology of animal consciousness in action. But in actual fact we know pretty little about animal consciousness. The specific religious interest comes in at the point where we seem to sense a difference in kind between animal and human consciousness. Humans appear to have a very specific kind of self-consciousness or, to be more precise, reflective self-consciousness. Human beings are not merely conscious, like the dog from whom Professor Wigner failed to elicit the desired reply. We are self-conscious in the sense that we are at one and the same time subjects as well as objects of (or to) ourselves. My own subjectivity is an object of enquiry to myself, ontologically and ethically (as also St. Augustine realized long ago). These two aspects could easily be presented as one were I speaking in Latin or French. But as I happen to be speaking in English at this moment, I am in the position of being capable to distinguish between "consciousness" and "conscience" where otherwise I'd only have *conscientia* or *conscience* at my disposal. In our very subjectivity we are objects to ourselves and of ourselves. In fact, subjectivity is always experienced in objectivity i.e., in a mediate, indirect fashion. I do not simply experience pain, or hunger, like a dog, but my experience of pain etc. is filtered through the reflective self-awarenss "I, Swi Werblowsky, am feeling pain, am hungry, am afraid" etc. This dialectic between objectivity and subjectivity can play a tremendous role in our understanding and classification of religions. There are religions which take this subjectivity and reify it—and then you get a human soul (immortal or otherwise) or something similar. If you prefer Kantian to theological language you will speak of the "transcendental personality". If you are a Buddhist then you know that talking about the absolute core of your personality—in connection with which you also have to take into account the crucial factor of memory—is rather like drawing perspectivistic lines on a blackboard which do not meet. They are drawn so as to create the illusion of converging somewhere outside the blackboard but in reality they don't meet because there is no point of convergence. The dissolution of the subject in the *annata*-doctrine ultimately also dissolves all objectivity. Or does the infinite regress of subjectivity behind subjectivity behind subjectivity etc. (because as soon as our subjectivity becomes an object there appears another subjectivity behind it that objectifies the previous one) lead us to a Nothing—with a capital N—which might, perhaps, as some Sufi thinkers would formulate it, be the ultimate religious reality?

The reproachful glances of our chairman compel me to cut short just as I am beginning to feel that I am happily launched on my course. Let me therefore conclude by saying that for the student of religion our problem resides in the fact that human consciousness functions on several levels. For sheer lack of time it must suffice here to mention the names of some of the philosophical anthropologists that have paid special attention to this subject e.g.

Hartmann. A. Gehlen and H. Plessner (especially in his *Die Stufen des Organischen und der Mensch*). Surely Darwin did not teach us that we were animals or naked apes. What he taught us was a better understanding of the specificities that make us human, and of the levels of spiritual existence which evolution constructs on the basis of the underlying ones. But these levels are very different from what the parapsychologists and the ESP and ASC chaps are trying to sell us. In fact, these latter are the real materialists since for them the spiritual is merely euphemism for the reality of certain material phenomena (though by now most of them have sufficient good sense to do without ectoplasms and similar crude notions). To those who postulate a connection between the alleged facts of parapsychology and religion I would say that if ever I have experienced anything approaching vague religious intimations, I was successfully cured of them by reading Rhine and his successors. Perhaps they really prove something, but it certainly has nothing whatever to do with religion. Their "researches" present not so much proof of spiritual realities in our lives but rather the ultimate victory of the most primitive and crude animistic materialism. They take us back to Edward Tylor. Let me therefore sum up by repeating that when we talk of consciousness, the major problem for the student of religion is not the subject of "religious consciousness" (what ever that may mean) but the religious implications and dimensions of the very fact of consciousness, and more especially of reflective self-consciousness in its human form. And perhaps all I have said was merely a misplaced footnote to Aristotle's definition of God as the thought that was thinking itself.

Section G:

Comparative Religious Responses to Modernization

— G1 —

The Problems of Modernization in 'Hinduism'
Ravi Ravindra

— G2 —

Religion and Modernization:
The General Problems and
Islamic Responses
Mohammed Al-Nowaihi

— G3 —

Modernism and Modernization
in Buddhism
R.J. Swi Werblowsky/David J. Kalupahana

Ravi Ravindra

— G1 —
The Problems of
Modernization in 'Hinduism'

WE, THE PEOPLE OF INDIA, having solemnly resolved to constitute
India into a SOVEREIGN, SECULAR, SOCIALISTIC* DEMOCRATIC
REPUBLIC and to secure to all its citizens:
JUSTICE, social, economic and political;
LIBERTY of thought, expression, belief, faith and worship;
EQUALITY of status and of opportunity; and to promote among them all
FRATERNITY assuring the dignity of the individual and the unity of the
Nation
　　IN OUR CONSTITUENT ASSEMBLY this twenty-sixth day of November 1949, do HEREBY ADOPT, ENACT AND GIVE TO OURSELVES
THIS CONSTITUTION.

Thus reads the preamble to the Constitution of Modern India.[1] It
also takes us immediately into the heart of our topic.

In India, modernization still means primarily Westernization, not
only in Socio-political institutions but quite comprehensively. India
seems to aspire towards Western modes of thought in education,
research and management, industrialization according to the procedures and developments of Western science and technology,
Western social values and goals, and Western institutions of
government, information and warfare. No doubt, all of these institutions, procedures and modes of thought are quite modern within the
Western world. But they show discernable continuities with earlier
Western sensibilities and practices. Arising out of the Western soil,
they are likely to be more in tune with the Western soul. However,
either owing to military and economic pressures or because of the
seduction of progress and success, these modern Western values
and aspirations have been adopted by the whole world. Thus,
although modernization is a universal phenomenon, leading to some
global promises and problems, in the non-Western world it still has a
peculiarly alien flavor and quite external character.

---

*These two words 'SECULAR SOCIALISTIC' were added, by a special, constitutional amendment, during the emergency imposed in India during 1975-77.

From the point of view of India, the initiative for any change or innovation has been for two hundred years or so outside her borders and control. And what is true of India is, of course, true of what Westerners and following them now most Indians, call 'Hinduism'; for 'Hinduism' without India is an abstraction, as is India with 'Hinduism.'

Something needs to be said about 'Hinduism' and the reason for my unease regarding this word. I am not clear what 'Hinduism' is.[2] The title of this talk was suggested to me by the organizers of the conference; my only innovation is the addition of the quotation marks around the word *Hinduism*. The word 'Hinduism' seems to suggest, at the very least, that it is a 'religion.' When I try to translate 'religion' into Hindi or Sanskrit, I cannot find any suitable word. In a recent paper,[3] I suggested that an appropriate Sanskrit word for 'religion' is *yoga*. This is so at least to the extent that we might assume that the Bhagavad Gita and Patanjali's *Yoga Sutra[s]* have something to do with what is meant by 'religion,' since their central concern is *moksa* (Liberation). Even the etymologies of 'yoga' and 'religion' have some close parallels in terms of 'uniting' (or making a bond between) what is human and what is divine, as well as in their explicit associations with 'diligence,' 'attention' and 'heedfulness.' The word 'yoga,' unlike 'religion,' has an associated verb form which is commonly used, as for example in the *Bhagavad Gita*, making its connotations closer to a process than to a doctrine. Since *yoga* is concerned with *sat (being)*, *jnana* (gnosis, knowledge) and *karma* (doing, action), it has as much to do with 'religion' as with 'science' as well as with 'art.' So, we might as well use expressions like 'hinduyoga' and 'Christianyoga' for what we now label as 'Hinduism' and 'Christianity.' From a Hindu[4] point of view, even more appropriate would be relatively more specific expressions, for different aspects within these traditions, like 'the yoga of *Katha Upanisad*' or 'the yoga of *Theologia Germanica*'; or a set of expressions like 'mantra yoga,' 'karma yoga' and 'yoga of the prayer of the heart.' If these expressions were widely used in connection with various religions and their developments, many of the apparently peculiar characteristics of 'Hinduism' would not appear so strange after all. For example, one should not feel so odd in being a Hindu and a Christian simultaneously; certainly no more than in a following *karmayoga* and *jnanayoga* at the same time. No easy eclecticism is advocated here. I am simply drawing attention to an obvious point, almost universally forgotten in practice, that our conceptual apparatus tries to cast all reality in its own mold. From another *darsana* (perspective, point of view), what appears very strange to us may seem quite normal. The chief value of comparative studies may lie precisely in their ability to make us aware of our presuppositions.

Another word which is sometimes used to render 'religion' into Sanskrit is *dharma. Dharma* has in it the connotations of 'order, law,' 'responsibility,' 'obligation,' 'duty' and 'righteousness.' No being is exempt from the workings and demands of *dharma.* Every aggregation of the constituents of *prakrti*, which we can understand to be the agency or the force responsible for making anything that can be an object, whether gross like a stone or subtle like thoughts and feelings, is subject to laws. But no manifestation whatsoever is wholly an object.[5] Every existence has a self, which partakes of the Self, and therefore has obligations in the general maintenance of the cosmic order. This interplay of order, law and obligation is what determines *dharma* for any creature. Thus, we act in accord with *dharma* if we respond to the obligations laid upon us by right order, as we understand it according to our capacity. Bees, snakes, trees and stars all act in accordance with their *dharma*, perhaps without conscious understanding and without complication. The *dharma* of a human being in any given situation is not easy to be sure about, as is amply illustrated by the complexities of the vast *Mahabharata*, and may require immense subtletly of thought and feeling to be understood. But Hindus seem to revel in these complexities, and none of their creations—mythologies, philosophies, arts or literature—are ever simple or straightforward. Since several large forces, cosmic, planetary, social and individual, make their demands simultaneously on a human being, each according to its own law, a precise understanding of his responsibilities in a given situation requires discrimination, dedication and effort.

This point is dramatically brought out and elaborated in the *Bhagavad Gita.* From the very first word in this remarkable text, the whole dialogue, as Krsna himself says towards the end (18.70), is about *dharma.* The root meaning of *dharma* in the Bhagavad Gita is much the same as in the *Rg Veda*, the earliest work known to India,

and also as in the writings of Sri Aurobindo in our own time, namely, the upholding of the orderly relatedness of all that is.[6] In this
tradition, which has been continuous for at least three thousand
years, *dharma* is said to be eternal (*sanatana*) since it is based on
truths which are timeless and therefore valid for all time, although
no doubt our interpretation of them and response to them may vary
in time. This *sanatana dharma* is not made by any man or any god;
it is prior to them, it is the support of the entire creation. It is the
ordering principle of all that exists; it is the first and the highest
principle of manifestation. There are tendencies and forces which aid
the maintenance of *dharma* and there are others which oppose it.
The whole cosmic drama is played out between these two large currents; one may choose to be in one current, or the other, but no one
may opt out of the game. No one, that is, who is bound by
manifestation (*maya*), gross or subtle. But it is possible for man to
be free of all specific *dharmas*, if he is able to identify himself completely with the highest *purusa* (spirit, person).[7] Then he is bound by
nothing, higher or lower. According to the *Bhagavad Gita* such a
person participates in Krsna's own mode of being, that of unconditioned freedom (*moksa*). This is the end of human *dharma*, and the
goal of man. The means appropriate for this end are called yoga.

Dharma has a large community component in it, whereas *yoga*
refers to a more individual search. The contrast can be understood
by the examples of 'marriage' and 'love'. Marriage is discussed at
length in the *dhatmasatras*, but only a *yoga* corresponds to love,
namely the *bhaktiyoga*. However, we can exaggerate the separation
of *yoga* and *dharma* a little too much, for they are quite related to
each other. Mythologically, sometimes Yoga is personified as the
son of Dharma and Kriya (action and performance). From the traditional Hindu point of view, the purpose of any specific *dharma* is to
lead beyond itself. Therefore, the purpose of the whole manifested
cosmos is, and of all social organizations and of all human activities
like philosophy, ritual and art ought to be, to help every creature
realize the identity of its self (*atman*) and the Great Self (*Brahman*).
Thus art is not for the sake of art itself; it is, if it is any good at all, a
way to what is beyond art and beyond any manifestation. Similarly,
a society functions properly only when it enables its members to
engage with concerns which are higher than social. On the in-

dividual level, a mind is healthy when it is able to know its proper place and is able to listen to what is above it.

According to the *Chandogya Upanisad* (VI. I. 1-4), when Svetaketu Arunaya was twelve years old, his father Uddalka asked him to live the life of a student, for no one in their family was unlearned and a brahman only by birth. He returned at the age of twenty-four, having studied all the sciences, greatly thinking himself well-read. His father then said to him, "Svetaketu, since you now are so greatly conceited, think yourself well-read and self-important, did you ask for that instruction by which the unhearable becomes heard, the unperceivable becomes perceived, the unknowable becomes known?" Svetaketu wondered, "How, Sir, can there be such teaching?" The generic name for all such teaching is *yoga*. A society functioning rightly according to *dharma* makes *yoga* possible; but only a society which heeds its integrated (*yukta*) men, can truly know what *dharma* is and function according to it.

Returning now to 'religion', we can perhaps say that from the point of view of the Hindus it may be more appropriately described in terms of *dharma* and *yoga*, neither of which need to have any exclusivist or sectarian meaning, nor any churchly implications. Also, both *dharma* and *yoga* are much more holistic than 'religion', particularly as the latter has come to be in the modern West, where it has become a matter of course to separate 'religion' from 'philosophy', 'science', 'politics', 'education' and 'art'.[8] Furthermore, and most importantly, *dharma* and *yoga* are not ends in themselves; their whole point is transcendence. Nor do they serve any 'social' ends. In the terms of *dharma* and *yoga* one cannot even properly raise the question similar to 'Is religion socially useful or relevant?' In the Indian context, the question is more: 'Is a given society sufficiently in accord with *dharma* that *yoga* can be practiced for the sake of *moksa* (Liberation)?'

To the extent 'Hinduism' means *dharma and yoga leading to moksa*, it is not really a 'religion', for all human aspirations and efforts towards transcendence can be so described. And, if it does not mean *dharma and yoga leading to moksa*, from the point of view of the above metaphysical perspective, 'Hinduism' is quite pointless, whatever it stands for. Perhaps, then, by 'Hinduism' is meant that cluster of understandings and forms of *dharma* and *yoga* which had their main inspiration and development in India. I say 'perhaps' because I am not really sure about this, especially because in the vast and ancient culture of India so many different forms and interpretations have emerged that with sufficient ingenuity most major ideas and practices can be discovered there. And given the general Hindu tendency to think that every form, however twisted and perverse it may seem to the majority, derives ultimately from Divine energy and is likely to elevate its sincere devotee, and given a very high level of tolerance among the Hindus for conceptual and aesthetic chaos, no form is ever completely eliminated. There is such an exuberant riot of imagination, cults, practices, gods, mythologies, philosophies—and everything on a stupendous scale— that no one addicted to logical and clear formulations in all spheres of life is likely to find 'Hinduism' satisfactory or palatable.

With these hesitations present in the background, we can come back to modernization. *Moksa* is, by definition, not analyzable in terms of any rational categories, nor any other temporal forms. Although it is the goal of 'Hinduism,' and of any other path in time based on *sanatana dharma,*[9] *moksa* refers to a timeless state, not opposed to time but independent of it. *Yoga* being a teaching "by which the unhearable becomes heard," is subject to change in time, but only in its beginning stages where the outermost personality of a seeker is predominant and the teacher adapts the teaching to suit the pupil's particular predilection. This outermost personality is what is most affected by social conditioning and therefore by contingencies of history and geography. To the extent that a given *yoga* is able to lead to truth it is an instrument that transforms an aspirant from his time-bound outermost self to his time-freed innermost Self. The varieties of *yoga*, which here means path or teaching for transformation, correspond to the different basic types of men and do not essentially change with time in their inner content, although it is true that in any given period of history a particular type of man may be in ascendency requiring the corresponding *yoga*.

What is most affected by history is cultural *dharma* which changes by a constant interaction of external and internal forces of innovation and preserving tendencies of the tradition. At the risk of being extremely simplistic, we may choose the traditional metaphor of the wheel: the center, which exists everywhere, indicates *moksa*, the spokes are like various *yogas* leading to the center and the rim is cultural *dharma* touching the road of history, but drawing its integrity and strength from inside. *Moksa* is neither personal nor social; nor, of course, non-personal or non-social. *Yoga* is personal in the beginning of a spiritual journey, and *dharma* is social.[10] This *dharma* is now subjected to a rapid change, largely initiated by strong external forces.

We may now return to the preamble to the constitution of modern India, a constitution which we "give to ourselves", and which has no transcendent reference. This constitution comes neither from heaven as *struti* (revelation) heard by the sages, nor from the ancestors as *smrti* (tradition) incorporating the cumulative experience of the community, dependent on *sanatana dharma* a perceived, understood and interpreted by the wisest among those whose social *dharma* the consitution attempts to represent. The constitution is, both in spirit and origin, entirely Western. "We wanted the music of Veena or Sitar," remarked a member of the Constituent Assembly responsible for approving the draft constitution, "but here we have the music of an English band."[11] In a reversal of the traditional order, the constitution self-consciously takes its stand on earth and not in Heaven. Its fundamental notion of social justice, liberty and equality were developed in a culture, the alien nature of which by itself is not at all an important issue, during the period when the center of gravity of that culture was unrealted to, if not in opposition to, transcendent concerns.

We can see this even in the effect that Christian missionaries, more pious than wise, had quite fantastic and absurd impressions about 'Hinduism,' often resulting from their definite, but innocent, convictions about idols, sexual symbolism and polytheism. Of course, as was said earlier, it is not easy to remain unconfounded in front of the gargantuan multi-dimensionality of 'Hinduism' in which everything from the most sublime to the most bizarre has its place. The venomous serpent Kaliya who had caused much panic and discomfort to everyone around the palace in the Yamuna river where he lodged himself, on being overpowered by Krsna claimed to have acted in accordance with his snake *dharma* in spreading his poison around. Krsna found this explanation quite acceptable and spared Kaliya's life, merely banishing him to the ocean, a more appropriate place for the serpent's activities. If one has a more straightforward notion about right and wrong, one is likely to be bewildered by all that can go on under the umbrella of 'Hinduism.' Many well-intentioned European Christians were quite scandalised by 'Hinduism,' and said some quite uncharitable and silly things in connection with it. Here is a remark made by the eminent missionary, Reverand Alexander Duff, who lived in India from 1830 to 1863 and did much to promote education and social reform: "Of all the systems of false religion ever fabricated by the perverse ingenuity of fallen man, Hinduism is surely the most stupendous . . . Of all systems of false religion it is that which seems to embody the largest amount and variety of semblances and counterfeits of divinely revealed facts and doctrines."[12]

In spite of all this, and largely because the above is hardly the whole truth about Christian activities in India, no external force has contributed more to the purification and reform of the Hindu society than Christianity. All internal reform movements among the Hindus in the last one hundred years or so had their explicit or implicit reference to Christianity, and came into existence in opposition to it, in imitation of it or in accomodation with it. Christian scriptures and many Christians dedicated to the care of the sick[13] and the poor leavened the awakening conscience among the Hindus about the plight of the downtrodden in their own society.

It is difficult to exaggerate either the necessity of these social reforms or their desirability. The understanding and practice of cultural *dharma* had gone awry and needed to be corrected, as it still does now. (And the constitution is also a necessary corrective.) Nevertheless, to the extent that Christ's "kingdom is not of this world," social reform, even at its best, cannot be considered as man's highest end. What gives religion significance, from the Hindu point of view, is beyond social good, although clearly not opposed to it. Christianity in India did not provide, what in any case would have been an astounding achievement anywhere, a functioning model of active engagement with social welfare and the transcendent concerns. It is difficult to escape the impression that in the modern world, in the West or the East, Christianity on the large has been basically a social force, which by itself could hardly be undervalued, and that its transcendent yearnings have not been able to challenge a society about its own *raison d'etre*. Perhaps this is just another way of saying that in the modern times, nominally Christian societies are basically secular in their aspirations.

Another aspect of modernization and the accompanying secularization needs to be mentioned, namely science and technology, for yesterday's 'rice Christians' in India are today's 'wheat technologists.' Science has been the major intellectual and social influence in the modern West, owing to its close relationship with technology, and therefore with military and economic power. And this sort of power is all that matters in the world, unless there is some moral or spiritual power in opposition to it or pointing in a different direction. Even within the Western world, modern natural science has driven itself like a wedge in the history of thought, creating a deep cleavage in the intellect of man.[14] It is a fact of Western intellectual history that every major poet and artist, since Newton's founding of natural science on a firm footing, has felt uneasy about the assumptions, procedures or results of the scientific enterprise. However, perhaps because of the separation among the domains of truth, beauty and goodness that prevails in the mind of the modern Western man, science has moved on, wholly indifferent to these critics, like a large iceberg unaffected by the thrashings of small fish.

In any case, modern science and technology have not arisen and developed in a metaphysical vacuum. Underlying their development there are many cultural values and metaphysical assumptions about the nature and purpose of man, the cosmos and knowledge.[15] These assumptions are products of Western European history and philosophy. Modern science and technology, not withstanding the recurring large scale uneasiness with them, are as European in character as European music or sculpture. Western science is as distinct from Indian science, in its fundamental attitude and purpose, as Western harmony is from the Indian *raga*. It is not often remarked that modern natural sciences represent one among many possible ways of approaching nature. This way is no more unique or exclusively God-given than Christianity was claimed to be by its adherents.[16] There can be, and have been, different approaches to the study of nature and man, informed by different purposes and yielding different results. An example of a branch of science developed in India is *yoga*, with its quite different basis, intention and consequences, as contrasted with its counterparts in Western science, namely physiology, psychology and medicine. One should have added, because of the discussion earlier in the paper, 'religion' also as a Western counterpart to the science of *yoga*. But 'religion' and science are wholly separated in the modern West, and whatever 'religion' may be it is not considered knowledge. One result of this situation is that modern science is completely divorced from any transcendent concerns, and has been the chief force of secularisation in the modern world.

The major problem faced by 'Hinduism' now is: How to reconcile the demands of time and the demands of what is timeless? or, to use a more individual language, how to meet the needs of the body as well as the spirit?[17] This question has a different pathos in India whose poverty has become as proverbial as her richness used to be. There, among the intelligentsia and among those with some social conscience, where the awareness of the problems and needs of the manifested world is overwhelming, any concern for the un-manifested reality is beginning to look indecent, immoral and even insane. And an important factor in the situation is the awareness of their presence of the Western culture with its immense material prosperity, military might, technical knowledge and virtual control over most global institutions and resources. This enormous worldly power of the West makes all its cultural styles and practice desirable and worthy of emulation in the eyes of a people who have not had a demonstrable worldly success in recent history. Whether drawn to the liberal democratic style or the Marxist-communist mode, almost everyone among the educated youth in modern India seems to consider social ideals as ultimate, and Western science and technology as the basic means.

Clearly, needs of the body cannot be denied; a starving man cannot attend to the spirit. The cry of the earth cannot be ignored. The West has obviously made, and will continue to make, significant contributions to human welfare throughout the world, and not the least in India. Still, if the body of the Hindu society were to survive and prosper, but without being at the same time a temple of the spirit, it would be an existence without significance. As long as modernization in India continues to be primarily Westernization, it is difficult to be sanguine about the triumph of the spirit. Not because the West is 'alien' (the time for such parochial sentiment is past in the emerging planetary culture), but because the modern West does not speak with the power of its own spiritual depths. For the sake of the whole planet, India and 'Hinduism' need to grow a new body for their ancient spirit to make a new response to the demands of the earth. The realm of technique and materiality cannot be neglected without the risk of subjugation or starvation. But the very purpose of which one exists, society exists, can be easily forgotten in the midst of social concerns and worldly success. If 'Hinduism' ceases to make room for those among men, the wild geese (*hamsa*), who respond to the call of the other shore, how would the world hear the dance of Siva, the Divine Outsider? The whole herd of starving lions in search of food and security may well be lured into cages, and be tamed to perform worldly tricks, forgetting the jungle-reverberating roar of a free lion like the Buddha. Arjuna the archer is needed for the protection of *dharma*, but he must always submit himself to the purposes of Krsna, the lord of *yoga*. In the imagery of the *Rg Veda*, our mother is Earth and our father is Heaven; who among the children will dare to hold Heaven and Earth in a new embrace?

NOTES

1. Quoted in B.M. Sharma, *The Republic of India: Constitution and Government* (Asia Publishing House, New York, 1966), p. 154.
2. My eminent colleague, Professor Wilfred Cantwell Smith, has written extensively, and with great insight, about this and other related matters. In particular, see his *Meaning and End of Religion* (Mentor Books, New York, 1964), Chapter 3, Section V, and footnote 25 to Chapter 5. I have arrived at my opinions independently, more from instict than from research. We have both more than once remarked to each other about the uncanny congruence of our opinions and conclusion given our very different cultural and intellectual backgrounds.
3. R. Ravindra, "Is Religion Psychotherapy? An Indian View"; paper presented at the annual meeting of the Canadian Society for the Study of Religion, Fredericton, May-June, 1977. (To be published in *Religious Studies*, Cambridge University Press.)

4. Even the label 'Hindu' is quite problematic. Until fairly recently it seems to have been a synonym for 'Indian'. Even these days it is often understood by exclusion as 'non-Muslim, non-Christian...Indian.'

5. See, for example, *Bhagavad Gita*, 13.26.

6. For the thesis that the root meaning of *dharma* as established in the *Rg Veda* has a demonstrable continuity in the *Bhagavad Gita*, see P.W.R. Bowlby, *The Lotus and the Chariot: A Study of the Root Meaning of Dharma in the Indian Religious Tradition*, Ph.D. Thesis, McMaster University, Hamilton Ontario, 1975. The importance of this thesis lies in its challenge to earlier Western scholarship which long accepted the opinion that, contrary to the convictin in the Hindu tradition, there is no discernible continuity in the fundamental concepts of the tradition from the *sruti* texts, of which the *Rg Veda* is the earliest, to the *smrti* texts to which the *Bhagavad Gita* belongs.

7. Christ for whom "I and my Father are one" (*John* 10.30), "is the end of the law for righteousness" (*Romans* 10.4).

8. In medieval Christendom also it would have been considered strange to think that one could engage seriously in any sphere of life without reference to God and thus to 'religion.'

9. One must not imagine that 'Hinduism' is synonymous with *sanatana dharma*. 'Hinduism' is at best an instance of *sanatana dharma* as understood, expressed and practised in time and space. Even if the whole of India were to disappear, along with 'Hinduism,' from the surface of the earth, *sanatana dharma* would still remain. The eternal remains, even if at any given moment it may not have any visible illustration. When Hindus say that all religions are essentially the same, what they are referring to is the transcendental unity of religions, and not to the unity of religious forms. It is their belief, and with someone at the level of realization of Ramakrishna it was a knowledge, that to the extent that a religion leads to transcendent reality it is because it is a form of *sanatana dharma* which is like a tree with its roots in heaven and with many branches on earth.

10. It is appropriate to say, as the *Bhagavad Gita* clearly implies, that an individual's *dharma* relates his social *dharma* and personal *yoga*. In our metaphor of the wheel, an individual human being is situated at the meeting pont of a spoke and the rim. From other points of view, the whole wheel, including the spokes although rarely the center, can be spoken as representing *dharma*.

11. Quoted in G. Austin, *The Indian Constitution: Cornerstone of a Nation* (Clarendon Press, Oxford, 1966), p. 325.

12. Quoted in R.C. Majundar (ed.), *The History and the Culture of the Indian People,* Vol. X, *British Paramountcy and Indian Renaissance* (Bharatiya Vidya Bhavan, Bombay, 1965), Part II, p. 155.

13. Even these days the one person who immediately comes to mind in this connection in India is Mother Theresa whose saintly selflessness in caring for the dying is exemplary.

14. See my review of *Visionary Physics: Blake's Response to Newton* by D.D. Ault (University of Chicago Press, Chicago, 1974), published in the *American Journal of Physics,* Vol. 43, 1975, pp. 1114-16.

15. Some of these assumptions are discussed in R. Ravindra, "Experiment and Experience: A Critique of Modern Scientific Knowing," *Dalhousie Review,* Vol. 55, 1975-76, pp. 655-674.

16. There are many interesting parallels between organized science of the twentieth century and organized Christianity of the nineteenth and earlier centuries, including the unilateral insistence on being the one true way. 'Pious' practising scientists cannot even understand that somebody can seriously raise a question about this. However, this topic cannot be pursued further here.

17. By 'spirit' is not meant 'mind' or 'heart.' According to the Hindu ideas, mind and heart, unlike the spirit, are in the realms of *prakrti* (Nature, materiality, objectivity). Since creation is from above, at birth the spirit takes on a *sarira* (body, including mind and hearet). At death, the spirit gives up the 'body' (*sarira tyaga*) rather than the body giving up the ghost. For some discussion of this point, see R. Ravindra, "Is Religion Psychotherapy? An Indian View," *op. cit.*

ACKNOWLEDGEMENTS

A research grant from the Canada Council is gratefully acknowledged. Professors Wilfred Cantwell Smith and Paul Bowlby kindly read the first draft and made several valuable suggestions.

Mohamed Al-Nowaihi

— G2 —
Religion and Modernization: The General Problem and Islamic Responses

I. The Case Against Religion

Before tackling specific Muslim responses, this paper will attempt a recapitulation of the general problem as the present writer understands it. This is not done as mere formal acknowledgement of the first word in the title of this Group B, viz. "Comparative Religious Responses to Modernization." That word itself can only be a recognition of the fact which must enlighten and control the discussion of problems of modernization in any particular religion: that modernization is not the exclusive dilemma of that religion; rather it is a predicament confronted by all the great, established religions in their endeavor to cope with the exigencies of the world of today. To be sure, each one of them has its own points of awkwardness and idiosyncratic devices for solution. But the starting point must be to have a clear and impartial vision of that general predicament. The adjective "impartial" is advisedly used. Many, but not all, men and women of religious faith are used to having the problem already slanted in favor of religion, the case against religion already belittled, ridiculed and refuted. The only profitable way of tackling the problem—not to dwell on its being the only honest way—is first to hear the anti-religious point of view; to try to understand the reasons why many—too many—men and women of good sense and upright character have stopped to believe, not only in one given religion, but in Religion. If we happen to be believers, this is the more reason that we should do so. If we are confident of the truth and validity of our faith, we should have nothing to fear. We shall not serve our religion—be it what it may—by any self-deception. A religion that can be upheld only by disregarding facts, cheating and lying—to oneself as well to other—is not worth keeping.

The case against religion in the modern age, which was the cause of all the attempts at accommodation, consists of three aspects: intellectual, moral and pragmatic. The three are intertwined; the one of them led to, and was in turn strengthened by, each of the other two. But before recalling them, one has to rid oneself of the illusion that what is often called the crisis of faith in the modern world is solely due to the wickedness of modern man, to his lapse from grace, to his ingratitude towards his Maker and Sustainer. Many atheists and agnostics have been, and still are, of the highest moral caliber. And, in fact, their chief objection to religion has been ethical. If one persists in denying this sobering fact, one will remain incapable of gauging the true dimensions of the problem their group is trying to study. And, in consequence, one will remain utterly incapable of doing any genuine service to one's faith—whatever it may be.

The case against religion, briefly expressed within the available time, is something as follows. Religion is little more than a myth, a myth which may have been acceptable or even necessary in the pre-scientific ages of man, but which is now invalid, injurious or at least redundant. It was the pre-scientific man's attempt to explain to himself the facts and forces of the universe and to define his position in and proper relations with that universe. This attempt we should be unfair to disrespect, just as it would be unfair of us to disrespect the child's imaginative but fallacious attempt to grapple with external reality, even though we as adults have fully or largely outgrown it. But still, we are justified in pronouncing it to be an imperfect and fallacious attempt.

This intellectual part of the anti-religious case was greatly strengthened on the one hand by the remarkable success of modern science in discovering the actual causes of many of the phenomena which used to baffle us and which we attributed to a mysterious, supernatural power or powers; and on the other hand by the sad history of opposition to scientific progress on the part of established religion. For the official representatives of religion, followed, of course, by the vast masses, felt bound to oppose ever scientific advance in modern history, from the Copernician view of the solar system to the Darwinian theory of evolution; from the attempts to discover the true facts about the circulation of the blood and the workings of our internal organs to the invention of anaesthetics for surgical operations, drugs for the treatment of syphilis or artificial methods of birth-control. What happened was that those spokesmen of the established churches always found the new scientific discovery or hypothesis to conflict with the letter of certain texts in their sacred scriptures, or with the philosophy of life and the ethical code for man which they had built upon their understanding of those texts. Now, it is another sobering fact of history that in every major conflict which they waged against the scientists, it was they who were in the end defeated and who had to accept that defeat as best they could—usually with a marked bad grace. About the latest issue, that of birth-control, which is still raging, we cannot prophesy; though many thinkers, guided by what they consider to be the general trend of modern history, are not in much doubt.

This intellectual rebellion was easily, one might say only too naturally, transferred from a struggle against the spokesmen of the established churches to one against religion itself. In this religious spokesmen had only themselves to blame, on account of their relentless and rabid opposition to every scientific advance, and because of the further fact that it was consistently they who started the fight. Little wonder, then, that the intellectual rebellion soon gave rise to, and was in turn immensely fortified by, the moral rebellion. For those religious spokesmen, or in any case the significant body of them, were seen to be little better than dogged obscurants who did their best, or rather their worst, to obstruct the truth and uphold the old errors and falsehoods. For that purpose they did not refrain from subjecting the individuals to dreadful torture and execution, banishment and excommunication, dismissal and imprisonment, and their writings to burning, banning and expurgation.

Religion, therefore, was held to be itself a vicious obscurantist force, bent on the maintenance of an interpretation of the cosmos and of the human condition that was not only invalid but suffocating and deadening, inherently inimical to the spirit of free inquiry, and irreprievably committed for that purpose to the use of the cruellest and most inhuman methods of repression. But this moral repulsion against religion gained considerably more ground when the record of the religious spokesmen was examined on the third field of the battle, that of man's progress in the practical affairs of his life and his struggle to solve the problems and cure the ills of his economic and social conditions. For here again, the official representatives of religion were, most of them and in most cases, for the preservation of the status quo with all its sufferings and glaring injustices: whether in the battle for the abolition of slavery or that of the feminists and suffragettes; whether in the struggles against unrestricted and irresponsible private enterprise, or the use of modern inventions and medical discoveries, or the application of new psychological treatments.

The issues in this respect are too multifarious to be even enumerated on the present occasion. If one issue is to be singled out as an example, let it be the economic. For, if it is true as has been said that the ethical consideration was the main cause of the thinkers' rebellion, it is equally true that the major force which drove thousands—millions?—of practical men and women away from religion has been its sad record on the question of economic equity; and it is this that is still giving the atheist-materialist philosophies their strongest prop against religious faith. Succinctly put, this is their case. The representatives of established religions keep on asking us to ignore this world, despise its pleasures, and eschew its ambitions. Religion, therefore, is an anti-social force, dedicated to the frustration of man's hopes and endeavors to improve his living conditions and attain a measure of comfort and happiness in this world. In this call of theirs, religion's spokesmen want us to accept our present injustices and submit to all inequalities as the ordained stated sanctioned by God, any attempt at righting which would therefore be a rebellion against His Divine Will. They console us by saying that we shall receive justice and recompense at the hand of God in the Hereafter, when we shall be given Heaven as a reward for our resignation and submission in this earthly life. Religion, is, therefore, in essence an opiate for the underprivileged masses. But why do the spokesmen of religion do this? Do they often practice the abstinence they preach? Consider how in most epochs of history they have allied themselves with cruel tyrants and selfish monopolizers of the world's wealth, and consider the worldly benefits that accrued to them from that unholy alliance: the great riches, the carnal luxuries, the pomp and circumstance, the vast estates which they held with tenacious greed, and on which they even refused to pay the due taxes to the state. In that unholy alliance they used their religion as an inducement for the have-nots to accept their miserable lot and give cringing obeisance to their God-appointed lords and masters, far more than they ever used it as an exhortation to the haves to do justice unto the robbed and oppressed. Religion, therefore, is little more than a fraudulent trick and a conspiracy to dissuade the poor from demanding their just share of the wealth of the world. Our overriding concern with religion is its practical influence on man, materially and morally. If such has been its actual influence on its chief upholders, what good can there be in it, what strength can its flaunted ethical value have, and what reasonable hope can still be placed in it for the salvation of tormented humanity?[1]

II. Western Responses to Modernization

These, in sum, were the roots of the religious predicament—the deep and surging forces that compelled modern religious men to undertake their painful processes of accommodation. To be sure, each and every point in the anti-religious case was hotly contested; but, as claimed earlier, on all the major issues it was the men of religion who had to accommodate themselves to the onward march of modernization. What that accommodation entailed was a heart-searching reconsideration of what religion is. What is the true essence of religious faith? What is the rightful domain of belief? What is the legitimate authority of the ancient scriptures, and of their time-honoured hermeneutics and exegeses? Are we bound to accept every *ispe dixit* in the latter—or even in the scriptures themselves—in order to maintain essential religious faith? It is now time to glance briefly at the main devices by which religious believers were able to achieve that accommodation; devices which now enable many intelligent and educated men and women in the West to accept the salutary modernist changes and yet with full sincerity and piety to keep their essential faith. The adjective "salutary" is meant to indicate that the present writer is not one of those who accept every development in modern life and society, and who are out to prove that it can be reconciled with their religion. To this writer, many—too many—of those developments are evil, and must be strenuously opposed.

The devices may be grouped under four categories.

First, there was the distinction between the official spokesmen and religion itself. This meant a realization that it may have been their particular interpretation of religion that was at fault, and not religion *per se*. They may have tended unnecessarily to associate their given state of knowledge, level of understanding, conceptions and personal whims with their sacred texts, which later may be capable of yielding a different interpretation altogether if approached from a different stance of knowledge, an interpretation that would be more in consonance with both modern knowledge and modern conscience. This was strengthened by the fact that in many of the battles they fought they quite obviously went beyond the reasonable limits of their legitimate concerns and intruded themselves into subjects outside their proper scholarly authority.

There was a further realization that, in addition to their intellectual limitations, they also had inevitable moral limitations, being but fallible humans who were subject to much of the ethical level current and acceptable in their time and place, and sometimes even going below it in certain respects. But these natural human shortcomings are not necessarily intrinsic defects in the religious faith nor an unavoidable concomitant of it.

For both these reasons, we may disagree with their opinion as much as we feel bound to, and even criticize and condemn their moral insensitivities and points of blindness, without us being considered to have gone beyond the pale. But what about the sacred texts themselves? Do these—or at least some of them—not give literal and palpable support to the dogmas of those spokesmen? Here the process was one of reinterpretation of those parts which in their letter conflicted with modern knowledge, ethics or practical needs. A non-believer would call this process, not one of reinterpretation, but one of "explaining away." There is little profit, however, in gainsaying the deep sincerity with which it was carried out. In this respect, a great resort was made to the metaphorical and symbolist approach. This is to say that much of what the scriptures pronounce is not meant literally, but is only metaphor and symbol intended to convey to human understanding a figurative or allegorical expression of the higher truth, the infinite truth which our finite brains encased in their inescapable material limitations are not capable of understanding unless it took on some concrete form. In time, however, this gave birth to an even bolder and much more radical approach whose gravity merits that it be allotted a new category.

This ultimate step was the contention that all those sacred texts, though indeed divinely inspired, were yet received by men and written down by men, who were subject to several human intellectual imperfections and who, moreover, used human languages which had certain inherent and inevitable limitations and characteristics. The outcome is that we may question even these texts themselves on some of the things they say without necessarily having to give up our belief in divine existence, as the atheists do, or in divine revelation, as the deists do. The present audience will be familiar with the successive strides made in this approach since the second half of the nineteenth century, in what is called Biblical Criticism, in comparative religion, and in contemporary interreligious dialogue. Not all the facts and theories propounded in this context issued from lay authors; many were advocated by rabbis and clergymen.

III. Why Respond to Modernization?

Before we come to consider how many of these devices have been used by the Muslim modernists or can possibly be used by them in any forseeable future, we must, I think, pause here to ask this fundamental question: Why all this bother? Why all these "devices" to accommodate religion to modernization? Why, instead of tinkering with that archaic, broken machine, not simply discard religion altogether as an outdated system of thinking and basis of behavior? Here I have to guard myself as best I can against allowing my faith to pervert my presentation, which I have endeavoured so far to make as objective as I can. I am quite aware of the atheist and communist answers to that question: that it is merely the pathetic struggle, the hopeless and doomed struggle, of ignorant and credulous humanity to perpetuate its beloved, age-old myths and legends; or that it is the selfish, wicked, cynical attempt of the privileged classes to preserve their illicit gains which are indissolubly bound with those fables, in collusion with established priesthoods and with the dumb consent of the deluded and hag-ridden masses, who are still duped by those capitalist blood-suckers, sharks, hyenas, pigs—and whatever.

The present writer is the last to deny the by no means negligible element of truth in both of these contentions; he has devoted not a small portion of his Arabic writing and lecturing to the cause of purifying religion from the accretions of superstition, and warning against its continued abuse for the preservation of privilege. But is this the whole story? Would one be guilty of religious prejudice if one claimed that it is more than that—that it is, in fact, not merely the crisis of religious faith, but a crisis of modern scientific thought itself? We may begin by a fact which few can gainsay: that modern Western civilization, in spite of its great and magnificent achievements, achievements which no sane person can deny or minimize, has not made the general lot of man much happier. With its tremendous emphasis on material and technological advance, and its relative or complete disregard of the spiritual side of man, a disregard which is either contemptuously avowed or but thinly veiled, it has failed to give man a greater feeling of security and to make him psychologically any more self-integrated. Witness the not inconsiderable number of young people in the West who have become thoroughly dissatisifed, indeed totally disillusioned, with this civilization; their unhappiness and frustration; their terrible feeling of a great spiritual vacuum, a feeling which they either accept in the most bitter frame of despair and cynicism, or which they try to escape in a fantastic variety of ways, ways that may seem unrelated and which are certainly conflicting, but which may be claimed to spring all from the same appalling spiritual void: whether in the taking of hallucinatory and psychedelic drugs to obtain fake ecstacy and uplift; or in the public display (not merely private practice) of utterly licentious promiscuity, to a degree whose shamelessness brings man much lower than the beasts; or in the following of the craziest occultist cranks and the embracing of the most *outre* sects; or in the joining and forming of gangs of rowdy hooligans who are out for sheer vicious destruction; or in the violent activism of extreme political wings, whether of the fanatical right or the fanatical left. In the meantime, the entire human race is reft and blood-spattered by savage fighting between states and internecine massacres within nations in almost every corner of the world; while they all live under the ominous shadow of that latest and most brilliant achievement of Western science and technology: the shadow of the nuclear explosion which may exterminate them all.

But let us move to another element, one that has arisen in scientific thought itself, and has caused a profound—some would say radical—change in what is called the scientific attitude. Please note carefully: this new phenomenon was not forced on science by an argument or refutation that the spokesmen of religion were able to make, but by the development and progress of science itself. Science being, supposedly, the most objective of man's endeavors to grapple with the realities of the universe and the realities of his own life, scientists therefore are, or ought to be, *par excellence*, the readiest of all men to admit their errors, accept new data and reformulate their hypotheses. And, periodically, they do just that, although, being themselves but humans, they may pass through a time-lag during which they, too, are obstinate and dogmatic. So it was they who realized the extravagance of their claims for science and for the capabilities of human reason. That extravagance had reached its summit in the heyday of nineteenth century rationalism, in the various mechanistic and other purely materialistic interpretations of the universe and of human social and individual behavior. But in the first decades of this, the twentieth century, the scientists became increasingly more diffident and truly humble. They realized the inevitable limitations and inherent imperfections of reason—including, of course, their own. They realized that the utmost they could hope to reach with strict scientific methods was probability, not certainty—a word they now do their best to avoid. They began to see the inconclusiveness of all purely materialist theories and their inadequacy to explain and account for all the phenomena of existence. From their own splendid advances in the

study of physics and mathematical physics, they realized that matter itself is not as solid or as permanent as they once thought it to
be. They became aware that matter, far from being the prime influence in and mover of the universe, of which everything else is but
a function or a reflection, is itself just one manifestation which
cosmic energy may take in a certain set of circumstances; itself "an
event," or "a group of events." They listened more attentively to
the evidence advanced by many men neither whose sanity nor
whose integrity could be doubted, the evidence for the existence of
another category of phenomena, which lies outside those categories
that can be gauged by science. Formerly, they used to condemn all
such evidence out of hand as the ravings of crackpots or the fabrications of charlatans. Now they were not so sure, and they became
more and more ready to admit the *possibility* of the existence of that
extra-sensory, or non-material or ultra physical or para-scientific
state or stratum or dimension—or call it what you will.

To expatiate on this element—though it is of grave importance to
us all—would be presumptuous on the part of the layman; in any
case, it will surely be discussed in other committees of this Conference, especially Committee IV. Now these two developments, the
terrifying ravages caused by modern man's spiritual void and the
profound change in scientific thought, combined to make scientists
as well as other scientifically imbued thinkers much less contemp-
tuous than they used to be towards man's evident hunger for
something above mere materialist interpretations; towards his
spiritual searchings and strivings and ideals. Hence a growing
number among them have come to admit that man may be basically
and indispensably in need of what he calls religious faith. As a
distinguished American social scientist[2] expressed it, man is by
means simply a rational animal, but also a mystical, non-rational being. So, as that social scientist expressed it, man is in need of a
myth—what others would rather express by saying that man cannot live by bread alone.

Whether one views this fact as a regrettable shortcoming in
human nature, or glories in it as the sign of the inner superiority of
man over all other living creatures, one has soberly to take account
of it. The attempt to rid man of his religious faith and eradicate his
religious instinct has been a favorite ploy of many of the prominent

liberators of the intellect of man, especially in the two greatest political revolutions in man's history, the French at the end of eighteenth century, and the Communist in the second decade of the twentieth. On this attempt they expended much zealous energy; but it may be wondered whether they did not waste it on a vain and Quixotic crusade, harming their emancipatory effort and causing it unnecessary diversion and delay of fruition. If religious faith, whether we like it or not, is, up till now at least, an indispensable need for the vast majority of men and women, it may be wondered whether that dedicated zeal could not have been more profitably directed towards another goal: to make sure that religion, that overpowering force for most human beings, is not used as a force for reaction and subjugation, but as one for progress and emancipation. The way to this goal is to stress the finer and more tolerant elements that exist in all the great religions, and give them preponderance over the elements of bigotry and fanaticism. In support of such a plea, one may not do better than point up the small, but possibly growing, number of thinkers among the Marxists themselves, outside the U.S.S.R. Writers like Garoudy and Rodinson, with all the minute differences between their approaches, are taking a new attitude to religion; not the traditional one of belligerency and the fight-to-the-death crusade, but one of reconciliation and peaceful coexistence. Their frank advocacy is for a mutual alliance oriented towards the search for the best means to implement humanity's hopes for justice, equity, universal peace, and the happiness of all men in their life on earth. In that advocacy they take note of the historical fact that all the great religions of the world started as powerful progressive, reforming, indeed revolutionary movements aiming at both the intellectual and the material liberation of man; and that they became forces of stultification and privilege only in later periods when their original revolutionary fervor had cooled and they were seized by the privileged classes and made into established churches.

If all this has a moral, it is surely this. In looking at the devices by which the Western modernizers sought to reconcile their faith with their acceptance of the advance of science and the requirements of modern society, and in looking at the Islamic devices which will shortly be explained, one ought not to scorn the devices or call them mere tricks and subterfuges, nor should one doubt the sincerity of their users and dub them dissemblers, hypocrites, opportunistic unbelievers—which, also, they have been dubbed, both the Westerners and the Muslims among them. In both the Western and the Islamic countries, they have been and are making the only attempt that has any chance of success, given the present nature of man, and making it selflessly and at great personal sacrifice, exposed as they are to the barbs of the traditional religionists on one side and the out-and-out materialists on the other.

IV. Islamic Responses to Modernization

A consideration of the Western devices mentioned above will soon reveal the purpose of the four of them: the attempt to rediscover the real essence of faith, the real "spirit" of religion, so to speak, and to isolate it from the many human accretions that had overlaid it and all but suffocated it. For the sad fact is that, although religion—according to believers—comes down from heaven pure, yet once it descends on earth, many human imperfections adulterate it. Those imperfections are born out of the—perhaps permanent—human fallibilites, but also out of the specific temporal and environmental limitations of the ages through which an ancient religion pased. So the attempt is to separate the core from the husk, the timeless meaning from the temporal letter, the "spirit" from "the Law." The established churches have historically held to the husk, the letter, the Law, and the reformers or modernizers tried to reassert their opposites. It is seemingly astonishing, but perhaps only too natural, that once a reformatory movement gains a measure of success and becomes established among its converts, itself, in turn, becomes rigid and is loath to modify the teachng of its founder. So a new reformative movement emerges; and so, apparently, *ad infinitum.* It is edifying to note that Christianity itself, as started and led by Jesus, was a rebellion on behalf of the spirit of religion against those Jews who had neglected it in favor of the letter of the Law—the Pharisees, scribes and hypocrites, as the New Testament has them. And the same happened in Islam.[3]

However, when we now come to consider the particular problem of Islam, we discover that, although the general predicament and its attempted solution were inherently similar, significant differences obtained, which made the task of the Muslim reformers tougher in some respects, and easier in others. To start with, the fourth device was not open to them—that which argues that although the Scripture was divinely inspired, it was written down by men who transmitted the inspiration according to their own ability to understand it and, moreover, using human languages that had definite historical limitations. For all Muslims now believe that their sacred book, the Qur'an, is the literal word of God. It is not the Prophet Muhammad's formulation or expression of truths with which God inspired him: its very consonants and vowels, syllables and words, sentences and passages, are the actual verbal composition and utterance of Allah Himself, speaking in the Direct Speech, First Person. True, in the early centuries of Islam there were individuals and groups of theologians who maintained that the Qur'an was only inspired in meaning and that the wording was Muhammad's. But these were stamped as heretics or even infidels, and their opinion became extinct, to be found only in rare books.

Second, there is the now predominant belief in the permanence and immutability of the *Sharica*, the Divine Law. God, just as He is the fount of all goodness, wisdom and knowledge, is also the fount of all law. He is the only law-giver, and His Law is embodied in two sources: the Qur'an, which is a collection of God's direct and verbal revelations to His prophet and messenger, Muhammad, and the *Hadith* or *Sunnah*, Muhammad's Tradition, which consists of the saying and actions of the Prophet. The sayings were admittedly Muhammad's own wording—as distinct from the Qur'an—but the Prophet was inspired by God in everything he said or did, so his Tradition has the same validity and authority as the Qur'an. Law, therefore, is not something arrived at by the patient ingenuity of man, through a long process of experiment and reasoning, and in response to actual experiences, needs and challenges which confront him in his earthly life. It is something divinely ordained, made once and for all, and meant to last unchanged for all time. This dogma found great support in the fact that, in both Qur'an and Sunnah, early Islam did legislate on quite a number of secular questions, both personal and social, which faced the Muslims during the life of Muhammad. Hence there is a certain amount of edicts on marriage and divorce, custody of the children, inheritance, profit and usury, and the life; as well as certain decreed punishments for such major crimes as homicide, adultery and theft. There are also some injunctions to regulate the relations of Muslims with others in times of peace, war and truce. The conservative Muslims refuse to admit that those injunctions were meant as temporary solutions to pressing problems that had confronted the contemporaries of the Prophet. They hold them to be of permanent and mandatory applicability. Some of them go further to claim that in the *Sharica* we have all the codes of law require or shall ever require, so that we have no need to resort to any other man-made law, civil, criminal, commercial, constitutional or international. While these lines are being written (in July 1977) there is a powerful call in the Egyptian press, started by the conservative elements three or four months ago and being energetically stepped up, to cancel all our secular codes of European origin and to go back to the old *Sharica* and establish it as our only source of law.

It may be remarked that both factors—the belief in the literal truth of the scriptures and in the exclusive validity of the divine law—existed in the Judao-Christian world. To this day there are the "fundamentalists" who accept the Holy Bible literally, and the belief in the immutability and permanence of God's law in every minor detail is not restricted to Talmudic Judaism but includes some Christian believers. However, since the seventeenth century the West has so developed as to steadily decrease the influence of those literalists, who now can hardly be said to constitute an unsurmountable obstacle in the path of reformers bent on modernizing the ancient religious pronouncements.

Nor were those two factors of much practical account in the early centuries of Islam, when Muslim civilization was still in its period of vital growth. Then they seldom acted as suffocating restrictions on the development of Muslim legislation. It was after that civilization had passed its zenith and started on its centuries of decline, from the fourteenth well into the nineteenth centuries A.D., that they combined to bolster up the dogma that the injunctions of the Qur'an and the Sunnah were lasting and unchangeable, suitable in the letter for all peoples, times and places.

And, in fact, this is the chief argument employed by our modernists in their debate with the fundamentalists: the attempt to demonstrate that the crude literalism, intolerance and refusal to change which now dominate most of our intellectual attitude are not the product of genuine, early Islam, but of our centuries of political, social, economic and cultural stagnation, when the original dynamic spirit of Islam had died down and bigotry and reaction ruled the field. Following is a summary of their representation of what actually happened in Islamic history. Far from the Qur'an and the Prophet's tradition containing all the laws ever needful to mankind, the both of them stopped to be sufficient very soon after the death of Muhammad. The rapid and radical change of conditions in the life of the growing Muslim community—a change brought about by the impetus of Islam itself—demonstrated the inadequacy of all the edicts in both Qur'an and Sunnah to meet the requirements of new situations. So, in orthodox Islam itself, two new sources of law-making were added to the *Sharica*, and considered integral parts of it: *Ijmac*, and *Qiyas*. *Ijmac* is consensus, that is, the general agreement of the Muslim community, as represented by its leading scholars, on a certain solution for a new problem—the contention being that God would never let the Muslims agree on a wrong. *Qiyas*, which means analogy, is for one scholar to solve a new problem by looking for one which he deems to be more or less similar and about which there is some ruling in the Qur'an or Sunnah, and deduce therefrom the appropriate answer which he believes to be applicable to the new question. These two new sources constituted *Ra'y*, human opinion, as an element in law-making to stand side by side with the two earlier, divinely ordained or inspired, sources. They resulted in a great proliferation of *Madhahib* (singular *madhhab*), schools of Islamic jurisprudence. There was hardly a question of *Fiqh*, Jurisprudence, about which those schools did not differ, to a lesser or greater degree. Now the remarkable thing is that the various schools exhibited the greatest mutual toleration, all being considered equally tenable, and the choice among them left to individual preference. Indeed, the dictum was asserted: *ikhtilafuhum rahmah* which means that the difference of opinion among the

a'immah (singular 'imam), the leaders of the schools of jurisprudence, is a mercy to Muslims, as it allows a person to follow
whichever opinion is more suitable to his particular needs or more in
accord with his intellectual bent.

That remarkable mutual toleration of the 'imams stemmed from
the fact that not one of them claimed infallibility for his opinion.
Each realized, and categorically declared with the most genuine
humility, that he was but a fallible human, liable to error. This is important to remember and needs continual stressing, for the conventional view has come to grant the right of passing individual judgements to those ancient jurists alone, and to deny it to anybody that
came after them. Yet, the modern reformers point out, *ijihad*, i.e. the
right of every scholar to make and express his own opinion, was
open to all scholars who could demonstrate by their learning and
uprightedness their fitness for exercising it. When the door of ijihad
was declared shut, this only happened in our centuries of decline and
stagnation, and it was wrong. Hence they call for *fath bab al-ijtihad*,
the reopening of the door of individual opinion. To support this call,
they remind Muslims of one of the cardinal creeds of Islam, a creed
to which all Muslims subscribe, and which none challenges. This is
embodied in the established dictum *la kahanut fi al-Islam*, i.e., no
priesthood in Islam. As different from several other religions, Islam
does not establish a priesthood, and recognizes none. No human being after the Prophet Muhammad, or group of human beings, can
claim any special sacerdotal quality or power of dispensation. None
after the Prophet can claim *ex-cathedra* infallibility for his pronouncements. From this it will be seen that the first and second
devices of Western modernizers, the distiction between religion and
its official spokesman in their intellectual and moral limitations,
were much easier to use in Islam while in the West they took centuries of bitter struggle and untold martyrdoms to establish. This is
not to say that, human nature being what it is, the fourteen centuries of Islamic history were totally devoid of certain individuals
and groups who attempted to claim for themselves a power and a
position which were, virtually though not avowedly, priestly. But it
was not hard to refute their claims and confound their presump-
tions. This is not to deny that the opinion of a scholar who has
devoted a lifetime to the study of religion has a certain prestige and

merits special attention. But this is no more than the special consideration due to the opinion of a physician, a scientist, a literary
critic, a grammarian, or any other expert in a branch of knowledge.
None of these can claim infallibility of opinion or immunity from error; he can be questioned, required to submit evidence, argued with,
differed from. This fact is pointed up in the very title we give our
religious scholars. They are not called the Arabic equivalents of
priests, clergymen or ministers. They are simply called *culama'*
(singular *calim*), learned men, from *cilm*, knowledge or learning.
Strong objection is made to calling them *rijal al-din*, men of religion
—a habit that has crept in and is being encouraged by some of them,
but denounced by others.They should only be called *culama' al-din.*

Now, going back to the belief that is now professed by all
Muslims that the Qur'an is the literal, binding word of God, our
modernizers do not contest this dogma; but they point out that,
although it is the literal word of God, this "word" is yet open to different understanding, on many though not all questions. Thus spake
God: that is true—but how shall we, humans, understand His correct and full meaning? It is obvious that we are limited by our ability to understand, which may change—which does change—from
time to time and from one environment to another. Here they point
to the very great variety in the process of classical *tafsir*, explanation of Qur'an. There were literally scores upon scores of those explanations, demonstrating the most extensive differences—once
more, all respectable, all tenable, the preference left to the individual
reader. Often the *tafsir* consisted in *ta'wil*, interpretation, which was
giving the Quranic verse other than its obvious or literal meaning,
when the literal meaning obviously contradicted the sensory experiences of man, or was not congruent with the interpreter's sectarian stand.

Both the amount and extent of differences in the classical explanations and interpretations were so great as to amaze or even
scandalize members of the contemporary Muslim community when
they were rediscovered and revealed to them. All this will show that
the third Western device, that of the metaphorical or symbolist explanation, was quite open to Muslim thinkers, and had, in fact, a
recognized and respected place in their traditional scholarship, thus,

in its own way, mitigating much of the rigidity that might have resulted from the belief in the literal revelation of the Qur'an. Indeed,
no less a person that the great thinker Ibn Rush, known to Europe
as Averroes (1126-1198), had categorically declared that, whenever a
contradiction arose between the literal meaning of a sacred text and
what sensory experience or rational thought can accept, preponderance should be allotted to the latter, and resort should then be made
to the *ta'wil.* he and several other classical Muslim thinkers, facing
Greek philosophy and other rich legacies of earlier non-Muslim
civilizations, had shown admirable receptivity and adaptability, and
attempted a number of reconciliations between faith and reason. In
fact, they had suggested some syntheses and solutions which were
made use of by European theologians and philosophers when, a few
centuries later, the conflict began in Europe between religious belief
and rational thought. Surely, our reformists argue, the right to differ in explaining and interpreting God's word was not restricted to
our ancient commentators? On the contrary, in view of the vast
development of modern knowledge, we may be more in need than
ever before to exercise that right, so as to be able to give a
metaphorical interpretation to certain Quranic verses which our
ancestors, not knowing many things we now know, were content to
understand literally. This may be the only means possible to us of
maintaining our belief in the divine origin of our holy scripture and
at the same time accepting the findings of modern knowledge.

V. Landmarks on the Path of Islamic Modernization

It has been stated above that the theoretical stand which considers *Al-Sharica* permanent and immutable never operated in the
early, dynamic centures of Islam, but only in our centuries of almost
total stagnation—our "dark ages," as we call them, borrowing a
term from Western history(but denoting quite a different period of
time, from the fourteenth to the mid-nineteenth century A.D., as
stated before). Nor was that stand powerful enough in our modern
era to stem the tide of new thought, social change and new legislation which was made imperative by the vastly altered conditions,
conditions resulting from our increased contact with the modern
Western World. This contact began with the Napoleonic invasion of

Egypt and progressed by leaps and bounds in the latter half of the nineteenth century. The Ottoman Empire, under whose suzerainty most countries of the Middle East lay, started, in the middle of that century, a great movement of new enactments, called *tanzimat* (organizations), most of which were borrowed from European sources. First came the Commercial Code in precisely 1850, to be followed in 1858 by the Penal Code, and soon to give rise in the various Arab countries to the codification of new civil, commercial and penal laws, all of which went markedly outside *Al-Sharica* and were taken from the Napoleonic Code, the English Common law and the Indian Law (made by the British for their great colony), with little attempt to claim that they were derived from the traditional Islamic Law. The only domain which was left to the jurisdiction of the *Sharica* was that of family relationships in what is called *Qanun al-ahwal al-shakhsiyya*, Law of Personal Status, limited to such matters as conjugal relations, guardianship of minors, custody of the children, succession and inheritance, and gifts and bequests. How was the orthodoxy inherited from our "dark ages" able to accept, or at least not actively resist, all those new laws of foreign origin, and yet, at the same time, hold fast to the theory of the imperativeness, perfection, sufficiency and immutability of the *Sharica*? This was achieved by claiming that it was no defect of Religious Law itself, but was rather the fault of times that had gone bad and men who had lapsed from grace. The *Sharica* was still the correct and good and proper Law, and we must just wait for the times to regain their former goodness and men to become once more worthy of the *Sharica*.

It would be unjust to accuse our conservative *culama'* of conscious hypocrisy: they were perfectly sincere in holding to that stand. This, however, does not exculpate it from the stigma of dangerous contradictoriness and a kind of intellectual schizophrenia which is very harmful to a community. The danger and harm will become more apparent when one realizes the device to which our modernists resorted to get their reforms enacted and which was accepted, or acquiesced in by the *culama'*. This is the device called *cadam samac*, denial of hearing. The decisions of the ancient jurists were not declared null, but any litigant who brought a lawsuit demanding their application was denied hearing in a court of law.

For instance, the classical jurists thought that the period of gestation could last between two and seven years. No attempt was made to challenge this opinion in the light of present medical knowledge. Instead, in the 1929 Law of Personal Status in Egypt, any woman was denied judicial hearing if she made a claim for inheritance resting on her infant being born more than one year after the death of her husband or her divorce from him. Thus the "legal fiction" of the rightness of ancient jurisprudence was declared to remain intact.

Be that as it may, the exigencies of life had worked their irresistible pressure on all the branches of Law except the Law of Personal Status; and it was this—in most Arab countries and in the majority of cases—that was left to our reformers to try to modernize. This archaic law, in which we were still bound by the verdicts and opinions of imams who had lived a thousand years ago, was not the least needful of reform, governing as it does some of the most vital problems in the lives of human beings, and causing untold injury and misery to millions of our men, women and children—but chiefly women and children, particularly in regard to our two major social evils, polygamy and unrestricted divorce.[4] It is not the purpose of this paper to enumerate the reforms that have been successfully introduced in many, but not all, Arab countries—a subject which, moreover, has been adequately studied by better qualified scholars, especially the distinguished Arabist the late Professor Joseph Schacht. What will be attempted here is to trace the successive steps by which our modernizers have tackled the immense problem which faced them. This may help us to discover the limitations that have so far restricted their efforts, and explore the barrier that has still to be courageously surmounted if we are ambitious of any significant new achievement.

Up to 1915, every one of our countries, in its official legislation and adjudication on matters of Personal Status, followed one or the other of the classical *madhahib*. This meant that its legislators and judges could not just follow the ancient *fiqh* in general, but were restricted to that one school and could not go outside it to consult the opinions of other schools. In Egypt, that was the *hanafi* School, after the name of its founder, Abu Hanifa. Not only that, but they were also bound on every point to follow *al-qawl al-rajih*, the "predominant opinion," in that particular school. (In every school there may be, and there usually is, a variety of opinions on any one point, and the "predominant opinion" would be the one preferred by most authorities who wrote the textbooks of the school.) Muhammad cAbduh, our leading modernizer in Egypt (1849-1905), had been for a number of years calling for the right to follow one of the "lesser opinions" in the same chosen school, whenever it was found to be more suitable for our new conditions. Then years after his death, the first such enactment was made, whereby, following a "lesser opinion" in the *hanafi* school, a wife was given the right to claim and obtain divorce if her husband had a dangerous disease of which she had no knowledge before the marriage. The next step was to go outside that one school and apply the predominant opinion in any of the three other main and extant schools of the Sunnah sect (considered to be the main orthodox body of Islam): the *maliki, shafici* and *hanbali* schools. From this they progressed to consider the suitability of certain lesser opinions in any of these major schools of "orthodoxy"; and the next step was to go outside the four major schools of the Sunnah in order to search in the opinions of the minor and less well-spread—or even extinct—schools, still within the orthodox sect.But a much bolder step was taken when our Egyptian legislators went outside the schools of the Sunnah altogether, whether major or minor, whether extant or extinct, to borrow opinions from schools belonging to other Muslim sects, until now considered "heretical." Such was the *ithna cashari imami* school of the *shica* sect, in the right of the testator to bequeath up to one third of his legacy to any one of his rightful heirs even without the consent of the rest of these heirs—up till then that right was allowed him only if he made the bequest to a person or persons outside the rightful heirs, or to one of the latter but with the consent of the rest of them. Another was the *ibadi* school of the *khawarij* sect, in giving the grandchildren whose parent had died that share of the legacy of their grandparent which their deceased parent would have inherited had he survived the grandparent. In the latter instance, the lack of any such provision in the orthodox schools of jurisprudence often caused grevious privations, since in our countries it is not infrequent for a son or daughter who had grown up, got married and had children, to die before his or her parent.

It will have been noticed that in all this reforming work, which, admittedly, alleviated some of the worst abuses and eased some of the most pressing problems, our modernizers did not see fit to challenge the basic contention that the ancient *sharica* was complete, sufficient and unchangeable. Nor could any of these achievements, valuable though they were, be considered a real *ithhad*, an exercise of the right to form a new opinion, since, for the advocation of any of their reforms, they had to quote the opinion and depend on the authority of some ancient scholar in one classical school or another. And that had often forced them to what is perhaps the strangest device of all, that of *talfiq*, literally "patching up." This consisted, in order to arrive at their sought verdict, in taking its first premise from one *'imam*, the second from another *'imam*, and drawing a conclusion which neither of those ancient scholars would have countenanced. To say all this is not to belittle their courage, but to point up the severe restrictions within which they had to work with any hope of success in the first four or five decades of this century. And, despite all this caution and gradualness, they often failed to convince the state authorities to enact their proposed reforms. The one move towards a radical reconsideration of the whole problem of the *sharica* was the argument advanced by the great Muhammad cAbduh, and developed by his disciples in what is called *al-manar* Group (after the name of their modernizing journal). The argument goes as follows. Religious questions are not all of the same order of importance. A distinction must be made between *'usul* and *furuc* (literally, roots and branches, meaning fundamentals and secondary points.) The *'usul* we are not entitled to change so long as we wish to remain Muslims. But these consist only of *caquida, cibada, and akhlaq*: respectively articles of creed, rites of worship, and principles of ethics. The *furuc*, however, include everything connected with *mucamalat*, that is, all mundane transactions among people, such as civil and commercial exchanges, inheritance, and even marriage and divorce. All these are non-essentials which form no fundamental part of religion, and we do not only have the right to change legislation concerning them, but it is, indeed, our bounden duty to effect the change if it would result in more benefit and happiness to people in their changed circumstances.

Muhammad cAbduh was a distinguished *c alim* in *al-Jami c al-Azhar* (the "Glorious Mosque," the great Islamic seminary established in Cairo just over one thousand years ago), and for a time he was even grand Mufti of Egypt (the chief counsellor to the government on religious affairs). Perhaps that was what enabled him to advocate that daring view; he was working from within the sanctum sanctorum of Islamic scholarship. But, although that argument of his won the approval of quite a few thinking men, it was never accepted by the formal body of the *culama*.' When, in the 1930s, another Azharite teacher, c Abd al-Muta c al al-Sa c idi, attempted to revive it, he was muzzled and demoted in the Azhar service.

However, the years that have elapsed since have seen much political and social change, starting with the success of the army coup in 1952 and its elevation to a declared Revolution. It seemed to the present writer that the times might be suitable for resuscitating Muhammad cAbduh's argument, and, perhaps, advancing it a step further, towards a radical confrontation with the established view of *al-Shari c a.* As long as that view was dominant: as long as we had to base all our new reforms on the opinion of some ancient 'imam, diligently extracted from some age-old tome or another, and sometimes after a resort to some sort of *talfiq*, it seemed to this writer that no significant progress could be made any more. In the numbers of February and March, 1970 of the Lebanese cultural monthly *al-Adab*, he published two articles under the title *wa'l an, ila al-thawra al-fikriyya* (And now, to the intellectual revolution). These articles rebuked our purportedly revolutionary regime in Egypt for restricting its reformative zeal to the political, military and economic fronts, and all but neglecting the intellectual emancipation, which, in the writer's view, was the *sine qua non* for all genuine and pervasive transformation of society. Then the articles outlined the needed changes in the current religious, ethical, nationalist and cultural attitudes. The repercussions of the articles induced that journal to devote its whole number of May 1970 to articles falling under the general title *nahwa thawra thaqafiyya carabiyya* (Towards an Arab cultural revolution). Writers from all over the Arab world contributed studies of the changes needed in the spheres of politics, economics, social institutions, philosophy, religion, art, literature and language. The present writer's contribution was entitled *nahwa thawra fi al-fikr al-dini* (Towards a revolution in religious thought). The rest of the present paper is devoted to an English condensation of some of the arguments used. This is done in the hope that it might be of interest to the members of this group to watch how a modernist Muslim writer addresses his readers and tries to win them over to his unfamiliar point of view: the caution he has to exercise, as well as the limit of boldness he may risk with any hope of getting away with it in the current intellectual and emotional state of mind in the Muslim world.[5]

VI. A Muslim Modernist
Addressing His Co-Religionists

In all the spheres covered by other writers in this special number, the first obstacle that is always raised in the way of any proposed reform is the religious obstacle. People do not ask whether the new proposal is in itself right or wrong, beneficial or harmful: they ask whether it agrees or disagrees with the requirements of religion—by which they mean the verdicts and opinions of the ancient 'imams. We cannot go on much longer spending time and effort in justifying every proposed reform by first proving that it does meet with such requirements. What is needed is to introduce a radical change in people's understanding of what the essence of religion is, what it intrinsically came for, what its rightful role in human society should be, so as to persuade them not to intrude it into spheres which lie outside its legitimate domain.

The claim is made that Islam contains a complete body of legislation which covers all civil, penal, commercial, political, constitutional and international fields, and which can provide a judgement for every case. This claim reveals an ignorance of how vast, multifarious and complex a modern code of law is; it even reveals a basic ignorance of what law is. The Quranic verses which may be considered to contain legal provisions are no more than five hundred, in the widest and most inclusive count. A law must define beforehand the limits of obligation and specify the degrees of punishment, from maximum to minimum, for their infringement. In all the laws or quasi-laws which the Qur'an contains, it specifies no more than five hudud (singular hadd, punishment): the well-known ones for homicide, brigandage, theft, adultery and slander—to say nothing about the differences regarding the circumstances of their applicability among the various sects and schools, differences that could not be tolerated in any one code. Those differences proliferate and get more contradictory and irreconcilable when the classical jurists debate other actions than those five crimes, some holding a certain action in certain circumstances *haram*, unlawful and punishable, others considering it only *makruh*, reprehensible and meriting rebuke but not actual punishment, and others still finding it *mubah*, completely permissible.[6] Reading, almost haphazard, one single section in a single chapter in any of the great classical works of *fiqh* will provide examples, often by the score.

Moreover, a careful consideration of the commands and prohibitions contained in both the Holy Qur'an and the Prophet's Tradition demonstrates most of them to be moral exhortations and not proper laws in the real sense of the word; hence, partly, that immense difference just alluded to. But let us ask this straight question: did either the Qur'an or the Sunnah, or the both of them together, ever attempt to laydown a complete code of law, as the claim is frequently made? On the contrary, both were greatly reluctant to tackle any but the most pressing questions which which resulted from the growth of the Muslim community in Medina after the Prophet Muhammad had fled to it (in the year 622 A.D.) from his native Mecca and started there to found his new state. This is proved by verses 101 and 102 in *sura* 5, which began: "O believers, question not concerning things which, if they were revealed to you, would vex you." These verses were occasioned by the early Muslim's propensity to rush to Muhammad demanding a solution to every problem that faced them. Likewise, the classical collections of the Prophet's *hadith* contain several instances where Muhammad was greatly annoyed by that propensity of his companions, and warned them against the consequences of asking too many questions. One such warning was: "Verily, the most sinning Muslim is he who asks about a matter that was not forbidden before his question, and which, in consequence of his asking, is declared *haram*."[7] The Pro-

phet clearly wanted people to exercise their own judgement and not
heap upon themselves commands and prohibitions to which they
would feel bound afterwards. This is exactly the explanation given
by the classical commentaries on the Quranic verses just quoted.

Was Muhammad himself an autocratic adjudicator who loved to
impose his opinion on everything? On the contrary, apart from matters of creed, worship and the higher ethics, he was given to con-
sulting his companions, and in many instances acceded to their
recommendations and abandoned his former opinions. This was
epitomized in the famous anecdote of *ta'bir al-nakhl*, fructification of
the date palms. He had expressed his opinion on the uselessness and
superstitiousness of that practice by which they cut the requisite
part off a male palm and grafted it in the opposite part of a female
tree; it was God who caused all trees to bear fruit. When their stopping this operation resulted in the trees going barren, he told them to
return to their practice; admitted his error; said that, in everything
not touching the Revelation, he was only a fallible mortal like them;
and added this admission: *Autum aclam bi umur dunyakum* (You
are more knowledgeable about the affairs of your worldly life).[8]
Although this saying is often quoted to illustrate Muhammad's pro-
bity, its full significance has seldom been gauged, and its moral has
certainly never been formally implemented. If Muhammad had the
integrity to admit that he was less knowledgeable than his contemporaries about their worldly affairs, and even in such an elementary
fact of their simple desert life, how much more knowledgeably we
must be in the affairs of our vastly more technical and complex life
in this twentieth century. Were he to come back to life, would he try
to interfere in these our worldly affairs as our religious dignitaries,
who have set themselves up as the spokesmen of his religion, are
continually doing?

If the Prophet himself could make mistakes about mundane affairs, could infallibilty be claimed for the opinions of the jurists?
They themselves never made such a claim: it was made on their
behalf in our centuries of bigotry and dogmatism. Their entire work
postulates the right of every scholar to form his own opinion and offer his own solution. Not only that, but an objective study of
classical legislation shows that the greater portion of it was not
primarily derived from any analogous deductions from the Qur'an

or the Sunnah: it was borrowed from the laws, customs and practices of the conquered lands which formerly belonged to the two great Persian and Byzantine empires. All the Muslim jurists did was that they culled that rich material from those much more developed lands which were the heirs to earlier, mature civilizations and which had sophisticated sedentary societies of agriculturists, craftsmen, traders and civil servants; and, finding that material good and beneficial, they declared that it did not conflict with the prerequisites of Islam and couched it in Islamic forms. Now, after our centuries of backwardness and underdevelopment, we find ourselves in a similar situation vis-a-vis the Western countries which have far outstripped us in material and cultural development. It does not seem just that we be denied the right which was exercised by our ancestors in their times of dynamic growth when, sweeping out of their arid Arabian desert into Iraq, Persia, Syria and Egypt, they settled in these countries and availed themselves extensively of their governmental, fiscal, economic, commercial, agricultural and industrial practices.

If neither the Qur'an nor the Sunnah attempted to lay down a complete code of law that "covers all needs for all eternity" as the claim is often phrased, did they yet intend the injunctions which they made on the mundane questions which they did tackle to be permanent and unalterable? Facing this thorny and perilous question, let us begin by noting a fact which is denied by none: the change of legislation within the Qur'an itself. In the ten years (622-632) which the Prophet spent in Medina founding, developing, bolstering and expanding the new Islamic state, the society went—as it was bound to do—into successive stages of development, and it was sometimes found that the edicts which were made in an earlier stage did not suit the later. So new verses were revealed modifying or completely annulling earlier pronouncements. This is known as the phenomenon of *al-nasikh wa al-mansukh*, the abrogating and the abrogated verses. And this phenomenon points up the dynamic, changing nature of Islamic legislation right from its very begining. Next, the historical fact that leaps to the mind is the action of cUmar, the second Caliph, in refusing on several occasions to implement certain Quranic injunctions when he believed that the changed times rendered them unsuitable. For instance, he refused to apply the Quranic punishment of theft (cutting off of the thieves' hands, as categorically decreed in the Qur'an, 5:38) in a year of famine, and, also, when he discovered that the thieves were the slaves of a rich and stingy master who did not pay them their rightful wages. (Instead, he severely castigated that master, imposed a heavy fine on him, and ordered him to remunerate the wretched slaves decently.) Likewise, he cancelled the share in public alms allotted by the Qur'an, (9:60) to the *mu'allafa qulubuhm*, those Arab chieftains whom the Prophet placated with gifts when the new Islamic state was not yet firmly established. When, protesting, they quoted the Qur'an, cUmar bluntly told them that Islam was no more in fear of their mischief-making. When questioned about these cancellations of categorical Quranic edicts, he simply answered that conditions had changed since the time of the Prophet—a time, let it be noted, which was only one decade earlier. (cUmar ruled from 634 to 644.) Our conservative *culama'*, who cannot deny those actions of cUmar, yet try to explain them away by arguments incompatible with the Islamic creed. For instance, they claim for the early Caliphs (successors of the Prophet), who were close companions of Muhammad, *fatwa al-sahabi*, the power to pronounce an opinion tantamount in authority to that of the Prophet himself. But, we must insist, nobody after the Prophet had any sacerdotal power of making *ex cathedra* pronouncements. As the established dictum has it, *al-numuwwa la tu—warrath*, Prophethood is not inherited. The Caliphs were successors to Muhammad only in his temporal capacity as political chief of state. Moreover, we have seen how in temporal affairs Muhammad himself claimed no infallibility. All those attempts by our *culama'* can only lessen cUmar's degree of courage, perspicacity, tolerance and breadth of view. They fear that cUmar's actions might be considered a transgression which detracted from the sanctity of the Qur'an. It may be wondered, however, whether cUmar was not the one who demonstrated a true understanding of the spirit of Islamic legislation, a spirit of continual development and dynamic change to suit)the ever changing conditions of human life, quite different from the rigid, inflexible strait jackets into which our conservatives want to force it.

In this respect, we need to consider more deeply than we have

ever done before the real and full significance of the classical principle of *al-maslaha*, the common weal or public good. The classical
theorists themselves declared it to be the overriding stipulation of
all *isharica* commands and prohibitions. According to it, any *sharica*
injunction whatever can be suspended if its implementation would
result in positive harm to the Muslim community. Hence, those
theorists allowed a ruler to make any change of law that would
result in *jalb nafc wa dafc darar*, the securing of a (public) benefit or
the preventing of a (public) harm. This principle was embodied in the
further dictum: *al-darurat tubih al-mahzurat*, necessities make permissible the things that were forbidden. For instance, in times of
famine, Muslims may eat pork, which is otherwise an abhorrent sin
to commit. However, since the start of our decline, this principle has
never been adequately implemented, and nowadays it receives little
more than lip-service. And yet, itself alone can justify all the
beneficial reforms which our modernizers are propagating. We must
hasten to declare that we do not wish this principle to be lightly or
irresponsibly exercised. We are not advocating that we rush to
cancel or suspend any law which we do not like, or simply to replace
it by a fancy new law from the glamorous West. We would insist
that, before the exercise of the principle of *al-maslaha* in any new
legislation, the most careful and thorough study must be made by
all our learned men who have something to say about the various
sides of the problem under discussion—jurists, economists, social
scientists, medical experts and any other concerned specialists.
However, once they reach consensus on the need to change the existing law or to enact the new provision, nothing should be allowed
to obstruct its enactment by due process of the law—not even a
Quranic or Prophetic text that carries a different provision.

To conclude: all the injunctions on the secular affairs which are
made in the Qur'an and the Sunnah were no more than temporary
provision meant for the Arabs of the time of the Prophet alone and
not intended to be everlasting and unalterable. All the findings of
the ancient 'imams were the opinions of human beings who did their
best in their limiting circumstances and who neither were infallible
nor claimed infallibility. Consequently, all the decisions and provisions of the classical *sharica* must be amenable to change. It will be

a happy day indeed when Muslims—or a significant and effective
body of them—come to admit this and at the same time realize that
it does not conflict with essential religious faith and need not cause
that faith any harm. It is, indeed, the only way to restore the Islamic
faith to its former dynamic and beneficial character. Thus, and only
thus, can Islam continue as a faith which claims the allegience and
sincere devotion of men through all the changes of time and place.

NOTES

1. A remark must be added here, taking note of a change that has
    been occurring since the 1960s. Learning the lessons of the bitter
    past, a (growing?) number of clegymen belonging to different chur-
    ches, have been actively campaigning against political, economic
    and social injustices, and lamenting the passive, if not inimical, at-
    titude adopted by their churches towards those issues. They want
    them more positively to fight the color bar, take the side of the vic-
    tims of colonial exploitation, speak for the poor against the rich,
    defend the civil liberties, and condemn the inequitable treatment
    still meted out to women in many spheres. Though still a minority
    and in most cases frowned upon by the official establishments and
    treated as rebels, or worse, they may be deemed to point the way
    to the future, and the success they have already achieved in stir-
    ring the conscience of Christians is not negligible. The strength
    which their protest has already assumed found an expression in no
    other than the fourth world Synod of Bishops held in the Vatican
    in October 1974. For the first time, a majority of its delegates
    came from the developing countries in Asia, Africa and Latin
    America. The synod's theme was "Evangelization in the Modern
    World", and it discussed the difficulties of preaching Catholicism
    in the ever more secularized West on the one hand, and, on the
    other hand, in an East where living memory still associates the
    church with colonialism's worst abuses. So the need was stressed
    for a radical "liberation theology" that is based on the admission
    that spiritual salvation cannot be effected without political and
    economic salvation. If it is the church's supreme objective to
    liberate men from sin, then the sins of hunger, war, oppression,
    slavery, eroticism and insufficient wages must not be neglected.
    Another topic raised was the need to upgrade the status of women
    in the church, while an impassioned plea was made on behalf of

married priests. Although the conclave's official summing-up report glossed over such detailed criticisms and talked rather generally on the church's role in the modern world (that report was rejected by an overwhelming majority of the bishops), yet, the mere fact that such views were boldly expressed in such a conclave, and in front of the Pope himself was indubitably significant, and, hopefully, indicative of future developments. But until this hope is fulfilled, this observation must be confined to a footnote, and the case against established religion must remain substantially as represented in the text above.

2. Professor Robert N. Bellah, "Islamic Tradition and the Problems of Modernization," a paper delivered in the Colloquium on Tradition and Change in the Middle East, Harvard University, January 16, 1968.

3. Of Islam, Professor Bellah has the following remarks to make in the paper just cited. He makes a sharp distinction between "the Quranic teaching" and the way Islamic law was later established. Regarding the Quranic teaching, he repeatedly describes its nature as one of "basic modernity." He even describes it as "universalist, progressive and indeed revolutionary." Why did it fail, to be replaced by the conventional view of *al-sharica*? His answer to this question is that "it was too modern to succeed." The present writer cannot help adding: and so, until this day, it remains to be, for the conservative majority of the Muslims—too modern to succeed.

4. For more detail on the campaign to reform the Law of Personal Status, see the writer's "problems of Modernization is Islam," *The Muslim World*, Hartford Seminary Foundation, LXV, No. 3, 1975, pp. 174-185.

5. This state of mind, it must be sorrowfully added, is now (middle of 1977) much more intolerant, for certain political reasons. Were that article to be published now, it would raise a greater storm than it did seven years ago. But the sensitive political pendulum swings continually, and with it the tolerated degree of freedom of expression goes up and down.

6. There are two other categories under which actions can be classified according to our *usul al-fiqh*, Principles of Jurisprudence: *fard*, mandatory, something a Muslim must do, otherwise he merits punishment; and *mandub*: commendable, something he ought, but is not forced to do. Here again, innumerable differences occurred among the classical jurists regarding the classification of certain actions *per se* or in given circumstances.

7. Readers of Arabic may consult the special section on this topic in

the chapter entitled *kitab al-fada'il* (Book of Virtues) in *Sahih Muslim,* one of the earliest and most trustworthy collections of the Prophet's *hadith.* The section in question is given a heading of which this is a translation: "The respect due to (Muhammad), and avoiding to ask him many questions about inessential things regarding which there are no injunctions."

8. Ibid. same Chapter, section heading translated "The duty to obey (Muhammad) in what he said in the way of religious law, but not in what he gave as his human opinion in the affairs of the worldly life."

R.J. Zwi Werblowsky

— G3 —
Modernism and Modernization in Buddhism

In the short space at our disposal we must forego the preliminary exercise—essential though it may be—of examining and defining the notoriously unclear terms 'modernity,' 'modernization and 'modernism.' Let us therefore simply take it for granted, somewhat naively and uncritically, that we are all living in a cultural climate characterized as 'modernity'; that processes are at work leading traditional, post-traditional and so-called "premodern" societies to this state of modernity; that these processes are generally subsumed under the name 'modernization'; and that religious movements trying to reformulate their traditions in the light of what they hold to be modernity are described as 'modernist'. Hence the expression *modernism*, first applied to certain tendencies in nineteenth century western Catholicism (and solemnly condemned by papal authority), was subsequently applied also to similar movements (Muslim, Hindu, Buddhist etc.) elsewhere. A few preliminary observations of a general nature are, however, unavoidable.

1. Whatever the criteria selected for defining, diagnosing, and measuring modernity and modernization (e.g., the indexical, typological, world-acculturative or evolutionary methods; criteria of rationalization, diffusion of secular-rational norms, degrees of self-sustaining growth, increase in mobility, decreasing importance of ascriptive status, urbanization, industrialization, changes in the proportions of primary, secondary and tertiary occupations etc.), we are—especially in the religious sphere—primarily concerned with what Robert Bellah has called the "modernization of the soul." This is a process far more difficult to describe than the other forms and levels of modernization.

2. Modernization is often held closely related (whether in a rela-

tionship of cause, or effect, or both, is a question that need not detain us here) to "secularization." Both terms are vague and in need of more precise analysis. There is a wide range of responses: the euphoric celebration of "secular theology" as the true because "modern" fulfillment of the Christian gospel; apologetic attempts to show that the "modernist" interpretation of a religion can handle and successfully overcome the challenges and dangers of secularism; the view that secularism, as an essential element of modernity, will combine with the latter to abolish religion; anti-modernist reaction as the only way to preserve religion from the poison of secularism, and so on. The spectrum is wide and each religious civilization exhibits its specific range of responses.

3. The terminology used becomes further complicated by the fact that it also has ideological functions and at times even serves ideological purposes. The words 'modern' and 'secular' are therefore not simply scientific, descriptive terms (in which case one could discuss whether they were adequate or happily chosen), but more often than not serve as slogans and even battle-cries in ideological warfare and hence are used with a different value-weighting by different protagonists in the debate.

4. Both modernization and secularization have often been equated with "westernization."Whilst this simple and uncritical identificaton is undoubtedly wrong, there certainly is a relationship and few observers would deny that the impact of the West (especially since the ninetenth century) and its colonial, military, economic and cultural expansion served as an important catalyst. The responses to western influence assumed a great variety of forms: adoption, imitation and emulation, enculturation, outright rejection and repudiation, selective adaptation and assimilation, and even such complex phenomena as outward repudiation of what was actually being adopted or the claim that the values which the "West" had brought (to the extent that they were any good at all) were "in reality" identical with those taught since time immemorial by one's own religion and culture. They merely had been (temporarily) forgotten as a result of historical decadence (caused, of course, by the western intrusion), and were now being rediscovered. At any rate it is important to keep in mind the strength of the anti-western affects operating in many "Third World" modernization processes. Quite

apart from analytical sociological reasons, these affects also lend subjective weight to the claim that modernization and westernization are not the same.

5. The rejection of the simplistic equation modernization=westernization (notwithstanding the undeniable and decisive role of western influence in every modernization process) leads to a further differentiation. In their excess of joy at the discovery of "modernity" as an historical and sociological category, scholars at first believed that the concept was unequivocal and clear-cut. Modernization processes everywhere would of necessity converge on one and the same type or model of modernity (probably the western one). This theory of convergence has by now been abandoned Modernization takes place within the context of specific cultural traditions and by way of mobilization of their specific resources, amongst which we should also count their specific symbol systems. We must, therefore, look in the various societies and cultures for the "possiblility of the development of parameters of modernity differing from the ones developed in Europe" (S.N. Eisenstadt). The current attitude has found expression in such dicta as e.g., that in order to understand modernization processes in contemporary North Africa you had better read Ibn Khaldun rather than Max Weber. This statement, like every good epigram, is undoubtedly a deliberate exaggeration, but it well illustrates the prsent trends in sociological thinking on the subject.

II.

Having cleared the ground, as it were, as regards the general problem and the terminologies generated by it, we may now turn to our immediate subject: Buddhism. In the limited space at our disposal we shall have to neglect the Mahayana forms of Buddhism where matters are very different in view of the diversity of historical and social realities as well as of doctrinal presuppositions. But Theravada Buddhism too is an elusive entity. Political, social, economic and cultural modernization processes have taken place in many Buddhist countries and societies (as distinct from "Buddhism" as an abstract entity), and contemporary scholarship is an unusually advantageous position. A great deal of comparative material has accumulated as a result of detailed studies of Buddhism in Ceylon (Sri Lanka), Burma, Thailand, Vietnam (which has Mahayana as well as Theravada Buddhists) and elsewhere, including the quantitatively insignificant but sociologically interesting so-called revival of Buddhism in India. Moreover we also benefit from the accumulated results of different types of research that are now available and can be co-ordinated and synthesized. The impressive achievements of the classical methods of historico-philological scholarship, with their emphasis on Buddhist philosophy and doctrine, can now be supplemented by work bearing on social and political theory and history as well as by intensive anthropological field-work. Those who read English only, have the work of Rhys-Davids, the translated Stcherbatsky, and the writings of e.g., Conze, Thomas and (more recently) Kalupahana for the philosophical and doctrinal history. This type of work can now be supplemented by the anthropolgical research of E.M. Mendelson and Spiro (Burma); Obeyesekere, Yalman and Gombrich (Ceylon); Tambiah (Thailand) and many others (Leach, Nash). For political and social theory as well as recent developments we have the work of Nash, D.C. Smith, W. King, and Sarkisyanz's important study of Burma. H. Bechert's impressive 3-volume *magnum opus* is available in German only, though many shorter papers and articles have been published in English.

Buddhism made an increasing impact on the West since the nineteenth century—whether it was correctly understood and interpreted by the enthusiastic recipients of the gospel is irrelevant to our present purpose. Germany (Schopenhaur!), England and France became centers not only of Buddhological scholarship but also of fascinated attention to the message. Not only chairs for Pali and Buddhist studies were established but also "Buddhist Societies" and the like. This fact is of crucial importance, because the "Feedback" from the West to Asia played a considerable role in the development of Buddhist modernism. It must sufficed here merely to mention the names Alexandra David-Neel (incidentally the first, to the best of my knowledge, to have coined and used the term "Buddhist modernism"), the Anagarika Dharmapala, the Bhikkhu

Ashoka (=Gordon Douglas), the Ven. Nyanatiloka and the Ven. Nyanaponika (both originally Germans). As late as 1973 the Buddhist Government of Sri Lanka commemorated the 66th anniversary of the death of Colonel Olcott (whose career was not limited to the theosophical movement but extended also to Buddhism) as a formal state occasion. There was a striking contrast, until the more recent period, between the contempt felt and voiced by the majority of Christian missionaries (who were the "experts" on the spot and compared their "advanced" civilization with the "superstitions" and "magical beliefs" of the native populations among whom they worked) on the one hand, and the more bookish and elitist enthusiasm for the Buddha's message, derived mainly from literary sources, on the part of the distant admirers on the other. Since then the role of the foreigner-on-the-spot has been taken over by the anthropolotists (supposedly more "value free" than missionaries), the missionaries themselves have become more "ecumenical" and "dialogual", and an increasing number of westerners have been ordained into the Sangha.

The preceding paranthesis regarding contacts with the West and the at times profound ambivalence accompanying these contacts is more germane to our subject than may appear at first sight. It caused Buddhist modernism to adopt and at times excessively apologetic attitude—and apologetics very often take the form of a counter-offensive and compensatory aggressiveness. After all, Buddhists had been exposed to a great deal of denigration e.g. the charge that Buddhist "love" was essentially self-love and selfishness (a statement, by the way, which no Buddhist child brought up on the *Jataka* stories would ever be able to understand). In the circumstances one takes note of criticisms and allegedly negative descriptions, and then proceeds to show that these are biased and wrong and that, in fact, Buddhism not only exhibits all the virtues which it was said to lack but that it possessed them to an even greater degree than the civilizations (or religions) of the critics. It is no discourtesy to Buddhist modernism to say that it is a reaction not only to a new objective (political, economic etc.) situation but also to a profound alienation on the part of an educated elite that had lost its traditional roots and had to rediscover them in a struggle with themselves as well as with the dominant "alien" culture. Thus it is not surprising to learn that the Buddha had "anticipated the UNESCO Charter by 2500 years" or that the Sangha "is the oldest democratic institution in the world." (In fact, some rules of procedure laid down in the Vinaya resemble certain parliamentary procedures). It is important to remember that Buddhism encountered western civilization when the latter was riding high on the wave of "progress" and presented itself as "scientific" (sometimes in the crudest forms of nineteenth century materialism). This gave some modernist writers a chance to emphasize the basic "materialism" of Buddhist metaphysics (there is no abiding spiritual essence or substance, only fleeting, momentary combinations of transitory "elements" tied together in accordance with certain laws of causality). Others would stress the spiritual challenges and promise of Buddhism (liberation from suffering and from ego-hood) over and against the poverty of modern western materialism. The watchword, repeated in ever so many forms and variations, was that Buddhism was the only truly "scientific" religion, especially since the difficulties under which western theistic religions were laboring could be shown to be non-existent within the framework of anonical scriptural doctrine (and by resolutely ignoring all forms of folk-Buddhism!) Indeed, by shutting one's eyes to the diverse forms of popular (animistic-magic) Buddhism, one could argue that western religions, and Christianity in particular, were but a farrago of unscientific superstitions, supernaturalism and the like, accepted on the basis of blind faith. Buddhism, on the other hand, was based on knowledge and insight, and did not suffer from the embarrassments of supernaturalism, revelation, and a personal God. As an "atheistic religion" (and not merely a philosophy), it lacked precisely all those features at which the modern mind boggled; yet it taught not only a lofty morality but also a way to salvation. Demanding maximum effort and mental discipline from its devotees, it was not only a scientific but also a humanistic religion with a noble record of tolerance. And it enabled man to encounter Transcendence (i.e., that which is beyond our human conceptualizations of Being and Non-Being) and to experience a spiritual dimension of life without having to swallow the anthropomorphisms and supernaturalisms in theology, psychology and ontology that mark the crisis of western religion.

Of course Buddhist villagers and farmers and ordinary folk were rarely obsessed with nirvana. They lived ordinary lives of joys and sorrows, desiring good harvest, if possible wealth (to love more comfortably and, above all, to be able to perform works of merit), and many children. They feared poverty, sickness and death. And they hoped for a better re-incarnation after death. Buddhism thus had evolved a two-tier religiousity: one for the virtuosi (i.e., the ideal monks) and one for the "householders." The latter would hardly have understood the learned disquisitions of western scholars who proclaimed that Buddhism was other-worldly and pessimistic. But when the western interpreters challenged the self-respect and pride of "identity" of Buddhist intellectuals, the latter hit back in modernist terms. Christopher Dawson in his Gifford Lectures still accused Buddhism of sacrificing material reality to a one-sided, exclusive spirituality and hence of being incapable of cultural creation and dynamism. Buddhist modernism replied that it was Christianity that was other-worldly whereas Buddhism sought "the meaning of life in life itself" (Malalasekera). The professional student may raise his eyebrows in amazement and wonder whether modernist over-reaction had not gone too far. But since the ideologies called "modern" (including the modern Christian theologies) seem to put a premium on this-worldliness, Buddhist modernism did not intend to lag behind and stand as a symbol of world-negation or—even worse—serve as a religion for cop-outs. The western sub-culture of the disaffected and alienated has provided ample evidence that this fear was not unfounded. Hence, according to the modernists, Buddhism was not only liberal and democratic (see above) but also socialist. A few extreme and revolutionary ideologists took up the afore-mentioned notion of Buddhist materialism and arrived at the theory of Buddhist Marxism. Buddha was a proto-Marx and Ashoka a proto-Lenin. Nirvana was nothing but the ideal, just and classless society. Other and more sensible Buddhist socialists held this view to be a fatal aberration. Marxism, as one modernist writer put it, was "a leaf taken out from the book of Buddhism, [but] a leaf torn out and misread." But all modernists agreed that Buddhism was a social gospel. "A reborn Buddhism. . . would be a social religion" because the Buddha was not only a religious reformer, launching a revolt in the brahminic temple; he was also a social rebel. Professional historians may feel that the historical Buddha (of whom we know very little at best) was socially and politically a rather conservative figure, but the modernist's need of social "relevance" makes him take a different approach. No doubt there is something about the Buddhist attitude to life that seems to be incompatible with capitalism and the accumulation of wealth for its own sake. Already Max Weber had noted the greater economic effectiveness of Hindu over Theravada social ethic. Buddhist "indifference," according to Weber, was incompatible with interest in this world, and Buddhist values were an obstacle to purely economic goals of rational accumulation, investment and wealth. The doctrine of karma can also be an obstacle to rational long-term planning and reform. After the malaria epidemic of 1935 a Ceylonese politican defended himself by arguing: "The people are suffering for their karma. A government cannot alter one's karma." Needless to say that this disingenuous remark drew angry protest from the modernists. Whether Buddhist economic ethic is really a relevant factor in the difficulties encountered on the road to development by Burma, Sri Lanka or (in a different manner) Thailand, is outside the scope of the present paper.

Most Buddhist countries—whether countries where Buddhism plays a dominant role as the State Religion (Sri Lanka, Thailand) or such where Buddhism, once the State Religion, has been deprived of its role but the majority of the population remains, at least for the time being, Buddhist (as e.g., Burma)—belong to what is generally called the Third World. We have already briefly touched on the question of the relationship—if any—between these countries' development problems and Buddhist economic ethics (viz. the complex of economic motivations as shaped by Buddhist culture). But the history of these countries in the modern age has been determined also by another factor: politics in the widest sense, by which I mean the struggle for liberation, independence and de-colonization as well as the political and social power struggles after independence. Unlike Judaism and Islam (to take extreme examples, and avoiding comparison with the geographically and culturally closer and more germane case of Hinduism), Buddhism can be said to have started out without a political doctrine. It certainly possessed no theory for legitimating political power.

Yet in due course there arose Buddhist kingdoms and "politics," and a Buddhist political ethos did develop. (Needless to add that Buddhist kingdoms were, for the greater part of their history, at each other's throats and carrying on wars, much like Christian kingdoms. Wars are evidently not a monpolistic invention of the wicked colonialist West). Limitations of space preclude a discussion of the Ashokan paradigm and its offshoots, except for briefly noting the fact that a Buddhist concept of state, polity and society did emerge and that this concept exhibits an interesting complementarity i.e. unity in duality. It presupposes the distinction between the "supra-mundane" values by protecting—and at times this meant supervising, reforming and 'cleaning up'—the Sangha. A synthesis, or if you are less enthusiastic: a compromise, had thus been developed in which a Buddhist polity could combine a sense of Buddhist responsibility toward the world with the Buddhist ideal of total renunciation.

The continuity of this synthesis was shattered by western colonialism and the years of colonial domination. The organic link between state—in absolute value terms inferior to the Sangha, but in both theory and fact responsible for its purity—and Buddhism was broken. The result was two-sided. On the one hand the revival of modern Buddhism is, to a large extent, a lay phenomenon. It was initiated by "laymen," many of whom had re-discovered their native Buddhism from which they had been alienated as a result of colonial educational influences. But the re-discovery too was due, to a large extent, to western interest in, and appreciation of Buddhism. On the other hand the Sangha had become more independent or, if you want, more unruly. It had developed political commitments, loyalties and vested interests, but the traditional mechanisms for supervising it and holding it in check had been destroyed. (Burma and the fate of U Nu's experiment in Buddhist socialism may serve as an example.)

This may be the point at which a word about the phenomenon of the "political monks" may be appropriate. A Buddhist upasaka is surely not supposed to withdraw from the world. On the contrary, he is supposed to be in the world and to support the Sangha who, in their turn, are definitely expected to renounce the world. Their master and exemplar, the Buddha, was after all a world-conqueror precisely because he was a world-renouncer. My present concern is not with the political role of the Sangha as a whole, or with meddling and power-hungry individual monks or temple-establishments, but with the fact that monks played a decisive part in anti-colonial liberation movements. The political activity of Buddhist monks in Vietnam is still fresh in everybody's memory. Even more relevant to our immediate purpose is the evaluation of the political activity of monks by some modernists. The Chief Abbot of the Malwatta Vihara, in his enthusiastic Foreward to one of the most vehemently polemical documents of modernism (D.C. Wijayawardhana's *The Revolt in the Temple*, 1953) proudly and unhesitatingly praised the political role of the Sangha, adding that monks were meant to be not mediators (an obvious dig at the Catholic Church and its priests) "but only [sic!] leaders." Dr. Walpola Rahula's writings seem to reflect the same attitude. This is a far cry from the admission made to me several years ago by a Vietnamese bhikkhu to the effect that situations may arise in which a monk felt in conscience bound to engage in politics, "but then he should disrobe first."

Buddhist modernism, not unlike its Christian counterpart, thus seems to embrace a political theology. But in terms of the Buddhist tradition it is caught in a permanent conflict—some would prefer to call it dialectic—with other authoritative elements of that tradition. Buddhism is a universal religion of salvation, yet it is closely associated with contemporary nationalisms. In addition to these more theoretical questions, modernity and the demands generated by it (such as long-term planning, scientific experimental research, pest controls and hygienic meaures) often clash with tradition. For example most modern Buddhists argue that birth-control is legitimate as long as no actual life is destroyed but new life is merely prevented from arising. But Buddhist medical and biological students have qualms about killing mice and rats and guinea-pigs in research laboratories, and Buddhist agricultural and health experts have real problems of conscience when it comes to pest-control and insecticides. Responsibility for the world—not only for humans but for all sentient beings—can draw legitimation from Buddhist sources, but its practical application into conflict with ever so many rules and deeply ingrained patterns. The concept of a Buddhist polity has historical antecedents which could be fruitful also in the modern situation but which also generate problems that can lead, as recent history has shown, to serious and even total breakdowns. The complementarity Sangha-laity may offer a paradigm for a more differentiated and realistic approach to a unified yet double-tiered value system, but his paradigm is endangered by the fact that the Sangha itself is still struggling to define its role, or rather to re-define its part in the dialectic—essential to Buddhism—between total renunciation on the one hand, and responsible contribution to a changing world on the other. Whether the Thai experiment of using monks for the implementation of limited modernization programs—often quite simply national programs in the interest of the state—can be called a success, and if so then by what criteria, is still a debatable point. There is, of course, also the possibility of total separation of religion (both Sangha and laity) and polity, but in such a way that everyone brings his sense of Buddhist values to the task in hand. It would be the Buddhist equivalent to what in neo-Protestant terminology might be called the Barthian approach. It is a perfectly legitimate Buddhist possibility, as long as it does not degenerate into a Third World version of primitive Machiavellism of the kind expounded to me recently by a Burmese diplomat: religion is something which the masses should fervently hold, but of which the leadership must be free.

Whether "modernism" can help religious traditions survive modernity, adapt to it or adapt it, we are not yet able to say at the present stage. There are problems with which all religions are faced. But Buddhism, at least theoretically, has resources to cope with the questions of modern man that many other traditions lack and which give it a relevance and superiority which many modernist writers have emphasized though their exaggerations have all but obfuscated their main point. But the distance from theory to practice is long, as Buddhists themselves know only too well.

NOTE

I have dealt more fully with the problems discussed in this paper in my book *Beyond Tradition and Modernity: Changing Religions in a Changing World*(London, 1976). On the problem of modernization in general see *ibid.*, pp. 1-20; on Buddhism, *ibid.*, pp. 92-100 and 127-8. To the bibliography given there, several more recent relevant titles should be added e.g., H. Dumoulin and D.C. Maraldo (eds.), *Buddhism in the Modern World*, 1976; S.J. Tambiah, *World Conqueror and World Renouncer*, 1976; H. Bechert, *Weltflucht oder Weltveranderung: Antworten des Buddhistischen Modernismus auf Fragen unserer Zeit.* 1976.

David J. Kalupahana

Commentary

It is not possible for me to make a detailed criticism of Professor Werblowsky's paper, since I was given very short notice (exactly one and one half hours) to read and comment on it. It is easy to agree with the views of a reputed scholar and difficult to find problems with which to disagree. Fortunately for me, there is one thesis that he presents in his paper on which I may be able to express a different point of view and, therefore, I shall confine my comments to this only.

Professor Werblowsky seems to *assume* that in all the Buddhist traditions there is a sharp dichotomy between a transcendent reality and the phenomenal and that this is the basis of the two-tier religiosity in Buddhism, one for the monks and one for the householder. The problem of modernization seems to me to be inextricably tied with the recognition of such a two-tier religiosity. I wish to show that, at least in the earliest Buddhist tradition, a sharp dichotomy between a transcendent reality and the phenomenal world was not made and, consequently, a theory of a two-tier religiosity is not to be found there. If so, modernization *of* Buddhism would mean gong back to the original message, a regression rather than a progression.

The Buddha claimed that his doctrine is timeless (*akalika*). By this he did not mean that his doctrine is fixed or permanent. What he meant was that it is not a message that is appliable to only one point in time. In other words, it can be adopted to the needs of any period of time and this is because there were no fixed dogmas. The absence of any specific dogmas made it a very flexible teaching and the result was the radical changes that it underwent, not only in India, but also in its passage to the Far East. Early Buddhism which began as a reaction against the transcendentalism or absolutism of the earlier Indian philosophico-religious systems, gradually came to adopt a transcendentalist point of view, both in Theravada and Mahayana traditions. The Theravada developed transcendentalism or absolutism as a result of philosophical speculation, and Mahayana as a result of speculating on religious matters. Both ended up with the kind of sharp dichotomy that Professor Werblowsky assumes and both traditions never satisfactorily resolved this dichotomy. Modern sociologists are, therefore, not doing anything new when they attempt to explain and resolve this problem-situation.

As far as I understand the original message of the Buddha, it is based on a very sophisticated philosophical theory of causation or "dependent arising" (*paticcasamuppada*). I must say that it is the only *religion* that I know of which rejected any form of absolutism or transcendentalism and based itself on an empirical doctrine of causation. By an empirical doctrine of causation I do not mean anything similar to what the British empiricist, David Hume, presented, but rather a doctrine of causation which would be more consistent with the radical empiricism enunciated by a philosopher like William James.

The doctrine of causation or dependent arising is based on an empirical theory of knowledge. Buddha did not claim to possess any transcendent knowledge or any form of omniscience. Highest knowledge, according to him, is knowledge through the senses, but which is free from prejudices. It is the knowledge of one who has no passions or desires. It is objective knowledge free from subjective prejudices. Such objective knowledge provides man with an understanding of the present situation, of what goes on now. This is called knowledge of phenomena (*dhamme nana*). On the basis of this experiential knowledge, the Buddha claimed that one could make reasonable inferences regarding the past and the future. Through such inductive knowledge one comes to recognize a causal uniformity. he distinguished between causation and causal uniformity. The former is something given in experience and the latter is inferred.

Using this knowledge of causation and causal uniformity the Buddha proceeded to explain human life. Human life, according to him is determined by a complex of causes and conditions. The combination of causes and conditions is important in that the variations in the effect can only be accounted for by the variations in the complexity of conditions. The Buddha maintained that past human dispositions or volitional actions have played a major role in determining the present life. It is possible for man to change his future provided he is able to understand this complexity of conditions that determines it. The Buddha admitted the difficulty of knowing beforehand with certainty this complexity of conditions. In such cases he seems to claim that one can be guided by the inductive inferences regarding the uniformity of dependence, that is called *dhammata*. Thus, as mentioned before, knowledge by experience and induction is practically essential and important for man to achieve the best possible form of life. Now the question can be raised at this stage, how do we determine what is good and bad, or which is the best possible form of life. Knowledge by experience and induction alone is not sufficient for this. One needs a different kind of knowledge. Such a form of knowledge has to be evaluative rather than factual. This evaluative knowledge the Buddha called *anumana*, or measuring accordingly. This measuring accordingly is based on knowledge by experience and induction, and not independent of it. *Anumana* is, therefore, knowledge by reflection and reasoning according to or based upon knowledge by experience and induction. Reflection will not be valid unless it is guided by the information yielded by experience and induction which, as we have already found, is the knowledge of causal dependence. Knowledge of good and bad can be had only by such a reasoning according to experience. The Buddha says:

> A disciple should evaluate himself thus. That person who is of evil desires and who is in the thrall of evil desires, that person is displeasing and disagreeable to me. Similarly, if I were to be of evil desires and in the thrall of evil desires, I should be displeasing and disagreeable to others. When a disciple knows this, he should make up his mind that I will not be of evil desires nor in the thrall of evil desires.

Reflective knowledge is thus evaluative or normative. It provides information regarding what is good and bad. It pertains to goodness. As is evident from the above passage, this reflective knowledge is not only evaluative but also directive. Evaluative knowledge would be useless unless it is followed by correct practice and action. The goal of learning by experience and reflection is to perfect one's personality, to be a perfect man. On the basis of the above-mentioned knowledge of facts and values, the Buddha came to the conclusion that human suffering in this world is due to excessive desire or attachment. A greedy and confused man not only harms others, but also harms himself. Using this criterion, it is possible to find four types of persons in the world: first is a man who harms himself; second is the man who harms others; third is the one who harms both oneself and others, and according to the Buddha, the best man is one who neither harms himself nor others. So the superman in Buddhism is one who neither harms himself nor others.

The goal of Buddhism is thus not the attainment of a transcendental or immortal state of existence after death, but happiness here and now. This is a very naturalistic view of life, where man is not subordinate to a supernatural power or principle. It recognizes the ability of man to attain freedom and happiness through the understanding of the nature of human life. The philosophy of Buddhism, as outlined above, represents one of the most systematic forms of humanism. It is based on the naturalistic metaphysic with causal dependence as its central theme. Rejecting any form of transcendentalism or strict determinism or fatalism, it emphasizes the ultimate faith in man and recognizes the ability to solve his problems through reliance, primarily upon empirical knowledge, reason and scientific method applied with courage and vision. It believes in the freedom of man not in a transcendental sphere, but here and now. The highest goal it offers is happiness to be attained here. This happiness is not attained by a denial of *human needs*, but by an elimination of human desires. If we can recognize this very important distinction between human needs and desires, then I'm sure we'll be able to make Buddhism very relevant to the modern world, to the modern society, and I do not see any problems about modernization.

Section H:

Religion and Science: Convergent or Divergent Definitions of Reality

— H1 —

Beyond Scientism: Science and Religion in Dialogue

Donald R. Ferrell/Morris I. Berkowitz

— H2 —

On the Structural Resemblances in Ultimate Religious Philosophical and Scientific Thought

Ben-Ami Scharfstein

Donald R. Ferrell

— H1 —
Beyond Scientism: Science and Religion in Dialogue

It was Alfred North Whitehead who predicted that the future of world history would be determined in large measure by the decision reached in his generation as to the relationship of science and religion (1925). Whitehead understood, perhaps better than most others of his time, that these two great expressions of human intellectual and spiritual experience were utterly crucial for the formation of human destiny. For Whitehead neither science nor religion should be underestimated in its significance for the human future, and, it seemed clear to him, that if the relationship between science and religion were to be ultimately defined by either indifference or antagonism, the consequences for humankind would be deeply destructive.

However the history of the interaction between science and religion is construed, there can be little doubt that the growth in scientific knowledge and the consequent creation of a scientific culture over the past three hundred years, phenomenae which constitute the very essence of modernity, have left the religious communities of Western culture in a profoundly disrupted state. If it is true, as Whitehead and others have asserted, that the Western religious tradition provided the conception of reality within which modern science as we now know it emerged, then surely one of great ironies of this history, as Kenneth Cauthen has pointed out (1969), is the displacement of religion as the primary energizing force within Western society by a social instrument which could not have come into being without the very religious tradition it displaced. The irony becomes even more poignant when seen in the light of Richard Rubenstein's thesis that the Judeo-Christian tradition not only made the rise of science as a theoretical enterprise possible, but it also created inadvertently the secularized, rationalized, disenchanted ethos which led to that bureaucratic objectivity culminating in the technology of extermination represented by the Nazi death camps (1975).

If the history of the relationship between science and religion contains these implications, i.e., that the rise of science in the West has
meant the gradual erosion of the structure of religious consciousness and its replacement by a secularized consciousness
whose logical expressions include not only the theory of relativity,
quantum mechanics, and visions of an expanding universe, of man
evolving, of matter transformed into energy and energy into matter,
of the structure of the biological cell and the death of our sun 5
billion years in the future, but also of ecological pillage, human
alienation from nature, a culture of waste and the design and execution of a technology of mass death, then it is possible that Whitehead's concern that we achieve a consensus in which the relationship
of science and religion be defined in positive and constructive terms
has even greater significance than he realized. Perhaps our very survival is in some way related to the dialogue between science and
religion.

To say that the Judeo-Christian community has been disrupted
by the rise of a scientific culture is not to imply a negative evaluation of the scientific enterprise. It is, however, to point to a fundamental crisis within the religious consciousness of the West which
has been clearly precipitated by the extraordinary impact science
has had upon our culture. Put quite simply the crisis is that modern
science has created a model of truth and reality that has rendered
the assertions of the Western religious traditions profoundly
suspect. While it has been pervasive within the religious community, the response to this crisis has not been uniform. In fact, David
Tracy (1975) has argued that within the contemporary Western
Christian theological community one can find five basic types or
models of theological inquiry, each of which has to some degree
achieved its distinctive identity and methodological self-
consciousness as it has sought to come to terms with the challenges
of the scientific era. These he identifies as the orthodox, the liberal,
the neo-orthodox, the radical and the revisionist models.

It is orthodoxy which has been least motivated to rethink the
meaning of its theological assertions in the light of scientific
knowledge. Although Tracy does not do so, if one includes Protestant evangelical theology within this model, one finds a vigorous
insistence that the adequacy of all forms of knowledge, including

scientific knowledge, is determined by the extent to which they are compatible with the absolute truth of Christian revelation as given in inerrant biblical form. While most recent evangelical theology rejects Rudoph Bultmann's attempt to demythologize Christian assertions as a way of taking account of the scientific worldview, and argues that scientific knowledge can in no way affect the content of Christian truth, some evangelical theologians argue that theology is itself a scientific enterprise. Carl F.H. Henry (1976), for example, has argued that theology is a presuppositional system of axiomatic truths from which the whole structure of Christian doctrine is deduced. Christian revelation makes theology as a science possible because its truth is fully rational and fully capable of verification by whatever valid criteria of truthfulness the human mind has yet conceived. Furthermore Christian revelation, Henry seems to argue, by providing information that is objectively certain and literally true as to the nature of reality bestows upon theology a more complete scientific status than the actual scientific enterprise itself because of the tentativity and incompleteness of the latter's actual cognitive achievements. Empirical science is in no position to raise cognitive objections to Christianity, Henry asserts, because of the uncertainty of its own conclusions.

The orthodox model constitutes one of the significant ways in which the religious mind within the Christian community has sought to deal with the crisis brought on by the rise of science. In its evangelical expression it asserts that divine revelation is given in objectivity valid, univocal, i.e., literal propositional form in which cognitive information about God, man, and the world is communicated, the content of which is absolutely certain and which constitutes the epistemological matrix in relation to which every human claim to have truth, including the claims of science, must be evaluated as valid or invalid.

Obviously much more needs to be said about this theological model, especially when one considers the attention the evangelical movement is now receiving in our culture. Without attempting to assess the adequacy of this model here, the following observation is in order. The resurgence of evangelical theology represents a radical rejection of at least two fundamental assumptions which are to be found more or less present within the remaining theological models Tracy identifies. Both of these assumptions emerged within the Christian theological community as direct outcomes of the religious encounter with modern science, and clearly represent the influence that science has had upon the religious mind.

Wolfhart Pannenberg (1976) has drawn attention to the first assumption. Pannenberg argues that as natural science destroyed the plausibility of the biblical-Aristotelian cosmology of the medieval Christian tradition by redefining the nature of physcial reality, both philosophy and theology lost that cognitive access to God based upon the existence of the world. By asserting the principle of natural causation, natural science undercut the cognitive basis for asserting God as the unmoved first cause of the world or its final purpose. Neither philosophy nor theology could any longer assume that the world pointed beyond itself to the reality of God.

This defeat for theology in particular led to the development of a new foundation for the construction of knowledge of God. After some faltering attempts in the eighteenth century to renew cosmological arguments for the existence of God, theology, Pannenberg asserts, turned increasingly to the view that the internal structure of the human self is the basis for knowledge of God. This assumption finds expression in the liberal theological model through Schleiermacher's emphasis upon religious experience as the primary source of man's consciousness of God, in neo-orthodoxy in Bultmann's explicit appropriation of Heidegger, and in Barth's and Tillich's claim that faith is the precondition and the self-verifying center for the knowledge of God, in radical theology through the influence of Feuerbach's and Nietzsche's uniquely modern form of atheism, and in the revisionist attempt to rethink both Christian theological categories and the meaning of modernity in relation to the phenomenological field of human existence, especially in relation to such experiences as trust and the human encounter with limits.

The second assumption which has emerged from the encounter of the religious mind with modern science has been stated by Langdon Gilkey (1970). According to Gilkey's analysis the triumph of science over the last two hundred years led to an even more fundamental development within the Christian theological community than the anthropocentric turn mentioned above. Gilkey reminds us that from the age of Galileo and Newton until early in the nineteenth century, it was widely believed by both scientists and theologians that science and religion were in fact complimentary systems of truth and that the revealed knowledge of religion contained factual information about the structure of the universe within whose framework science could understand itself. This revealed knowledge included assertions concerning the origin of life forms and the catastrophic invention of God within the formative processes of the earth in relation to which late eighteenth and early nineteeth century geologists made their fossil discoveries intelligible to themselves.

With the development of both geology and biology, however, this view that revealed knowledge contained empirical information that was continuous with and complimentary of scientific knowledge and that religious language referred literally to factual states of affairs was thoroughly discredited. Hence, the second assumption developed within the theological community in its encounter with science, namely, that religious truth could no longer be defended as conveying information about or entailing any empirical matters of fact and thus must now be understood as a system of symbolic meanings which has no authoritative significance for the interpretations of factual states of affairs. In coming to see its most fundamental assertions as thoroughly symbolic, the Christian theological mind defined its relationship to science in a new way. Now it acknowledged that only science could provide valid information concerning the empirical order and it further recognized that theology had no basis for challenging properly scientific assertions. Furthermore, it gradually became clear to the theological community, Gilkey argues, that the validity of whatever empirical states of affairs might be presupposed in theological assertions, for example historic events, could not be established by theological assertions themselves but only by the deliverances of scientific inquiry. As is well known this situation has had radical implications for theology's subsequent career,as the debate over the historical Jesus, for example, has made clear.

It was within the framework of these two basic assumptions, the primacy of the self in theological inquiry and the symbolic character of religious assertions, that liberalism and neo-orthodoxy worked out their theological programs, both deeply influenced, as Gilkey has shown, by the scientific age. Liberalism accepted the scientific culture as normative for theological construction and both subjected the Christian tradition to thorough criticism and worked out its own theological affirmations in relation to fundamental scientific contructs, especially the theme of cosmic and human evolution. Neoorthodoxy, especially in the person of Karl Barth, rejected the liberal attempt to reconstruct Christian doctrine in the light of scientific knowledge and asserted theology's freedom from the scientific enterprise by virtue of its grounding in divine revelation. Science and religion cannot conflict because they deal with two entirely different orders of reality. Neo-orthodoxy accepted the authority of science over the empirical order and eschewed any appeal to science to support religious belief. Theological truth, it asserted, has no relationship to scientific truth, and while the object of theologcial assertions is fully real as disclosed in the biblical documents, it can be neither confirmed nor disconfirmed by scientific evidence. God's action in the world can be discerned only by the eyes of faith and asserted paradoxically "in spite of" the absence of scientific evidence that God is so acting.

It is widely agreed today that the liberal attempt to reconcile religion and science failed because of the inability of the liberal theologians to direct the critical drive they appropriated from the scientific enterprise toward science itself and the secular culture science made possible (Tracy, *op. cit*). And, if Gilkey's argument is correct, neo-orthodoxy has lost its influence, in part, because, in-seeking to free religious truth from both scientific inquiry or metaphysical thought it could find no way of rooting its assertions, especially the assertion that God acts in history, in reality except in the existential structure of faith. Religious assertions may thus have been rendered invulnerable to criticism but at the expense of intersubjective discourse. This is Pannenberg's criticsm of both Barth and Tillich.

As many observers have pointed out one of the primary values of the radical movement in theology was its confronting the religious community with the full extent to which the scientific culture of the first half of the twentieth century had rendered traditional religious assertions, especially assertions about the reality of God, profoundly problematic if not totally meaningless. Two assumptions about the scientific enterprise seem to have convinced the radical theologians that belief in and assertions about the God of Judeo-Christian tradition are no longer possible. The first is the assumption, seen, for example, in Paul Van Buren's *The Secular Meaning of the Gospel*, that science constitutes the definitive paradigm of knowledge and truth. Thus, only empirical propositions have cognitive status and only that which can be known by scientific means can be said to be real in any meaningful sense. Since God, as traditionally conceived, is not an object within the spatio-temporal nexus, then at the very least He is beyond the reach of cognitive discourse and therefore a dead issue for the secular mind. The second assumption is that science has given persons such power and control over nature that it is impossible, out of their new sense of autonomy, for most contemporary men and women to conceive of themselves as either in need of or dependent upon God as limit to and ground of their own existence. This is a familiar theme in William Hamilton's reflections on the meaning of the death-of-God. Thus, for the radical theologians science has destroyed epistemologically and psychologically the grounds for meaningful religious assertions about the God of the Judeo-Christian tradition. Religious life may still be possible for Jews and Christians but certainly not in the service of God as their traditions have defined Him.

The last model Tracy identifies is the revisionist model, and it is the one he, himself, advocates. Since it is also the model that informs the perspective of this paper, its main features will be discussed briefly and the remainder of the paper will be an attempt to indicate the insights the revisionist approach makes available to the task of defining the relationship between science and religion.

While stressing the value of the pluralistic situation in theology today, the revisionist model, as Tracy develops it, stands in creative tension with the other models discussed above. Perhaps this tension wil become explicit when the basic program of revisionist theology is made clear.

With liberalism and radical theology, the revisionist model shares the assumption that something decisive has happened within the intellectual and spiritual life of western people within the last three hundred years which theology can afford neither to ignore nor underestimate. The creation of a secular consciousness through the agency of scientific enterprise, a consciousness which has become increasingly anti-theistic and anti-Christian, is, as it is for liberalism and radical theology, the primary datum which Christian theology must analyze and interpret. In carrying out this task, however, the revisionist model rejects the attempt of orthodoxy to isolate itself from any critical interaction with the scientific culture, particularly those intellectual disciplines which undergird secularity, as well as the recent attempt of evangelical theology to interact with the scientific culture by reviving, albeit in a highly sophisticated form,the doctrine of God as a supernatural being who communicates to persons literal cognitive information about the nature of reality in propositional form as contained within the structure of an infallible body of scripture. At the same time it rejects the fideism of neo-orthodoxy, which sought, like orthodoxy to separate itself from science through asserting the inaccessibility of the Word of God to human reflection.

The revisionist model accepts what is authentic within secular culture as a constitutive element within its own self-understanding, namely, the secular faith "which affirms the ultimate significance and final worth of our lives, our thoughts, and actions, here and now, in nature and in history" (Tracy, p.8). This secular faith of our common humanity the revisionist theologian shares and thereby acknowledges in himself the radical demystification of the religious tradition it has been the destiny of the modern experiment to accomplish. But the revisionist model also commits the theologian to the view that, when properly interpreted, the Christian faith in its full theistic intention, is the most adequate structure of religious meaning within which to make the secular faith of our common humanity fully intelligible and symbolically persuasive.

Revisionist theology, then, wishes to continue the dialogue with the scientific culture which liberalism began; however, it wishes to do so in full recognition that liberal theology must be transcended, that not only must the demystification of the religious tradition continue, thus continuing the liberal enterprise, but that, as Tracy puts it, there must be "disenchantment with disenchantment," that is, revisionist theology must also demystify the secular, scientific cul-

ture which the revisionist theologian, at the same time, wishes to affirm. This twofold task it seeks to accomplish by bringing
philosophical, that is, metaphysical analysis to bear upon the structure of common human experience, thus continuing the "turn to the
subject" common to theology's encounter with science, and by
deriving from Christian texts the symbolic re-presentation of the
human encounter with limits, thus challenging the secular attempt
to eliminate the transcendent from the field of human experience.

The critical character of this two-fold commitment of the
revisinist theologian to the secular enterprise and the Christian faith
must be kept in mind. Revisionist theology is in tension with the orthodox and neo-orthodox models because it rejects literalism and
supernaturalism in religion as well as the claim of an exclusively
religious form of knowledge. It is in tension with liberal and radical
theology because it does not exempt the scientific culture from
critical scrutiny nor does it accept the conclusion that there can be
no viable conception of the God of Jews and Christians once one
understands the inherent meaning of secularity itself. With this obviously inadequate account of the revisionist program, let us explore
the way science and religion are related within this model.

Van Harvey (1966) has cast considerable light upon the unfortunate history of the religious encounter with science by pointing out
that theologians and scientists, in their disputes with each other, actually experienced the collision of two conflicting moralities of inquiry. The theologian, on the one hand, approached the cognitive
task from the perspective of the preestablished authority of the Bible and the religious tradition derived from it, and thus was committed to a morality of knowledge which celebrated the primacy of
belief and faithfulness to the doctrinal consensus of the religious
tradition. The scientific conception of inquiry, on the other hand,
asserted the objectivity of knowledge and required that the knower
be free of all forms of external authority in order to exercise his own
judgements in accordance with public criteria of validity. This
meant that scientific inquiry could not accept any proposition as
true in advance of the radical process of inquiry itself, and every conclusion which emerged as true from this process must also be subjected to further criticism.Hence, scientific knowledge was defined

as tentative, proximate and open to new evidence. Not only then, did science challenge the world-view of traditional religion, but it also confronted the theologian with a moral dilemma: either to subject the faith already believed to be true to critical scientific scrutiny thus entertaining uncertainty and doubt, or to be accused of sacrificing one's intellect in order to keep one's faith intact. Certainly the theologian, aware of the nature of the scientific enterprise, could not, in good conscience continue to hold that his faith was secure simply because it was believed by the religious community in which he stood.

In seeking to resolve this dilemma, revisionist theology makes explicit the critical character of its methodological commitment. It asserts in the first place its commitment to the morality of inquiry exemplified in the scientific paradigm of knowledge as an authentic and abiding achievement of the human mind and spirit. Revisionist theology, then, is morally obligated to defend the autonomy of the theologian, to examine the evidence for and against its own claims following the evidence wherever it and rethinking its own assertions accordingly always within the context of public criteria of meaning and validity. In making this commitment the revisionist theologian rejects the notion of Christian existence as assent to a body of absolute, immutable and final propositions as fallacious and illusory and a profound violation of the new morality of knowledge which has emerged from the scientific age.

Revisionist theology, then, finds itself in harmony with the scientific-secular culture of our time at the point of its affirming that culture's conception of truth and the modes of inquiry by which truth is achieved. And yet, it must face a serious objection which may be formulated as follows: is it not a violation of the demand for objectivity that the new morality of knowledge requires that the revisionist theologian comes to the task of the search for truth committed to the scientific mode of knowing and at the same time to the Christian paradigm? How are the revisionist theologian's secular faith and Christian self-understanding to be reconciled?

In dealing with this objection revisionist theology argues that the conception of objectivity which requires the complete and total emptying of the knowing subject of any concrete perspective before the truth can be known is inconsistent with the actual process of inquiry. What objectivity does require, however, is the willingness of the knower to subject to sustained critical analysis whatever perspective is brought to the task of knowing such that the concept of warranted belief stands as a constant corrective over one's will to believe. It is this latter conception of objectivity to which the revisionist theologian is committed and which he believes makes an authentic dialogue between religion and science possible as two distinctive communities of inquiry and interpretation which are both committed to a common morality of knowledge.

This assertion of methodological and epistemological unity between science and religion at the level of a common morality of knowledge leads to the further delineation of their relationship to each other. From the revisionist perspective the structural similarity between science and religion seen, in the first instance, in their commitment to a common morality of knowledge, means that both science and religion seek to make cognitive assertions about the nature of reality. As Ian Barbour (1974) has persuasively argued it is a mistake, once the logic of models and paradigms is understood, to assert that the fundamental difference between science and religion is that the assertions of the former are cognitive and impersonal and those of the latter noncognitive and self-involving. Barbour argues that both science and religion carry out their cognitive tasks with the help of theoretical models in relation to their own peculiar paradigm traditions, and while these theoretical models are not literal or pictorial representations of reality, but rather symbolic conceptual entities, they are, nonetheless, genuinely cognitive structures, which claim to assert something true about the nature of reality. While it is true that religious language does perform important non-cognitive functions which scientific language does not, thus constituting a major difference between science and religion, revisionist theology is deeply restless with the view that religious language can make no cognitive claims.

In stressing this unity between science and religion, however, revisionist theology does not wish to ignore their obvious differences. Yet it does not want to interpret these differences to mean that science and religion are totally unrelated; however, it is willing to grant that while there are significant similarities between them, they do, in fact, serve different ends. Thus, revisionist theology does not seek to derive a natural theology from scientific constructs nor does it seek to continue the liberal program of making the scientific worldview normative for theological construction.

Rather revisionist theology thinks it sees within the scientific enterprise a genuinely religious dimension, which, while present there only implicitly, points to a universal religious dimension within the whole of human experience which it is the task of religion to make as explicit as possible through its own symbolic language, models and paradigm traditions. This approach fully affirms the freedom of science and at the same time suggests how religious life is possible in a scientific culture.

There is no one way to understand the religious dimension of our common experience. David Tracy has argued that it can best be seen in our encounter with a sense of limit, a sense of limit-to our existence given in the experiences of finitude and contingency and a sense of limit-of our existence given in the awareness of the horizon that transcends us. These experiences are religious in the fundamental sense that they confront us with the question of the ultimate meaning of our lives and of the cosmic matrix of which we are a part. The religious dimension within the scientific enterprise becomes visible wherever this limit experience becomes real in terms that are intrinsic to science itself.

It should be clear that the concept of limit as it is used here does not refer to what is ordinarily called the limits of science, that is, those methodoligcal boundaries within which science carries out its legitimate tasks. Rather the concept of limit as the religious dimension of science refers to those transcendental elements which often lie hidden in any given human activity and which constitute the conditions that make the particular activity possible. As these transcendental elements are made explicit through analysis, revisionist theology argues, they point to a dimension of ultimacy within science itself.

It should be clear that the concept of limit as it is used here does not refer to what is ordinarily called the limits of science, that is, those methodological boundaries within which science carries out is legitimate tasks. Rather the concept of limit as the religious dimension of science refers to those transcendental elements which often lie hidden in any given human activity and which constitute the conditions that make the particluar activity possible. As these transcendental elements are made explicit through analysis, revisionist theology argues, they point to a dimension of ultimacy within science itself.

Revisionist theologians recognize these limit experiences of a number of points within the scientific enterprise. In the formulation of scientific questions, the scientist transcends himself toward a world of meaning outside himself. This world of meaning acts as limit-to the scientist's own subjectivity and can lead the scientist to ask the question of the totality of meaning which stands as limit and ground of the particular meanings which science discovers. In making scientific judgments the scientist must establish a determinant conclusion in the face of an indeterminant realm of possibilities. He discovers that he has achieved what Bernard Lonergan (1970) calls "virtually unconditioned affirmation," that is, a conditioned judgment whose conditions are fulfilled to such a degree of probability that no further questions remain and thus virtual certainty has been attained. But, as Tracy points out, this judgment is not the ultimate ground of itself but merely an instance of the possibility of such judgments. In reflecting upon the structure of scientific judgments, then, the scientist might be led to ask how such judgments are possible without an unconditioned ground of judgment which stands as both limit-to and limit-of the act of scientific judgment. Finally, the scientist is inevitably involved in ethical questions about the nature and scope of scientific inquiry. Not only must he ask whether a particular scientific procedure should be carried out, but under what conditions and to what purpose. In having to ask the question of the larger good to be served or thwarted by his work, the scientist cannot escape the moral dimension of the scientific enterprise. But such moral questions can lead the scientist to question not only the ethical rules for conducting scientific research but the very value of science itself, that is, whether the values of intelligent inquiry, belief based upon evidence alone, rational discussion with one's colleagues, honesty in reporting one's findings and the hope that the order and pattern of the world can be discovered by scientific means are themselves of value and whether they are sup-

ported by an intelligent and rational source of value in which the
values of science are grounded.

These limit questions are not imposed upon science by religion.
Rather they seem to be implied with the scientific enterprise itself
and when they are explored the religious dimension within science
as a human activity is made manifest. It is the task of religion to articulate this common religious dimension within human experience
and activity, since it can only be brought to full expression through
myth and symbol and reflected upon through the conceptual structures religion generates.

Revisionist theology seeks to carry out the dialogue with science
by calling attention to this dimension of ultimacy and by resisting
the drive within science to deal with this dimension by developing
its own myths and claiming an ultimacy for science which it does
not itself possess but only manifests when it reflects upon its own
foundations. This dialogue has led thinkers like Theodore Roszak,
E.F. Schumacher, Frederick Ferre, Harold Schilling and Huston
Smith, among others, to challege the tendencies within modern
science toward reductionism, materialism, an alienating attitude
toward man and nature, a worship of technology and a willingness
to define as unreal those levels of reality that lie outside the reach of
science. These thinkers have seen with significant clarity that the
profound cultural crisis which has begun to overtake us is directly
related to the impact of modern science upon us, especially its deeply ambiguous capacity to generate a mythic structure in relation to
which the religious needs of large numbers of moderns find fulfillment. This crisis has led these same thinkers to call for the development of a post-modern consciousness in both science and religion as
the basis of our salvation from the most aversive consequences of
science in its modern form. Revisionist theology shares this emerging
consensus and argues that it is precisely in its dialogue with the
scientific community that the Judeo-Christian tradition can articulate the grounds, along with the other major religious traditions
of mankind, for the emergence of this new consciousness which
must take us beyond scientism.

But this task cannot be carried out if science alone receives our
criticism. The Judeo-Christian tradition must also undergo profound criticism, especially the classical conceptions of God, revela-

tion, and the nature of the religious life. Our secular faith in the worthwhileness of our lives here and now and the freedom and responsibilty we human beings now possess for ourselves and our planet cannot find expression in a God who is unmoved by our suffering, unaffected by our decision, and invulnerable to our destiny, in a doctrine of revelation that requires a sacrifice of our intellects or a surrender of our autonomy to a heteronomous authority, and in a conception of the religious life that lures us away from the pursuit of justice and peace for our global village. Thus, we must also achieve a consciousness that takes us beyond orthodoxy and literalism while finding the resources within the religious traditions through which a new clarification of values and a genuine sense of transcendence may become a possibilty for our age.

This last comment invites one final, though far too brief, observation. This paper has focused rather exclusively upon the Christian community in its attempt to understand the relationship between science and religion. In doing so, however, it has not been my intention to assert a superior role for the Christian faith in the dialogue between science and religion. Revisionist theology welcomes the insights that the other religious traditions have to contribute to this dialogue, but it also wishes to transcend the tendency within liberalism to obscure the very real and crucial differences which obtain among the world religions.

Recognizing that religious truth is expressed in symbolic form, revisionist theology sees in this recognition the possibility of genuine tolerance among the world religions; and yet, it would also bring to bear its own methodology upon the analysis of the other religious traditions in seeking to explicate the resources they possess that might further the dialogue between science and religion, that is, revisionist theology would seek to discover the forms through which the limited experience is articulated within the other world religious traditions and what they may tell us about the authentic place of science within the larger human enterprise itself. At the same time revisionist theology seeks to be open to the criticism of its approach which the other religious traditions are in a position to offer.

Such dialogue between the world religions and science has only just begun but its promise should not be underestimated.

WORKS CONSULTED

Barbour, Ian. *Issues in Science and Religion*. Englewood Cliffs, N.J.: Prentice-Hall, 1966.

. . . . *Myths, Models and Paradigms*. New York: Harper & Row, 1974.

Cauthen, Kenneth. *Science, Secularization and God*. Nashville: Abingdon Press, 1969.

Ferre, Frederick. *Shaping the Future: Resources for the Post-Modern World*. New York: Harper & Row, 1976.

Gilkey, Langdon. *Religion and the Scientific Future*. New York: Harper & Row, 1970.

Harvey, Van A. *The Historian and the Believer: The Morality of Historical Knowledge and Christian Belief*. New York: The MacMillan Co., 1966.

Henry, Carl F.H. *God, Revelation and Authority*, Vol. 1. Waco, Texas: Word Books, 1976.

Lonergan, Bernard. *Insight*. New York: The Philosophical Library, 1970.

Pannenberg, Wolfhart. *Theology and the Philisophy of Science*. Tr. Francis McDonagh. Philadelphia: The Westminster Press, 1976.

Rosak, Theodore. *The Making of a Counter-Culture*. Garden City, N.J.: Doubleday, 1969.

Rubenstein, Richard. *The Cunning of History: Mass Death and the American Future*. New York: Harper & Row, 1975.

Schilling, Harold K. *The New Consciousness in Science and Religion*. Philadelphia: The United Church Press, 1973.

Schumacher, E.F. *Small is Beautiful: Economics as if People Mattered*. New York, Harper & Row-Perennial Library, 1973.

Smith, Huston. *Forgotten Truth: The Primordial Tradition*. New York: Harper & Row, 1977.

Tracy, David. *Blessed Rage for Order: The New Pluralism in Theology*. New York: Seabury Press, 1975.

Whitehead, Alfred North. *Science in the Modern World*. New York: The New American Library, 1925.

Morris I. Berkowitz

Commentary

Physical scientists, since Einstein and Heisenberg, give every evidence in the way in which they approach their work of being unsure, tentative, and involved in a world of probability and possibility, as opposed to the world of law and certainty which seemed to prevail in the post-Newtonian scientific revolution. Religionists, if Professor Ferrell's provocative paper is any indication, seem to be also entering that world. The conditions for dialogue should be ripe—but, alas, his paper also illustrates many of the problems of proceeding with that dialogue.

First, although he partially recognizes the former and persisting rigidities of thought of some scientists, and of some religionists, he seems to project upon "science" more of the rigidities than its ablest practicioners now manifest, while assuming that scientism only existed on the side of science: certainly there is a corresponding rigidity, which perhaps the distasteful name "religionism" can bring to mind, which has pervaded religious thinking and made religious thinkers far less amenable to discourse than the scientists have been. The work of many religious thinkers, ably reviewed in Professor Tracy's study, is suitable not for dialogue with their scientific counterparts, but much more for fighting what can only be described as a rear guard action in defense of traditional faith.[1]

Professor Ferrell's own paper exemplifies a major part of the problem of establishing dialogue. Ferrell states that he is concerned with what religionists must do to prepare themselves for a dialogue with scientists. However, one looks in vain for references to more modern scientists than Alfred North Whitehead. Instead, the frame of reference of scientists is only imputed from the thoughts of religious thinkers and philosophers. He seems, then, to be preparing for this dialogue only on his own terms. It is quite possible, and even likely, that many scientists will not be willing to come to dialogue within this frame of reference because they will have little to say which they would regard as meaningful within it. There will be, I suspect, an appreciable lack of sympathy for this point of view because it overlooks some of the fundamental concerns of the scientist.

First and foremost, "science" is not a monolithic whole as Ferrell seems to see it, but only an abstraction which refers to a commonly understood method of knowing (as he points out) and the accumulated cognitive findings of individuals working under this self-imposed and demanding discipline.[1] The reification of the scientific enterprise within his paper is analytically very unsound. Individual scientists, like individual religionists, may be reflective or non-reflective, rigid or non-rigid, competent or non-competent. The dialogue will only come between individuals who are concerned and interested. Who are the scientists with whom Ferrell would have his dialogue, and who are the religionists who would participate? If it is only to be the theologically revisionist within the dialogue, perhaps there is little need for it—they have already converted in large measure to a partially scientific methodological self-discipline.

Secondly, scientists work only within a very limited and mundane world. Their subject matter must, given the nature of scientific method, be observable, repetitive, and clearly distinguishable from any other subject matters. Much of what traditional religious discourse has explicated is well beyond the limits of current scientific methods to even investigate. Thoughtful scientists have never suggested that science is an instrument which can explore men's "ultimate concerns." Some scientists have, of course, done so, the name of Einstein coming to mind most prominently. Einstein, however, never pretended in his concern with ethics and morality that he was anything more than another concerned citizen with a scientific background.[3] One cannot take as mundane an enterprise as science, an enterprise so bounded by physically observable phenomena and extend it far beyond the data themselves. Certainly scientists, like all human beings, have values, and are as free to express them as any other human beings, but they leave their role as scientists when they do this. There is no guarantee that a competent scientist will be any better a philosopher than any other competent human being.

Thirdly, one must also quibble with the whole notion that it is science which has produced the tone of non-believing that seems to pervade western society. I frankly doubt it very much—we are not looking at a scientifc reformation as much as we are at a reformation which has its roots in the destruction of both man's ties to the soil and his ties to other human beings based upon a village communalism, and his growing relationship with a marvelously satisfying technological revolution which, although based on science, reveals itself through modern engineering. The rationalism which seems to pervade modern society is a pragmatic, problem-solving rationalism, not a truly scientific investigative rationalism.

Notwithstanding my criticisms of some of Ferrell's assumptions, I agree with him that dialogue would be a useful thing. But then I must ask—what kind of dialogue and to what purpose? Dialogue between scientists and religionists can proceed to the enlightenment and enrichment of both regardless of whether the consequences for the human community will be great, small, or none at all. I think most social scientists would share with me one of my concerns: to assess the importance of any discussion with regard to what goes on in the world outside of the realm of the scholars and the academics.

I found it hard, as a sociologist, not to notice that Ferrell did not consider the role in this dialogue which might be played by social scientists. The social scientific enterprise has been concerned with looking at both science and religion in terms of the kinds of roles which both these institutional structures play in the greater society. Perhaps here there is the ground for starting discourse. After all, ultimately we would all hope that whatever scientists and religionists have to say to one another should be assessed in terms of its lasting impact on social life, and whatever dialogue develops must be a dialogue which goes beyond the concerns of the participating scientists and religionists to, in fact, have some impact on the greater public. Otherwise it would be purely ivory tower dialogue, and both the religionists and the scientists would probably increasingly find themselves more and more fascinating to one another, but totally irrelevant to anyone else.

The social scientist could come to this dialogue with a series of reasonably respectable findings and a bag of methodological techniques. Both resources could help. The social scientific study of religion has been an ongoing concern ever since the harsh judgements of Karl Marx about religion and its role in society.[4] The social scientific study of the role of science in society has not quite that depth of history, but since the end of the second world war has made some interesting and promising steps forward. The words of Hirsch and Barber are good evidence to this effect.[5] Both of these sub-specialties point to a way around the dilemma of deciding upon the grounds for a discourse between scientists and religionists—whose frame of reference, whose analytic models shall be the first on the platter for dissection. Most social scientists would say, we can forget about what either scientists or religionists *believe* they are doing in the real world, and begin talking about the measurable consequences of their activities. In brief, forget for a moment about intentions, designs, and motivations, and worry about results, impacts, and the consequences of actions. The dialogue could become one in which the participants discuss not their very esoteric models but the results of their work for a wider public. Then the dialogue can be broadened to include those who must finally be concerned—the lay people whose lives and well-being may be profoundly affected by the activities of their scientific and religious brethren. Certainly Liston Pope and Gerhard Lenski have provided models, however imperfect, for the examination of the relevance and importance of religion, although similar models for the impact of science (as opposed to technology) are evident.[7] The models for the study of religion have provided significant results.

There are decisions which need to be taken: what kind of dialogue do we want; who should participate? If what is desired is a comfortable academic dialogue, I fail to see the difficulty of beginning it. A grant from some generous agency would allow a few days of conference between distinguished scientists and religionists, with perhaps even the publication of a volume of the proceedings. Interesting and profitable to the participants in terms of their intellectual development perhaps, but we should not pretend that these kinds of events have anything but very long term and very difficult to diagnose consequences, if they have consequences for anyone but the participants at all. If we are concerned with a dialogue which is meaningful then we must follow the lead of Kurt Lewin and involve those individuals on whom ultimately we wish to have an impact.[8] That may mean that we will have to use the services of some of our social scientific colleagues to both participate in these conferences and to design the impact studies which result from them.

This three-way dialogue would have other beneficial effects as well. Some of the frequently obtuse and unnecessarily vague language used by all participants would have to disappear and communication could proceed in plain English. We might, by this simple amendment to our normal procedures, come closer to grips with what it is we all really want to talk about. We would all profit if we had to drop our disguises, come out from behind the smokescreen of status, pretension, and don't rock the boatism, and stand face to face as human beings engaged in human enterprises, rather than as scientists, religionists, or social scientists..

Ben-Ami Scharfstein

— H2 —

On the Structural Resemblances in Ultimate Religious, Philosophical and Scientific Thought

Religion, philosophy, and science have complex historical ties. I will ignore these in favor of the ties that depend upon creative imagination. My description of a number of them will be, I am afraid, too rapid. To be genuinely persuasive, my argument would require more and better-analyzed evidence than I can give here. But I hope that even my too-rapid sketch will prove stimulating.

Let me, then, begin abruptly, with the trait of curiosity, in the absence of which neither religion, philosophy, nor science would have developed. As we see most easily in the case of children, curiosity is biologically necessary. Not unlike the thinkers who will be our subject, children prefer, within measure, to expose themselves to the unknown, and to alter and destabilize both themselves and the world, become familiar, as they do so, with the world and with their powers in relation to it. Like the thinkers I am referring to, the more children are able to create, understand, and master instability, the deeper the stability they sense within themselves.[1]

Curiosity is both initiatory and creative. On its urging, we explore our surroundings, that is, we give the world shape, content, color, and power. It is out of curiosity that we elicit the reciprocal construction of self and world and become, at once, more richly subjective and more powerfully objective. The world therefore grows in relation to the perceptions and needs of each human being who has elicited it, or, so to speak, completed its creation.

In such stubbornly curious people as those we are considering, curiosity accepts no limits; it penetrates into details radically; or it arouses such radically general questions as, "How did the world come into being?" or, "Why is there something rather than nothing?" Some of the answers, I suspect, may even precede the explicit asking of the questions. One, anthropomorphic answer, that of the Winnebagos, was that in the beginning the great father, Earth-maker, could not think what to do and so began to cry; but when he looked down he saw that his tears had become the waters of the earth and realized that he could wish whatever he liked into existence. The Indians of ancient India, having a sometimes more abstract cast of mind, imagined the time when there was neither Non-Being nor Being; but, as if by the ardor stimulated by this very absence, the empty principle, the One, was born, so to speak, from itself, and the process that may be called the self-creation of the world had begun. On a less abstract, perhaps proto-scientific level, the ancient Indians learned to describe the world's construction in terms both of the very minute and the enormous. The Buddhists, for example, hypothesized a particle, a *paramanu* so small that 1,975,226,743 of them fitted into a measure equivalent to our three-quarters of an inch; while the worlds, infinite in number, were organized, they thought, into walled-off groups of 1,000; 1,000,000 and 1,000,000,000.[2]

Even in the few answers I have repeated, it is possible to discover the potential theologian, potential philosopher, and potential scientist. To judge by the history of religion and philosophy, of all the answers given to the question, "Why is there something rather than nothing?" the most successful philosophical one was that of Plotinus, paralleled in India by that given by the eighth-century philosopher, Shankara. Put without its philosophical justification, the answer was that the infinite plentitude of being, the One, existed necessarily, and was in no way diminished by the ceaseless emanation from it of the world.

Christian thinkers, though they adapted Plotinus's answer to their own needs, followed the passage in the *Second Book of Maccabees* (7:28) that represented God as making heaven and earth "not from things existent." They therefore rejected both the eternity of Aristotle's world and the pre-existence of matter, which Plato assumed in the *Timaeus*. Yet the idea of creation *ex nihilo* was difficult enough to tempt some Christian thinkers to identify it with the Plotinian emanation of reality from, as the Christians put it, the essence of God.[3] Creation *ex nihilo* naturally raised intellectual problems. Following Aristotle, the medieval philosophers defined time as

the measure of motion, so that before creation there could have been
no time, and so (they hoped) it made no sense to ask, "Why did God
create the world at one rather than at another moment of time?"

The attempt to understand ultimates evidently made some medievals uncomfortable, and they expressed their discomfort in the
form of principles that I take to be both expressive and defensive.
We find such a principle, I think, in the fifteenth-century church-
man, scientist, and mystic, Nicholas of Cusa, who emphasized, in a
certain Plotinian vein, that reality could be expressed only in paradoxical terms. Thus the absolute maximum, he said, being infinite,
had no degrees of "more" or "less," so that, unable to be smaller
than it was, it must be identical with the absolute minimum. This
identity of maximum and minimum, he said, "is far and away
beyond our understanding, which is fundamentally unable by any
rational process to reconcile contradictories."[4]

Now, after mentioning Nicholas, I turn to the twentieth century.
I turn, more exactly, to 1927, when the Belgian cosmologist,
Georges Lemaitre, proposed the theory that the universe, because it
was taken to be expanding, had once been concentrated in a huge,
dense "atome," with which the space and time themselves
orginated. The universe, he held, was the sequel of this atom's explosion. The parallel between the moment of explosion and the moment, as the medievals saw it, of creation, by no means escaped
Lemaitre, who was, as it happens, a priest. Both, of course, were the
moments at which time began.

The rival of Lemaitre's and then Gamow's equivalent theory, the
steady-state theory of Bondi and Gold, was also significantly
analogous to an old view of creation, that of Plotinus. Bondi and
Gold's assumption that the universe must be basically uniform over
space and time, but sustained eternally by the creation of new matter, is surely like the Plotinian universe, which emanates uniformly
and eternally from the infinite plenitude of being. Bondi and Gold's
notion that the energy of the universe did not run down because extracted from a negative energy reservoir, which became more
negative, that is, denser, as it was used, would have pleased the
paradox-oriented Nicholas of Cusa. How, too, Nicholas would have
been pleased by the contemporary talk of "black holes" containing

"singularities" at which matter is concentrated to a mathematical point of infinite density. And how particularly pleased he would have been by the speculation, exemplifying the coincidence of maximum and minimum, that the whole universe might be warped and concentrated to such a singularity. Nicholas believed in only a single, though unlimited universe, but Bruno, who was permeated by Nicholas's thought, would have been endlessly exhilarated by John Wheller's timeless superspace embedding an infinite number of universes, which enter and leave space-time by way of singularities. On second thought, however, Bruno might have felt that Wheeler's scheme violated the perfect cosmological principle in which he, Bruno, implicitly believed.

We have heard the answers of the Winnebagos, the ancient Indians, Plotinus, the medieval Christians, and some modern cosmologists. But there is a point at which they all fail, and, I take it, must fail. Philosophers have now and then explained why reason cannot grasp the question at issue, let alone answer it. When we attempt to understand anything, they have pointed out, we consider its origin, development, and use, we observe how and to what it reacts, we analyze it into its constituents, and we compare and contrast it with something else of its own or a different kind. To understand it is to set it within a variable web of relationships. But what of existence or being as such? Where and how does it begin, what does it react to, and with what can it be compared and contrasted? What is its place in any variable web of relationships? Of course there are answers. Theology and philosophy are filled with them, and contemporary cosmology makes and remakes its conjectures every day. But it is a question whether the absence of being or existence as a whole can even be conceived and whether or not there is anything to compare it with as a whole. It is even a question whether such general questions about existence make any abstract sense.

Although I do not want to engage directly in the classical debate on existence as such, I find that it begins to make clear sense only when transposed into a problem that I have so far not mentioned, the problem of life and death. For very nearly all of us, living or living well is all our hope and dying or dying badly all our fear, and the vocabulary of "existence" and "non-existence" is the abstract counterpart of our hope and fear and the thoughts and imaginings that cluster around them. When we transpose the problem, being or existence is, of course, equated with life, and non-being or non-existence with death. "True" existence then becomes equivalent to that in life which demands the most attention or gives the greatest rewards, while "illusory" being or existence to that which, in fact or feeling, does not or ought not to demand attention or give any reward we value. To say that existence as a whole is "illusory" is thus to express disappointment in life, to find it not to have fulfilled its promise and therefore to be painful, repulsive, insipid, or thin.

Such questions as, "Why is there anything?" are therefore not susceptible of simply rational or objective responses. If the response is not dogmatic or conventional, it must be subjective. The response of creative men, I believe, expresses either the fantasy of perfect intimacy, or the related, equally powerful fantasy of destruction and creation, that is, of death followed by rebirth or renewal.

Let me begin to explore my contention, that fantasies and subjective needs underlie religious, philosophical, and scientific thinking by comparing the thought mechanisms of two types of apparently antithetical persons, the philosophical mystic, who is a possible amalgam of the religious man and philosopher, and the physicist.

Like other mystics, the philosophical mystic makes a sharp distinction between inauthentic and authentic experience. The inauthentic is this varied world we sense and live or appear to live in. The authentic, which is indescribably simple and satisfactory, lies behind it. We are really, that is, in the authentic world, but to realize its satisfaction we must learn to see through the illusion to the truth.

So much is common to philosophical and other mystics. But the philosophical mystic, depending on his intellectual and cultural circumstances, supports his mysticism by making use of one of at least four different intellectual mechanisms. These I shall call, "the singularizing mechanism," "the dissociating mechanism," "the relativizing mechanism," and "the ranking mechanism."

Let me explain each of these briefly. The singularizing mechanism is meant to reduce the plural world to a single, essentially unvarying spiritual substance. In the West, Plotinus makes free use of this mechanism, and his disciple, Proclus, singularizes the world with great intensity and pseudo-Euclidean exactness.[5] In India, Shankara is prominent among those who argue that everything is constituted by consciousness, the creative ability of which we experience in dreams. At its greatest intensity and purity, he argues, consciousness is the steady unvarying reality that is common to all the manifestations of consciousness. Sadly, although consciousness is reality and bliss, in us it tends to misapprehend itself.[6]

The dissociating mechanism is especially popular among Buddhists. They deny that anything, whether soul, body, or object has any genuine coherence of its own, any genuine existence apart from that of its most elementary constituents. From a technical standpoint, their method of dissociating resembles that of the (unmystical) Moslem theologians, the Mutakallimun, who use it against the causal determinism of the Aristotelians.[7] This is also, of course, the method used by Hume against speculative metaphysics in general, and is therefore the most obvious link between mystical and Positivistic philosophers.

Another, somewhat analogous dissociating mechanism is what I shall call, for obvious reasons, "quantization." It is exploited in particular by certain Buddhists, the seventh-century philosopher, Dharmakirti, for example, who argues that nothing, not even time and space, are continuous, but that the continuous appearance of the spatial and temporal world is constructed of point-instants, briefer, perhaps, even than our physicists' "resonances," for the real, "momentary thing represents its own annihilation."[8]

The relativizing mechanism is used in one version by Nagarjuan, a second or third-century South Indian, who begins with the assumption that really to exist is to be independent, to have "own-being." He then tries to demonstrate that all human perceptions and ideas are relative and therefore, in themselves, empty. Furthermore, they all involve contradictions or, in the Kantian sense, antinomies, so that they cannot be said to exist, not to exist, to both exist and not exist, or not to both exist and not exist. The world we appear to live in is, to put it briefly, incoherent and therefore impossible.[9]

The ranking mechanism is common to all Neoplatonic philosophies and to many Oriental ones. It is exemplified by Plotinus and,

more systematically, by Proclus, who say that all that exists proceeds from a single first cause. The One, which is identical with the
Good. They add that every order begins in a monad, from which
emanate subsidiary beings, which remain linked to one another and
to the monad by the desire or tension to return to the primary
unity.[10]

In spite of their differences, all the mechanisms I have described
share a quite general aim. That is, they all transform the world of
space, time, matter, and plurality (as ordinarily understood) into an
epiphenomenon or illusion. The metaphysical, or, I should say,
psychological results are impressive, for when everything has been
either singularized, dissociated, relativized, or referred for its existence to a monad, past and future are abolished, and, with them,
past and anticipated evil. Furthermore, because selfhood has either
been abolished or made absolute, the difficulties in associating with
something or someone else must vanish.

Now let me turn to the comparison of the thought mechanisms of
the philosophical mystics with those of the physicists, by whom I
mean the great theoretical physicists of the twentieth century.
Singularizing seems to me quite characteristic of these physicists.
Certainly Einstein wanted to penetrate to a deeper constancy and
simplicity, a universe without either quanta or accidents, a universe
as geometrical, symmetrical, invariant, unified, and fieldlike as
possible, in consonance with what he himself called his "cosmic
religion" and "mystical emotion." Pauli, generalizing, claimed that
the desire for a greater unification of the world was universal among
scientists. He explained the happiness men feel in understanding
nature as the discovery that inner images correspond with outer
reality, the difference between inner and outer therefore being
revealed as superficial.[11]

The dissociating, like the singularizing mechanism is a legacy to
Western thought from Greece, where it was most radically developed by the skeptics, who used it to deprive substances of their
substantiality and causes of their causal force. No doubt as a result
of its own internal development, but also, perhaps, as the result of
the philosophical arguments of Hume, Mach, Russell, and the
Positivists, this dissociative emphasis on correlations rather than

causes became usual in modern physics. It may be speculated that the breaking of causal continuity into separate occurrences made it easier to arrive at the idea of the quantum. Interestingly, the modern union of the idea of quanta with that of causal uncertainty recalls the dissociative tactics of the Moslem theologians I have mentioned. Buddhist philosophers, though no less dissociative, usually retained their belief in uniform laws of causality.

Philosophical relativizing certainly has come parallel with the theory of relativity, which not only translated matter and energy into one another, but which tended to attenuate matter into geometry. Relativity even inspired such a thinker as Hermann Weyl to claim that we are now aware that becomeing is no more than a subjective, psychological phenomenon, for the presentness of time has lost its objectivity. But the parallel is not only with the theory of relativity. The antinomical relativizing of Nagarjuna, like Chuang Tzu's, and like Nichoas of Cusa's, recalls the complementarity principle of modern physics. Reasoning in the vein of these philosophers, and, in fact, influenced by their likes, Bohr maintained that language was inherently ambiguous and dialectical,as was, from the human standpoint, reality itself.[12] I am sure that Nagarjuna, Chuang Tzu, and Nicholas would all have been gratified by the demonstration of the complementarity of waves and particles and would have found it to confirm the paradoxical philosophy they shared with Bohr.

The ranking mechanism, too, has its analogies in physics. It is involved, of course, in the idea that the universe is constituted of minimal unities arranged in an order of increasing complexity and held together by a network of reciprocal tensions. Just as the Neo-Platonists assumed that the minimum in rank resembled the maximum, or, in other words, that the microcosm resembled the macrocosm, so modern physicists have attempted to understand the universe by analogy with the atom. In saying this, I am referring to the attempts of Jordan, Eddington, and Dirac to discover universal dimensionless constants. There is something, too, in the exclusion principle that reminds me of the Neo-Platonic hierarchy. In both, that is, there is a principle of levels that allows differentiation and energy transfer without collapse. I find it therefore interesting that Pauli, the formulator of the exclusion principle, was philosophically, at least in later life, an adherent of a kind of Neo-Platonism, who

found that the archetypical images in our psyche were essential to
relate sense perceptions with ideas, that is to say, outer with inner
reality.[13]

I am not sure how far the analogies I have been suggesting can be
reasonably pursued. Of all the analogous mechanisms, the most fundamental, to my mind, is that which depends on the desire to penetrate, simplify, and singularize the world. But however far the analogies can be pursued, I am convinced that they are not superficial, for
they rest, as I have said, on analogous needs, fantasies, and creative
impulses. No doubt faulty but suggestive empirical studies have
convinced me that the creative impulses of scientists have been
stimulated by the attempt to transcend the sense of isolation.
Isolated, that is, by anything from heart trouble, difficulties in seeing and hearing, physical clumsiness, or neurotic disturbances, they
withdraw into a world of investigation and speculation, which
creates a compensatory intimacy with themselves, the world, and, in
time, others like themselves, and which endows them with a sense of
creative power.[14] The theoretical physicist, Yukawa, for example,
may have become one in part because so physically clumsy and so
poor at dealing with other people.[15] The child who is to become a
physicist is likely to find unusual satisfaction in reacting to objects
as such, spaces as such, and motions as such.[16] The deprivations of
the size he happens to be are perhaps relieved by his excursions into
atomic and galactic sizes; and he may escape his painful closeness to
or distance from other persons by withdrawing into atomic and
galactic spaces.[17] In paying tribute to Max Planck, Einstein said
that he himself had been led to art and science largely in order to
escape the painful crudity, hopeless dreariness, and shifting desires
of life. In compensation, he said, "man tries to make for himself in
the fashion that suits him best a simplified and intelligible picture of
the world; he then tries to some extent to substitute this cosmos of
his for the world of experience, and thus to overcome it.... The
state of mind which enables a man to do work of this kind is akin to
that of the religious worshipper or the lover."[18] Yukawa, with a different emphasis, confessed that he had searched in a science for a
ray of light in order to dispel the darkness within himself.[19]

I do not contend that great physicists must be philosophical or other mystics. On the other hand, it should not be surprising to find mystics or quasi-mystics among them. Some of them, Einstein, Pauli, and Weyl, for example, passed through a Positivistic stage. Others no doubt remained Positivists, though I do not think Positivism as distant from mysticism as may first appear. At any rate, Einstein and Pauli can be situated on the border of mysticism, Pauli in the end supposing that human beings must remain in tension between the Positivistic and mystical poles. [20] Schrodinger, at the very time he made his greatest contributions as a physicist, was an avowed Vedantist, that is, a follower of Shankara; and it is fitting that, as a Vedantist, he disliked the idea of quanta and hypothesized a kind of continuous vibrating "cloud" not quite unlike Shankara's reality.[21] Weyl was at times an explicit mystic.[22] Weizsacker went so far as to say, "Physics is possible only on the background of negative theology."[23]

I have been emphasizing scientists because, on a first view, their lives might be supposed to have been, so to speak, direct and positive, not compensatory and isolated. Religious thinkers are too many in type to be characterized briefly, but if I confine them, as I have in fact done, to those with philosophical and mystical tendencies, I find that I cannot understand their development in the absence of a crucially difficult personal isolation.[24] As for philosophers, my own relatively intensive examination of the lives of some twenty of the greatest has convinced me that their need to create philosophy has been a response to anxiety and isolation, perhaps the result of the early death of a parent.[25]

I have been able to say part of what I wanted. I have certainly not wanted to conceal the often fundamental differences between religious, philosophical, and scientific thought; but I have been trying to point out some deep, perhaps unobvious similarities. Religious, philosophical, and scientific thinkers have often had similar implicit aims, or, as I should like to call them, psychic rules. Although I cannot now elaborate on the theme, I feel I will be understood when I say that the psyche rules of fundamental, that is, deeply theoretical science, are roughly these: Things cannot be just as they appear. As they appear, they are not sufficiently intelligible. In the end, they *must* be intelligible. In the end, they will be grasped in somehow simple, intelligible formulas.

Like philosophy, science is meant to be a process of both simplification and penetration, which are meant, as in most classical philosophy, to be or to give access to the truth and the healing, stabilizing pleasure with which it is experienced. Of course, the philosophical mystics I have mentioned would not agree (any more than Plato) that the healing truth can be reached by sheerly, that is, narrowly intellectual means; and some of them would deny that the intellect can reach truth in their sense at all; but they, like the scientists and philosophers, agree that things cannot be just as they appear, and that one must penetrate beneath or beyond them.

If the psychic rules I have stated are approximately right, and if my remarks on the effect of personal isolation have been well taken, then the religious thinker, the philosopher, and the scientist have been impelled to follow the rules by their struggle against clumsiness and for precision and power; against depression and for stimulation; against ambivalence and for a whole self; against loneliness and for closeness at least to oneself; and against death and for permanence. Their struggle takes what is, for the usual adult, the unusual form of serious, even obsessive play with ideas and things, in order to bridge the distance between personal and impersonal reality. If, as I assume, they are genuinely creative, they invest their ideas with narcissistic intensity, because their love and hope for them are their love and hope for themselves, and they dream of the discovery or experience that will grant them rebirth and reunion. The very intensity of their creative effort is a form of isolation, which may both exhilarate and frighten them because it may reawaken early experiences of loneliness, abandonment, and weakness.

In all seriousness, I suggest that it is such a desire to invent by and for oneself, but within and for the sake of a deep human mutuality, that underlies the creation of religion, philosophy, and science, not to speak of art in all its forms. It underlies the professional activities of thinkers of all kinds, the papers and books they write and the reactions and counter-reactions these solicit, the lectures, seminars, and congresses they hold, and the pleasure that many of them take in teaching and in preaching. We invent in solitude in order to people and escape it, in order to renew ourselves, in order—of course—to understand better, but also—of course—to feel better.

I find it interesting to make out to what a degree our needy, primitive fundamental selves are inextricably bound up in our complex, sophisticated, professional selves, and to see how professional differences that have evolved by what appears to be an irreversible process leave such different professions and structures of ideas, not merely different, but, as Hindu philosophers say, identical in their difference, which is to say, different in their identity.

NOTES

1. D.E. Berlyne, "Laughter, Humor, and Play," in G. Lindzey & E. Aronson, eds., *The Handbook of Social Psychology*, 2nd. ed., vol. 3 (Reading, Mass.: Addison-Wesley, 1969). J.S. Bruner, A. Jolly & K. Sylva, eds., *Play* (Harmondsworth: Penguin Books, 1976).
2. W.M. McGovern, *A Manual of Buddhist Philosophy*, vol. 1, *Cosmopology (London: Kegan Paul Trench & Trubner, 1923, pp. 41ff. R.F. Gombrich, "Ancient Indian Cosmology," in C. Blacker & M. Loewe, eds., Ancient Cosmologies* (London: Allen & Unwin, 1975).
3. "The Identification of *Ex Nihilo* with Emanation in Gregory of Nyassa" and "The Meaning of *Ex Nihilo* in the Church Fathers, Arabic amd Hebrew Philosophy and St. Thomas," In H.A. Wolfson, *Studies in the History of Philosophy and Religion*, vol. 1 (Cambridge, Mass.: Harvard University Press, 1973).
4. Nicholas Cusanus, *Of Learned Ignorance*, trans. G. Heron (New Haven: Yale University Press, 1954), chap. 4, pp. 12, 13.
5. Proclus, *The Elements of Theology*, trans. E.R. Dodds, 2nd ed. (London: Oxford University press, 1963)).
6. *The Vedanta Sutras of Badarayana, with the Commentary by Sankara*, trans. G. Thibault, 2 vol. (reprint New York: Dover, 1962). E. Deutsch, *Advaita Vedanta: A Philosophical Reconstruction* (Honolulu, University of Hawaii Press, 1969).
7. H.A. Wolfson, *The Philosophy of the Kalam* (Cambridge Mass.: Harvard University Press, 1976).
8. Th. Stcherbatsky, *Buddhist Logic*, vol. 1 (reprint The Hague: Mouton, 1958), pp. 79-118.

9. F.J. Streng, *Emptiness* (Nashville: Abingdon Press, 1967).
10. Proclus, ibid.
11. W. Pauli, "The Influence of Archetypal Ideas on the Scientific Theories of Kepler," in C.G. Jung & W. Pauli, *The Interpretation of Nature and the Psyche* (New York: Pantheon, 1955). p. 152.
12. L. Rosenfeld, "Niels Bohr in the Thirties," in S. Rozental, ed., *Niels Bohr* (Amsterdam, 1967), p. 121
13. Pauli, op. cit., "Wolfgang Pauli's philosophische Auffassungen," in W. Heisenberg, *"Schritte uber Grenzen* (Munich: Piper, 1971), pp. 48-51.
14. A. Roe, *The Making of a Scientist* (New York: Dodd, Mead & Co., 1953), summarizing earlier, more technical studies. B.T. Eiduson, *Scientists: Their Psychological World* (New York: Basic Books, 1953). F. Bello & A. Roe, in P.C. Obler & H.A. Estrin, ed., *The New Scientist* (New York: Anchor Books, 1962). L.S. Kubie, "Some Unsolved Problems of the Scientific Career," in M.R. Stein, A.J. Vidich & D.M. White, eds., *Identity and Anxiety* (Glencoe, Ill.: Free Press, 1960). P. Greenacre, *Emotional Growth*, vol. 2 (New York: International Universities Press, 1971).
15. H. Yukawa, *Creativity and Intuition* (Tokyo: Kodansha, 1973), pp. 24, 26.
16. A.E. Michotte, "The Emotional Significance of Movement," in M.B. Arnold, ed., *The Nature of Emotion* (Harmondsworth: Penguin Books, 1968), pp. 263-68.
17. A. Roe, *The Making of a Scientist*, p. 88. R. Eckstein, *Children of Time and Space* (New York: Appleton-Century-Crofts, 1966), p. 340.
18. A. Einstein, *Ideas and Opinions* (New York: Crown Publishers, 1954), p. 225.
19. Yukawa, op.cit., pp. 131-32.
20. W. Heisenberg, op. cit., p. 48.
21. E. Schrodinger, *What is Life? and Other Scientific Essays* (New York: Anchor Books, 1956); *My View of the World* (Cambridge: Cambridge University Press, 1964).
22. H. Weyl, "Insight and Reflection," in T.L. Saaty & F.J. Weyl, eds., *The Spirit and Use of the Mathematical Sciences* (New York: McGraw-Hill, 1969).
23. C.F. von Weizsacker, *Die Einheit der Natur* (Munich: Hanser, 1971), pp. 319-19.
24. B.A. Scharfstein, *Mystical Experience* (Baltimore: Penguin Books, 1974).
25. This examination is contained in a book, *Philosophers as Human Beings*, to be published by Blackwell in England and Oxford in the USA.

Index

Paragon House Publishers and the International Conference on the Unity of Sciences (ICUS) are divisions of the International Cultural Foundation, Inc. The International Cultural Foundation is an independent, non-profit organization dedicated to promoting academic, scientific, religious and cultural exchange among the countries of the world. Founded in 1972 by the Reverend Sun Myung Moon, the Foundation is now headquartered in New York with branch offices located throughout the world.